RAISING
CAIN

How *the* BIBLE
SHAPES *the* THINGS YOU SAY

To Joan

DEWEY: 220.3
SUBHD: FIGURES OF SPEECH \ANECDOTES-
-DICTIONARIES \ BIBLE--ANECDOTES

ISBN: 978-0-8054-9592-8

Printed in The United States of America

1 2 3 4 5 6 7 • 17 16 15 14 13

RP

INTRODUCTION

A DROP IN THE BUCKET | Adam's rib | **CRYSTAL CLEAR** | Flesh and blood | **ALL THINGS MUST PASS** | Count the cost | **HE WHO IS NOT WITH ME IS AGAINST ME** | Inherit the wind | **LIVE OFF THE FAT OF THE LAND** | Labor of love | **A LITTLE BIRD TOLD ME** | Many are called but few are chosen | **KNOWLEDGE IS POWER** | Armageddon | **OLD WIVES' TALES** | Powers that be **RIGHT-HAND MAN** | Suffer fools gladly | **SAFETY IN NUMBERS** Den of thieves | **BURNING BUSH** | Fly in the ointment

We recognize and often use these and other idioms, allusions, and sayings as a part of our everyday language. Many of these expressions are generations old, some go back even centuries. We may not know their origins or who coined them but they are an important element of our language, providing us a verbal shorthand to express ourselves more colorfully, more easily, and more effectively than without them.

For four hundred years the King James Version of the Bible and its interpretation have been major sources for English idioms, allusions, and sayings, either directly or indirectly. *Raising Cain* lists and describes over 900 expressions (some of which are listed above) that demonstrate the Bible's continuing influence on the language and cultures of peoples whose primary language is English. Some of these expressions will be recognized by many English speakers while some will be less familiar. All of these terms, however, are currently being used, a fact that contemporary citations in this book demonstrate. I discovered many by reading the King James Version of the Bible, of course, but also by simply being observant. These expressions surround us; one has only to read or listen carefully to find them in English-language newspapers and magazines, on television and radio, and on web sites throughout the world.

You'll discover, I think, that becoming familiar with these terms will help you understand the English language better and also discover the perennial relevance of the Bible to our culture.

Definitions of terms

The expressions in *Raising Cain* are of three broad types: idioms, allusions, and sayings.

An *idiom* is an expression whose meaning cannot be inferred from the meanings of the words that compose it. In fact, the words that compose an idiom often make no sense in themselves. For example, "living off the fat of the land" does not mean that one literally eats fat and "putting one's hand to the plow" requires no plow at all.

An *allusion* is a reference to a person, place, statement, or event from the Bible. Examples are "wisdom of Solomon," "Eden," "flesh of my flesh," and "Armageddon."

A *saying*:

- Is a concise expression setting forth wisdom or truth
- Is an often-repeated and familiar expression
- Can stand alone as an independent unit, not needing other words or expressions to make a sentence

Examples are "All things must pass," "Eat, drink, and be merry," and "Fight the good fight."

The King James Version

The King James Version of the Bible is the primary source of these terms because it is arguably the version most recognized by English speakers and is the most influential on Western civilization. Translated by a team of Bible scholars appointed by King James of England and published in 1611, the version has continued to be popular after four hundred years, in spite of the increasing availability of new translations and paraphrases. We owe much to the KJV translators but even more to William Tyndale, whose translation was a primary source for them, and other courageous English translators who risked and even gave their lives in order to make the Bible available to all English readers.

Origins

Some terms found in or influenced by the Bible were not used for the first time in the Bible. In some cases translators used terms that were already being used in their own time and placed them in the Bible, much as modern translators do now. A discussion of these pre-translation origins, however, is beyond the scope of this book.

Semantic Distance

Although most terms in this book come directly from the Bible, some, as noted above, come from interpretation of biblical terms. Some terms' definitions do not coincide with their biblical context, having changed over time. "The mark of Cain," for example, is generally understood now to mean an indication of one's guilt, yet its biblical meaning was different, meaning instead a sign of God's protection of Cain against anyone who might consider killing him. "Arrows in one's quiver" originally referred to a large number of children, especially sons, implying one's power against aggressors. Now the term is generally understood to refer to the indirect sense of the term, to one's power, especially military might.

Format

The following format elements illustrate terms in both their biblical and contemporary contexts, using "all of one mind" as an example.

1. The term, either an idiom, allusion, or a saying (e.g., "all of one mind")

2. A contemporary definition of the term, explaining what it means to contemporary English speakers
   (e.g., to be in accord, harmony, or agreement)

3. Citations from the Bible where the term or its derivative appears
   (e.g., 1 Peter 3.8 KJV "Finally, be ye *all of one mind*, having compassion one of another, love as brethren, be pitiful [or, sympathetic], be courteous.")

4.   <u>Current quotations, primarily non-religious, publications</u> in a variety of contexts (e.g., "He was pleased and heartened by the unity of his community over this issue and he felt that 'the battle was already won since we are *all of one mind* and one heart.'" "Community Calls on Board of Education to Embrace Diversity," Neal Abunab, May 28, 2004, *Arab American News*)

How terms qualify for inclusion

All terms in this book must meet two criteria in order to qualify for inclusion:

The term must appear in or be influenced by the Bible. (To be "influenced by" means that the term is derived from a biblical term or comes from a common interpretation of a term or idea from the Bible.) Some terms—e.g., "Good Samaritan" and "Damascus road experience"—do not appear in the Bible but are influenced by biblical narrative, events, or interpretation of a biblical text. In these two examples, they are influenced respectively by Jesus' parable about a Samaritan who helped a stranger (Luke 10.30–37) and by Paul's encounter with Jesus on the road to Damascus (Acts 9.1–19).

The term must be used in current, non-religious writing. One would expect that terms in the Bible would appear in religious publications. But the inclusion of biblical terms in non-religious publications and contexts demonstrates that these terms have been adopted by the broader secular culture, an important point for understanding and appreciating the Bible's continued influence on and relevance to our contemporary culture. I use examples from secular contemporary sources such as newspapers, magazines, books, and web sites and from such social realms as sports, business, recreation, government, and literature. Noteworthy is the fact that many of the contemporary citations come from international publications, indicating even further influence on the English language.

If you are already familiar with the Bible, I hope that this book will add to your enjoyment of it and to your spiritual insight and understanding. If you are not yet acquainted with the Bible, I hope that this book will stimulate you to explore it for its riches in language and in knowing its Author.

Wayne Harvey
September 14, 2012

RAISING CAIN

A

"ADAM'S APPLE"

A

Abaddon

Means: The angel of the bottomless pit; associated with hell and Satan

Biblical Text: *And they had a king over them, which is the angel of the bottomless pit, whose name in the Hebrew tongue is **Abaddon**, but in the Greek tongue hath his name Apollyon* (Revelation 9:11).

Example of Use: Even before the album starts spinning, the juxtaposed theme of Pinback's latest release, "Summer in **Abaddon**," is already making noises. Sure, **Abaddon** sounds like a nice place to spend all that summer vacation time, but as translated, **Abaddon** is actually a Hebrew word referring to a place of eternal damnation. ("CD Review: New Pinback Album Takes Vacation from Mediocrity," Drew Tabke, Dec. 1, 2004, *Daily Utah Chronicle*, Salt Lake City)

Abomination of desolation

Means: That which is so disgusting or detestable that it brings great misery or destruction (based on the foreign introduction in the Jerusalem temple of a pagan idol as referred to in the book of Daniel)

Biblical Text: *But when ye shall see the **abomination of desolation**, spoken of by Daniel the prophet, standing where it ought not, (let him that readeth understand,) then let them that be in Judaea flee to the mountains* (Mark 13:14).

Example of Use: Madonna reacted with surprise recently when people who hold such things sacred took offense at her performing while adorned with distinctive Hindu markings that symbolize purity.

These critics thought the rest of her revealing costume, not to mention her suggestive gyrations, bespoke a different message. . . . Something close to the logical conclusion occurs when, for example, Christians conduct their own Passover Seder meals and in the process stuff themselves with pork barbecue. (I've witnessed such a thing. It may not match the proverbial **abomination of desolation**, but it's somewhere on the way.) ("Sacred Rites Should Be Revered," Sept. 26, 1998, *Post-Tribune*, Merrillville, Indiana)

Abraham's bosom

Means: A place where the faithful will enjoy the peace of heaven after death (based on the Jewish concept of a place of contentment, peace, and joy after death with Abraham, father of the Jews)

Biblical Text: *There was a certain rich man, which was clothed in purple and fine linen, and fared sumptuously every day: And there was a certain beggar named Lazarus, which was laid at his gate, full of sores, And desiring to be fed with the crumbs which fell from the rich man's table: moreover the dogs came and licked his sores. And it came to pass, that the beggar died, and was carried by the angels into **Abraham's bosom**: the rich man also died, and was buried; And in hell he lift up his eyes, being in torments, and seeth **Abraham** afar off, and **Lazarus in his bosom** (Luke 16:19–23).*

Example of Use: In anticipation of living beyond my sixty-five years, and gambling that before I am gathered into **Abraham's bosom** I may need to use some form of prescription drugs, I must contribute an additional $35 per month, with an annual $250 deductible, and pay 25 percent of additional costs up to $2,250 for this service. I will then be required to pay 100 percent of any prescription drug costs that range from $2,250 to $3,600. As I understand my benefits, on June 30, 2004, when I am officially retired and beginning to live on a fixed income, if I wish to have minimum preventive health care, I must begin to pay $93.70 per month, plus a potential $350 per year deductible for Medicare coverage. ("Medicare: Seniors Must Pay Plenty for Free Care," James C. Coomer, Mar. 10, 2004, *The Atlanta Journal and Constitution*)

Absent in body, present in spirit

Means: Applies to persons who are apart from one another physically while one or more enjoy thoughts of the other

Biblical Text: *For I verily, as **absent in body, but present in spirit**, have judged already, as though I were present, concerning him that hath so done this deed* (1 Corinthians 5:3).

Example of Use: I have been sustained by the unconditional love of my wife of thirty-three years, Gwendolyn McZeek Campbell, who is this morning **absent in body but present in spirit.** ("EPA, Commerce Application Commission Nominations: Arthur C. Campbell Confirmation," June 13, 2000, *Congressional Testimony*)

Accord, In one

Means: To agree, to be unified

Biblical Text: *That they gathered themselves together, to fight with Joshua and with Israel, with **one accord*** (Joshua 9:2).

Example of Use: Strumming the heartstrings of a city, Nashville's harmony runs deep. Priding itself on the moniker Music City USA, nowhere else but here can you hear the diverse sounds of Americana—country, rockabilly, jazz, blues, gospel, and rock 'n' roll—playing **in one accord**. ("Nashville, Host of the 2003, CoC—a City of Note," July 14, 2003, *Nation's Cities Weekly*)

Act of God

Means: An act of nature attributed to God, e.g., lightning, a hurricane, a tornado

Biblical Text: *And know ye this day: for I speak not with your children which have not known, and which have not seen the chastisement of the LORD your God, his greatness, his mighty hand, and his stretched out arm, And his miracles, and **his acts**, which he did in the midst of Egypt unto Pharaoh the king of Egypt, and unto all his land; . . . But your eyes have seen all the great **acts of the LORD** which he did* (Deuteronomy 11:2–3, 7).

Example of Use: Now, eight weeks after the storm, all three breaches are looking less like **acts of God** and more like failures of engineering that could have been anticipated and very likely prevented. ("When the Levee Broke\Was It an **Act of God** . . . or a Poor Design?" Joby Warrick and Michael Grunwald, Oct. 26, 2005, *The Cincinnati Post*, OH)

Adam and Eve

Means: (1) The first man and woman, especially in a state of innocence, disobedience, or beginning or (2) nakedness

Biblical Text: *And the LORD God formed man of the dust of the ground, and breathed into his nostrils the breath of life; and man became a living soul. . . . And the rib, which the LORD God had taken from man, made he a woman, and brought her unto the man. . . . And they were both naked, the man and his wife, and were not ashamed* (Genesis 2:7, 22, 25). *And **Adam** called his wife's name **Eve**; because she was the mother of all living* (Genesis 3:20).

Examples of use: In many Ugandan villages, children go about their ravaged lives in **Adam**'s **and Eve**'s suits—naked. ("Rather Walk Naked but Protect Museveni," David Ouma Balikowa, Oct. 8, 2004, *The Monitor*, Kampala, Uganda)

Héloïse and Abelard are sometimes referred to as the Romeo and Juliet of early medieval France or, as Antoine Audouard calls them in his fictionalized retelling of their story, "the **Adam and Eve** of love." ("Snooping on Two Star-Crossed Lovers," Joanna Kavenna, May 10, 2004, telegraph.co.uk)

Adam's ale

Means: Water, so named because Adam apparently had only water to drink

Example of Use: We've all heard of the Pepsi challenge. But yesterday dozens of shoppers trying a similar test at a North supermarket couldn't tell tap water from bottled spring water. ("**Adam's Ale** Put to the Tap Taste Test," June 5, 2003, *The Journal,* Newcastle, England)

Adam's apple

Means: The projection in the throat of the thyroid cartilage of the larynx. This protuberance in the front of a man's throat commonly called the "Adam's apple" is not referred to in the Bible yet the term comes from the legendary explanation for it. It exists, as it is told, to represent a piece of the forbidden fruit that Adam ate and that became lodged in his throat (Genesis 3:2–7).

Example of Use: Joe Crawford, a fifteen-year resident of Indianapolis, is finally realizing his dream. Originally from St. Louis, Crawford is the owner of **Adam's Apple** Menswear specialty clothing store, catering to the upscale man. ("**Adam's Apple** Gulps Slice of Menswear Market," Kenneth Snorten, June 17, 1995, *Indianapolis Recorder*)

Adam's curse

Means: Work

Biblical Text: *And unto Adam he said, Because thou hast hear-kened unto the voice of thy wife, and hast eaten of the tree, of which I commanded thee, saying, Thou shalt not eat of it:* **cursed is the ground for thy sake; in sorrow shalt thou eat of it all the days of thy life; Thorns also and thistles shall it bring forth to thee; and thou shalt eat the herb of the field; In the sweat of thy face shalt thou eat bread, till thou return unto the ground;** *for out of it wast thou taken: for dust thou art, and unto dust shalt thou return* (Genesis 3:17–19).

Example of Use: Work is a very, very important theme. America is a work culture, but Russia was not. In Russia, work was the **curse of Adam**. So you have to ask yourself: What is everybody in this novel doing? There is the whole question of work versus pleasure. ("One Classic, but Many Anna Kareninas," Jacob Stockinger, Sept. 14, 2005, *The Capital Times,* Madison, WI)

Adam's rib

Means: Woman

Biblical Text: *And the Lord God caused a deep sleep to fall upon Adam, and he slept: and he took one of his ribs, and closed up the flesh instead thereof; And* **the rib, which the Lord God had taken from man,** *made he a woman, and brought her unto the man* (Genesis 2:21–22).

Example of Use: Whether it's the anti-heroics of Hellboy or The Punisher or the classic valor of Spider-Man, testosterone seems vital to the formula for breaking out of the comics subculture and into the mainstream. But in the midst of all this busting, where are the women? ("Superheroines, Especially, Have a

A

Reputation As Lowly Spinoffs, the **Adam's Rib** of Their Male Counterparts," John Jurgensen, Apr. 26, 2004, *The Hartford Courant*)

Add a cubit

Means: To add to or increase, e.g., one's lifetime or height, generally meaning what is possible for God alone. A cubit is an ancient measure of length based on the length of the forearm.

Biblical Text: *Which of you by taking thought can **add one cubit** unto his stature? And why take ye thought for raiment? Consider the lilies of the field, how they grow; they toil not, neither do they spin: And yet I say unto you, That even Solomon in all his glory was not arrayed like one of these* (Matthew 6:27–29).

Example of Use: Though his last film, *Blankman*, did not fare well, Wayans isn't deflated by every disappointment. "This is just my job," he shrugs. "It's not gonna **add a cubit** to my life, it's not going to cure cancer. I could be a plumber, and if I did good work as a plumber, they should applaud." ("*In Living Color*'s Damon Wayans Returns to Big Screen in 'Major Payne,'" Luaine Lee, Mar. 20, 1995, Knight Ridder/Tribune News Service)

All flesh is grass

Means: All human beings are fragile and short-lived.

Biblical Text: *The voice said, Cry. And he said, What shall I cry? **All flesh is grass**, and all the goodliness thereof is as the flower of the field: The grass withereth, the flower fadeth: because the spirit of the LORD bloweth upon it: surely the people is grass. The grass withereth, the flower fadeth: but the word of our God shall stand for ever* (Isaiah 40:6–8).

Example of Use: The truth is, I have two cars. A silly Los Angeles extravagance, I know, but in my defense, one of them is an old wreck. It runs intermittently, makes peculiar noises, and at speeds under 50 miles per hour emits an odor like neither gasoline nor oil but, instead, like burning human flesh. I think of it as my weekend car, my take-the-dog-to-the-beach car. So when I bought my German sleekmobile, I kept the wreck in the garage alongside it. I like to think that, after some initial sniping, they've reached an understanding, sitting there quietly in the dark. Perhaps the wreck keeps the German car honest and humble, in an **all-flesh-is-grass** sort of way. ("Hard-Times Hollywood," Rob Long, June 10, 2002, *Newsweek International*)

All men are liars

Means: Everyone is a liar.

Biblical Text: *I believed, therefore have I spoken: I was greatly afflicted: I said in my haste,* **All men are liars** (Psalm 116:10–11).

Example of Use: All men are liars. If women just accepted that as one of life's truisms, the happier they would be. The problem for men is that they are not very good liars, and women, being much better skilled in the art, see through everything, even if they choose not to act upon their discoveries. ("I've Fallen for Those Lies Again; Television," Jaci Stephen, Sept. 14, 2003, *Mail on Sunday*, London)

All of one mind

Means: In accord, harmony, agreement

Biblical Text: *Finally, be ye* **all of one mind**, *having compassion one of another, love as brethren, be pitiful [or, sympathetic], be courteous* (1 Peter 3:8). See also Rom. 12:16; Php. 1:27; 2:2.

Example of Use: We were not **all of one mind**. But we were all determined, even at that late date, to carry on with that continual and fearless sifting and winnowing by which alone the truth can be found. And we all knew that this, more than any line on a map, was what made us Wisconsinites. ("Wisconsinites Still Sift and Winnow," John Nichols, Dec. 16, 2003, *Wisconsin State Journal*)

All things are lawful but all things are not expedient

Means: Although all activities for a person or a group might be acceptable behavior, they might not help others or serve as a good example of moral behavior for them

All things are lawful unto me, but all things are not expedient: all things are lawful for me, but I will not be brought under the power of any (1 Corinthians 6:12). See also 1 Cor. 10:23.

Example of Use: There is a Scripture in the Bible that says: "**All things are lawful. But all things are not expedient.**" That is to say, that there is a time and place for everything. ("What Black America Has to Say about 9/11," Sept. 1, 2002, *Black Issues Book Review*)

All things are possible

Means: The power of faith is unlimited

*Jesus said unto him, If thou canst believe, **all things are possible** to him that believeth* (Mark 9:23). See also Mark 10:27.

Example of Use: It's all new again for the [Kansas City] Royals [major league baseball team], as it is every spring, and it beckons as always with the timelessly alluring promise that **all things are possible**. ("Gauging Success: Team's Temperature Will Be Measured by More Than Just Wins," Bob Dutton, Feb. 16, 2007, *Kansas City Star*)

All things in common

Means: The sharing of interests, possessions, or characteristics among a group

Biblical Text: *And all that believed were together, and had **all things common**; And sold their possessions and goods, and parted them to all men, as every man had need* (Acts 2:44–45).

Example of Use: [Sol Hicks, Atlanta, says that] MDRT has enriched my life by giving me the ability to network with other agents around the world who have **all things in common**. That helps us all become better and better and allows us to provide enhanced service to our clients. ("Salute to MDRT! (Million Dollar Round Table)," Barry Higgins, Dec. 2, 2002, *National Underwriter Life & Health-Financial Services Edition*)

All things to all men

Means: A condition of attempting to satisfy or appeal to everyone

Biblical Text: *To the weak became I as weak, that I might gain the weak: I am made **all things to all men**, that I might by all means save some* (1 Corinthians 9:22).

Example of Use: March brought the long-anticipated arrival of Conde Nast's *Cargo*, which came in just about on target—a slick shopping magazine that tries to be **all things to all men** (from cosmetics to computers). ("A Bumper Crop," Samir Husni, Apr. 1, 2004, *Folio: the Magazine for Magazine Management*)

All things work together for good

Means: Despite one's negative life experiences, overall, positive ones will displace them

A

Biblical Text: *And we know that **all things work together for good** to them that love God, to them who are the called according to his purpose* (Romans 8:28).

Example of Use: "I wasn't sure if Kobe was going to chase that 40 points so bad that he was going to hurt our chances there at the end of the game," Coach Phil Jackson said. "It got a little bit tenuous. But **all things work together for good** to those who want to hustle. And he hustled up the points." ("Streak at 9, Lakers at 7[;] Bryant Scores 41, Ties Jordan; L.A. Improves Seeding in West[;] Lakers 106, Seattle 101," Howard Beck, Feb. 24, 2003, *Daily News,* Los Angeles)

Almost thou persuadest me

Means: A remark to someone who has made a persuasive, yet not totally convincing, argument

Biblical Text: *King Agrippa, believest thou the prophets? I know that thou believest. Then Agrippa said unto Paul, **Almost thou persuadest me** to be a Christian* (Acts 26:27–28).

Example of Use: When Tories begin talking like this, I'm almost tempted to think that a Conservative government in Britain might be a good thing. ("**Almost Thou Persuadest Me to Be a Conservative,**" Oct. 5, 2006, methodius.blogspot.com)

Alpha and Omega

Means: (1) The beginning and the end of something or (2) the crucial element of something

Biblical Text: *I am **Alpha and Omega**, the beginning and the end, the first and the last* (Revelation 22:13).

Example of Use: What we want is less work-life balance, more a recognition that the **alpha and omega** of good living is to know how to play—and to insert the play ethic into everything we do. ("Slow Down, Tune Out, Make Peace," Will Hutton, Sept. 11, 2004, *Guardian Unlimited*, UK)

Am I my brother's keeper?

Means: A rhetorical question implying that one is not responsible for anyone else

Biblical Text: *And the* Lord *said unto Cain, Where is Abel thy brother? And he said, I know not:* **Am I my brother's keeper?** (Genesis 4:9).

Example of Use: "This is a team game and these guys are a real team," Watford said. "It is like their t-shirts say, '**Am I my brother's keeper?**'—Yes, I am. I am my brother's keeper. We support each other and pick each other up no matter what is going on." ("Reserves Carry the Load at Homecoming Game," Kent Bush, Sept. 18, 2004, *Express Star*, Chickasha, OK).

Ananias's club

Means: Liars and deceivers

Biblical Text: *But Peter said,* **Ananias**, *why hath Satan filled thine heart to lie to the Holy Ghost, and to keep back part of the price of the land? . . . And* **Ananias** *hearing these words fell down, and gave up the ghost: and great fear came on all them that heard these things. And the young men arose, wound him up, and carried him out, and buried him* (Acts 5:3, 5–6).

Example of Use: Teddy Roosevelt dismissed his opponents as the "lunatic fringe" and members of the "**Ananias Club**," a reference to the biggest liar in Scriptures. ("A Bare-Knuckle Political Heritage. (Criticism of Political Figures)," Ralph De Toledano, Apr. 23, 2001, *Insight on the News*)

Anathema

Means: A ban, curse, or excommunication

Biblical Text: *If any man love not the Lord Jesus Christ, let him be **Anathema*** (1 Corinthians 16:22).

Example of Use: Today's complex enterprise architectures can be **anathema** to anyone assigned with wringing the most performance out of an application. ("Symantec's i3 Homes in on Problem Transactions," David Worthington, Sept. 1, 2007, *Software Development Times*)

Ancient and honorable, The

Means: People who are revered and hold power by virtue of that reverence, especially when old or relatively old; reference to things with iconic value

Biblical Text: *Therefore the LORD will cut off from Israel head and tail, branch and rush, in one day. The **ancient and honourable**, he is the head; and the prophet that teacheth lies, he is the tail. For the leaders of this people cause them to err; and they that are led of them are destroyed* (Isaiah 9:14–16).

Example of Use: The first historical references to fruitcake go back to Roman times. During the Middle Ages, soldiers in the Crusades ate fruitcakes for sustenance during battle. Fruitcakes, which became especially popular during Victorian England, have an **ancient and honorable** tradition. ("Web Site Offers 'Virtual Fruitcake' for Holidays," Nov. 25, 1997, PR Newswire)

Angels unawares, Entertain

Means: An admonition to show hospitality or generosity to strangers and, by so doing, possibly enjoy the presence of angels

Biblical Text: *Let brotherly love continue. Be not forgetful to entertain strangers: for thereby some have **entertained angels unawares*** (Hebrews 13:1–2).

Example of Use: No facet of etiquette is left untouched [in the *Book of Courtesy*]. . . . For example, one particularly fine piece of advice and observation: "Never let it be said of you, 'She is a snob.' Snobs never **entertain angels unawares**. They care only for those from whom they can get something. Snobs measure most things by money." ("Accepting an Uncommon Courtesy," Stephen Good, June 4, 2001, *Insight on the News*)

Angels, A little lower than

Means: To be subordinate to God

Biblical Text: *But we see Jesus, who was made **a little lower than the angels** for the suffering of death, crowned with glory and honour; that he by the grace of God should taste death for every man* (Hebrews 2:9). See also Ps. 8:5.

Example of Use: "I draw the most strength from the victims," Attorney General Janet Reno told a victims' rights conference on Aug. 12, "for they represent America to me: people who will not be put down, people who will not be defeated, people who will rise again and stand again for what is right. . . . You are my heroes and heroines. You are but **little lower than the angels**." ("Victims & Vengeance: Why the Victims' Rights Amendment Is a Bad Idea," Bruce Shapiro, Feb. 10, 1997, *The Nation*)

Ant, Consider the (or Go to the)

Means: An appeal to be responsible, prepared for any circumstances, and to become wise

Biblical Text: *Go to the ant, thou sluggard; consider her ways, and be wise* (Proverbs 6:6). See also Prov. 30:25.

Example of Use: Let us for a minute **consider the ant**. The ant is an individual being in the universe. However, the ant is a crucial part of the colony. Here is a duality of individual and group. The ant is one, and part of many. . . . From this small ant comes a philosophy that can grow to encompass all things. ("Philosophy of the Ant," Sept. 23, 2004, www.pyrobix.com/2004/09/philosophy-of-ant.html)

Antichrist

Means: Someone who is an enemy of Christ or of some other person or ideology held supremely dear or in great esteem

Biblical Text: *Little children, it is the last time: and as ye have heard that **antichrist** shall come, even now are there many antichrists; whereby we know that it is the last time* (1 John 2:18).

Example of Use: [In his movie, *The Golden Compass*,] "My point is that religion does most good when the **Antichrist** is furthest away from political power and that when it gets hold of power, say to send people to war, or condemn them to death, or to rule every aspect of our lives, it rapidly goes bad. That is what I am trying to describe." ("Author Who 'Killed God' Is Labelled the **Antichrist**; It's Friday! Don't Miss," Michael Hellicar, Nov. 23, 2007, *Daily Mail*, London)

Appeal to Caesar, I

Means: To appeal to a higher power or authority

Biblical Text: *For if I be an offender, or have committed any thing worthy of death, I refuse not to die: but if there be none of these things whereof these accuse me, no man may deliver me unto them.* **I appeal unto Caesar** (Acts 25:11).

Example of Use: Attorney General McDonnell notwithstanding, we really have no political leadership in Richmond. In the next several days, I'm going to write a letter to my representative in the Virginia House of Delegates. Maybe something could be done there. While I'm not optimistic about that, it couldn't hurt to try. An **appeal to Caesar** may be our only recourse at this point. ("Homo-Fascists Win at CNU," Cultural Insurrectionist, Feb. 26, 2007, joshdermer.blogspot.com)

Apple of one's eye

Means: One who is particularly dear to another, being the favorite object of one's affection

Biblical Text: *Keep me as **the apple of the eye**, hide me under the shadow of thy wings, From the wicked that oppress me, from my deadly enemies, who compass me about* (Psalm 17:8–9).

Example of Use: A friend said: "Marti was so close to his mum. He always spent lots of time with his family. He was **the apple of his mum's eye**. She always knew he would be a star and always had faith in him." ("Singer Mourns the Woman Who Knew He'd Be a Star," Karen Bale, *Daily Record*, Glasgow, Scotland)

Ark of the covenant

Means: Something highly regarded or considered sacrosanct

Biblical Text: *And Joshua spake unto the priests, saying, Take up the **ark of the covenant**, and pass over before the people* (Joshua 3:6).

Example of Use: Two civilians were killed and 14 policemen injured here as a result of bomb attack and stoning by "irresponsible individuals" while Orthodox followers were escorting the **Ark of the Covenant** replicas to their respective churches, police said Saturday. ("2 Killed, 14 Injured in Ethiopian Unrest: Police," Jan. 21, 2006, Xinhua News Agency)

Armageddon

Means: Any great battle, decisive or catastrophic conflict, or destructive confrontation

Biblical Text: *Behold, I come as a thief. Blessed is he that watcheth, and keepeth his garments, lest he walk naked, and they see his shame. And he gathered them together into a place called in the Hebrew tongue* **Armageddon** (Revelation 16:15–16).

Example of Use: For many months now, my brother, John Zogby, has been calling this year's presidential contest the "**Armageddon** election." Both sides, Republicans and Democrats, he has written, "are acting as if a loss will mean the end of the world as we know it." ("The **Armageddon** Election," James Zogby, Sept. 9, 2004, mediamonitors.net)

Arrows in one's quiver

Means: (1) A large number of children, especially sons, and (2) power

Biblical Text: *Lo, children are an heritage of the LORD: and the fruit of the womb is his reward. As* **arrows** *are in the hand of a mighty man; so are children of the youth. Happy is the man that hath* **his quiver full of them***: they shall not be ashamed, but they shall speak with the enemies in the gate* (Psalm 127:3–5).

Example of Use: Tomorrow's college graduates better be prepared to out-think, out-prepare, and out-work their competitors to be successful—and be willing to take risks, according to John Cushman III. "I never wanted to be on a level playing field. I always wanted **more arrows in my quiver**. With more **arrows in my quiver** I can outshoot the other side," a dapper Cushman told about 50 business students and staff on the Cal Poly campus Tuesday. ("Competitive Success," Nov. 5, 2003, *The Tribune*, San Luis Obispo, CA)

As a dream when one awakes

Means: Impermanence

Biblical Text: *Surely thou didst set them in slippery places: thou castedst them down into destruction. How are they brought into desolation, as in a moment! they are utterly consumed with terrors. As a dream when one awaketh; so, O Lord, when thou awakest, thou shalt despise their image* (Psalm 73:18–20).

Example of Use: last night i dreamt we were finally together and it was a feeling so sweet i could have died from it. but just **as a dream when one awakes** and is no more, so the heart deeply sank in ache. ("Last Night," Jen, Dec. 16, 2006, big-bluesky.typepad.com)

As a man thinks in his heart, so is he

Means: A person's real character is defined by his opinions, attitudes, and thought

Biblical Text: *For as he thinketh in his heart, so is he: Eat and drink, saith he to thee; but his heart is not with thee* (Proverbs 23:7).

Example of Use: Fear is one of several options available to us. We can choose not to be afraid. We can choose to define ourselves as dynamic, competent and resourceful beings ready to take on the challenges of life. "**As he thinketh in his heart, so**

A

is he." ("Overcome Fear to Achieve Greatness," Mar. 7, 1997, *Philadelphia Tribune*)

As for me and my house

Means: A phrase indicating a person's convictions on an issue and those of his family, friends, or group

Biblical Text: *As for me and my house, we will serve the Lord. And the people answered and said, God forbid that we should forsake the* LORD, *to serve other gods* (Joshua 24:15–16).

Example of Use: As for me and my house we have no air conditioning. We find that we have 1–5 days of really uncomfortable heat each year. ("How Do You Beat the Heat?" July 20, 2006, *Wisconsin State Journal*, Madison)

As many as the sand

Means: A huge number

Biblical Text: *Judah and Israel were* **many, as the sand** *which is by the sea in multitude, eating and drinking, and making merry* (1 Kings 4:20).

Example of Use: The stars seem to number **as many as the sand** particles you can't count. ("Sand Dunes Pay Homage to Natural Beauty," Don Kennedy, Oct. 19, 2000, *The Gazette*, Colorado Springs, CO)

As old as the hills

Means: Very old

Biblical Text: *Art thou the first man that was born? or* **wast thou made before the hills?** (Job 15:7).

Example of Use: Lawyer-bashing is **as old as the hills** and as fashionable this election season as ever. ("How Many Lawyers Does It Take . . . ?" Sept. 20, 2004, *Denver Post*)

As one man

Means: In complete agreement; to be unanimous; working as a unit

Biblical Text: *And all the people gathered themselves together* ***as one man*** *into the street that was before the water gate* (Nehemiah 8:1).

Example of Use: At the bark of a command, the ranks of soldiers with closely cropped hair froze. Then, **as one man**, they roared: "Bir Turk dunyaya bedel dir!"—"One Turk is worth the whole world!" ("Turkish Military Takes Backseat, for Now; EU Puts Curbs As Membership Debate Nears," Andrew Borowiec, Oct. 10, 2004, *The Washington Times*)

As was his custom

Means: A pattern of one's behavior

Biblical Text: *And he came to Nazareth, where he had been brought up: and,* ***as his custom was****, he went into the synagogue on the sabbath day, and stood up for to read* (Luke 4:16).

Example of Use: On Dec. 6, 1973, there was a vice presidential inauguration of sorts and **as was his custom**, Mr. Ford spoke with modesty and presence. President Ford: I'm a Ford, not a Lincoln. (Soundbite of laughter and applause) ("Gerald Ford's Legacy As a Likable President," Robert Siegel, Dec. 27, 2006, *All Things Considered*, National Public Radio)

As you sow, so shall you reap

Means: One's behavior determines one's results

A

Biblical Text: *Be not deceived; God is not mocked: for **whatsoever a man soweth, that shall he also reap**.* (Galatians 6:7).

Example of Use: Senior executives who choose to disregard shoddy treatment of their managers are making a conscious decision to place the company in jeopardy. ("**As You Sow, So Shall You Reap**," Scott Clark, Sept. 27, 1999, *The Journal Record*, Tulsa, OK)

Ask and it shall be given

Means: One's request shall be accepted

Biblical Text: *Ask, and it shall be given you; seek, and ye shall find; knock, and it shall be opened unto you* (Matthew 7:7).

Example of Use: There comes a time in the field of development that we must "get back to the basics" if we are going to advance and do our jobs properly. **Ask, and it shall be given you; seek, and ye shall find**. . . . Money does not come in, it must be gone after." ("Ask . . . the Secret to Fund Raising," Charles V. Watts, May 1, 2001, *Fund Raising Management*)

Asleep, To be

Means: To be deceased

Biblical Text: *After that, he was seen of above five hundred brethren at once; of whom the greater part remain unto this present, but some are **fallen asleep*** (1 Corinthians 15:6).

Example of Use: In daily conversations the deceased tend to pass or fade away . . . meet their eternal reward . . . or merely **fall asleep**. (deathreference.com)

Asunder

Means: In separate pieces, places, or parts

Biblical Text: *What therefore God hath joined together, let not man put **asunder*** (Mark 10:9).

Example of Use: No matter who you are, no matter whether you initiate the split or have it forced on you, divorce is a painful, tedious, heart-rending process. It takes its toll not only on the soon-to-be-**torn-asunder** couple, but on friends who are forced to choose sides, on relatives and, worst of all, on children. ("What Our Congress Has Joined Together, Let No Activist Judge **Tear Asunder**," Allen Johnson, June 11, 2006, *The News & Record*, Piedmont Triad, NC)

At ease in Zion

Means: Living in ease and luxury

Biblical Text: *Woe to them that are **at ease in Zion**, and trust in the mountain of Samaria, which are named chief of the nations, to whom the house of Israel came!* (Amos 6:1).

Example of Use: The main drive and directing imagination came from the magazine's founding editor Elliot Cohen, and Cohen was, to put it mildly, someone far from **at ease in Zion**. ("Remembering Robert Warshow. (The Immediate Experience)," Midge Decter, Apr. 1, 2002, *Commentary*)

At hand

Means: (1) Near in time or place; (2) deserving immediate attention

Biblical Text: *And as ye go, preach, saying, The kingdom of heaven is **at hand*** (Matthew 10:7).

Example of Use: "The Latest in Wireless Technology Is Close **at Hand**," Tricia Duryee, Sept. 23, 2006, *Seattle Times*

Avenger of blood

Means: A person responsible for exacting revenge on the murderer of a relative or a friend

Biblical Text: *These were the cities appointed for all the children of Israel, and for the stranger that sojourneth among them, that whosoever killeth any person at unawares might flee thither, and not die by the hand of the **avenger of blood**, until he stood before the congregation* (Joshua 20:9).

Example of Use: Batista also is known as a free spirit who is passionate about poetry, writing, philosophy and music. He has written a book of poetry in Spanish and recently published a thriller about a serial killer called *The **Avenger of Blood***. ("Mariners, Batista Agree to Terms[;] Charismatic Right-Handed Pitcher Will Take Physical Thursday to Complete the Deal," David Andriesen, Dec. 12, 2006, *Seattle Post-Intelligencer*)

Ax is laid at . . . , The

Means: Judgment is near

Biblical Text: *And now also **the axe is laid** unto the root of the trees: therefore every tree which bringeth not forth good fruit is hewn down, and cast into the fire* (Matthew 3:10).

Example of Use: Second, expenditures have to be cut. But in doing so, hardly anything can be done to trim salaries and other absolutely necessary current expenses. So, the **axe is laid** on capital expenditures. ("We Are Kidding Ourselves," Jan. 19, 2003, *Manila Bulletin*)

RAISING CAIN

B

"BESIDE ONESELF"

Babel (or Babel, Tower of)

B

Means: A confusion of sounds or voices, especially when loud or disagreeable, or a scene of noise and confusion

Biblical Text: *The* LORD *scattered them abroad from thence upon the face of all the earth: and they left off to build the city. Therefore is the name of it called* **Babel***; because the* LORD *did there confound the language of all the earth: and from thence did the* LORD *scatter them abroad upon the face of all the earth* (Genesis 11:8–9).

Example of Use: "Foreigners on U.S. airwaves have traditionally been Canadians. But South Florida—with its **Tower of Babel** of languages and nationalities—is a more accepting arena for different sounds, broadcast industry insiders say." ("There's a Little Bit of Britain in the Air," Carl Juste, Oct. 14, 2004, *Miami Herald*)

Babylon

Means: A place or a group notorious for its corruption or depravity

Biblical Text: *And upon her forehead was a name written,* MYSTERY, **BABYLON** THE GREAT, THE MOTHER OF HARLOTS AND ABOMINATIONS OF THE EARTH (Revelation 17:5). See also Rev. 14:8; 16:19; 18:1–3.

Example of Use: Like any great metropolis, London can sometimes seem a **Babylon** of squander. The attractions of recycling, of sustainable ways of producing and using organic foods, are a great antidote. ("Go Green in the City," July 5, 2006, *Evening Standard*, London)

Babylonian captivity

Means: A long period of subjugation or exile

Biblical Text: *Behold, the days come, that all that is in thine house, and that which thy fathers have laid up in store unto this day, **shall be carried into Babylon**: nothing shall be left, saith the LORD* (2 Kings 20:17). See also 2 Kings 24:15–20.

Example of Use: In New York City, where the founder [Bill Clinton] has entered the difficult years of his **Babylonian Captivity**, the first signs of outright impiety were visible. ("Bill and Hill Are Pills: The Negative Publicity That Followed the Clintons from the White House Has Turned Some Former Supporters against Them," John Leo, Feb. 19, 2001, *U.S. News & World Report*)

Balaam's ass

Means: Someone who makes others aware of the truth in a particular situation, often with opposition, disbelief, or resentment, or who protects others from unseen danger

Biblical Text: *And when the **ass** saw the angel of the LORD, she fell down under **Balaam**: and **Balaam's** anger was kindled, and he smote the **ass** with a staff. And the LORD opened the mouth of the **ass**, and she said unto **Balaam**, What have I done unto thee, that thou hast smitten me these three times?* (Numbers 22:27–28).

Example of Use: "I will bind myself to the truth/And speak it like **Balaam's ass** once more." (Bill Mallonee, 2007, talking-donkey.worldmagblog.com/talkingdonkey)

Balm in Gilead

B

Means: A remedy of a powerful nature

Biblical Text: *Is there no balm in Gilead; is there no physician there? why then is not the health of the daughter of my people recovered?* (Jeremiah 8:22). See also Jer. 46:11.

Example of Use: "[T]ell me truly, I implore[.] Is there—is there **balm in Gilead**?—tell me—tell me, I implore!" Quoth the raven, "Nevermore." (Edgar Allan Poe, "The Raven") Financial missteps at the city of Leesburg are turning into one giant stumblefest. ("'Nevermore' Not a Good Way to Run a City," Lauren Ritchie, Feb. 11, 2007, *Orlando Sentinel*)

Baptism of fire

Means: The experience of any severe or painful ordeal, particularly an initial negative experience

Biblical Text: *John answered, saying unto them all, I indeed baptize you with water; but one mightier than I cometh, the latchet of whose shoes I am not worthy to unloose: he shall **baptize** you with the Holy Ghost and **with fire*** (Luke 3:16).

Example of Use: A resident whose roof had taken flight in the storm demanded that Dr. Wong "come at once . . . that's what I elected him for." It was sort of a **baptism of fire** for this new assemblyman who is still tidying up loose ends from the effects of the storm. ("**Baptism of Fire** for Wakil Rakyat," Joceline Tan, Mar. 19, 2000, *New Straits Times*, Kuala Lumpur, Malaysia)

Barabbas

Means: One who is guilty but escapes punishment as an innocent person takes his place

Biblical Text: *And so Pilate, willing to content the people, released **Barabbas** unto them, and delivered Jesus, when he had scourged him, to be crucified* (Mark 15:15).

B

Example of Use: "Just deserts for prison inmates should mean no dessert, especially in lean times," a legislator said Thursday. "Why are we giving **Barabbas**-like characters pound cake?" said Rep. Marty Seifert, R-Marshall, referring to a biblical robber. "We have to make sure the rapists and murderers sacrifice like everyone else." ("Bill Would Put Prison Desserts on the Budget-Cutting Table," Conrad DeFiebre, Mar. 21, 2003, *Star Tribune,* Minneapolis, MN)

Be fruitful and multiply

Means: An exhortation to reproduce

Biblical Text: *And God blessed them, and God said to them, **Be fruitful and multiply*** (Genesis 1:28).

Example of Use: Why do investments that you own continue to **be fruitful and multiply?** Why do people invest? Because of what's known as the "eighth wonder of the world"—compounding. In fact, consider it the investor's best friend. ("The Power of Compounding," Takita Mason, Oct. 1, 2000, *Black Enterprise*)

Be not righteous over much

Means: Avoid false piety

Biblical Text: *Be not righteous over much; neither make thyself over wise: why shouldest thou destroy thyself?* (Ecclesiastes 7:16).

Example of Use: My father mentioned Solomon's admonition to **be not righteous over much** nor be overwise, which, to a certain degree, put the smack down on my argument, and I didn't have much good to say. ("Addenda," Mar. 22, 2007, Lincoln Davis, lincolndavis.blogspot.com)

Be sure your sin will find you out

Means: An exhortation warning that one's misdeeds will eventually be revealed

Biblical Text: *But if ye will not do so, behold, ye have sinned against the LORD: and* **be sure your sin will find you out** (Numbers 32:23).

Example of Use: The United States-to-be, which received 5 percent of all slaves brought to the Americas, is now home to about 30 percent of the persons of African descent in our hemisphere. Even so, Bender claims that slavery is central to American history. He may be right. Rest assured—**your sins will find you out!** ("Half-Brother to the World: The United States Has Been More like Other Nations than We Like to Think. [*A Nation Among Nations: America's Place in World History*] [Book Review]," Eugen Weber, June 22, 2006, *American Scholar*)

Bear the burden and heat of the day

Means: Do hard work in difficult circumstances

Biblical Text: *Saying, These last have wrought but one hour, and thou hast made them equal unto us, which have* **borne the burden and heat of the day** (Matthew 20:12).

Example of Use: The Rev. Ian Paisley agreed with Mr. Trimble that the disbandment of the Full-Time Reserve would be a disaster. "We would have no policing at all in Northern Ireland because the stream of new recruits would not be tried and proved and those that have stood **the burden and heat of the day** would have been sacrificed on the altar of political expediency," he said.

("Police Board Takes Shape," Gavin Jennings, Sept. 22, 2001, *The News Letter*, Belfast, Northern Ireland)

Beat one's plowshares into swords

Means: Prepare for war

Biblical Text: *Proclaim ye this among the Gentiles; Prepare war, wake up the mighty men, let all the men of war draw near; let them come up:* ***Beat your plowshares into swords*** *and your pruning-hooks into spears: let the weak say, I am strong* (Joel 3:9–10).

Example of Use: A conservative today is a reactionary ready to **beat plowshares into swords**. (Dean C, May 20, 2007, blog. 360.yahoo.com)

Beat one's swords into plowshares

Means: Prepare for peace

Biblical Text: *And he shall judge among the nations, and shall rebuke many people: and they shall* ***beat their swords into plowshares***, *and their spears into pruninghooks: nation shall not lift up sword against nation, neither shall they learn war any more* (Isaiah 2:4). See also Mic. 4:3.

Example of Use: In a ghostlike performance, the small cluster of white deer slip in and out of sight, peacefully weaving among the hummock-shaped bunkers that once held America's war weapons. The striking image is one Dennis Money wants others to see. "It's a classic moment to see one of these deer on top of an ammunition bunker," he said. "You go back to that old saying about **beating your swords into plowshares**. You put a military base to bed and turn it into a conservation park." ("Animal News to Conserve: Deer or Energy?" William Kates, Apr. 8, 2007, *The Virginian Pilot,* Hampton Roads)

Beat the air

Means: To fail, to make no progress; to work to no purpose; to labor in vain

Biblical Text: *I therefore so run, not as uncertainly; so fight I, not as one that **beateth the air**: But I keep under my body, and bring it into subjection: lest that by any means, when I have preached to others, I myself should be a castaway* (1 Corinthians 9:26–27).

Example of Use: KCNA accused U.S. conservatives of using Hwang to escalate a smear campaign against North Korea and eventually topple the communist regime. "But this is as foolish an act as trying to **beat the air**," it said. ("North Korea Slams Top Defector's Visit to United States," Nov. 7, 2003, AP Worldstream)

Become a byword

Means: To be an object of reproach, representing that which is inferior or negative

Biblical Text: *Then will I pluck them up by the roots out of my land which I have given them; and this house, which I have sanctified for my name, will I cast out of my sight, and will **make** it to be a proverb and a **byword** among all nations* (2 Chronicles 7:20).

Example of Use: Zimbabwe has **become a byword** for economic and political meltdown. ("Chronicle of a Death Foretold; Journalism in Zimbabwe," Geoffrey Nyarota, Oct. 7, 2006, *The Economist*)

Become like little children

Means: Become humble and compliant

Biblical Text: *And Jesus called a little child unto him, and set him in the midst of them, And said, Verily I say unto you, Except ye be converted, and **become as little children**, ye shall not enter into the kingdom of heaven* (Matthew 18:2–3).

Example of Use: Their trust is whole-hearted, their hope is maxxed out, their love is so strong and their pain is so raw . . . and there's nothing complicated about that. It's what we're asked to be and to do . . . shed the skins of politics and correctness, etiquette and dress for success, all these socially encoded behaviours that we honestly hate . . . and **become like little children**. ("Beth Rhyme and Color—Trivial Pursuits[:] Perceptions and Reflections," May 31, 2007, rhymeandcolor. blogspirit.com)

Beginning of wisdom

Means: Insight; the ability to discern what is true, right, or enduring

Biblical Text: *The fear of the* Lord *is **the beginning of wisdom**: a good understanding have all they that do his commandments: his praise endureth for ever* (Psalm 111:10). See also Prov. 9:10.

Example of Use: For the 19 military administrators of the northern states, the fear of Shiite fanatics, a group of Islamic puritans, is the **beginning of wisdom**. ("War against Shiites," Feb. 24, 1997, *The Week*)

Behemoth

Means: Something or someone unusually large

Biblical Text: *Behold now **behemoth**, which I made with thee; he eateth grass as an ox. Lo now, his strength is in his loins, and his force is in the navel of his belly. He moveth his tail like a cedar: the sinews of his stones are wrapped together. His bones*

B

are as strong pieces of brass; his bones are like bars of iron (Job 40:15–18).

Example of use: "Working with **behemoth** beams is routine for the 10 Hamilton Construction employees on hand for the installation Tuesday; the company also installed the slightly larger beams in Chemult, construction manager Con O'Connor said. ("Heavyweight Beams Arrive at Bridge Replacement Site. [The Concrete **Behemoths**, Each about 61 Yards Long, Will Provide Stability]," Andrea Damewood, Nov. 28, 2007, *The Register-Guard*, Eugene, OR)

Behold the man!

Means: An exhortation meaning, "Look at him!"

Biblical Text: *Then came Jesus forth, wearing the crown of thorns, and the purple robe. And Pilate saith unto them, **Behold the man!*** (John 19:5).

Example of Use: Three days after his final Throne Speech, Prime Minister Jean Chretien announced he would expand the National Parks system by half. Would this be his "legacy"? **Behold the man**, he replied. "I do my job the best I can." So perhaps he will leave no legacy. Would we think better of him if he did? ("An Illusion of Action; Look for Chretien's 'Legacy' in the Throne Speech, but You Won't Find It," Kevin Michael Grace, Oct. 21, 2002, *The Report Newsmagazine*)

Believe until one sees with one's own eyes, Not to

Means: Refusal to believe what seems incredible until one actually verifies it by seeing it

Biblical Text: *The other disciples therefore said unto him [Thomas], We have seen the Lord. But he said unto them, **Except***

I shall see in his hands the print of the nails, and put my finger into the print of the nails, and thrust my hand into his side, *I will not believe* (John 20:25).

Example of Use: I probably won't believe Lemieux will play in 70 games **until I actually see it with my own eyes**, but as of right now—with the shape he appears to be in—it's hard not to give him the benefit of the doubt. ("NHL Hockey: Hopefully, Mario Can Keep It Up," Matt Canamucio, Oct. 17, 2002, *Sports Network*)

Belshazzar's feast

Means: An occasion of decadent indulgence

Biblical Text: *Belshazzar the king made a great feast* to a thousand of his lords, and drank wine before the thousand (Daniel 5:1).

Example of Use: Rich, rich Saul Steinberg's party may have been a gaudy feast of consumption, but news stories left the woman in no doubt that Malcolm Forbes' party was the most extravagant blowout since **Belshazzar's feast**. ("Parties for Rich and Famous Vital Public Service," Russell Baker, Sept. 5, 1989, *The Journal Record*)

Belshazzar's wall

Means: The location of a message of impending doom or catastrophe

Biblical Text: *In the same hour came forth fingers of a man's hand, and wrote over against the candlestick upon the plaister of the **wall** of the king's palace: and the king [**Belshazzar**] saw the part of the hand that wrote* (Daniel 5:5).

Example of Use: It is the fashion now at exhibitions to embellish the display of paintings with an artist's aphorisms writ as large as *Mene Mene Tekel* on **Belshazzar's wall**. ("Bondage, Eroticism, the Supernatural—Late 18th-Century Gothic Fantasies Are Shown to Titillating," Brian Sewell, Feb. 17, 2006, *Evening Standard*, London)

Beside oneself, To be

Means: To be extremely excited or agitated; to lose control of one's senses

Biblical Text: *And the multitude cometh together again, so that they could not so much as eat bread. And when his friends heard of it, they went out to lay hold on him: for they said, He is **beside himself*** (Mark 3:20–21).

Example of Use: Tom Hicks was **beside himself**. He couldn't sit in one place. And he couldn't stand. He couldn't even bear to watch at times, but the buoyant CEO and chairman of Hicks Muse Tate & Furst, the giant buyout firm, also couldn't afford to turn away, because this deal could go either way. . . . This was really big. This was Saturday afternoons in the fall. This was perky cheerleaders flying through the air, and high-stepping marching bands. This was college football. This was Texas. ("How One College Program Runs the Business," Dec. 20, 1999, *Fortune*)

Better is the end of a thing than the beginning

Means: The conclusion or product of something is more satisfactory than its commencement

Biblical Text: *Better is the end of a thing than the beginning thereof: and the patient in spirit is better than the proud in spirit* (Ecclesiastes 7:8).

Example of Use: "**Better is the end of a thing than its beginning.**" Sure is in this instance. Just posted my two copies of the Docetism essay (one to the Institute and one to my marker) and it's out of my hands now. It's been particularly difficult this week with losing my first draft and notes in the computer crash. ("Voila," Ukok's Place, Feb. 25, 2006, innominepatriset-filiietspiritussancti.blogspot.com)

Beulah land (or Beulah, Land of)

Means: A place of ease and plenty

Biblical Text: *Thou shalt no more be termed Forsaken; neither shall thy land any more be termed Desolate: but thou shalt be called Hephzibah, and thy land **Beulah**: for the LORD delighteth in thee, and thy land shall be married* (Isaiah 62:4).

Example of Use: His [a woodchuck's] burrow emerged from underground, exactly between two hilled rows of potatoes. And for 10 days after he broke through to daylight, he must have thought he'd arrived in Shangri-La in **Beulah Land**. ("Hard Work Needed to Maintain One's Garden," Robert Siegel, Aug. 24, 2000, *All Things Considered*, National Public Radio)

Beware of false prophets

Means: An exhortation to avoid people who teach or preach false doctrine or who would otherwise lead one astray

Biblical Text: *Beware of false prophets, which come to you in sheep's clothing, but inwardly they are ravening wolves* (Matthew 7:15).

Example of Use: Cyberspace is thy lord and master—thou shalt have no other gods before it. There is no way to be partially committed to getting online. The process requires

B

time, money and energy. **Beware of false prophets** from the online industry who promise a heavenly experience with little or no work. First, estimate the amount of resources you think you'll spend on the project—then double it. ("The 10 Commandments of Cyberspace," William F. Allman, Sept. 15, 1995, *Folio: the Magazine for Magazine Management*)

Beyond measure

Means: In excess; without limit

Biblical Text: *For ye have heard of my conversation in time past in the Jews' religion, how that **beyond measure** I [Paul] perse-cuted the church of God, and wasted it* (Galatians 1:13).

Examples of use: "Strength **Beyond Measure**: Naperville Woman Refuses to Let Aneurysm Beat Her," Beth Sneller, Aug. 22, 2002, *Daily Herald,* Arlington Heights, IL.

Birthright, Sell one's

Means: To give up a right, possession, or privilege that is one's due by birth (To "sell one's birthright for a mess of pottage" is often used, meaning to accept some trivial gain while losing something far more valuable.)

Biblical Text: *And Jacob said, **Sell me this day thy birthright**. And Esau said, Behold, I am at the point to die: and what profit shall this birthright do to me? And Jacob said, Swear to me this day; and he sware unto him: and **he sold his birthright** unto Jacob. Then Jacob gave Esau bread and pottage of lentiles; and he did eat and drink, and rose up, and went his way: thus Esau despised his **birthright** (Genesis 25:31–34).

Example of Use: "The [George H. W.] Bush administration was born of the Reagan revolution," said Morton Blackwell, head of the conservative Leadership Institute. "He has now

sold his birthright for a mess of pottage laced with cyanide."
("Bush's Big Gamble: The '92 Suburban Strategy," Thomas B.
Edsall, July 15, 1990, *The Washington Post*)

Birthright, Steal one's

Means: To take a right, possession, or privilege owned by
someone else to whom it is due by birth

Biblical Text: *And he said, Is not he rightly named Jacob? for he
hath supplanted me these two times: he **took away my birthright**; and, behold, now he hath taken away my blessing. And he
said [to his father, Isaac], Hast thou not reserved a blessing for
me?* (Genesis 27:36).

Example of Use: Looking back on what drove him to arrange
the meeting, Joel, 52, says: "When my father told me the story
of my grandfather, that the Nazis had stolen our company and
given it to one of their placemen, that my grandparents had
been threatened by the Gestapo unless they relinquished
everything, and that they were forced to flee from all the things
they held dear with only the clothes on their backs, I simply
couldn't believe it." . . . But it is the Neckermanns' unfeeling,
almost defiant attitude that Billy Joel finds so painful, rather
than the blatant **theft of his birthright**. ("Billy Joel: The Day I
Confronted the Woman Whose Nazi Grandfather **Stole My
Birthright**," Allan Hall, Feb. 24, 2002, *The Mail on Sunday*,
London)

Bitter end

Means: The final extremity, no matter how painful or
time-consuming

B

Biblical Text: *For the lips of a strange woman drop as an honey-comb, and her mouth is smoother than oil: But her **end is bitter** as wormwood, sharp as a two-edged sword* (Proverbs 5:3–4).

Example of Use: "Capitals-Rangers: Mirror Images to the **Bitter End**," Jesse Spector, *Sporting News*, May 9, 2012.

Blessed are . . .

Means: Fortunate or happy

Biblical Text: *Blessed are the poor in spirit: for theirs is the kingdom of heaven* (Matthew 5:3).

Example of Use: "**Blessed Are** the Liberals for They Love to Tax," Joseph F. White Jr., Jan. 26, 1997, *Rocky Mountain News*, Denver

Blessed are the meek

Means: A blessing on those who are humble and unpretentious

Biblical Text: *Blessed are the meek: for they shall inherit the earth* (Matthew 5:5).

Example of Use: I called to thank him and ask where he got that phrasing and what exactly it meant. He told me he had never liked the beatitude that says "**Blessed are the meek**," because "it reminded me of a bunch of 'hangdog' kind of people, which I didn't much like. Then I found a French Bible where the translation, instead of 'meek,' uses the French word 'debonair.' I translated that as 'Blessed are the happy-go-lucky.'" ("Open-Hearted in Fiction and Friendship," Apr. 29, 2007, *The Boston Globe*)

Blessed are the peacemakers

Means: A blessing on those who establish peace among people or groups who have been at war with each other

Biblical Text: *Blessed are the peacemakers: for they shall be called the children of God* (Matthew 5:9).

Example of Use: "[Linda Flynn Beekman] kissed her son goodbye and got on a plane bound for Bosnia as a peace witness, to volunteer—she wasn't quite sure how—to help the people of Sarajevo. "She didn't speak the language, didn't know where her help might be needed. She had only a connection to an Italian peace organization, **Blessed Are the Peacemakers**." ("Everyday Life in a War Zone," Colette Bancroft, Sept. 28, 2004, *St. Petersburg Times*, FL)

Blind leading the blind

Means: A condition in which one who is uninformed and incompetent leads others who are similarly incapable

Biblical Text: *Let them alone: they be blind leaders of the blind. And if the **blind lead the blind**, both shall fall into the ditch* (Matthew 15:14). See also Luke 6:39.

Example of Use: No, journalists—including Broder—have been trying to lead the rest of us down the same dark path toward the Leviathan State for more than a century. Except for those few people who understand the horrors of unchecked government, it has been a long and dreary episode of **the blind leading the blind**. ("End of Another Progressive-Era Relic," William Anderson, Oct. 7, 2004, www.mises.org)

Blinds the eyes of the wise, A gift

Means: Offerings, whether bribes or not, create partiality in judges.

Biblical Text: *Thou shalt not wrest judgment; thou shalt not respect persons, neither take a gift: for **a gift doth blind the eyes of the wise**, and pervert the words of the righteous* (Deuteronomy 16:19).

Example of use: As in the Koran of the Muslim faith, the sacred Judeo-Christian texts also make anti-corruption references. According to the Old Testament, Moses told his peoples more than 2,300 years ago: "Do not accept bribes, because **bribes blind the eyes of the wise** and pervert the words of the just." ("Corruption: First U.N. Treaty to Fight a Global Vice," Diego Cevallos, Dec. 12, 2003, Inter Press Service English News Wire)

Blood cries out

Means: A condition in which revenge is called for because of murder

Biblical Text: *And the LORD said unto Cain, Where is Abel thy brother? And he said, I know not: Am I my brother's keeper? And he said, What hast thou done? the voice of **thy brother's blood crieth unto me from the ground*** (Genesis 4:9–10).

Example of Use: We all contain the seeds of kindness or the seeds of violence. The death of my wonderful daughter, Rachel Joy Scott, and the deaths of that heroic teacher and the other 11 children who died must not be in vain. Their **blood cries out** for answers. ("Columbine Tragedy Shows Nation Must Return to a Trust in God," Darrell Scott, May 1, 2000, *Insight on the News*)

Blood on one's hands, To have

Means: To be responsible for someone's death

Biblical Text: *And when ye spread forth your hands, I will hide mine eyes from you: yea, when ye make many prayers, I will not hear: your **hands are full of blood*** (Isaiah 1:15).

Example of Use: A chill went down my spine when I read the Feb. 7 article "Nazi-Era Filmmaker Riefenstahl Defends Herself at Rare Appearance" and saw a photograph of 96-year-old Leni Riefenstahl, Nazi propaganda film director par excellence. And for good reason: She has **blood on her hands**, including mine. ("Nazi-Era Director Has **Blood on Hands**," Feb. 17, 1999, *The Palm Beach Post*)

Blood on one's head

Means: To be responsible for someone's death

Biblical Text: *And David said unto him, **Thy blood be upon thy head**; for thy mouth hath testified against thee, saying, I have slain the LORD's anointed* (2 Samuel 1:16).

Example of Use: Peace activists demonstrated yesterday at the home of Avigdor Eskin, who was convicted last week of violating the Prevention of Terrorism Act by putting a curse on prime minister Yitzhak Rabin a month before he was assassinated. The demonstrators carried signs that read "His **blood is on his head**," and "We will not forget who incited and who was murdered." Eskin's wife came out on her porch carrying a sign saying "Free Dror Adani and Haggai Amir." ("News in Brief," Raine Marcus Itim, June 2, 1997, *Jerusalem Post*)

Book of life

B

Means: (1) The general experience of life; (2) the record of one's life; (3) a record indicating those who will find favor or disfavor by someone in authority

Biblical Text: *He that overcometh, the same shall be clothed in white raiment; and I will not blot out his name out of the **book of life**, but I will confess his name before my Father, and before his angels* (Revelation 3:5). See also Rev. 20:12–15; 21:27.

Example of Use: Who, or what, wrote the **Book of Life**? That was the unasked question that nevertheless got answered at the June 26, 2000, press conference announcing the decoding of the human genome. ("Who Wrote the **Book of Life**?" Thomas W. Clark, Sept. 1, 2000, *The Humanist*)

Books there is no end, Of making many

Means: Books will always be published.

Biblical Text: *And further, by these, my son, be admonished: **of making many books there is no end**; and much study is a weariness of the flesh. Let us hear the conclusion of the whole matter: Fear God, and keep his commandments: for this is the whole duty of man* (Ecclesiastes 12:12–13).

Example of Use: Before snuggling into bed too cozily with Xlibris, Random House's admiralty might consult Ecclesiastes, which along with its famous estimation that "all is vanity" offers even more pertinent advice: "My child, beware. **Of making many books there is no end.**" ("All Is Vanity," Tom Bissell and Webster Younce, Dec. 1, 2000, *Harper's Magazine*)

Born again

Means: Characterized by renewal, resurgence, or return; a condition in which one makes a renewed commitment or a conversion, especially from one direction or philosophy to its opposite

Biblical Text: *Jesus answered and said unto him, Verily, verily, I say unto thee, Except a man be **born again**, he cannot see the kingdom of God. . . . Marvel not that I said unto thee, Ye must be **born again*** (John 3:3, 7). See also 1 Pet. 1:23.

Example of Use: Some of these historic barns . . . are being saved. ("**Born-Again** Barns," Ellen Mitchell, Jan. 10, 2002, *Newsday*, New York)

Bottomless pit

Means: (1) A hopeless situation; (2) a reference, usually humorous, to someone who seems able to eat far more than others

Biblical Text: *And when they shall have finished their testimony, the beast that ascendeth out of the **bottomless pit** shall make war against them, and shall overcome them, and kill them* (Revelation 11:7).

Example of Use: Mark Hughes has been warned that Blackburn [soccer team] are no longer the **bottomless pit** of cash that they were a decade ago—but the new Rovers manager will have some money to spend when the transfer window reopens in January. ("No Blank Cheque; Hughes Must Sell before Spending Big at Rovers," Martyn Ziegler, Sept. 18, 2004, *Daily Post*, Liverpool)

Bowels of compassion

Means: Feelings of deep pity or sympathy

Biblical Text: *But whoso hath this world's good, and seeth his brother have need, and shutteth up his **bowels of compassion** from him, how dwelleth the love of God in him?* (1 John 3:17).

Example of Use: These ministers make religion a cold and flinty-hearted thing, having neither principles of right action, nor **bowels of compassion**. They strip the love of God of its beauty, and leave the throne of religion a huge, horrible, repulsive form. It is a religion for oppressors, tyrants, man-stealers, and thugs. ("What to the Slave Is the Fourth of July?" July 25, 2001, *The New York Beacon*)

Breach of promise

Means: Failure to carry out one's promise, especially to marry

Biblical Text: *After the number of the days in which ye searched the land, even forty days, each day for a year, shall ye bear your iniquities, even forty years, and ye shall know my **breach of promise*** (Numbers 14:34).

Example of Use: The patient specifically asked that she not be sedated, and Dr. Murphy promised the patient that he would not sedate her. Barring the occurrence of an emergency requiring sedation, Dr. Murphy was clearly subject to liability for his **breach of promise** to the patient. ("TX: Anesthesiologist Promises Not to Sedate Patient: Sedated Patient Sues for **Breach of Promise**," A. David Tammelleo, Sept. 1, 2002, *Hospital Law's Regan Report*)

Bread of life, The

Means: Food required for life

Biblical Text: *Verily, verily, I say unto you, He that believeth on me hath everlasting life. I am that **bread of life*** (John 6:47–48).

Example of Use: The store, called Foods for Life Natural Foods, in Glendale, Calif., lent its back room to bake bread. The specialty was a bread made with only sprouted organic grains, seeds and beans, and no flour, a difficult feat for sure. The company named its bread Ezekiel 4:9, after the Scripture, and it took off. ("Grains Make **Bread of Life**," Cynthia Hizer, Oct. 21, 1999, *The Atlanta Journal-Constitution*)

Break bread

Means: To eat with someone

Biblical Text: *And upon the first day of the week, when the disciples came together to **break bread**, Paul preached unto them, ready to depart on the morrow* (Acts 20:7).

Example of Use: The Rapprochement Center of Beit Sahour in the West Bank, as its name implies, wants to bring people closer to each other and develop friendly relations between Palestinians and Israelis. ("Let Us **Break Bread**, Not Bones," Mari Ternbo, Dec. 1, 1994, *Women Magazine*)

Break forth

Means: To happen, appear, or open

Biblical Text: *Then shall thy light **break forth** as the morning, and thine health shall spring forth speedily: and thy righteousness shall go before thee; the glory of the LORD shall be thy reward* (Isaiah 58:8).

Example of Use: "Consumers are emerging from their self-involved, self-centered cocoons to reconnect with the outside world. As they **break forth** from the cocoon, they are assuming a new leadership position in the social, political, cultural landscapes that define their identity in relation to the outside world," said Pam Danziger, president of Unity Marketing, and author of *Why People Buy Things They Don't Need . . .* today at the National Retail Federation Convention, Jacob K. Javits Convention Center, New York. ("'Butterfly' Consumers Emerge from their Cocoons, 'Connecting' Seen As the Dominant Consumer Trend of the Future," Jan. 14, 2003, *Business Wire*)

Break of day

Means: Morning, as the sun rises

Biblical Text: *When he therefore was come up again, and had broken bread, and eaten, and talked a long while, even till* **break of day***, so he departed* (Acts 20:11).

Example of Use: In the dust-doused city of Khost, where roosters compete with gunfire to announce the **break of day**, it is often hard to tell who is calling the shots. ("Tribal Ties Bind Afghan Army: The U.S. Says within Four to Six Weeks Its Troops Will Arrive to Train a New Afghan National Army," Ilene R. Prusher, Mar. 27, 2002, *The Christian Science Monitor*)

Bricks without straw, Make

Means: To work in unusually difficult conditions without the tools or material needed

Biblical Text: *And Pharaoh commanded the same day the task-masters of the people, and their officers, saying,* **Ye shall no more give the people straw to make brick, as heretofore***: let them go and gather straw for themselves* (Exodus 5:6–7).

Example of Use: Virginia opened its 2006 General Assembly last week with a House Republican majority still looking to **make bricks without straw**, a Senate Republican leadership that wouldn't mind chucking a few bricks at the House and a

Democratic governor whose architectural skills have yet to be measured. ("Mr. Kaine Goes to Richmond: Act I," Jan. 19, 2006, *The Virginian Pilot*)

Bring down

Means: To overcome or destroy

Biblical Text: *Understand therefore this day, that the LORD thy God is he which goeth over before thee; as a consuming fire he shall destroy them, and he shall **bring them down** before thy face: so shalt thou drive them out, and destroy them quickly, as the LORD hath said unto thee* (Deuteronomy 9:3).

Example of Use: A person who normally visits a Web site once a day might direct his or her bot to visit once an hour or even once every five minutes, generating as many visits as hundreds of once-a-day visitors. That's a lot of traffic—enough to **bring down** some Web sites, not just for people using RSS, but for everyone. ("Kick Back and Let the Web Come to You," Brian Kladko, Dec. 7, 2004, *The Record,* Bergen County, NJ)

Bring to light

Means: To make something known; to discover facts, often about something incorrect, immoral, or illegal

Biblical Text: *Therefore judge nothing before the time, until the Lord come, who both will **bring to light** the hidden things of darkness, and will make manifest the counsels of the hearts: and then shall every man have praise of God* (1 Corinthians 4:5).

Example of Use: A groundbreaking national campaign designed to **bring to light** the link between depression and suicide is being developed and will be test marketed this fall, with a national launch planned for spring 2003. ("Prevent Suicide. Treat Depression," Oct. 7, 2002, PR Newswire)

Bring word

B

Means: To tell someone news

Biblical Text: *And he sent them to Bethlehem, and said, Go and search diligently for the young child; and when ye have found him,* ***bring me word*** *again, that I may come and worship him also* (Matthew 2:8). See also Gen. 37:14.

Example of Use: Last week **brought word** of a shakeup at the state's largest advertising and public relations firm, Cranford Johnson Robinson Woods of Little Rock. ("Shaken, Stirred. [Outtakes: An Inside Look into Arkansas Media] Frank Cox and Boyd Blackwood Resigned from Cranford Johnson Robinson Woods," Lance Turner, Dec. 6, 2004, *Arkansas Business*)

Broken cistern

Means: Someone or something with no substance; something that does not serve the purpose for which it was made

Biblical Text: *For my people have committed two evils; they have forsaken me the fountain of living waters, and hewed them out cisterns,* ***broken cisterns***, *that can hold no water* (Jeremiah 2:13).

Example of Use: The political wannabes of Tararua, seeking their places in history in the upcoming local body elections, are all nodding their heads like toy dogs in the back windows of cars, and mumbling about priorities and fixing faulty infrastructure, while ignoring the fact the water problem has been stuck in the **broken cistern** of excuses for as long as I can remember. ("The Proposed Cycleway between the Boondock Towns of Eketahuna and Shannon Sounds Flash and Expensive," Sept. 7, 2010, *Manawatu Standard*)

Broken reed

Means: Someone or something that is unreliable or undependable

Biblical Text: *Lo, thou trustest in the staff of this **broken reed**, on Egypt; whereon if a man lean, it will go into his hand, and pierce it: so is Pharaoh king of Egypt to all that trust in him* (Isaiah 36:6).

Example of Use: By creating the Financial Services Authority, I set the scene for the bonanza of the good years. I regret the FSA has turned out to be a **broken reed**. ("Dear Voters, I Trust That You'll Always Feel Indebted to Me," Nov. 25, 2008, *Belfast Telegraph*)

Build on a rock

Means: To establish oneself or one's enterprise on sound principles

Biblical Text: *Therefore whosoever heareth these sayings of mine, and doeth them, I will liken him unto a wise man, which **built his house upon a rock*** (Matthew 7:24).

Example of Use: The foundation for today's quality control structure was **built on the rock** known as W. Edwards Deming, the person most credited with introducing innovative quality control techniques to U.S. industry. ("Returning to Sound Ideas: The Ideas of W. Edwards Deming Can Help Companies Survive Today's Business Challenges," Joe Cappello, Feb. 1, 2002, *Industrial Distribution*)

Bulls of Bashan

B

Means: Strong, bold men

Biblical Text: *Many bulls have compassed me:* ***strong bulls of Bashan*** *have beset me round* (Psalm 22:12).

Example of use: A series of concerts will be performed across South Devon this weekend. . . . The programme includes Lutoslawski's *Livre pour Orchestre*, Gavin Bryar's *Violin Concerto The **Bulls of Bashan*** with young violinist Benjamin Marquise Gilmore as soloist and Tchaikovsky's *6th Symphony The Pathetique.* ("State School Is Match for Eton," Nov. 24, 2006, *Western Morning News*, The Plymouth, UK)

Bulrushes, From the

Means: From an unexpected source

Biblical Text: *And when she could not longer hide him, she took for him an ark of **bulrushes**, and daubed it with slime and with pitch, and put the child therein; and she laid it in the flags by the river's brink* (Exodus 2:3).

Example of Use: He dropped out of school at 15, got pushed into a job as a newspaperman—the closest he has ever come to actually being a mutant—then struggled for many years to emerge **from the bulrushes** of British provincial theater. Stewart may have been driven to play powerful figures on stage by his own feelings of inferiority. ("Commanding Presence: 'X-Men' Star Says He's More Mellow Off-Screen," Bruce Newman, July 14, 2000, Knight Ridder/Tribune News Service)

Burn with lust

Means: To want something with great feeling, usually related to sexual desire

Biblical Text: *And likewise also the men, leaving the natural use of the woman,* **burned in their lust** *one toward another; men with men working that which is unseemly, and receiving in themselves that recompence of their error which was meet* (Romans 1:27).

Example of Use: The choices he presents are clear: "to be selfish or selfless, to forgive or to hate, to **burn with lust** or with love, to defend your personal power or dismantle it." ("*Escape Routes*: For People Who Feel Trapped in Life's Hells," Johann Christoph Arnold, 2007, www.bruderhof.com)

Burning bush

Means: A source of important revelation, especially of a supernatural nature

Biblical Text: *And the angel of the* LORD *appeared unto him in a* **flame of fire out of the midst of a bush**: *and he looked, and, behold, the* **bush burned** *with fire, and the bush was not consumed* (Exodus 3:2).

Example of Use: Though she didn't encounter a crying statue or a **burning bush**, Linda Wanaski is sure the heart-shaped potato she found on Super Bowl Sunday is a sign from God. "We were having some hard times, and I asked God to give us some sort of sign," said Wanaski, a 49-year-old school-bus driver from Schaumburg. ("Forget the Hearts 'n' Flowers. Couple Finds Romance in a Sack of Potatoes," Michael Levine, Feb. 14, 2001, *Daily Herald*, Arlington Heights, IL)

Burnt offering

Means: An overcooked meal (whimsical)

Biblical Text: *And Abraham rose up early in the morning, and saddled his ass, and took two of his young men with him,* *and Isaac his son, and clave the wood for the **burnt offering**, and rose up, and went unto the place of which God had told him* (Genesis 22:3).

Example of Use: Even if you present a **burnt offering**, it doesn't matter, as long as you present it with a big smile. You'll probably get a laugh out of your partner. It's not what you cook, but the fact that you did cook, which counts. ("Even if You Present a **Burnt Offering**, It Doesn't Matter, As Long As You Present It with a Big Smile," Jan. 9, 2006, *Western Mail*, Cardiff, Wales)

Business, Mind one's own

Means: To avoid prying into someone else's affairs

Biblical Text: *We beseech you, brethren, that ye increase more and more; And that ye study to be quiet, and to **do your own business**, and to work with your own hands, as we commanded you* (1 Thessalonians 4:10b–11).

Example of Use: A good piece of advice my mom passed on to me was **tend to your business** and leave everyone else's alone. ("What She Said: We Don't Always Listen, but We Always Hear," Lori Price and Kathy Flanigan, May 14, 2006, *Milwaukee Journal Sentinel*, Milwaukee, WI)

Butter, As smooth as

Means: Literally: to be especially free of uneven parts; figuratively: to be insincerely convincing or to be refined and appealing

Biblical Text: *The words of his mouth were **smoother than butter**, but war was in his heart: his words were softer than oil, yet were they drawn swords* (Psalm 55:21).

Example of Use: Robben Ford is capable of dealing the average guitarist a double-whammy ego blow. Not only can he conjure both stinging and **smooth-as-butter** tones while employing sophisticated phrasing that straddles both blues and jazz, he also has pop songwriting savvy and a sweet singing voice. ("Robben Ford (Interview)," Shawn Hammond, Feb. 1, 2008, *Guitar Player*)

By all means

Means: Certainly; expresses certainty with a positive meaning

Biblical Text: *But bade them farewell, saying, I must **by all means** keep this feast that cometh in Jerusalem: but I will return again unto you, if God will. And he sailed from Ephesus* (Acts 18:21).

Example of Use: Yes, **by all means**, bring back Scottie Pippen. Bring him back to the Bulls because during the 40 games he might play, he should help win some games and be a great influence on the young players. ("Really Now, Pippen Great Fit for Bulls?" Barry Rozner, July 17, 2003, *Daily Herald,* Arlington Heights, IL)

By and by

Means: At some future, indefinite time

Biblical Text: *And she came in straightway with haste unto the king, and asked, saying, I will that thou give me **by and by** in a charger the head of John the Baptist* (Mark 6:25).

Example of Use: Let your weeds grow high and **by and by**, the city will come around and make you cut them down. ("City Wants Weed Warnings Whacked: Owners to Get 10 Days to Clean Up Property, Then Straight to Court," Tim Chitwood, Sept. 6, 2006, *Columbus Ledger-Enquirer,* OH)

By no means

Means: In no sense; certainly not

Biblical Text: *Keeping mercy for thousands, forgiving iniquity and transgression and sin, and that will* **by no means** *clear the guilty* (Exodus 34:7).

Example of Use: The Taiwan issue is China's internal affair and should **by no means** be deliberated in the framework of the security alliance between the United States and Japan, said Chinese Foreign Minister Li Zhaoxing here Sunday. ("Urgent: Taiwan Issue **by No Means** to Be Considered in U.S.-Japan Security Arrangement: Chinese FM," Mar. 6, 2005, Xinhua News Agency)

By their fruits you shall know them

Means: One's true nature or character is revealed by his behavior and its results

Biblical Text: *Beware of false prophets, which come to you in sheep's clothing, but inwardly they are ravening wolves.* **Ye shall know them by their fruits** (Matthew 7:15–16a).

Example of Use: True, it will remain hard for a lot of discriminating people to admire much, if anything, that Dali did after the end of the 1930s, when he took New York by the throat and the wallet. And yet: **by their fruits you shall know them**. ("Dear Salvador . . . An Apology; Dali Was a Dodgy Surrealist Showman with an Eye for the Main Chance—Which, Kevin Jackson Now Realises, Is Precisely Where His Genius Lies," Kevin Jackson, Mar. 25, 2007, *Independent on Sunday*, London)

RAISING CAIN

C

"CITY ON A HILL"

Cain and Abel

Means: A relationship between brothers, marked by strong disagreement or opposition

Biblical Text: *And **Cain** talked with **Abel** his brother: and it came to pass, when they were in the field, that **Cain** rose up against **Abel** his brother, and slew him. And the* LORD *said unto **Cain**, Where is **Abel** thy brother? And he said, I know not: Am I my brother's keeper?* (Genesis 4:8–9).

Example of Use: In [the film] *Undertow*, . . . Mulroney is a taciturn pig farmer raising two sons in the Georgia wastelands. When his long-lost brother . . . pays a call, dark stuff gets stirred up. Think **Cain and Abel**, Southern gothic-style. ("*Sideways* Was Director's Idyll in Wine Country," Steven Rea, Oct. 31, 2004, *The Philadelphia Inquirer*)

Cain, Mark of

Means: A distinguishing sign that displays some quality about its bearer, usually guilt

Biblical Text: *And the* LORD *said unto him, Therefore whosoever slayeth Cain, vengeance shall be taken on him sevenfold. And the Lord set **a mark upon Cain**, lest any finding him should kill him* (Genesis 4:15).

Example of Use: Brewer made repeated reference to Gen. 4:15–16 in exhorting the jury to return a guilty verdict, saying Patty Jo Pulley had put a **mark of Cain** on Rick Pulley when she left fingernail scratches on his face. ("Pulley Found Guilty of Murder," Lauren Chesnut, Oct. 30, 2004, *Register & Bee*, Danville, VA)

Calvary

Means: A place or experience of great suffering or anguish

Biblical Text: *And when they were come to the place, which is called **Calvary**, there they crucified him, and the malefactors, one on the right hand, and the other on the left* (Luke 23:33).

Example of Use: [He] left a brief, loving [suicide] note for his wife, in which he proclaimed his innocence and said he wanted to end his "**calvary**." The situation had continued for at least ten years since he had first been accused of the crime and during which he had twice been held in prison, once for four months in 1996–97 and again briefly last December. ("Scandal Figure Suicide," Dick Leonard, June 1, 2002, *Europe*)

Camel to go through the eye of a needle, It is easier for a

Means: An expression denoting how extremely difficult, if not impossible, something is to do

Biblical Text: *Then said Jesus unto his disciples, Verily I say unto you, That a rich man shall hardly enter into the kingdom of heaven. And again I say unto you, **It is easier for a camel to go through the eye of a needle**, than for a rich man to enter into the kingdom of God* (Matthew 19:23–24).

Example of Use: Just waiting for the draft would be a mistake. Finding the go-to guy in the draft is like getting **a camel to go through the eye of a needle**. ("Jazz Fans Sound Off on Team's Woes," Feb. 17, 2005, *Deseret News*, Salt Lake City, Utah)

Can anything good come out of Nazareth?

Means: An expression denoting the improbability of someone or something from a place with little general recognition or notoriety making great accomplishments

Biblical Text: *And Nathanael said unto him,* ***Can there any good thing come out of Nazareth?*** *Philip saith unto him, Come and see* (John 1:46).

Example of Use: Many people say **can any good thing come out of Trent State?** Well, something is about to come out of Trent State that's good. ("The Exoneration of Larry Peterson," Michele Norris, June 12, 2007, *All Things Considered*, National Public Radio)

Carved in stone

Means: To be fixed or unchangeable

Biblical Text: *But if the ministration of death, written and* ***engraven in stones****, was glorious, so that the children of Israel could not stedfastly behold the face of Moses for the glory of his countenance; which glory was to be done away* (2 Corinthians 3:7).

Example of Use: The way President Reagan and his wife, Nancy, would carry on about their love for each other, one might have gotten the impression their romance was **carved in stone**—and it turns out it was. ("Reagans' Romance **Carved in Stone**," Mar. 28, 2005, AP Online)

Cast lots

Means: To make a decision by a chance device, such as rolling dice or flipping a coin

Biblical Text: *And they said every one to his fellow, Come, and let us **cast lots**, that we may know for whose cause this evil is upon us. So they **cast lots**, and the lot fell upon Jonah* (Jonah 1:7).

Example of Use: He might play down the significance of his heroic wartime escape from Singapore, but Bill Parkes' remarkable story wouldn't be out of place in a Hollywood film. "We had no training in jungle habitation and didn't know what we could or couldn't eat. We **cast lots** each day to see who would try the fruit and if he didn't take sick we would all eat it." ("Bill's Great Escape after the Fall of Singapore. [Lest We Forget]," Nov. 14, 2005, *The News Letter,* Belfast, Northern Ireland)

Cast one's bread on the waters

Means: To do good without expecting gratitude or immediate reward; to give freely to others in the belief that one's good deeds will ultimately benefit someone or oneself

Biblical Text: *Cast thy bread upon the waters: for thou shalt find it after many days* (Ecclesiastes 11:1).

Example of Use: Westering's experience as a Marine Corps drill instructor forms the basis for his coaching philosophy: Bring out the best in yourself and your teammates, and the score will take care of itself. Or, as his wife, Donna, once put it: "**Cast your bread upon the waters**. It comes back with strawberry jam." ("Lutes Want to Win, But in a Nice Way," Pam Schmid, May 25, 2000, *Star Tribune,* Minneapolis, MN)

Cast one's lot

Means: To ally oneself closely with or share the fate of a person or a group

Biblical Text: *My son, if sinners entice thee, consent thou not. If they say, Come with us, let us lay wait for blood, let us lurk*

privily for the innocent without cause: . . . ***Cast in thy lot*** *among us; let us all have one purse: My son, walk not thou in the way with them; refrain thy foot from their path: For their feet run to evil, and make haste to shed blood* (Proverbs 1:10–16).

Example of Use: Two-time All-Bergen County football player Joe Robinson of River Dell has decided to attend Princeton. ("RD Football Standout **Casts Lot** with Princeton," Ron Fox, Feb. 9, 2000, *The Record*, Bergen County, NJ)

Cast the first stone

Means: To blame, criticize, or punish another, even though one is equally guilty

Biblical Text: *And the scribes and Pharisees brought unto him a woman taken in adultery.* . . . *But Jesus stooped down, and with his finger wrote on the ground, as though he heard them not. So when they continued asking him, he lifted up himself, and said unto them, He that is without sin among you, let him* ***first cast a stone*** *at her* (John 8:3, 7).

Example of Use: "On Adultery Issue, Many Aren't Ready to **Cast First Stone**," Carey Goldberg, June 9, 1997, *New York Times*

Certain lewd fellows of the baser sort

Means: Persons who live a life of crime or other form of illegal or immoral behavior, being unacceptable to law-abiding society

Biblical Text: *But the Jews which believed not, moved with envy, took unto them* ***certain lewd fellows of the baser sort****, and gathered a company, and set all the city on an uproar, and assaulted the house of Jason, and sought to bring them out to the people* (Acts 17:5).

Example of Use: Lord Tancred, master of all he surveyed, hauled them before the magistrates—"**lewd fellows of the baser sort**" said the charge—and had them thrown out of their tied cottages. ("Dreaming of a Country Paradise," Mike Amos, Nov. 13, 2004, *The Northern Echo*)

Chariot of fire

Means: A means of overcoming a natural obstacle or other difficulty

Biblical Text: *And it came to pass, as they still went on, and talked, that, behold, there appeared a **chariot of fire**, and horses of fire, and parted them both asunder; and Elijah went up by a whirlwind into heaven* (2 Kings 2:11).

Example of Use: As warrior queen Boudica, Alex Kingston was on the rocky road to ruin. The ER star looked fearsome enough with her wild curls, a blood-curdling rebel yell and a **chariot of fire**. But dear, oh dear, oh dear, that dialogue. ("Frances Traynor: Did You See?" Oct. 2, 2003, *Daily Record*, Glasgow, Scotland)

Charity never fails

Means: Loving and giving to others, especially those with little, is always beneficial and meritorious

Biblical Text: *Charity never faileth: but whether there be prophecies, they shall fail; whether there be tongues, they shall cease; whether there be knowledge, it shall vanish away* (1 Corinthians 13:8).

Example of Use: Geraldine was an artist in every sense of the word. She was an elegant, refined woman of faith. She epitomized the Relief Society's motto, **"Charity Never Faileth."**

("E. Geraldine West: Obituaries," Oct. 15, 2004, *Daily Herald,* Arlington Heights, IL)

Cheer, Be of good

Means: An exhortation to hold a bright and pleasant demeanor

Biblical Text: *These things I have spoken unto you, that in me ye might have peace. In the world ye shall have tribulation: but **be of good cheer**; I have overcome the world* (John 16:33).

Example of Use: Vice President Atiku Abubakar expressed hope for the survival of democracy in the country, saying "As we meditate for the survival of democracy in our country, let us **be of good cheer** because after darkness comes the dawn. May God answer our prayers for the sustenance of democracy in our country." ("Count Me Out of May 29 Inauguration— Atiku," May 29, 2007, *All Africa Global Media*)

Child shall lead them, A little

Means: Someone, not necessarily a child, who is considered unlikely to take charge of an enterprise will succeed in doing so

Biblical Text: *The wolf also shall dwell with the lamb, and the leopard shall lie down with the kid; and the calf and the young lion and the fatling together; and **a little child shall lead them*** (Isaiah 11:6).

Example of Use: Start listening to young people. Amy Smolek's postelection advice (letters, Nov. 12) suggesting that we emphasize our being alike rather than our differences is right on. What a novel idea! Folks, there are many teenagers out there whose values and insights are so impressive. . . . "And **a little child shall lead them**." ("Letters in the Editor's Mailbag (Letter to the Editor)," Nov. 19, 2004, *The Register-Guard,* Eugene, OR)

Child, With

Means: To be pregnant

Biblical Text: *And the angel of the LORD said unto her, Behold, thou art **with child** and shalt bear a son, and shalt call his name Ishmael; because the LORD hath heard thy affliction* (Genesis 16:11).

Example of Use: "We are not **with child**," a statement from the celebrity couple claimed, but we are pregnant with ideas. ("Sandra Bullock Dismisses Pregnancy Rumors," Dec. 1, 2006, United Press International)

Children of light

Means: Especially enlightened or virtuous people

Biblical Text: *While ye have light, believe in the light, that ye may be **the children of light**. These things spake Jesus, and departed, and did hide himself from them* (John 12:36).

Example of Use: From the 1950s through the end of Soviet Communism in 1991, that crusade was portrayed as a contest between "the free world" and "godless communism." In other words, the **children of light** against the children of darkness. ("Civil Religion or Public Philosophy," Richard John Neuhaus, Dec. 1, 2000, *First Things: A Monthly Journal of Religion and Public Life*)

Children of this world

Means: (1) People in general; (2) People opposed to God and his people

Biblical Text: *And the lord commended the unjust steward, because he had done wisely: for the **children of this world** are in their generation wiser than the children of light* (Luke 16:8).

C

Example of Use: In the Renaissance, Walter Pater explains that "we have an interval, and then our place knows us no more. Some spend this interval in listlessness, some in high passions, the wisest, at least among '**the children of this world**,' in art and song." ("Graham R. Rosamund Marriott Watson, Woman of Letters. [Book Review]," Linda K. Hughes, Mar. 22, 2006, Ohio University Press)

Chosen few

Means: A select group who enjoy particular favor

Biblical Text: *For many are called, but **few are chosen*** (Matthew 22:14).

Example of Use: Everyone has a chance in summer camp. That's the line. The reality is that one, two, maybe three of these guys who aren't already Denver Nuggets will be invited to Nuggets training camp in October. Others will head to other NBA camps. ("Summer Camp Inviting for a **Chosen Few**," Michael BeDan, July 19, 2000, *Denver Rocky Mountain News*)

Chosen people

Means: Any people believing themselves to have special status conferred by a higher source

Biblical Text: *For thou art an holy **people** unto the* LORD *thy God: the* LORD *thy God hath **chosen** thee to be a special people unto himself, above all people that are upon the face of the earth* (Deuteronomy 7:6). See also Deut. 14:1–2.

Example of Use: Forgive me, Father, for I have sinned. I have been celebrating the misfortune of your **chosen people**, the Fighting Irish. Georgia Tech beat them 33–3 and I can think of only one thing to say. "HA! HA! HA! HA!" ("Fighting Irish

"Lack Punch These Days," David Whitley, Sept. 5, 2007, *Orlando Sentinel*)

City of refuge

Means: Safe place to flee for a person who has accidentally killed another

Biblical Text: *The LORD also spake unto Joshua, saying, Speak to the children of Israel, saying, Appoint out for you **cities of refuge**, whereof I spake unto you by the hand of Moses: That the slayer that killeth any person unawares and unwittingly may flee thither: and they shall be your refuge from the avenger of blood* (Josh. 20:1–3).

Example of Use: The City Council unanimously approved a resolution Tuesday condemning immigration raids, but it refused to make the town a "**city of refuge**" or call it a place where a "majority" of undocumented workers live. ("Mendota Council Condemns Raids: City Leaders Pass Resolution Denouncing Recent Arrests of Undocumented Workers," Mar. 21, 2007, *The Fresno Bee*)

City on a hill

Means: A community or a group that is exemplary to others, especially as approved of by God or some other authority

Biblical Text: *Ye are the light of the world. **A city that is set on an hill** cannot be hid* (Matthew 5:14).

Example of Use: As any third-grade tyke could tell you, the United States is a country of immigrants. It is a part of our national story. Our ancestors came here, fleeing persecution, to build a "**city on a hill**." And, despite the bumps and miscues along the way, they did just that. ("Column: Immigration: We

Should Close the Border," Jamie Weinstein, Apr. 10, 2006, *University Wire*)

C Clay in the potter's hand

Means: Someone or something pliable or malleable

Biblical Text: *O house of Israel, cannot I do with you as this potter? saith the LORD. Behold, as the **clay is in the potter's hand**, so are ye in mine hand, O house of Israel* (Jeremiah 18:6).

Example of Use: "Make sure that he's comfortable, will you, dear?"—Well, add Hermione's mother to the growing list of "Hermione Crookshanks awesome characters." The way you breathe life into the original characters or at least people we don't know too much about is beyond ingenious. Like **clay in the potter's hands**, so are the characters under the pen of HC. ("7: The Granger Home Review," by "bdrman," Apr. 8, 2007, www.harrypotterfanfiction.com)

Clean hands

Means: To be uninvolved and/or blameless with regard to an immoral or illegal act

Biblical Text: *Who shall ascend into the hill of the LORD? or who shall stand in his holy place? He that hath **clean hands**, and a pure heart; who hath not lifted up his soul unto vanity, nor sworn deceitfully* (Psalm 24:3–4).

Example of Use: The Supreme Court Collegium is expected to shortly decide on the fate of elevation of Karnataka High Court Chief Justice P. D. Dinakaran who rushed to Indian national capital New Delhi and claimed that he would come out of the muddle with his **hands clean**. ("'I Will Come out with **Clean Hands**,' Justice Dinakaran," Dec. 6, 2009, The Press Trust of India Ltd.)

Clear one of guilt

Means: To free someone from a legal charge or imputation of guilt; to acquit

Biblical Text: *Keeping mercy for thousands, forgiving iniquity and transgression and sin, and that will by no means **clear the guilty*** (Exodus 34:7).

Example of Use: In December, a man was **cleared of guilt** through DNA after spending nearly eight years behind bars for his mother-in-law's 1998 rape and murder in Barberton. ("Fighting Crime Evolves with DNA: Growing Offender Data Bank Key to Unlocking Akron Mysteries," Andale Gross, Mar. 11, 2006, *Akron Beacon Journal*, OH)

Clearer than day, or Clear as day, As

Means: To be obvious

Biblical Text: *And thine age shall be **clearer than the noonday**: thou shalt shine forth, thou shalt be as the morning* (Job 11:17).

Example of Use: "**Clear As Day**: Lakers Reign over Nuggets Bryant's 30 in 130–95 Rout Help L.A. Win 15th in Row" Dave Krieger, Jan. 11, 2000, *Rocky Mountain News*

Closer than a brother

Means: To have a special relationship and emotional bond with another person, not necessarily a relative or a male

Biblical Text: *A man that hath friends must shew himself friendly: and there is a friend that sticketh **closer than a brother*** (Proverbs 18:24).

Example of Use: You do it because that guy standing next to you is now **closer than a brother**. They did what they did because their squads, their brothers, were in danger, and that's why they're heroes of mine. ("For Those Who Served, These Are Real Heroes," Joe Fitzgerald, Oct. 24, 2001, *The Boston Herald*)

Clothed and in one's right mind

Means: To be prepared for social interaction

Biblical Text: *Then they went out to see what was done; and came to Jesus, and found the man, out of whom the devils were departed, sitting at the feet of Jesus, **clothed, and in his right mind**: and they were afraid* (Luke 8:35).

Example of Use: So I accepted, on the premise of trying to do what little I could toward the cause of women's membership. I thought that if I used my best Southern accent with my white hair and what I like to think of as Junoesque proportions, they might conclude that women, **fully clothed** and **in** more or less **their right mind**, could be taught to behave themselves and not sprawl on the sofa or comb their hair and put on lipstick at the table. ("The Clubs: When Men's Were Men's; Recollections of an Intrepid Girl Reporter," Sarah Booth Conroy, June 26, 1988, *The Washington Post*)

Cloud by day, a pillar of fire by night, A

Means: Reference to the pillar and cloud of the Exodus, sometimes meaning protective advice or guidance

Biblical Text: *And the LORD went before them **by day in a pillar of a cloud**, to lead them the way; and **by night in a pillar of fire**, to give them light; to go by day and night* (Exodus 13:21).

Example of Use: Neither Mr. Blair's goal nor his certainty of achieving it was in question. The new Labour leader was guided by his reforming **pillars of cloud by day and fire by**

night, and we all vastly approved. ("A Danger Lurking for Mr. Hague," Matthew Parris, June 28, 1997, *The Spectator*)

Cloud of witnesses

Means: A large group of people serving as witnesses to an event

Biblical Text: *Wherefore seeing we also are compassed about with so great* ***a cloud of witnesses****, let us lay aside every weight, and the sin which doth so easily beset us, and let us run with patience the race that is set before us* (Hebrews 12:1).

Example of Use: More recent research, restoring oral testimony taken from Lincoln's own time, has brought back into view two "major depressive episodes" in Lincoln's life, as well as providing a **cloud of witnesses** to his melancholy disposition. ("The Mournful Giant; A New Book Argues That a Towering Presidency Was Rooted in Terrible Gloom," William Lee Miller, Oct. 2, 2005, *The Washington Post*)

Cloud without rain (or water)

Means: A boastful person with no basis for his boasting; an idea without a credible basis

Biblical Text: *Whoso boasteth himself of a false gift is like* ***clouds*** *and wind* ***without rain*** (Proverbs 25:14).

Example of Use: The BW book states in the chapter on crying, "Marisa's mom has been bombarded by clichés: 'You can't hurt a baby by picking her up whenever she cries.' 'You can't spoil her by loving her too much.' Such clichés are **clouds without water**. . . . Yes, you can hurt a baby by picking him or her up too much." ("Analysis of Gfi Vs. Aap Comparison Chart," Matthew T. Aney, Jan., 2001, www.ezzo.info)

Cloven hoof

Means: A physical sign of an evil nature

Biblical Text: *And the swine, though he **divide the hoof**, and be **clovenfooted**, yet he cheweth not the cud; he is unclean to you. Of their flesh shall ye not eat, and their carcase shall ye not touch; they are unclean to you* (Leviticus 11:7).

Example of Use: "Washington Republicans Exhibit Forked Tongues and **Cloven Hooves**," D. F. Oliveria, July 6, 2000, *The Spokesman-Review*, Spokane, WA

Coat of many colors

Means: A multicolored garment, especially when a sign of distinction

Biblical Text: *Now Israel loved Joseph more than all his children, because he was the son of his old age: and he made him **a coat of many colours*** (Genesis 37:3).

Example of Use: Bruce Schantz was a man who wore a **coat of many colors**. Not only was he a principal in the Schantz Organ Company, but he was involved in many community affairs such as chairing the fund-raising drive that brought Wayne College to Orrville. ("Bruce Schantz (1913–2007)—Reminiscences," Jack L. Sievert, July 1, 2007, *The American Organist*)

Cockatrice

Means: A monstrous or treacherous person

Biblical Text: *Rejoice not thou, whole Palestina, because the rod of him that smote thee is broken: for out of the serpent's root shall come forth a **cockatrice**, and his fruit shall be a fiery flying serpent* (Isaiah 14:29). See also Isa. 11:8; 59:5.

Example of Use: As Bettina Schmitt, the curator, was visiting friends in Florence, she came across an ivory lapdog in the Palazzo Pitti and immediately recognised the hand of the master. The lapdog, with its haughty stare and one paw half-raised, is no cuddly companion—more a **cockatrice** whose eyes can turn you to stone. ("Thundering Ivory; Master of the Furies," May 13, 2006, *The Economist*)

Come short (or Fall short)

Means: To prove inadequate or insufficient; to fail to meet expectations or standards

Biblical Text: *[F]or all have sinned and **come short** of the glory of God* (Romans 3:23).

Example of Use: The risks of manned space flight had receded from public consciousness as shuttle launches and landings became almost routine, but everyone understood that the dangers were still there. Human beings and the machines they build will always **come short** of perfection. ("A Nation Mourns, Again. [Shuttle Crew Represented America's Best]," Feb. 2, 2003, *The Register-Guard*, Eugene, OR)

Come to oneself

Means: To realize one's predicament, a condition not apparent earlier

Biblical Text: *And when **he came to himself**, he said, How many hired servants of my father's have bread enough and to spare, and I perish with hunger!* (Luke 15:17).

Example of Use: "I missed a turn, a turn as well known to me as my driveway," Linda tells me. When she **came to herself**, she saw that she was not in the mountains. "I was down in some industrial area, utterly lost." ("Praying for Time: Alzheimer's at

Any Age Is a Tragedy—but for a 47-Year-Old Woman with Six-Year-Old Twins, It's a Very Special Fight: To Be a Mother with Everything She's Got, for Every Day She's Got Left," Melissa Fay Greene, Nov. 1, 2002, *Good Housekeeping*)

Come to pass

Means: To happen or to result

Biblical Text: *And it shall* **come to pass***, that every one that findeth me shall slay me* (Genesis 4:14).

Example of Use: "IFW Funding Crisis So Dire, Sunday Hunting May **Come to Pass**," Deirdre Fleming, Jan. 16, 2005, *Portland Press Herald*, ME

Commandments

Means: Laws, especially those with little or no allowance for deviation

Biblical Text: *If ye keep my* **commandments***, ye shall abide in my love; even as I have kept my Father's* **commandments***, and abide in his love* (John 15:10).

Example of Use: As it turns out, the "10 **Commandments** for Women in Mechanical Construction" apply to the male of the species as well. Traits that both women and men need to succeed in the contracting business include a sense of humor and knowing when to pick your fights. ("Women Hear 10 **Commandments** for Success in Construction," Bob Miodonski, Mar. 1, 2002, *Contractor*)

Common people

Means: People in general, as opposed to people of unusual notoriety and/or influence

Biblical Text: *David therefore himself calleth him Lord; and whence is he then his son? And the **common people** heard him gladly* (Mark 12:37).

Example of Use: The short rib was once known as affordable meat for **common people**. But what the aristocracy didn't understand was that, with enough coaxing, this tough meat could unleash a flavor surprisingly tender. ("Unleashing the Power and Flavor of Short Ribs," Cindy Arora, Oct. 18, 2006, *Record*, Stockton, CA)

Conscience seared with a hot iron, To have one's

Means: To become desensitized to an evil way of life and its effects and to persist in it

Biblical Text: *Now the Spirit speaketh expressly, that in the latter times some shall depart from the faith, giving heed to seducing spirits, and doctrines of devils; Speaking lies in hypocrisy; **having their conscience seared with a hot iron*** (1 Timothy 4:1–2).

Example of Use: Chancellor of Covenant University, Ota (Nigeria), Dr. David O. Oyedepo, has lashed out at leaders who have turned the country's vast resources into their private estates. According to him, "Covetousness has also become the cancer of our leadership structure across the length and breadth of our great continent," adding, "the **conscience of many has been seared with a hot iron**." ("Bishop Oyedepo Lashes Out at Corrupt Leaders," Jan. 22, 2007, *All Africa Global Media*)

Corners of the earth

Means: The most remote parts of any place, especially the earth

Biblical Text: *And he shall set up an ensign for the nations, and shall assemble the outcasts of Israel, and gather together the dispersed of Judah from* **the four corners of the earth** (Isaiah 11:12).

Example of Use: Manchester United will spread their net to the **four corners of the earth** to find Sir Alex Ferguson's replacement. ("Football: 'We'll Scour the World for New Fergie' United Chief Eyes Foreign Legion," Steve Bates, Jan. 14, 2001, *The People*, London)

Cornerstone

Means: An important fundamental principle or underlying concept

Biblical Text: *Therefore thus saith the Lord* GOD, *Behold, I lay in Zion for a foundation a stone, a tried stone, a precious* **corner stone**, *a sure foundation: he that believeth shall not make haste* (Isaiah 28:16).

Example of Use: Someday, they'll speak of the young left tackle and his formidable center, how they were plucked from the same rookie class to form the **cornerstone** of the Raiders' offensive line for years to come. ("Raiders Hope the G-Men Take No Prisoners in Years Ahead," Janny Hu, Nov. 14, 2004, *San Francisco Chronicle*)

Count the cost

Means: An exhortation denoting the need to consider the ultimate price for some decision

Biblical Text: *For which of you, intending to build a tower, sitteth not down first, and **counteth the cost**, whether he have sufficient to finish it?* (Luke 14:28).

Example of Use: "Farmers **Count the Cost** of Flood Chaos," Laura Winn and Claire Barratt, Dec. 15, 2000, *Coventry Evening Telegraph,* England

Cows of Bashan

Means: Indulgent women

Biblical Text: *Hear this word, ye **kine of Bashan**, that are in the mountain of Samaria, which oppress the poor, which crush the needy, which say to their masters, Bring, and let us drink* (Amos 4:1).

Example of Use: I reject the **fat cows of Bashan**, dressed in their designer sweat suits grazing the aisles for low-fat foods, while their daughters with frizzed hair eye grocery clerks. ("Revelation on a Plain Jar," Ken Wheatcroft-Pardue, 2007, www.poetsagainstthewar.org)

Cross to bear

Means: A burden or trial for which one consciously chooses to take responsibility

Biblical Text: *And whosoever doth not **bear his cross**, and come after me, cannot be my disciple* (Luke 14:27).

Example of Use: The Braves have won 13 consecutive division titles, but postseason failure has become their **cross to bear**. They've won one World Series title and haven't been back to one since 1999. ("NL Division Series: Game 5: Astros 12, Braves 3: Over . . . and Over Blowout Brings an Unmerciful End," David O'Brien, Oct. 12, 2004, *The Atlanta Journal-Constitution*)

C

Crown of life

Means: The greatest state or condition of one's life

Biblical Text: *Blessed is the man that endureth temptation: for when he is tried, he shall receive the **crown of life**, which the Lord hath promised to them that love him* (James 1:12).

Example of Use: (Harold) Ickes, the former deputy chief of staff for President Bill Clinton, inherited from his father, who served FDR as cabinet officer and confidant, a belief that doing for a president is the **crown of life**. ("Poor Harold, Lucky George," Mary McGrory, Oct. 19, 1997, *The Washington Post*)

Crown of one's head

Means: The top of one's head

Biblical Text: *But in all Israel there was none to be so much praised as Absalom for his beauty: from the sole of his foot even to the **crown of his head** there was no blemish in him* (2 Samuel 14:25).

Example of Use: Nate wears a fitted short-sleeve shirt and a yellow "Livestrong" bracelet around his left wrist. His hair, thinning slightly around **the crown of his head** from treatments, is spiked with gel. ("Spirit of a Fighter: Music. Dance. Friends. His Daughter. That's What Keeps Nate Barrell Here," Aug. 26, 2007, *The Sacramento Bee*)

Crown of thorns

Means: Any condition that causes great suffering, especially if unwarranted

Biblical Text: *And when they had platted a **crown of thorns**, they put it upon his head, and a reed in his right hand: and they bowed the knee before him, and mocked him, saying, Hail, King of the Jews!* (Matthew 27:29). See also Mark 15:17; John 19:2, 5.

Example of Use: Andy Robinson won a gold World Cup medal three years ago and the nation duly showed its gratitude by making him an officer of the Order of the British Empire. Now that the bed of roses has turned into a **crown of thorns**, his credibility as the architect of the new England will be on the line as never before at Twickenham tomorrow. ("The Gods Owe Honest Robbo a Lucky Break; The World of Rugby," Peter Jackson, Nov. 10, 2006, *The Daily Mail,* London)

Crumbs from the table

Means: That which is of little value

Biblical Text: *And she said, Truth, Lord: yet the dogs eat of the **crumbs which fall from their masters' table*** (Matthew 15:27).

Example of Use: A recently-released autobiography is an attempt to set the record straight, and stop an unofficial book cashing in on the pair's success. . . . Of course, this leaves anyone interviewing them now with **crumbs from the table**, but the pair are planning to crack the American market, with rumours of a film and plans for a U.S. series to be aired next year. ("Next Stop, Cracking the States for Little Britain," Phil Crossey, Sept. 22, 2006, *The News Letter,* Belfast, Northern Ireland)

Crying in the wilderness, A voice of one

Means: A lone expression of protest or disagreement with prevailing opinion, especially if met by opposition or indifference

Biblical Text: *As it is written in the book of the words of Esaias the prophet, saying, The voice of one **crying in the wilderness**, Prepare ye the way of the Lord, make his paths straight* (Luke 3:4).

Example of Use: Peyton Wolcott is either a lone **voice crying in the wilderness** or the vanguard of a revolution sweeping through school districts across America. I hope it's the latter, but I fear it's the former. ("Web Watchdog Keeps Eye on School Spenders," Scott Parks, May 8, 2006, *Dallas Morning News*)

C Crystal clear (or Clear as crystal)

Means: To be easily seen or understood; without obstruction or obfuscation

Biblical Text: *Having the glory of God: and her light was like unto a stone most precious, even like a jasper stone, **clear as crystal*** (Revelation 21:11). See also Rev. 22:1.

Example of Use: Bruce Springsteen is singing "Thunder Road" on a **crystal-clear** Bose stereo, the top's down, the road is open and the world is full of possibilities. ("While New, '05 'Vette Stays True to Its Heritage," Mark Phelan, Sept. 25, 2004, Knight Ridder/Tribune News Service)

Cup runneth over, My

Means: One's circumstances are filled with possibilities

Biblical Text: *Thou preparest a table before me in the presence of mine enemies: thou anointest my head with oil; **my cup runneth over*** (Psalm 23:5).

Example of Use: I'm acutely aware that being able to shop online I am among the fortunate individuals who are prone to pronounce, "**my cup runneth over**." ("When **Cup Runneth Over**, Give to the Hungry," Adrienne T. Washington, June 7, 2005, *The Washington Times*)

Curse God and die

Means: Renounce God or some other high authority, especially as one's circumstances seem to be without hope, and be prepared to accept whatever happens.

Biblical Text: *Then said his wife unto him, Dost thou still retain thine integrity?* ***curse God, and die*** (Job 2:9).

Example of Use: Larry David is just like a modern-day Job, except that he has the patience of a fruit fly and he isn't covered in boils. Also, he is very rich and his wife never tells him to **"curse God and die."** ("Sympathy for the Misanthrope," Carina Chocano, Sept. 17, 2002, salon.com)

Cut the baby in half

Means: A proposed compromise that satisfies no one because it is ridiculous, impractical, or futile and does not solve the problem at hand

Biblical Text: *[Solomon] said, Bring me a sword. And they brought a sword before the king. And the king said,* ***Divide the living child in two****, and give half to the one, and half to the other. Then spake the woman whose the living child was unto the king, for her bowels yearned upon her son, and she said, O my lord, give her the living child, and in no wise slay it. But the other said, Let it be neither mine nor thine, but divide it. Then the king answered and said, Give her the living child, and in no wise slay it: she is the mother thereof* (1 Kings 3:24–27).

Example of Use: It is going to be a real plus for intelligence (with Robert Gates as U.S. Defense Secretary, replacing Donald Rumsfeld) because it'll put to rest a lot of this nonsense about turf wars between the secretary of defense and the national intelligence director. There's just no way you can **cut that baby in half**, and he is the man in the Pentagon that could make that work. ("The Man Who Would Be in Don Rumsfeld's Chair," J. R. Labbe, Nov. 12, 2006, *Fort Worth Star-Telegram*)

Cut to the heart

Means: (1) To deeply wound or hurt one's sensibilities; (2) To proceed to or to focus on the most important matter of the moment

Biblical Text: *When they heard that, they were **cut to the heart**, and took counsel to slay them* (Acts 5:33). See also Acts 7:54.

Example of Use: Surveying the wreckage of the 4–2 midweek home loss to Crystal Palace, the Serbian millionaire left nothing out in his criticism. . . . He said: "The scars from that Palace game won't heal for a long time. They've **cut to my heart**. I'm sure it's the same with the supporters. "The players let everyone down and I feel betrayed. I'm disgusted. The way they played wasn't acceptable." ("I Feel Betrayed; Portsmouth Chief Blasts 'Team Who Let Us Down,'" Ivan Speck, May 5, 2001, *Daily Mail*, London)

RAISING CAIN

D

"DOVE OF PEACE"

Daily bread

Means: Sustenance, not necessarily bread, needed to live

Biblical Text: *Give us this day our **daily bread*** (Matthew 6:11).

Example of Use: By mid-morning, the beneficiaries of the women's efforts and Wegmans' community spirit start to sign in to pick up their **daily bread**. By day's end, the bread, yogurt and dry goods are gone, and someone from an after-school program in the village has come to pick cakes and cookies for their children. ("**Daily Bread**, for Others; Volunteers Take Food from Wegmans to P.E.A.C.E. Inc.," Jim McKeever, Nov. 26, 2003, *The Post-Standard,* Syracuse, NY)

Damascus road or Damascus-road experience

Means: An experience of sudden revelation causing a radical change in one's opinions or beliefs

Biblical Text: *And as he [Saul] journeyed, he came near **Damascus**: and suddenly there shined round about him a light from heaven: And he fell to the earth, and heard a voice saying unto him, Saul, Saul, why persecutest thou me? And he said, Who art thou, Lord? And the Lord said, I am Jesus whom thou persecutest: it is hard for thee to kick against the pricks. And he trembling and astonished said, Lord, what wilt thou have me to do?* (Acts 9:3–5).

Example of Use: [Dr. Seuss's] Grinch is part Ebenezer Scrooge, part pre-**Damascus-road**-St. Paul and part outcast-turned-bully. ("How 'Grinch' Stole My Heart as Easter Favorite," Cathleen Falsani, Dec. 20, 2002, *Chicago Sun-Times*)

Dan to Beersheba, From

Means: From one end of a place to the other, or the full extent of a place

Biblical Text: *Then all the children of Israel went out, and the congregation was gathered together as one man, **from Dan even to Beersheba**, with the land of Gilead, unto the* LORD *in Mizpeh* (Judges 20:1).

Example of Use: Together with Shuka Dorfman of the Israel Antiquities Authority, the Vatican is currently in the process of cataloguing all its Jewish items, said Sambi. What the Vatican will never be able to do, he said—"And I hear it **from Dan to Beersheba**"—is to produce the sacred menora looted by Titus when he destroyed the Temple. ("Cultural Understanding," Greer Fay Cashman, Oct. 3, 2005, *Jerusalem Post*)

Daughter of Zion

Means: A resident of Jerusalem or, more specifically, a female Jew

Biblical Text: *This is the word that the* LORD *hath spoken concerning him; The virgin the **daughter of Zion** hath despised thee, and laughed thee to scorn; the daughter of Jerusalem hath shaken her head at thee* (2 Kings 19:21).

Example of Use: Given a rare day off from practice last week, Criddle described his day's activities to a Utah newspaper: "I slept in. Lifted weights. Sat in an ice tub. Went to Panda Express. Then to Baskin-Robbins. Played some video games. Then got a Jamba Juice with a lovely young **daughter of Zion**." ("There's No Question: Tuitama Better Than Counterpart at QB-Factory BYU," Greg Hansen, Sept. 1, 2007, *Arizona Daily Star*, Tucson)

David and Goliath

Means: A real or apparent mismatch of foes with one party being decidedly stronger than the other

D

Biblical Text: *And as he talked with them, behold, there came up the champion, the Philistine of Gath, **Goliath** by name, out of the armies of the Philistines, and spake according to the same words: and **David** heard them. . . . And **David** said to Saul, Let no man's heart fail because of him; thy servant will go and fight with this Philistine.* (1 Samuel 17:23, 32).

Example of Use: In what had been described as a "**David and Goliath** type battle," the perceived little guy won a lawsuit Thursday against City Hall in a dispute over the construction of a sidewalk outside Bass Performance Hall. ("Sidewalk Builder Wins Suit against Fort Worth, Texas," Jack Douglas, Jr., Apr. 26, 2002, *Fort Worth Star-Telegram*)

Day is coming, One's

Means: A point of culmination or climax is in one's future

Biblical Text: *The wicked plotteth against the just, and gnasheth upon him with his teeth. The Lord shall laugh at him: for he seeth that **his day is coming*** (Psalm 37:12–13).

Example of Use: "Investigation Ultimately Will Reach the Top[;] [George] Ryan May Not Be Indicted before His Term in Office Ends, but the **Day Is Coming**," Mark Brown, May 22, 2002, *Chicago Sun-Times*

Day of small things

Means: Apparently insignificant matters that may lead to greater prospects

Biblical Text: *For who hath despised the **day of small things**? for they shall rejoice, and shall see the plummet in the hand of Zerubbabel with those seven; they are the eyes of the LORD, which run to and fro through the whole earth* (Zechariah 4:10).

Example of Use: The presidents of all the railroads have known the **day of small things** and been many years reaching their positions. ("How to Succeed in the Railroad Business," Chauncey M. Depew, Mar. 1, 2002, *Popular Mechanics*)

Day of the Lord

Means: A time of reckoning

Biblical Text: *For the **day of the LORD** of hosts shall be upon every one that is proud and lofty, and upon every one that is lifted up; and he shall be brought low* (Isaiah 2:12).

Example of Use: prayon777.com/_wsn/page10.html—I won't comment on this one either except to say that this piece warns that today is the "Great and Dreadful **day of the Lord**." Although I personally doubt that today is the beginning of the end or the first day of the second coming, it's clear that there are those that truly do believe. If nothing else, this makes for an interesting read. ("Looking at 'Lucky Sevens' on 7/7/07," July 7, 2007, *The Cincinnati Post*, OH)

Day of wrath

Means: A time when judgment will be applied for one's misdeeds

Biblical Text: *The great day of the LORD is near, it is near, and hasteth greatly, even the voice of the day of the LORD: the mighty man shall cry there bitterly. That day is a **day of wrath*** (Zephaniah 1:14–15a).

Example of Use: It has often been noted that Verdi was not a traditional religionist—quite the contrary, in fact—but he certainly evokes the most vivid and horrifying "**day of wrath**" in the repertory. ("Stephane Deneve's Passionate Requiem," Tim Page, Mar. 25, 2005, *The Washington Post*)

Days of our years

Means: A lifetime or many years

Biblical Text: *The **days of our years** are threescore years and ten; and if by reason of strength they be fourscore years, yet is their strength labour and sorrow; for it is soon cut off, and we fly away* (Psalm 90:10).

Example of Use: Often before I leave for work, my eyes wander to the fridge, three sides covered with photos and memorabilia charting the **days of our years** together, mostly moments large and small from our daughters' lives—bubble baths and new bikes, egg coloring and holiday hats, beach trips and Little League cards. (Larry Blakely, Feb. 13, 2007, www.chicago sportsreview.com)

Dead and buried

Means: To be dead or defunct beyond doubt; to be completed

Biblical Text: *Men and brethren, let me freely speak unto you of the patriarch David, that he is both **dead and buried**, and his sepulchre is with us unto this day* (Acts 2:29).

Example of Use: "New Labour '**Dead and Buried**' As Tories Surge 20 Points Ahead," Nicholas Cecil, June 25, 2008, *The Evening Standard*, London

Dead dog

Means: Someone or something of no consequence

Biblical Text: *Then said Abishai the son of Zeruiah unto the king, Why should this **dead dog** curse my lord the king? Let me go over, I pray thee, and take off his head* (2 Samuel 16:9).

Example of Use: There is no second place in American politics, no silver medal, no pat on the back for the good try. If you lose, nobody remembers that you were once an underdog. They only remember that you are now a **dead dog**. ("Now, It's Put-Up Time," Roger Simon and Major Garrett, Jan. 17, 2002, *U.S. News & World Report*)

Dead lion

Means: Someone or something that is (1) of no consequence or powerless or (2) without hope

Biblical Text: *For to him that is joined to all the living there is hope: for a living dog is better than a **dead lion*** (Ecclesiastes 9:4).

Example of Use: And the day after a new president is sworn in on May 29, Nigeria's people will awake as impoverished, disadvantaged and disaffected as ever. They've yet to see the promised benefits of civilian rule—and don't expect to soon. "All this is just a waste," said 32-year old Lawrence Akro, looking at electoral material during the vote. "It's like a **dead lion**, no use to anyone." ("Democracy Disappoints in Nigeria," Apr. 25, 2007, Associated Press/*AP* Online)

Dead Sea fruit

Means: A bitter disappointment, thing, or event

D

Biblical Text: *For their vine is of the vine of Sodom, and of the fields of Gomorrah: their grapes are grapes of gall, their clusters are bitter* (Deuteronomy 32:32).

Example of Use: His father was dogged by bad luck, the parents' marriage like **Dead Sea fruit**. His mother once told him, "Never marry for love—it's not enough, Adrian," but, as his poetry shows, he was obsessed with love and often lucky in it. ("Obituary: Adrian Henri," George Melly, Dec. 22, 2000, *The Independent,* London)

Dearly beloved

Means: Someone who is especially adored; sometimes used sarcastically

Biblical Text: *Again, think ye that we excuse ourselves unto you? we speak before God in Christ: but we do all things, **dearly beloved**, for your edifying* (2 Corinthians 12:19).

Example of Use: John Nichol, a former RAF navigator who was shot down over Iraq in 1991 and held captive for the duration of the war, told Sky News: "Faye was clearly coerced into making the TV broadcasts that we saw yesterday and today. She was clearly coerced into writing the letter. . . . No serviceman or woman is going to pick up a pen and write to their **dearly beloved** MP. It's a nonsense." ("Continuation: Letter Escalates Diplomatic Crisis," Mar. 30, 2007, *The Independent,* London)

Death's door, At

Means: So ill that one may die or to appear so

Biblical Text: *Have the **gates of death** been opened unto thee? or hast thou seen the doors of the shadow of death?* (Job 38:17).

Example of Use: Mark Nowacki knows what it's like to be **at death's door**. Four times since 1996, when he was diagnosed with AIDS, he says he's been told, "You're going to die in the next four to six months and there's nothing you can do about it." ("What's in a Name?" Sept. 21, 2007, *Isthmus*)

Decently and in order, Let everything be done

Means: Arrange someone or something's circumstances or conditions in a proper way

Biblical Text: *Let all things be done decently and in order* (1 Corinthians 14:40).

Example of Use: The truth is that our peace walkers in the St. Patrick's Day Parade never had any intention to cause disruption. It was all done happily, peaceably, **"decently and in order."** ("Letters," Apr. 1, 2007, *The Gazette,* Colorado Springs, CO)

Deep calleth unto deep

Means: A profound spiritual or philosophical understanding between two or more people, especially when they are esteemed for their special knowledge or achievements

Biblical Text: *Deep calleth unto deep at the noise of thy waterspouts: all thy waves and thy billows are gone over me* (Psalm 42:7).

Example of Use: Out of the chaos of this world, above the din, the shattering explosions of violence and hate—a Voice speaks. It calls us to move to a new realm, an interior world where truly **deep calls to deep**. ("Song: 'Deep Calls unto Deep (WhaleSong 1),'" jon, Mar. 12, 2007, www.acidplanet.com)

D

Delilah

Means: A seductive woman with evil intentions

Biblical Text: *And **Delilah** said to Samson, Tell me, I pray thee, wherein thy great strength lieth, and wherewith thou mightest be bound to afflict thee* (Judges 16:6).

Example of Use: Sitting in his new chair, in his new office, in his new school, new Lakes Community High School athletic director Troy Parola is talking about a new way they can test high school athletes for drugs. For some, it's literally a hair-raising experience, a **Delilah** delight. Hair today, gone tomorrow, so to speak. ("They're Stylin' at Lakes, and Parola Is a Perfect Fit," Joe Aguilar, Aug. 26, 2005, *Daily Herald,* Arlington Heights, IL)

Deliver us from . . .

Means: A request to be relieved of some onerous task or difficult circumstances

Biblical Text: *And lead us not into temptation, but **deliver us from** evil: For thine is the kingdom, and the power, and the glory, for ever. Amen* (Matthew 6:13).

Example of Use: If you had that sinking feeling when you got up today, help is at hand. The Church of England has just the thing to help chase away those Monday morning blues. ("**Deliver Us from** Mondays," Sept. 3, 2007, *The Daily Mail,* London)

Den of thieves

Means: An establishment or group of people involved in illegal or immoral activity

Biblical Text: *And he taught, saying unto them, Is it not written, My house shall be called of all nations the house of prayer? But ye have made it a **den of thieves** (Mark 11:17).*

Example of Use: Richard Scrushy is not guilty of a crime. That doesn't mean he didn't do anything wrong. . . . But Scrushy's incompetence went far beyond allowing a **den of thieves** to run amok in the finance department. ("Richard Scrushy Found Innocent," Loren Steffy, July 1, 2005, *Houston Chronicle*)

Depart in peace

Means: An exhortation for one to leave with a feeling of serenity and calm

Biblical Text: *Lord, now lettest thou thy servant **depart in peace**, according to thy word (Luke 2:29).*

Example of Use: We must try to establish some form of democracy in Iraq and create a police force able to give the people and government the security they need. After we have done that, we can **depart in peace** and leave the fate of Iraq in the hands of the Iraqi people. ("Destructive Criticism," Peter J. Riga, Feb. 11, 2005, *Commonweal*)

Desert shall blossom, The

Means: Literally: Arid land will bring vegetation unexpectedly; figuratively: unpromising conditions will bring unexpectedly positive results

Biblical Text: *The wilderness and the solitary place shall be glad for them; and **the desert** shall rejoice, and **blossom as the rose** (Isaiah 35:1).*

Example of Use: I remember, when I was in my 20s, going to a lecture at Sheffield University about the future of work. The steel mills and coal mines had begun to shut and, like a lot of people, I wondered what was going to replace them. The lecture was given by a bloke who looked like a professor, with an explosion of white hair and glasses as thick as jelly. He pointed at us with a long professorial finger. **"The desert will bloom!"** he said, dramatically. ("A Moonstruck Boy Who Thought He Had It Taped," Aug. 1, 2006, *Yorkshire Post*)

D

Devil can cite Scripture for his purpose, The

Means: Even someone who does not hold certain beliefs can be familiar with them and express them when doing so is favorable to him.

Biblical Text: *And [Satan] saith unto him [Jesus], If thou be the Son of God, cast thyself down: **for it is written**, He shall give his angels charge concerning thee: and in their hands they shall bear thee up, lest at any time thou dash thy foot against a stone* (Matthew 4:6). See also Luke 4:9–13.

Example of Use: One of the most famous passages in the Buddhist canon, from a text regarded by scholars as early, states, "Abstain from all unwholesome deeds, perform wholesome ones, purify your mind: this is the teaching of the buddhas." But *the devil can cite Scripture for his purpose*; it is admittedly tiresome to select this statement from among the thousands attributed to the Buddha as proof that his teachings were not "beyond good and evil." The more interesting question is the role that Nietzsche and other European thinkers play in Mishra's attempt to catapult the Buddha into modernity. ("A Buddha for the Blue States. [Book Review]," Donald S. Lopez Jr., Feb. 21, 2005, *The Nation*)

Die before one's time

Means: To die before one's appointed time, based on the supposition that each person is preordained to die at a particular time

Biblical Text: *Be not over much wicked, neither be thou foolish: why shouldest thou **die before thy time**?* (Ecclesiastes 7:17).

Example of Use: "With the storms here, we get so many, you can't run from every one of them," says Hawkins, a brawny 6-footer with a white mustache and clear, blue-grey eyes. "I'm a firm believer you don't **die before your time**." ("Ivan Survivor Refuses Evacuation Order," Allen G. Breed, July 9, 2005, AP Online)

Dishonest gain

Means: Acquisition by illegal means

Biblical Text: *Behold, therefore I have smitten mine hand at thy **dishonest gain** which thou hast made, and at thy blood which hath been in the midst of thee* (Ezekiel 22:13–16).

Example of Use: Always prefer a loss to a **dishonest gain**; the one brings pain at the moment, the other for all time. ("Mother Maps. [Fond Memories of a Mother, and Her Advice]," Laura B. Randolph, May 1, 1999, *Ebony*)

Divided against itself

Means: A body split by internal interests

Biblical Text: *And Jesus knew their thoughts, and said unto them, Every kingdom **divided against itself** is brought to desolation; and every city or house **divided against itself** shall not stand* (Matthew 12:25).

D

Example of Use: Yes, they were out of contention and apparently out of motivation, and they had spent the past two days dealing with the perception they have a clubhouse that is **divided against itself**. ("Not Much Fight Left; L.A. Goes Quietly in 7th Straight Loss: Arizona 6, Dodgers 2," Tony Jackson, Sept. 23, 2007, *Daily News*, Los Angeles)

Do unto others as you would have them do unto you

Means: A rule of ethical conduct that exhorts people to behave toward others in the way they themselves would want to be treated by them

Biblical Text: *And as ye would that men should do to you, do ye also to them likewise* (Luke 6:31).

Example of Use: I've tried to live my life according to the gospel of Will Rogers. In particular, I am inspired by his observation: "Everything is funny as long as it is happening to somebody else." It's not as worthy a life philosophy as, let's say: **"Do unto others as you would have them do unto you,"** but it sure beats the heck out of "Live fast, die young and leave a good-looking corpse." ("Laughing at Hollywood Is Fun, Most of the Time," Barry Koltnow, Apr. 2, 2007, *Orange County Register,* Santa Ana, CA)

Doers of the Word, not hearers only, Be

Means: Live and act according to what one believes and avoid inaction.

Biblical Text: *But be ye doers of the word, and not hearers only, deceiving your own selves* (James 1:22).

Example of Use: Citing passages from the Book of James, [John] Kerry asserted, "The Scriptures say, 'What does it profit my brethren if some say he has faith but does not have works?' When we look at what's happening in America today, where are the works of compassion? Because it is also written, 'Be doers of the word and not hearers only.'" ("Bush, Kerry Spar over Use of Religion in Presidential Race," May 1, 2004, *Church & State*)

D

Dog, A

Means: Someone or something of little importance or ability; someone or something that is unattractive

Biblical Text: *And the Philistine said unto David, Am I **a dog**, that thou comest to me with staves? And the Philistine cursed David by his gods* (1 Samuel 17:43). See also Eccl. 9:4.

Example of Use: There are those who do treat the president poorly. But, on balance, he has gotten a much softer ride from the press than any other president in my lifetime, with the exception of John Kennedy. And even though Obama is having trouble solving some vexing problems, most of the media are still rooting for him, sometimes openly. If he's **a dog**, he's Lassie. ("Being Dogged Comes with Being Chief Executive, Mr. President," Sept. 13, 2010, *The Examiner,* Washington, DC)

Dogs, Go to the

Means: To be ruined or to degenerate

Biblical Text: *Him that dieth of Jeroboam in the city shall the **dogs eat**; and him that dieth in the field shall the fowls of the air eat: for the LORD hath spoken it* (1 Kings 14:11).

Example of Use: Before our English **goes to the dogs** as evidenced by the drop in the percentage of passes in the 1999 Sijil Pelajaran Malaysia examination, the Ministry of Education should take immediate remedial action as English is a compulsory second language in the school curriculum. ("Don't Let Our English **Go to the Dogs**," Tunku Ismail Jewa, Apr. 11, 2000, *New Straits Times*, Kuala Lumpur, Malaysia)

D Dogs, Throw something to the

Means: To desert, discard, or abandon someone or something as if useless

Biblical Text: *And ye shall be holy men unto me: neither shall ye eat any flesh that is torn of beasts in the field; ye shall **cast it to the dogs** (Exodus 22:31).

Example of Use: The civil suit settlements "took the thirst for justice out of the palate" of a Senate Judiciary Committee that investigated Ruby Ridge, the authors say. "I can easily see why it was destined (that) there would be no justice at Ruby Ridge," Tony Brown writes. "It was the instinct to survive." "The Justice Department doesn't cut off its right arm, the FBI, and **throw it to the dogs**," the author says. ("Ruby Ridge Book Takes Personal Look at '92 Siege; Authors Allege Government Blocked Justice through Payoffs to Participants," Bill Morlin, Aug. 20, 2001, *The Spokesman Review*)

Dorcas

Means: A generous woman, especially one who makes clothes for the poor

Biblical Text: *Now there was at Joppa a certain disciple named Tabitha, which by interpretation is called **Dorcas**: this woman was full of good works and almsdeeds which she did* (Acts 9:36).

Example of Use: She [Kate Douglas Wiggin] was a pioneer in the American kindergarten movement who helped open San Francisco's first free kindergarten, and was a president of the Buxton/Hollis area chapter of the **Dorcas** Society, a women's group dedicated to working for good causes. ("'Rebecca' Revisited; Tour the Home of the Author of *Rebecca of Sunnybrook Farm* As Well As the One That Provided the Book's Setting—Even See the Old Movie—This Weekend," Ray Routhier, Oct. 4, 2009, *Portland Press Herald*, ME)

Doubting Thomas

Means: Someone who will not believe something without tangible evidence

Biblical Text: *But Thomas, one of the twelve, called Didymus, was not with them when Jesus came. The other disciples therefore said unto him, We have seen the Lord. But he said unto them, Except I shall see in his hands the print of the nails, and put my finger into the print of the nails, and thrust my hand into his side, I will not believe* (John 20:24–25).

Example of Use: There are . . . government forecasts predicting 20 percent alternative engines in 20 years. Maybe, but when it comes to alternative engines, I've always been a **Doubting Thomas**. ("**Doubting Thomas** and the Hybrids," Jerry Flint, May 1, 2001, *Ward's Auto World*)

Dove of peace

Means: A symbol of peace and reconciliation

Biblical Text: *And it came to pass at the end of forty days, that Noah opened the window of the ark which he had made: And he sent forth a raven, which went forth to and fro, until the waters were dried up from off the earth. Also he sent forth a **dove** from him, to see if the waters were abated from off the face of the ground; But the **dove** found no rest for the sole of her foot, and she returned unto him into the ark, for the waters were on the face of the whole earth: then he put forth his hand, and took her,*

D

*and pulled her in unto him into the ark. And he stayed yet other seven days; and again he sent forth the **dove** out of the ark; And the **dove** came in to him in the evening; and, lo, in her mouth was an olive leaf pluckt off: so Noah knew that the waters were abated from off the earth. And he stayed yet other seven days; and sent forth the **dove**; which returned not again unto him any more* (Genesis 8:6–12).

Example of Use: More than 300 young students keen to show their determination to reject war and violence picked up hammers and smashed dozens of toy pistols to pieces. . . . Sadichha Shrestha, a senior high school student from Nepal, took part in a 10,000-meter picture scroll drawing activity, in which the young people painted a **dove of peace** with an olive branch in its beak. ("Youngsters' 'Ode to Peace' Plea for a Warless World," Aug. 23, 2006, Xinhua News Agency)

Down to the sea in ships, Those who go

Means: People who go to sea

*Biblical Text: **They that go down to the sea in ships**, that do business in great waters; these see the works of the* LORD, *and his wonders in the deep* (Psalm 107:23–24).

Example of Use: Through dozens of recordings and accompanying songbooks, Bok has become what *Time* magazine calls "the poet laureate of **those who go down to the sea in ships**." ("Gordon Bok Herrings in the Bay," Mary DesRosier, Sept. 22, 2003, *Sing Out!,* Bethlehem, PA)

Drink the cup, To

Means: To either endure pain or enjoy pleasure associated with a choice one makes; to make a full commitment to someone or something

Biblical Text: *Then said Jesus unto Peter, Put up thy sword into the sheath:* **the cup which my Father hath given me, shall I not drink it?** (John 18:11).

Example of Use: Next week, Bertarelli and his well-fed crewmen will pound out a victory over Team New Zealand or lose and **drink the cup** of humiliation to the dregs. Either way, they'll get their name in lights for a while. ("Africa's Inspiring Entry," Angus Phillips, June 15, 2007, *The Washington Post*)

Drop in the bucket, A

Means: A small, and thereby relatively insignificant, part of a whole

Biblical Text: *Behold, the nations are as **a drop of a bucket**, and are counted as the small dust of the balance: behold, he taketh up the isles as a very little thing* (Isaiah 40:15).

Example of Use: Given everything John Studley has been through in his life, executing a two-minute drill to defeat Cambridge is a mere **drop in the bucket**. ("Studley Performance; Peabody QB Beats Odds," Dan Ventura, Oct. 30, 2004, *The Boston Herald*)

Dry and thirsty (or "weary" or "desert") land, A

Means: A desolate place or condition, used often in jest

Biblical Text: *O God, thou art my God; early will I seek thee: my soul thirsteth for thee, my flesh longeth for thee in **a dry and thirsty land**, where no water is* (Psalm 63:1).

Example of Use: The discriminating would be drawn from Sarasota, Manatee, Pinellas and Hillsborough counties, to Riverside Drive. Presumably such good taste would not be found in Palmetto, itself; we were **a dry and weary land**. My mind filled with Gatsbyesque visions of limousines delivering valuable cargo for an evening of sophisticated, pampered pleasure. ("Letters to the Editor," Aug. 20, 2006, *Bradenton Herald*, FL)

D Dry bones

Means: Someone or something that is hopeless or dead, literally or figuratively

Biblical Text: *The hand of the LORD was upon me, and carried me out in the spirit of the LORD, and set me down in the midst of **the valley which was full of bones**, And caused me to pass by them round about: and, behold, there were very many in the open valley; and, lo, **they were very dry*** (Ezekiel 37:1–2).

Example of Use: "Putting Flesh on the **Dry Bones** of History; Author Diana Preston Revisits China's Boxer Rebellion," Ken Ringle, Aug. 10, 2000, *The Washington Post*

Dry ground

Means: A place of safety or stability

Biblical Text: *But lift thou up thy rod, and stretch out thine hand over the sea, and divide it: and the children of Israel shall go on **dry ground** through the midst of the sea* (Exodus 14:16).

Example of Use: Laws are meant to define the parameters of what you cannot do and what you must do. You must pay your taxes, and you can't kill your boss. But the whole process of lawmaking is to define a "**dry ground** of freedom" within which you are able to make your own choices. That expression of free choice is critical for a healthy society—yet our "**dry ground** of freedom" has been shrinking for many decades. ("Our Country Has Greatly Changed; [Letter to the Editor]," June 4, 2010, *Seattle Post-Intelligencer*)

Dry up

Means: To disappear or become depleted

Biblical Text: *And he shall pass through the sea with affliction, and shall smite the waves in the sea, and all the deeps of the river shall **dry up**: and the pride of Assyria shall be brought down, and the sceptre of Egypt shall depart away* (Zechariah 10:11).

Example of Use: Noting that the US-Pak ties is all set to enter a difficult phase, post Osama bin Laden, an influential U.S. think tank has said that the American tolerance for Pakistani hedging or having it both ways would soon **dry up**, if Islamabad does not change its approach or policy with regard to terrorism. ("U.S. Tolerance for Pak Hedging to Dry Up Soon," May 3, 2011, PTI—The Press Trust of India Ltd.)

Due season, In

Means: At the appropriate time

Biblical Text: *And let us not be weary in well doing: for **in due season** we shall reap, if we faint not* (Galatians 6:9).

Example of Use: Joel wrote a statement that he had forgiven this man. He put it in the family safe box as a reminder of his decision. So **in due season**, like a butterfly in a chrysalis, Joel emerged from his spiritual darkness, into the light, revealing a glowing confidence, liveliness, and inner joy and peace beyond expectation. ("**In Due Season** Beauty Emerges from Darkness," Nancy Berntsen, 2007, awesomebutterflies.com)

Dunghill, A

Means: An extremely unpleasant place or situation bringing humiliation

D

Biblical Text: *Also I have made a decree, that whosoever shall alter this word, let timber be pulled down from his house, and being set up, let him be hanged thereon; and let his house be made a **dunghill** for this* (Ezra 6:11).

Example of Use: I have just entered Amsterdam's red-light district in—honest!—an attempt to visit the Oude Kerk, the medieval "old church" that is the capital city's oldest stone building. . . . The Oude Kerk sits in the middle of this cesspool, a faded jewel in a steaming **dunghill**. ("On Tiptoe through the Tulips: Why Holland Is Nervous—and an Alarming Case for the Entire West," Rod Dreher, July 15, 2002, *National Review*)

Dust from one's feet, To shake

Means: To depart in anger or disdain, especially decisively or in haste; to end a relationship with someone, especially in an unpleasant situation or to express one's displeasure

Biblical Text: *And whosoever shall not receive you, nor hear your words, when ye depart out of that house or city, **shake off the dust of your feet**. Verily I say unto you, It shall be more tolerable for the land of Sodom and Gomorrha in the day of judgment, than for that city* (Matthew 10:14–15).

Example of Use: After spending his vacation licking his wounds, the deposed Vivendi mogul Jean-Marie Messier was back, media-wise at least in *Paris Match* magazine, making it known that he intends to settle in New York. That move comes as no surprise in Paris, where business circles see no French future for Messier, who bears the stigma of wrecking his trans-Atlantic media and entertainment empire. . . . "Clearly, he is financially distressed and needs a job," a friend said. On Labor Day, Messier **shook the dust of France off his shoes**, taking his wife, Antoinette, and five kids to New York. ("The Global

Class: Summertime for Messier," Joseph Fitchett, Sept. 5, 2002, *International Herald Tribune*)

Dust to dust

Means: The cycle of life, signifying death, the end for every person

Biblical Text: *In the sweat of thy face shalt thou eat bread, till thou return unto the ground; for out of it wast thou taken: **for dust thou art, and unto dust shalt thou return*** (Genesis 3:19).

Example of Use: A week before, Fred, head gringo in charge of the Alamo grounds, fell victim to the joy of drink. Jose lifted him from the dirt, brushed him off and dragged him to a porch chair. Fred seemed to stick, but then tumbled over, bounced on the concrete and rolled off the porch, the chair clattering after him into the bushes. **Dust to dust**. Fred returned to his natural state. ("Opinion: At the Alamo, We Hear Sirens of Salvation," Phil Lucas, Apr. 8, 2007, *News Herald*, Panama City, FL)

Dust, Eat

Means: To be humbled abjectly

Biblical Text: *And the LORD God said unto the serpent, Because thou hast done this, thou art cursed above all cattle, and above every beast of the field; upon thy belly shalt thou go, and **dust shalt thou eat** all the days of thy life* (Genesis 3:14).

Example of Use: The race has not yet been run, and already they are stacking sour grapes in crates. Just in case. Now, having **eaten dust** in the first two classics, the losers have adopted a new explanation, which is sort of an old explanation. ("Great Field or Not, Winning Triple Crown a Very Special Case," John Clay, June 2, 2002, Knight Ridder/Tribune News Service)

D

Dust, Lick the

Means: To die; to be defeated in battle; to be humiliated

Biblical Text: *They that dwell in the wilderness shall bow before him; and his enemies shall **lick the dust*** (Psalm 72:9).

Example of Use: One *Malay Mail* reader used profanities when describing the bullies in the recent ragging incident at the Royal Malaysian Air Force camp in Jitra, Kedah, and demanded that they should be made to **lick the dust** while a Malay tabloid likened it to torture meted out at the infamous Abu Ghraib prison in Iraq. ("The Military Knows Best," Saiful Azhar Abdullah, Mar. 6, 2007, *The Malay Mail*, Malaysia)

Dust, Lie in the

Means: To die or to be ruined

Biblical Text: *His bones are full of the sin of his youth, which shall **lie down with him in the dust*** (Job 20:11).

Example of Use: Little did those first century rulers of Rome ever think that, long after their mighty empire **lay in the dust**, the Jewish faith, and even more so the Christian religion which had come out of it, would be flourishing, and have their adherents in all parts of the world! ("Theme for the Day," Feb. 15, 2000, *The Birmingham Post*, England)

Dust, Make something

Means: To destroy something completely

Biblical Text: *Neither did he leave of the people to Jehoahaz but fifty horsemen, and ten chariots, and ten thousand footmen; for the king of Syria had destroyed them, and had **made them like the dust** by threshing* (2 Kings 13:7). See also Deut. 9:21.

Example of Use: Over this year, one of the biggest obstacles to buying a high-definition TV **crumbled into dust**. Even if you're looking for a big, flat-panel plasma or a liquid-crystal display screen, you no longer have to spend more than the cost of a good laptop computer. ("LCD or Plasma? Consider Size, Weight, Glare," Nov. 26, 2006, *The Washington Post*)

D

Dust, Raise from the

Means: To rescue or exalt

Biblical Text: *He **raiseth up the poor out of the dust**, and lifteth up the beggar from the dunghill, to set them among princes, and to make them inherit the throne of glory* (1 Samuel 2:8).

Example of Use: So much of worldwide culture has been enriched by the Celts, through music, writing, a sense of egalitarianism, and an emphasis on justice. It is thrilling to see those characteristics being **lifted up from the dust** of history! ("Celtic Realm. [Letter to the Editor]," Wilson Strand, July 1, 2006, *National Geographic*)

Dust, Return to

Means: To die

Biblical Text: *Remember, I beseech thee, that thou hast made me as the clay; and wilt thou **bring me into dust** again?* (Job 10:9).

Example of Use: Gee, it's a big crazy world. But it always has been. Throughout the ages, people have argued and loved and lusted and suffered, and at last, died. And their survivors wept and then pressed on until they, too, **returned to dust**. ("Trying to Figure out the Rest of My Life," July 9, 2005, *Lexington Herald-Leader*, KY)

Dust, Sit in the

Means: To languish; to suffer humiliation

Biblical Text: *Come down, and **sit in the dust**, O virgin daughter of Babylon, sit on the ground: there is no throne, O daughter of the Chaldeans: for thou shalt no more be called tender and delicate* (Isaiah 47:1).

Example of Use: "We had dollars **sitting in the dust**," Newman said. "Stocked repair parts were sitting around way too long and we were looking for ways to automate and better manage our inventory. Then, Jeff Johnson showed up and everything changed." ("Inventory System Enables First-Rate Maintenance Team," Janet Howells-Tierney, Mar. 1, 2001, *Fleet Equipment*)

Dust, Sleep in the

Means: To die or no longer exist

Biblical Text: *And many of them that **sleep in the dust** of the earth shall awake, some to everlasting life, and some to shame and everlasting contempt* (Daniel 12:2). See also Job 7:21.

Example of Use: Americans visiting our overseas military cemeteries will find themselves enriched in ways I can only partially explain. At a minimum, the visit will prompt a renewed, and awesome, appreciation of those who **sleep in the dust** below. ("Cemetery Visit Is Invaluable," Aug. 15, 2007, *Albany Times Union*, NY)

RAISING CAIN

E

"IF THINE EYE OFFEND THEE"

Ears but do not hear, To have

Means: To have the facility to understand but to fail to do so

Biblical Text: *Son of man, thou dwellest in the midst of a rebellious house, which have eyes to see, and see not;* ***they have ears to hear, and hear not****: for they are a rebellious house* (Ezekiel 12:2).

Example of Use: Speaking before the pastor, Mr. Kerry, as he often does at religious gatherings, tried to put Mr. Bush and his administration into a biblical context, though never mentioning them by name. "Maybe these are the folks from Jeremiah [actually, Isaiah], who are reminded they have eyes but do not see; they **have ears, but do not hear**," he said. ("Kerry, Jackson Tell Blacks to Ignore Gay 'Marriage' Issue," Stephen Dinan, Oct. 11, 2004, *The Washington Times*)

Ears tingle

Means: To feel a ringing or thrilling sensation in the ear; to feel a thrilling sensation, especially as a result of becoming aware of an extraordinary event

Biblical Text: *Therefore thus saith the* LORD *God of Israel, Behold, I am bringing such evil upon Jerusalem and Judah, that whosoever heareth of it, both his* ***ears shall tingle*** (2 Kings 21:12).

Example of Use: Also in 1964, "Louie, Louie" by the Kingsmen was declared pornographic by the governor of Indiana . . . who, while admitting he couldn't understand the lyrics, said the song "made his **ears tingle**." ("A Look at What Happened in Years Past on This Day in Popular Music," Feb. 1, 2003, United Press International)

Ears to hear, let him hear, He who has

Means: An admonition to listen carefully

Biblical Text: *And other fell on good ground, and sprang up, and bare fruit an hundredfold. And when he had said these things, he cried,* ***He that hath ears to hear, let him hear*** (Luke 8:8).

E

Example of Use: "We think the hearing-impaired population will take hold of this technology because it is so new and effective," Hawkins said. The devices will be sold for $2,000 to $4,000 or about the cost of traditional hearing aids, he said. The company plans to keep the costs comparatively low, Hawkins said, in keeping with Hough's and the company's mission: **"He who has ears to hear, let him hear."** ("Oklahoma City High-Tech Firm Seeks Approval for New Hearing Aid," Sonya Colberg, Apr. 13, 2001, Knight Ridder/Tribune Business News)

Ears, Itching

Means: To want to hear what pleases one

Biblical Text: *For the time will come when they will not endure sound doctrine; but after their own lusts shall they heap to themselves teachers, having* ***itching ears***; *and they shall turn away their ears from the truth, and shall be turned unto fables* (2 Timothy 4:3–4).

Example of Use: Recently, while discussing the need for a new set of relational and conversational skills for advisors, an editor at a financial services magazine interrupted me to say, "No, that's not what they want to hear. We need to give them new ways to sell." He continued a monologue on selling strategies to **itching ears** that made me feel like I was in a scene from the movie, "Glengarry Glen Ross." ("The Warring Hand: After Years of Scandal and Ensuing Loss of Trust, Advisors Must

Abandon for Good the Aggressive Practices of the Past," Mitch Anthony, Oct. 1, 2003, *Research*)

Ears, Open (or Ears, Open one's; or Ears opened, To have one's)

Means: A willingness to be exposed to ideas and thoughts besides one's own

Biblical Text: *The Lord GOD hath **opened mine ear**, and I was not rebellious, neither turned away back* (Isaiah 50:5).

Example of Use: The pianist, however, points out the album was recorded more than two years ago and he's since moved on to other worlds. It's all part of the evolution of a musician who at 8 started with contemporary jazz, at 11 was knocked out by Art Tatum, soon afterwards immersed himself in Oscar Peterson, Gene Harris and Phineas Newborn, Jr., and now has completely **open ears**. ("Tanglewood Showcase Taylor-Made for Teen Piano Phenom Eigsti," Bob Young, Sept. 1, 2004, *The Boston Herald*)

East of Eden

Means: (1) A desolate place; (2) a place of exile

Biblical Text: *And Cain went out from the presence of the LORD, and dwelt in the land of Nod, on the **east of Eden*** (Genesis 4:16).

Example of Use: *In response to the letter writer wanting more stores east of Interstate 75. Why do people move east of I-75, where there are no grocery stores, no shopping malls, and less fast-food delivery, then complain?* ("Conveniences **East of Eden**," Apr. 7, 2001, *Sarasota Herald Tribune*)

Eat up, To

Means: To consume completely; to destroy

Biblical Text: *Have all the workers of iniquity no knowledge? Who **eat up** my people as they eat bread, and call not upon the LORD* (Psalm 14:4).

Example of Use: As fuel prices and student numbers balloon, transportation continues to **eat up** cash for classrooms. ("Buses **Eat up** Classroom Dollars," Amy Hsuan, Oct. 8, 2006, *Orian*, Portland, OR)

Eat, drink and be merry

Means: An exhortation to enjoy life

Biblical Text: *And I will say to my soul, Soul, thou hast much goods laid up for many years; take thine ease, **eat, drink, and be merry**. But I said unto him, Thou fool, this night thy soul shall be required of thee: then whose shall those things be, which thou hast provided? So is he that layeth up treasure for himself, and is not rich toward God* (Luke 12:19–21).

Example of Use: Eat, drink and be merry is only an old maxim for air passengers, especially in Delhi. . . . "There is no move to relax the no-alcohol-on-domestic-flights rule as of now," union civil aviation minister Praful Patel said. ("Domestic Flights to Stay a Dry Affair," Saurabh Sinha, May 22, 2006, *Times of India*, New Delhi)

Eden

Means: An unspoiled idyllic place

Biblical Text: *And the LORD God planted a garden eastward in **Eden**; and there he put the man whom he had formed* (Genesis 2:8).

Example of Use: In the beginning it was just a wild scheme thought up by an aging rock musician and his friends at an English country inn. Nine years later, the idea of creating a "garden of **Eden**" in the heart of Cornwall has not only come to fruition, it has blossomed into the biggest attraction in southwest England. ("The 'Garden of **Eden**' Is in England?" Doug Alexander, July 9, 2003, *The Christian Science Monitor*)

E

Egyptian darkness

Means: (1) Severe obscurity or confusion; (2) severe depression of the mind

Biblical Text: *And the* LORD *said unto Moses, Stretch out thine hand toward heaven, that there may be **darkness over the land of Egypt, even darkness which may be felt*** (Exodus 10:21).

Example of Use: Parenthetically, we may note that today, when Latin is no longer a required subject for students of the humanities at Swedish universities, many incipient researchers are unable to read Swedish historical documents and scholarly literature in the original, since they were all written in Latin. There are many ways of ensuring that an **Egyptian darkness** descends over contemporary society. This is one of them. ("On Translation and Being Translated," Kerstin Ekman, Apr. 1, 2003, *World Literature Today*)

Eleventh hour

Means: The latest possible time prior to a deadline

Biblical Text: *For the kingdom of heaven is like unto a man that is an householder, which went out early in the morning to hire labourers into his vineyard. And when he had agreed with the labourers for a penny a day, he sent them into his vineyard. And about the **eleventh hour** he went out, and found others standing* *idle, and saith unto them, Why stand ye here all the day idle? They say unto him, Because no man hath hired us. He saith unto them, Go ye also into the vineyard; and whatsoever is right, that shall ye receive* (Matthew 20:1–2, 6–7).

Example of Use: The last minute: "The water bombers arrived at the **eleventh hour**—just in time to prevent the forest fire from engulfing the town." ("Ailing Program Gets Help: **Eleventh-Hour** Donations Keep Youth Center Open for Now," Nov. 25, 2006, *The Sun News*, Myrtle Beach, SC)

Elijah

Means: A bold or visionary person, especially one who foresees coming disaster

Biblical Text: *And he came thither unto a cave, and lodged there; and, behold, the word of the LORD came to him, and he said unto him, What doest thou here, **Elijah**? And he said, I have been very jealous for the LORD God of hosts: for the children of Israel have forsaken thy covenant, thrown down thine altars, and slain thy prophets with the sword; and I, even I only, am left; and they seek my life, to take it away* (1 Kings 19:9–10).

Example of Use: And that's enough to make any of us depressed. When it seems like bad things keep happening no matter how hard we try to succeed, we're prime for an **Elijah** Complex. "I alone am left," we say. ("The Elijah Complex," Mike Bellah, 2007, www.bestyears.com)

End is near, The

Means: A final, usually climactic, stage is about to be reached, especially regarding an important development.

Biblical Text: *They hunt our steps, that we cannot go in our streets: our **end is near**, our days are fulfilled; for our end is come* (Lamentations 4:18).

Example of Use: Shannon Sharpe can see the writing on the wall. It might still be a bit illegible at this point, but he knows that it's telling him **the end is near**. The annoying aches he shook off with little trouble 10 years ago have evolved into chronic pains that dog him constantly. ("Sharpe Aware End Is Near[;] Broncos Veteran Still Trying to Decide if He Has Will to Return," Pat Rooney, Dec. 30, 2002, *Rocky Mountain News*, Denver)

End is not yet, The

Means: The termination of something has not happened, implying that the outcome is not yet determined

Biblical Text: *And ye shall hear of wars and rumours of wars: see that ye be not troubled: for all these things must come to pass, but **the end is not yet*** (Matthew 24:6).

Example of Use: The end is not yet. Not since John Dean has a single ex-official, disenchanted if not disgruntled, had such a powerful impact on the fortunes of a president. ("Clarke: Bush's John Dean?" Daniel Schorr, Apr. 2, 2004, *The Christian Science Monitor*)

Ends of the earth, To the

Means: To the utmost limit

Biblical Text: *For so hath the Lord commanded us, saying, I have set thee to be a light of the Gentiles, that thou shouldest be for salvation **unto the ends of the earth*** (Acts 13:47).

Example of Use: Think of the employee you hired most recently: Would you go **to the ends of the earth** with that person? ("HR **at the End of the Earth**," Patrick Mirza, June 1, 2004, *HR Magazine*)

Envy and strife

Means: The desire for what someone else possesses and the vigorous or bitter conflict, discord, or antagonism that results

Biblical Text: *Who is a wise man and endued with knowledge among you? let him shew out of a good conversation his works with meekness of wisdom. But if ye have bitter **envying and strife** in your hearts, glory not, and lie not against the truth* (James 3:13–14).

Example of Use: Internal racism has taught Blacks that supporting their own is against the American way. Blacks have been taught to tear down one other rather than build each other up. Jealously, **envy and strife** flourish within the Black community. However, if we look around at other racial and ethnic groups that prosper, we can see that they support their own whenever possible. ("Changing the Future by Supporting Black-Owned Businesses," Ervin Milton, Feb. 8, 2007, *Chicago Defender*)

Esau

Means: Someone who foolishly parts with something of value, receiving little in return, because of disregard for its value

Biblical Text: *Then Jacob gave **Esau** bread and pottage of lentiles; and he did eat and drink, and rose up, and went his way: thus **Esau** despised his birthright* (Genesis 25:34).

Example of Use: Downtown supporters are probably suffering an **Esau** complex these days, feeling cheated out of their birthright to the very projects downtown needed most. ("Editorial:

Downtown Deserves Chance to Shine," July 15, 2007, *Messenger-Inquirer,* Owensboro, KY)

Every idle word, Shall give account for

Means: One will be held accountable eventually for what he says in his lifetime.

Biblical Text: *But I say unto you, That **every idle word that men shall speak, they shall give account** thereof in the day of judgment* (Matthew 12:36).

Example of Use: "**Every idle word that men shall speak, they shall give account** thereof in the day of judgment," warns the Gospel of Matthew. Matthew is referring to eternal judgment, though his words apply equally to Supreme Court nominees appearing before the Senate Judiciary Committee. ("Alito's College Days; Reading His Senior Thesis on the Italian Constitutional Court," Joseph Lindsley, Dec. 5, 2005, *The Weekly Standard*)

Every knee shall bow

Means: Every person shall acknowledge authority.

Biblical Text: *That at the name of Jesus **every knee should bow,** of things in heaven, and things in earth, and things under the earth; And that every tongue should confess that Jesus Christ is Lord, to the glory of God the Father* (Philippians 2:10–11).

Example of Use: But I shall be accused of dancing around the most important issue of our time, the issue at the name of which **every knee shall bow.** Global warming, we are told, will have its most devastating effects on the world's disadvantaged. ("Climate, Class, and Claptrap," Garret Keizer, June 1, 2007, *Harper's Magazine*)

Every man did right in his own eyes

Means: A condition in which anarchy replaces order

Biblical Text: *In those days there was no king in Israel: **every man did that which was right in his own eyes*** (Judges 21:25).

Example of Use: We have made the jump from choosing whether or not we would keep a child to whether or not we would keep a child with Down's Syndrome to choosing what gender we would like. But with this logic, if you want a child, why not design it yourself? Are we en route to another Arian race? "And **everyone did what was right in their own eyes**." ("Will the Fetal Sex-Selection Experiment Be Fatal?" July 5, 2007, drewskibobaluski.spaces.live.com)

E

Evidence of things not seen, The

Means: Faith in someone or something

Biblical Text: *Now faith is the substance of things hoped for, **the evidence of things not seen*** (Hebrews 11:1).

Example of Use: The only thing keeping people going is hope and optimism about the future that is unknown. The hope is **the evidence of things not seen**. ("Amid Misery and Tragedy, Africa Still Optimistic," Lydia Polgreen, Mar. 7, 2006, *International Herald Tribune*)

Evil communications corrupt good manners

Means: Association with the wicked threatens the diligence of moral people.

Biblical Text: *Be not deceived: **evil communications corrupt good manners*** (1 Corinthians 15:33).

Example of Use: We have this knack of bundling together the very best and the very worst aspects of the unique nature and talents of our species. Think of the wonders of the Information Superhighway. Then contemplate all the dirty jokes and e-mail trivia that clog up its side roads. And as every burgher of Lichfield knows, **evil communications corrupt good manners**, as 1 Corinthians puts it. But that's the deal with us. The good, the bad and the utterly trivial come wound together like a bundle of two-ply wool. ("Post Style: The World according to . . . ," Sid Langley, June 7, 2000, *The Birmingham Post,* England)

Evil Eye

Means: An eye or glance believed to be capable of inflicting harm, often used in jest

Biblical Text: *Eat thou not the bread of him that hath an **evil eye**, neither desire thou his dainty meats* (Proverbs 23:6).

Example of Use: Sitting on a chair in a crowded clubhouse on Wednesday with his arms splayed and teammates crowded around him, Luis Matos took one look at a reporter and gave him the **evil eye**. ("Matos Hoping for Healthy Improvement," Jorge Arangure Jr., Mar. 31, 2006, *The Washington Post*)

Evil in the eyes of someone, To do

Means: To do what is wicked

Biblical Text: *For our fathers have trespassed, and done that which was **evil in the eyes of the LORD** our God, and have forsaken him, and have turned away their faces from the habitation of the LORD, and turned their backs* (2 Chronicles 29:6).

Example of Use: During the 1980s, the great **evil in the eyes of** such groups was the use of saturated fats, which are found in beef tallow and butter. Therefore, trans fat was preferred.

("Deep-Fried Do-Goodism," William P. Hoar, Feb. 5, 2007, *The New American*)

Evil that good may come, Do not do

Means: An admonition not to do what is wrong in order to create a good result; "the end does not justify the means."

Biblical Text: *And not rather, (as we be slanderously reported, and as some affirm that we say,)* **Let us do evil, that good may come**? *whose damnation is just* (Romans 3:8).

Example of Use: Bill Lockyer (former California state attorney general and now state treasurer) says there are 600,000 kids with gambling problems. St. Paul challenges us in his epistle to the Romans, "And why not say, '**Let us do evil that good may come?'**" Every argument for the legalization or expansion of gambling from a governmental official, to me, has a common thread, "We can do so much good with the money we get from gambling." ("Internet Gambling Regulation: Gregory J. Hogan Sr.," June 8, 2007, *Congressional Testimony*)

Exodus

Means: A journey by a large group to escape from a hostile environment

Biblical Text: *By faith Joseph, when his end was near, spoke about the* **exodus** *of the Israelites from Egypt and gave instructions about his bones* (Hebrews 11:22).

Example of Use: An alliance of organizations composed of overseas Filipinos and their families warned the local aviation industry yesterday that the current **exodus** of pilots and airline workers will worsen unless a comprehensive response is formulated. ("Action to Stem **Exodus** of Pilots Sought," Mar. 14, 2006, *Manila Bulletin*)

Extra mile

Means: Beyond what is expected or anticipated

Biblical Text: *And whosoever shall compel thee to go a **mile**, go with him twain* (Matthew 5:41).

Example of Use: To go the **extra mile**, all packages offer the winner and his guests a VIP tour of Richard Childress Racing, including a private lunch with world-class NASCAR driver Jeff Burton, along with $10,000 cash. ("Lenox® and NASCAR's Jeff Burton Team Up for the **Extra-Mile** Experience," May 7, 2007, PR Newswire)

Eye for an eye, a tooth for a tooth, An

Means: A law of retribution calling for a judgment to be commensurate with an offense

Biblical Text: *And thine eye shall not pity; but life shall go for life, **eye for eye, tooth for tooth**, hand for hand, foot for foot* (Deuteronomy 19:21).

Example of Use: An eye for an eye and a tooth for a tooth. That was the theme for this weekend's baseball series between No. 22 UF [University of Florida] (20–15, 8–4 Southeastern Conference) and No. 5 South Carolina (26–7, 7–5 SEC). ("Tense Gamecocks Series Leaves UF Baseball with 2 Losses," Alex Weintraub, Apr. 9, 2007, *University Wire*)

Eye offend thee, pluck it out, If thine

Means: Gain control of what leads one to sin

Biblical Text: *And **if thy right eye offend thee, pluck it out**, and cast it from thee: for it is profitable for thee that one of thy members should perish, and not that thy whole body should be cast into hell* (Matthew 5:29). See also Matt. 18:9; Mark 9:47.

Example of Use: "And **if thy right eye offend thee, pluck it out**, and cast it from thee. . . ." We've all been offended at one point or another—that's part of the price of admission to the land of the free and the home of the brave. But what personally offends each of us, and how we respond to the offense, is different. ("Offensive Line: Baise-Moi; Feminist Empowerment, Hardcore Porn or Both? Baise-Moi," Nov. 6, 2001, *Santa Fe Reporter*, NM)

Eye on the sparrow

Means: Attention to even the most minor people or matters

Biblical Text: *Are not two sparrows sold for a farthing? and one of them shall not fall on the ground without your Father. But the very hairs of your head are all numbered. Fear ye not therefore, ye are of more value than many sparrows* (Matthew 10:29–31).

Example of Use: It is much easier to understand the lovely phrase **"His eye is on the sparrow"** when we remember that He can hardly avoid seeing the sparrow because He made so many of them. ("Amid the Splendor, the Lowly Sparrow," Nick Clooney, Nov. 9, 2007, *Cincinnati Post*)

Eyeless in Gaza

Means: A hopeless state in a hostile environment

Biblical Text: *But the Philistines took him [Samson], and put out his eyes, and brought him down to Gaza*, and bound him with fetters of brass; and he did grind in the prison house (Judges 16:21).

Example of Use: One brazen settler, looking at the cluster of Israeli troops and cops below, winged rocks at the Arab house next door while shouting, "They're throwing stones!" Other settlers held up body-length mirrors to reflect the blazing sun into the eyes of Palestinians, soldiers, police and journalists—an appalling rush of light and heat that rendered the victims, however briefly, **eyeless in Gaza**. ("Unsettled in Gaza; The Pullout That's Dividing Israelis," Warren Bass, July 17, 2005, *The Washington Post*)

Eyes but do not see, To have

Means: To fail to understand

Biblical Text: *Hear now this, O foolish people, and without understanding;* **which have eyes, and see not;** *which have ears, and hear not* (Jeremiah 5:21).

Example of Use: Much of the vitamin content of the potato is in the skin. Some potato salad recipes have you remove the skin, others don't. It's up to you, but why would anyone who doesn't dislike the skin go through the bother of taking it off and losing the vitamins in the process? (As has been said of heathens—and potatoes—**"They have eyes, but do not see."**) ("A World of Potato Salad; A Fourth of July Visit to One of the Favorite Foods of Summer Takes Us to Many Nations," Al Sicherman, July 2, 1997, *Star Tribune*, Minneapolis, MN)

Eyes open (or opened), To have one's

Means: To become aware of someone or something

Biblical Text: *Let thine ear now be attentive, and* **thine eyes open,** *that thou mayest hear the prayer of thy servant, which I pray before thee now, day and night, for the children of Israel thy servants, and confess the sins of the children of Israel, which we have sinned against thee: both I and my father's house have sinned* (Nehemiah 1:6).

Example of Use: Stereotypes were dispelled and **eyes were opened** when two formerly homeless people spoke to students to raise awareness of homelessness. ("Formerly Homeless People Speak at U. Connecticut," Freesia Singngam, Nov. 10, 2006, *University Wire*)

Eyes to see and ears to hear, To have

Means: To have the ability or will to learn or understand

Biblical Text: *Son of man, thou dwellest in the midst of a rebellious house, which have* **eyes to see***, and see not; they have* **ears to hear***, and hear not: for they are a rebellious house* (Ezekiel 12:2).

Example of Use: [General] Taguba's report made it clear to anyone with **eyes to see** or ears to hear that what was going on at Abu Ghraib went beyond abuse to torture—and went far beyond the isolated misdeeds of a couple of twisted reservists. ("Truth-Telling and Abu Ghraib: General Pays the Price," June 20, 2007, *The Philadelphia Inquirer*)

Eyes, Heavy

Means: A facial expression, particularly of the eyes, showing a variety of emotions or conditions, such as sleepiness, fatigue, or earnestness

Biblical Text: *And they came to a place which was named Gethsemane: and he [Jesus] saith to his disciples, Sit ye here, while I shall pray. . . . And when he returned, he found them asleep again, (for their* **eyes were heavy***,) neither wist they what to answer him* (Mark 14:32, 40).

Example of Use: Once while tutoring a sleepy little Burmese boy who kept falling asleep with his face down in the book, I grilled him on the importance of sleep. "You need to get enough sleep every night so your brain is awake and ready to learn when you come to school. You don't need TV, you need sleep. Tell your parents that you should be in bed by 8 o'clock every night." He looked at me with **heavy eyes** and said, "But my parents no speak English." ("Feeling Drowsy Is Lousy," Lori Borgman, Mar. 1, 2011, *Buffalo News*)

E

RAISING CAIN

F

"FLY IN THE OINTMENT"

Faith as small as a mustard seed, To have

Means: A very small amount of faith in someone or something

Biblical Text: *And Jesus said unto them, Because of your unbelief: for verily I say unto you, If ye have **faith as a grain of mustard seed**, ye shall say unto this mountain, Remove hence to yonder place; and it shall remove; and nothing shall be impossible unto you* (Matthew 17:20). See also Luke 17:6.

Example of Use: "All You Need Is **Faith the Size of a Mustard Seed**: The Franchise Community Can Attract More Minority and Women Entrepreneurs by Using Faith—Focus, Anticipation, Initiative, Time and Harmony. (Minorities and Emerging Markets)," Robert Wallace, Nov. 1, 2001, *Franchising World*

Faith to move mountains

Means: Extraordinary faith to accomplish the apparently impossible

Biblical Text: *And though I have the gift of prophecy, and understand all mysteries, and all knowledge; and though I have all **faith, so that I could remove mountains**, and have not charity, I am nothing* (1 Corinthians 13:2). See also Matt. 17:20.

Example of Use: Tich Smith believes in miracles. How else would the former . . . Springbok cricketer have arrested a life of partying, drinking and gambling almost 20 years ago? Fifty-nine-year old Smith is a fervent believer. Just as well, he's going to need **faith to move mountains** if he wants to succeed in his quest to create a village for 1000 AIDS orphans in Durban. ("A Tich in Time Will Save Numerous Lives," Apr. 4, 2010, *Sunday Tribune*, South Africa)

Faith without works

Means: Beliefs without corresponding actions

Biblical Text: *Yea, a man may say, Thou hast faith, and I have works: show me thy **faith without thy works**, and I will show thee my faith by my works. . . . For as the body without the spirit is dead, so **faith without works** is dead also* (James 2:18, 26).

Example of Use: Walk into a Wal-Mart store, and you'll see giant banners proclaiming a commitment to "Wal-Mart Good Works" before you see the first "Rollback" placard. It's marketing from the Book of James, as in the Bible's broadside against **faith without works**, rather than the Book of Sam, as in Walton, legendary "Mr. Sam" to the Wal-Mart nation. ("Image Efforts Cut into Wal-Mart Sales; Good for PR, but Takes Focus Off of Low Prices," Jack Neff, Dec. 13, 2004, *Advertising Age*)

Faith, hope, and charity (or love)

Means: Characteristics of Christian love

Biblical Text: *And now abideth **faith, hope, charity**, these three; but the greatest of these is charity* (1 Corinthians 13:13).

Example of Use: You might think seed firms are selling seeds pure and simple. In fact, they are also introducing you to a horticultural version of **faith, hope and charity**. . . , faith in the idea of a more colourful garden, hope that the seeds will germinate and flower, and charity if they don't perform well. ("Plant with Flying Colours; Gardening Club—Peter Surridge Discovers Ravishing Shades and Tones among the Seed Catalogues for 2002," Peter Surridge, Nov. 24, 2001, *Daily Post*, Liverpool, England)

Fall away

Means: To stray from a prescribed course, especially acceptable or necessary behavior, or away from friends

Biblical Text: *They on the rock are they, which, when they hear, receive the word with joy; and these have no root, which for a while believe, and in time of temptation **fall away*** (Luke 8:13).

Example of Use: "I no longer want to belong to the church. I no longer want to attend Mass," Fontaine told his somber audience. "I wish it wasn't so, but it is." Therein lies the ultimate challenge facing Malone, who this week became the 11th bishop of the Diocese of Portland. As he takes the crozier and tries to lead his new flock out of the controversy that has raged for the past two years, how can he persuade **fallen-away** Catholics like Fontaine to follow? ("Skeptics Pray New Bishop Has Healing Touch," Bill Nemitz, Apr. 2, 2004, *Portland Press Herald*, ME)

Fall from grace

Means: To experience reduced status, prestige, or favor

Biblical Text: *Christ is become of no effect unto you, whosoever of you are justified by the law; ye are **fallen from grace*** (Galatians 5:4).

Example of Use: "Fallen Angel? Is that what they're calling it? That's ridiculous—they should have called it triumphant angel," exclaims Jonathan Shalit, one-time manager of teenage diva sensation Charlotte Church. Jonathan, one of the talking heads in a documentary on the Cardiff opera star's career, is seemingly unaware that he has contributed to a programme charting the supposed **fall from grace** of the girl whose angelic voice conquered the classical album charts when she was 12. ("The Angel Who **Fell from Grace**; Gareth Bicknell on the

Teenager Who Wooed the World with Her Voice," Gareth Bicknell, Feb. 14, 2004, *Daily Post*, Liverpool)

Fall on stony ground

Means: To receive an unfavorable reaction

Biblical Text: *Hearken; Behold, there went out a sower to sow: And it came to pass, as he sowed, some fell by the way side, and the fowls of the air came and devoured it up. And **some fell on stony ground**, where it had not much earth* (Mark 4:3–5).

Example of Use: The fans were after nostalgia, pure and simple. And Wings, finding their new material **falling on stony ground**, eventually gave in and made the most of it. The McCartney magic was as powerful as ever when it came to putting across the old hits. ("Wings on Song for Nostalgia; Review," Jackie Bailey, Nov. 24, 2007, *Birmingham Mail*, England)

Fallen angel

Means: (1) Someone formerly respected by others but who now is considered disreputable or of lower social status, especially because of his indiscretions; (2) a high-quality bond or stock that is now of significantly lower quality

Biblical Text: **How art thou fallen from heaven, O Lucifer,** *son of the morning! how art thou cut down to the ground, which didst weaken the nations! For thou hast said in thine heart, I will ascend into heaven, I will exalt my throne above the stars of God* (Isaiah 14:12–13a). See also Rev. 12:7–11.

Example of Use: When bond rating agencies downgraded General Motors in May, the world's largest automaker joined an exclusive club, or rogues' gallery, if you prefer. In recent years, a number of other household-name companies—Xerox, AT&T, Kodak, Maytag, Enron, Tyco, Lucent, WorldCom,

RJR—saw their debt securities drop from investment grade to speculative grade, or "high yield." They became **fallen angels**, in the parlance of the bond market. ("Many **'Fallen Angels'** Soar to New Heights," July 31, 2005, *Chicago Tribune*)

False prophets

Means: (1) Someone who claims authority illegitimately, especially one who claims to represent orthodoxy of some kind; (2) someone proven wrong in making a prediction

Biblical Text: *But there were **false prophets** also among the people, even as there shall be false teachers among you, who privily shall bring in damnable heresies, even denying the Lord that bought them, and bring upon themselves swift destruction* (2 Peter 2:1).

Example of Use: For as long as anybody can remember, spiritual con-artists have ripped off the faithful, preying on the sick, the elderly, the lonely and the desperate. But there is at least one organization that is successfully exposing spiritual chicanery—the Dallas-based Trinity Foundation. ("The Abuses of Televangelism: Man on a Mission to Root out **False Prophets**," July 29, 2006, *Lexington Herald-Leader*, KY)

Fashion of this world, The

Means: Ways of living that do not acknowledge or respect God or godly values

Biblical Text: *The fashion of this world passeth away* (1 Corinthians 7:31b).

Example of Use: As TV shows from *The Jetsons* to *Star Trek* have shown, futuristic fashion predictions have missed the mark before. What's cool now and what's cool in the future could be quite different. Still, anything's better than those jumpsuits! Lost in Polyester: In the 1960s, TV's *Lost in Space* Had a Vision of Future Fashion. Reality Check[:] **Fashion of This World** Still Rules. ("Future Shock," Kimberly Cihlar, Dec. 13, 1999, *New York Times Upfront*)

Fat of the land

Means: The best or richest of anything

Biblical Text: *And take your father and your households, and come unto me: and I will give you the good of the land of Egypt, and ye shall eat the **fat of the land*** (Genesis 45:18).

Example of Use: The Oscar-winning director Francis Ford Coppola has taken a swipe at the trio, saying they have become lazy, stopped taking risks and are "living off the **fat of the land**." ("Coppola Criticises De Niro, Pacino and Nicholson As 'Lazy,'" Emily Dugan, Oct. 19, 2007, *Belfast Telegraph*)

Father, forgive them; for they know not what they do

Means: Jesus' words of forgiveness on the cross to his tormentors

Biblical Text: *Then said Jesus, **Father, forgive them; for they know not what they do**. And they parted his raiment, and cast lots* (Luke 23:34).

Example of Use: Magee waves the heathen meddling away with a benign **"Father, forgive them, they knew not what they did"** kind of attitude and hopes his company will be back when the curtain rises on the last act of the Lincoln resurrection. ("'Teaser' Is Just Tip of the Iceberg for Theater Restoration," Tony Reid, June 26, 2006, *Herald & Review,* Decatur, IL)

Father's house are many mansions, In my

Means: The heavenly residence promised by Jesus to his followers

Biblical Text: *In my Father's house are many mansions: if it were not so, I would have told you. I go to prepare a place for you* (John 14:2).

Example of use: Among the best-known of the artists in the Addison show is Howard Finster, who died in October after devoting his life to creating images of the heavenly city, the New Jerusalem. His **"In My Father's House Are Many Mansions"** is a 6½-foot-tall, shimmering, mirror-encrusted building, its many windows revealing more structures inside, giving the sense of infinite buildings within buildings. ("Seeing the World with a Self-Taught Vision," Christine Temin, Mar. 1, 2002, *The Boston Globe*)

Fatted calf, Kill the

Means: To celebrate

Biblical Text: *And bring hither the fatted calf, and kill it; and let us eat, and be merry: For this my son was dead, and is alive again; he was lost, and is found* (Luke 15:23).

Example of Use: As a firm believer in the separation of church and state, I am uncomfortable with the postgame prayer by the OSU players in full view of the public. Didn't Jesus teach us to pray in private? Of course, the OSU-Michigan game is another matter—anything goes. **Kill the fatted calf** and burn it at the goal posts if it helps, and for good measure toss in a couple of cars and an old couch. Go Bucks. ("Fans Sink Their Teeth into a Couple of Juicy Items and Give Them a Shake," Ray Stein, Nov. 19, 2006, *Columbus Dispatch*, OH)

Fear and trembling

Means: Agitation and anxiety caused by the presence or imminence of danger

Biblical Text: *Servants, be obedient to them that are your masters according to the flesh, with **fear and trembling**, in singleness of your heart, as unto Christ* (Ephesians 6:5).

Example of Use: There seems to be an epidemic of **fear and trembling** for which there is no cure or vaccine. Take, for example, a recent conversation with an elderly relative who was afraid of returning her census form for fear of what the government might do with the information. As tactfully as possible, I pointed out that, with the exception of her race, all of the requested information was already on numerous tax forms she had filed, and was already possessed by every bank, utility, and credit card issuer she'd ever dealt with. ("Fear and Trembling and Electricity. [Occupational Safety and Health]," Richard Babyak, May 1, 2010, *Appliance Design*)

Fear not

Means: An exhortation not to be afraid, despite threatening circumstances

Biblical Text: *But when Jesus heard it, he answered him, saying, **Fear not**: believe only, and she shall be made whole* (Luke 8:50).

Example of Use: It is a recognized fact that Valentine's Day is a wily commercial scheme spearheaded by Tiffany's, FTD and Hallmark. **Fear not**[,] impoverished students, with less than $20 and a little creativity, you and your valentine can have a romantic (and cheap) date. ("**Fear Not**: Dirt Cheap Valentine's Day Deeds," Laura Newman, Feb. 13, 2003, *University Wire*)

Fear of God

Means: A feeling of profound fear and awe of someone or something, not necessarily of God

Biblical Text: *The transgression of the wicked saith within my heart, that there is no **fear of God** before his eyes* (Psalm 36:1).

Example of Use: "Fear only two: God, and the man who has no **fear of God**." (Hasidic Proverb)

Fearfully and wonderfully made, To be

Means: To be made in grand and sublime fashion

Biblical Text: *I will praise thee; for I am **fearfully and wonderfully made**: marvellous are thy works; and that my soul knoweth right well* (Psalm 139:14).

Example of Use: "African American people are embracing their natural hair more and more everyday," Coleman Holmes said. "We have stopped accepting what our culture has said about us and realized that we are '**fearfully and wonderfully made**.'" ("Local Women Open Salon Celebrating Natural Hair, The Nappy Kitchen Opens in Tower Grove Area," Nov. 15, 2010, PRWeb Newswire)

Feed the five thousand

Means: Provide food for a large number of people

Biblical Text: *And he commanded the multitude to sit down on the grass, and took the five loaves, and the two fishes, and looking up to heaven, he blessed, and brake, and gave the loaves to his disciples, and the disciples to the multitude. And they did all eat, and were filled: and they took up of the fragments that remained twelve baskets full. **And they that had eaten were about five thousand** men, beside women and children* (Matthew 14:19–21).

Example of Use: And so how have I coped with five? First and foremost is to get things sorted in the kitchen. The house is almost always full of people who want to be fed. It is impossible to tell how many people you are cooking for. One minute you think you are going to have to **feed the five thousand** and the next minute everyone has disappeared to a football match and you have two delicious roast chickens—one for you and one for the baby. ("Life and Strife in the Club of Five; a New Report Says Children Looked after by Mothers Thrive Far Better Than Those in Nurseries. But What Happens if You've Got Five? It's Fraught but Fantastic," Martine Oborne, Oct. 4, 2005, *The Evening Standard*, London)

F

Feet of clay

Means: A personal weakness or flaw, especially one that contributes to one's defeat or downfall

Biblical Text: *This image's head was of fine gold, his breast and his arms of silver, his belly and his thighs of brass, his legs of iron, his **feet** part of iron and part **of clay*** (Daniel 2:32–33).

Example of Use: The QC [Queen's counsel] said eyewitnesses had given very different accounts in 1994 and in court and urged the jury to be wary of evidence from experts, saying they often turn out to have "**feet of clay**." He cited the cases of the Birmingham Six, the Shirley McKie fingerprint case and the Hitler Diaries as occasions when experts got it wrong. ("Webster Is 'a Liar and Philanderer . . . but Not a Killer,'" May 18, 2011, *Daily Mail*, London)

Feet on (someone or something), Put one's

Means: To show severe disdain for someone or something

Biblical Text: *And it came to pass, when they brought out those Kings unto Joshua, that Joshua called for all the men of Israel, and said unto the captains of the men of war which went with him, Come near,* **put your feet upon the necks** *of these kings* (Joshua 10:24–26).

Example of Use: First the crowd of Iraqis sledgehammer the sculpture of Saddam Hussein. With the help of American soldiers, they yank it to the ground and drag the severed head through the streets. And then, in a gesture of pure cultural insult, they begin **pounding** the stew out of **the statue with their shoes**. . . . It is one of the strongest insults in the Arab world—sticking the sole of your shoe in somebody's face, in a culture where the foot is considered the dirtiest part of the body. ("Worst Foot Forward: A Guide to Foreign Insults," Linton Weeks, Apr. 11, 2003, *The Washington Post*)

Feet, Fall at one's

Means: (1) To express obeisance, sometimes by actually bowing or falling prostrate before someone; (2) to receive something unexpected, desirable, and without effort

Biblical Text: *And Esther spake yet again before the king, and* **fell down at his feet***, and besought him with tears to put away the mischief of Haman the Agagite, and his device that he had devised against the Jews* (Esther 8:3).

Example of Use: Just two short years ago, Slim Lambright's future literally **fell at her feet**. She was at her local supermarket when an advertisement for a $20 writing class, being offered as community service by Temple University, dropped off the bulletin board in front of her. She saw it as an act of divine intervention. Slim took the class, began writing in September of 1996 and completed a first draft in 1999. And a few months later, the fifty-plus-year-old Slim landed a book deal. That book, *The Justus Girls*, will be published by HarperCollins on July 1, 2001. ("On the Bookshelf: *The Justus Girls*," Dec. 12, 2001, *The New York Beacon*)

Feet, Lay someone or something at one's

Means: To make someone responsible for someone or something

Biblical Text: *And great multitudes came unto him, having with them those that were lame, blind, dumb, maimed, and many others, and **cast them down at Jesus' feet**; and he healed them* (Matthew 15:30). See also Acts 4:34–35.

Example of Use: Blix's defenders say the Iraqi nuclear-weapons mess does not prove anything about the kind of job he would do in weapons-inspections today. The problem in 1991, they say, was not Blix, but rather the inspection regime that existed at the time. "I don't think you can **lay it at his feet**," says Ewen Buchanan of UNMOVIC. "You have to **lay it at the feet** of the system that was in place." ("Blix-krieg: How Not to Fight Saddam Hussein," Byron York, Oct. 14, 2002, *National Review*)

Feet, Sit at one's

Means: To study under the tutelage of another, especially one esteemed in a particular field

Biblical Text: *I am verily a man which am a Jew, born in Tarsus, a city in Cilicia, yet brought up in this city **at the feet** of Gamaliel, and taught according to the perfect manner of the law of the fathers, and was zealous toward God, as ye all are this day* (Acts 22:3).

Example of Use: [Camille Cosby:] "I do not want my generation to be the last that **sat at the feet of** our elders with admiration, respect and an open mind and heart to what they could teach us. I have walked away from every interview with a deep sense of excitement about what I have learned." ("A Wealth of Wisdom," Kam Williams, Jan. 30, 2004, *Baltimore Afro-American*)

Fiery furnace

Means: A horrible punishment, especially one that leaves the intended victim unharmed but harms the punisher

Biblical Text: *Then Nebuchadnezzar came near to the mouth of the burning **fiery furnace**, and spake, and said, Shadrach, Meshach, and Abed-nego, ye servants of the most high God, come forth, and come hither* (Daniel 3:26).

Example of Use: Many college coaches have gone from the **fiery furnace** of the college football field to the safe haven of the press box. ("Bad Coaches Make Mediocre Commentators," Ronnie McLellan, Oct. 27, 2004, *University Wire*)

Fig leaf

Means: Something meant to conceal one's errors or flaws, usually inadequately

Biblical Text: *And the eyes of them [Adam and Eve] both were opened, and they knew that they were naked; and they sewed **fig leaves** together, and made themselves aprons* (Genesis 3:7).

Example of Use: Using "tax fairness" as his **fig leaf**, the governor is trying to disguise a proposed gross-receipts tax on business that clearly is a very naked power play, one that may well kneecap job growth here, clobber middle-class consumers in the wallet, or some of both. ("Rod's **Fig Leaf**; Governor Uses Anti-Biz Facade to Disguise His Tax Flip-Flop," Greg Hinz, Mar. 12, 2007, *Crain's Chicago Business*)

Fight the good fight

Means: Contend vigorously for worthy principles

Biblical Text: *Fight the good fight of faith, lay hold on eternal life, whereunto thou art also called, and hast professed a good profession before many witnesses* (1 Timothy 6:12).

Example of Use: As if the pressure of delivering harmony (in the form of flowers) to hundreds of relationships in a single day wasn't enough, local florists yesterday had to do it in a blinding snowstorm. "We understand it's an important day for these people," Jeff Decoteaux, co-owner of Flowers by Albert in Lowell, said yesterday morning. "We're just trying to **fight the good fight** here." ("Weather Was Snow Help for Florists," Tom Spoth, Feb. 15, 2007, *Sun*, Lowell, MA)

Filthy lucre

Means: Money or monetary gain, especially when given more importance than is good for its possessor or when gotten by illegal or immoral means

Biblical Text: *A bishop then must be blameless, the husband of one wife, vigilant, sober, of good behaviour, given to hospitality, apt to teach; Not given to wine, no striker, not greedy of **filthy lucre**; but patient, not a brawler, not covetous* (1 Timothy 3:2–3)

Example of Use: Apparently piquing your interest in **filthy lucre** is the new porn of the '00s. Forget about "Hot, Hot, Hot," messages like: Earn Big $$$$$$, Find the LOWEST Mortgage and Inve$t Now, have started relentlessly attacking our inboxes. ("Bodacious Profits. [Spam in Canada]," Rod Lamirand, June 1, 2001, *BC Business*, British Columbia)

F

Finger of God

Means: Divine guidance or action

Biblical Text: *And if I by Beelzebub cast out devils, by whom do your sons cast them out? therefore shall they be your judges. But if I with the **finger of God** cast out devils, no doubt the kingdom of God is come upon you* (Luke 11:19–20).

Example of Use: Robert Rosenberg's rooftop apartment in Tel Aviv was his front-row seat in the Persian Gulf War—the fiery clash of Iraqi Scud and U.S. Patriot missiles playing out nightly overhead. "It looks like the **finger of God** going up in the sky— the Patriots firing, the Scuds," says Rosenberg, now one of Tel Aviv's many Internet entrepreneurs, then both hapless target and fascinated spectator. ("Gulf War Tied Israel's Hands," Ellen Knickmeyer, Jan. 14, 2001, AP Online)

Fire and brimstone

Means: Vociferousness; a means of punishment by God or another high source with punitive powers

Biblical Text: *The sun was risen upon the earth when Lot entered into Zoar. Then the LORD rained upon Sodom and upon Gomorrah **brimstone and fire** from the LORD out of heaven; And he overthrew those cities, and all the plain, and all the inhabitants of the cities, and that which grew upon the ground* (Genesis 19:23–25).

Example of Use: Growing up a devout Methodist, Wally Harrelson vowed that whatever he did with his life, it would be serving others—a minister perhaps. Turns out the ministry wasn't his calling. But that hasn't kept Harrelson from dishing out his share of **fire and brimstone**. At 32 years and counting, Harrelson is North Carolina's longest-serving public defender. ("**Fire and Brimstone**: From a Courtroom Pulpit; Wally Harrelson Has Been

Defending the Underdog Longer Than Anyone Else in the State's History," Mike Fuchs, Dec. 15, 2002, *The News & Record,* Piedmont Triad, NC)

Fire that is not quenched

Means: An uncontrolled, harmful factor

Biblical Text: *And if thy hand offend thee, cut it off: it is better for thee to enter into life maimed, than having two hands to go into hell, into the **fire that never shall be quenched**: Where their worm dieth not, and the **fire is not quenched*** (Mark 9:43).

Example of Use: Breyten Breytenbach, 5 p.m. Monday, Bagley Wright Theatre. This longtime South African activist, who spent a decade behind bars for his beliefs, provides testament to the power of poetry. He uses words and wit and outrage as his weapons of choice, with an **unquenched fire** that is still raging. ("Diversity and World Events Help Shape Literary Lineup," John Marshall, Aug. 30, 2002, *Seattle Post-Intelligencer*)

Firebrand

Means: An agitator or agitating factor that creates unrest or strife

Biblical Text: *And Samson went and caught three hundred foxes, and took **firebrands**, and turned tail to tail, and put a **firebrand** in the midst between two tails* (Judges 15:4).

Example of Use: The sari-wearing **firebrand** who for two decades has fiercely fought biotechnology in her native India was complaining yet again about the men in lab coats who say they know best how to manage the world's food supply. ("Indian **Firebrand** Battles Biotech," July 31, 2004, *Little India*)

First shall be last and the last shall be first, The

Means: Those who are greatest now will at some time become the least and vice versa.

Biblical Text: *And he sat down, and called the twelve, and saith unto them,* ***If any man desire to be first, the same shall be last of all****, and servant of all* (Mark 9:35).

Example of Use: [Texas senior cornerback Aaron] Ross winning the Thorpe seemed improbable six years ago, when a clerical error in his high school transcript turned into an NCAA Clearinghouse issue that delayed his enrollment at Texas for two years. Ross also didn't become a full-time starter until this season. He had 10 takeaways in his last 10 games. Ross was joined at the awards Thursday by his girlfriend of three years, Sanya Richards, a former Longhorn and the American record-holder in the 400-meter dash. "My mom always told me during that difficult time, **'The first shall be last and the last shall be first,'**" Ross said. "She was right." ("Hogs' McFadden Wins Doak Walker Award," Chip Brown, Dec. 8, 2006, *Dallas Morning News*)

Firstfruits

Means: The first products or results of a project or endeavor, especially when offered to someone in gratitude

Biblical Text: *Honour the* LORD *with thy substance, and with the* ***firstfruits*** *of all thine increase* (Proverbs 3:9).

Example of Use: Kwanzaa is a **firstfruits** celebration. In fact, that's where the name Kwanzaa comes from, the phrase my *matunda ya kwanzaa* or my *sura ya kwanzaa*, which means **firstfruit**. ("Interview: Kwanzaa Creator Maulana Karenga Discusses the Evolution of the Holiday and Its Meaning in

2004," Tony Cox, Dec. 26, 2003, Tavis Smiley, National Public Radio)

Fishers of men

Means: Those who seek other people, not necessarily males, to become involved in some enterprise or cause

Biblical Text: *And Jesus said unto them, Come ye after me, and I will make you to become **fishers of men**. And straightway they forsook their nets, and followed him* (Mark 1:17–18).

Example of Use: It's that feeling of fatherly bonding that Rodgers and his group, African-American Men of Unity, are trying to recreate on the river. All of his young fishermen are part of Rites of Passage, a mentoring program run by African-American Men of Unity that aims to turn at-risk boys into mature men. "We're not the typical mentoring program," Rodgers said. "We're not trying to be the kids' best friends. We're taking the place of a father." ("The **Fishers of Men**," Elisabeth Kilpatrick, Aug. 17, 2008, *The Beacon News*, Aurora, IL)

Flaming sword

Means: An effective weapon, especially useful in preventing access to something

Biblical Text: *So he drove out the man; and he placed at the east of the garden of Eden Cherubims, and a **flaming sword** which turned every way, to keep the way of the tree of life* (Genesis 3:24).

Example of Use: As we were leaving, a young man dining alone at a nearby table looked up and declared that he could eat at this place every night. "In fact," he went on, "they'd have to use a **flaming sword** to keep me away." ("Burrito Loco, Commack's Fine Little Tex-Mex Grill," Joan Reminick, Sept. 26, 2007, *Newsday,* Melville, NY)

Fleece, Put out a

Means: To conduct a test as a means of seeking guidance for making a decision

Biblical Text: *And Gideon said unto God, If thou wilt save Israel by mine hand, as thou hast said, Behold, I will **put a fleece** of wool in the floor; and if the dew be on the fleece only, and it be dry upon all the earth beside, then shall I know that thou wilt save Israel by mine hand, as thou hast said* (Judges 6:36–37).

Example of Use: Amanda Hicks and Martin Vitale II hooked up in an Internet chat room nearly five years ago. . . . After dating more off than on for a couple years, Hicks of Thomasville and Vitale of Lewisville didn't become seriously involved until she **put out a fleece**—a biblical term requesting a signal from God about what to do—aboard a cruise ship in May 2002. Hicks got her answer, and Vitale, back home in Forsyth County, was unaware of what was happening on that ship. He soon found out the once-hesitant Hicks was ready for a serious commitment in their relationship. ("**'Fleece'** Leads Hesitant Couple to Tie the Knot," Bob Burchette, May 1, 2004, *The News & Record*, Piedmont Triad, NC)

Flesh and blood

Means: (1) One's offspring or relatives; (2) the human body; a person

Biblical Text: *For we wrestle not against **flesh and blood**, but against principalities, against powers, against the rulers of the darkness of this world, against spiritual wickedness in high places* (Ephesians 6:12).

Example of Use: "A press card does not provide you with an invisible shield. You're **flesh and blood**." (Jessica Savitch. BrainyQuote.com, Xplore Inc, 2012, http://www.brainyquote.

com/quotes/quotes/j/jessicasav313957.html, accessed July 20, 2012.)

Flesh is weak, The

Means: One's resistance to temptation is weak

Biblical Text: *Watch and pray, that ye enter not into temptation: the spirit indeed is willing, but **the flesh is weak*** (Matthew 26:41). See also Mark 14:38.

Example of Use: The cool factor maxed out this spring when I spied Vibram's fivefingers. These are the slippers that look like gloves for your feet, with grippy soles and a separate pocket for each toe. I tried them on, resisted the impulse to purchase, spent five weeks visualizing how they might be good for improving foot strength and biomechanics, then took the plunge. Hey, **the flesh is weak.** ("Shoe Fetish," David Medaris, July 20, 2007, *Isthmus*)

Flesh of my flesh

Means: One's children, especially with the normal filial emotional bond

Biblical Text: *And the rib, which the LORD God had taken from man, made he a woman, and brought her unto the man. And Adam said, This is now bone of my bones, and **flesh of my flesh**: she shall be called Woman, because she was taken out of Man* (Genesis 2:22–23).

Example of Use: We've learned that adoption is not a second-best option. It's an amazing, loving way to become the mom I always wanted to be. When Margaret Workman presided over our final adoption hearings for both girls, I'll never forget her words: "She is now your blood daughter, as though you gave birth to her yourself." I cried.

There's a plaque on the wall in my home that reads, "Not **flesh of my flesh**, nor bone of my bone. Nevertheless, you're still my own. Never forget for a single minute that you weren't born under my heart, but in it." ("Adoption Is Not a Second-Best Option," Cathy Gallagher, Nov. 25, 2007, *Sunday Gazette-Mail*)

Flesh, All

Means: All mankind and animals

Biblical Text: *And God looked upon the earth, and, behold, it was corrupt; for **all flesh** had corrupted his way upon the earth* (Genesis 6:12).

Example of Use: Home to rabbit is no different from home to man. Familiar surroundings are comfort and strange surroundings are stress to **all flesh**, as well to all plants. ("We're like Plants; It Takes a While to Adjust to a Change of Circumstances," Perry Mann, Jan. 4, 2009, *Sunday Gazette-Mail*, Charleston, WV)

Flesh, Become one

Means: To be married

Biblical Text: *And said, For this cause shall a man leave father and mother, and shall cleave to his wife: and they twain shall be **one flesh**? Wherefore they are no more twain, but **one flesh**. What therefore God hath joined together, let not man put asunder* (Matthew 19:5–6).

Example of Use: I've just had my first Christmas as a married woman and I'm not at all sure I got it right. **Becoming one flesh** is one thing. Sending one Christmas card is something else. At the start of Advent, I had a chat with my partner about whether we were going to send Christmas cards separately or as a couple. He hesitated and in that space I leapt right in and said it would be better if we each did our own thing. So he sent Christmas cards to his friends and his family and I sent Christmas cards to my friends, my family, his friends and his family. I know I've only got myself to blame. I couldn't help myself. ("Perspective: And It Came to Pass That Women Did Everything," Jo Ind, Dec. 27, 2001, *The Birmingham Post*, England)

Flood, Noah's

Means: An extraordinary inundation of water

Biblical Text: *And **Noah** was six hundred years old when the **flood** of waters was upon the earth. And Noah went in, and his sons, and his wife, and his sons' wives with him, into the ark, because of the waters of the **flood*** (Genesis 7:6–7).

Example of Use: It would take "**Noah's flood**" to threaten Green Diamond, Burroughs & Chapin, levee consultant Gary Dyhouse said in his presentation to business and community leaders, which included members of the Columbia City and Richland County councils. But critics of the project say there are only two kinds of levees: those that have failed and those that will. They point to 1976, when floodwater broke through a city-maintained section of the levee, flooding Manning's fields. The city had to pay Manning $4.1 million. ("Development Requests Levee for Construction Along Columbia, S.C.-Area River," Apr. 27, 2001, Knight Ridder/Tribune Business News)

Fly in the ointment

Means: A small but irritating flaw that spoils the entire element of which it is part

Biblical Text: *Dead flies cause the ointment of the apothecary to send forth a stinking savour: so doth a little folly him that is in reputation for wisdom and honour* (Ecclesiastes 10:1).

Example of Use: The Gulfport Housing Authority "thought twice last week," said *The Daily Herald*, when a suggestion was made that it do a good turn for the community under a new $600,000 grant. The money would enable the city to "put out insect poison." But there was a possible **fly in the ointment**. Executive Director Huston Carter said that, as fine as that may sound, an out-of-state court ruling should also be noted. It seems that after a child accidentally swallowed some of the poison the judge ruled for the child's family and the local housing authority lost $20,000. ("**A Fly in the Ointment**," Jimmie Bell, Aug. 23, 2006, *The Sun Herald*, Sydney)

Follow in one's steps

Means: To imitate someone or to do what he has done, especially in important matters

Biblical Text: *For even hereunto were ye called: because Christ also suffered for us, leaving us an example, that ye should **follow his steps**: Who did no sin, neither was guile found in his mouth: Who, when he was reviled, reviled not again; when he suffered, he threatened not; but committed himself to him that judgeth righteously: Who his own self bare our sins in his own body on the tree, that we, being dead to sins, should live unto righteousness: by whose stripes ye were healed* (1 Peter 2:21–24).

Example of Use: Rather than keep searching [for a job], Specht decided to start her own business, a personal shopping service that runs errands and shops for people. She started slowly and began building up her business—based in her home, in Liverpool—to include a regular customer base of about seven clients. It wasn't long before Specht began thinking that spouses of other Army soldiers might like to **follow in her steps**. With her husband assigned to the U.S. Army's Syracuse Recruiting Battalion, she got involved in the Family Support and Assistance Center and soon began talking to other spouses about what it takes to start and run a successful small business. ("Spreading the Word; Irina Specht Helps Others Who Want to Start Small Businesses," Elizabeth Doran, Feb. 7, 2002, *The Post-Standard,* Syracuse, NY)

F

Fool according to his folly, Do not answer a

Means: An exhortation to avoid arguing with a fool

Biblical Text: *Answer not a fool according to his folly, lest thou also be like unto him* (Proverbs 26:4).

Example of Use: Nothing to prove has kept me silent in the presence of foolish words. I learned such sound wisdom from one of my favorite books—Proverbs 26:4 **Answer not a fool according to his folly**, lest thou also be like unto him. ("Nothing to Prove," Artist Niko, May 1, 2007, nikoonline. com)

Fool says in his heart . . . , The

Means: A foolish person believes something, whether stated or not

Biblical Text: *The fool hath said in his heart, There is no God. Corrupt are they, and have done abominable iniquity: there is none that doeth good* (Psalm 53:1).

Example of Use: I agree with the ultimate sentiment in my heart. That being said, proximate judgments and assessments are made with the head. **The fool hath said in his heart**, "Religion is just another silly belief system." It isn't. ("Taking

Religion As a 'Natural Phenomenon' Seriously," Razib, May 13, 2007, scienceblogs.com)

For such a time as this

Means: An important entry of someone or something into a particular situation in which help is needed

Biblical Text: *For if thou altogether holdest thy peace at this time, then shall there enlargement and deliverance arise to the Jews from another place; but thou and thy father's house shall be destroyed: and who knoweth whether thou art come to the kingdom **for such a time as this**?* (Esther 4:14).

Example of Use: With so many issues facing South Florida—from cultural tensions to environmental concerns to educational challenges—it seems Kneip was born **for such a time as this**. His passion for learning, business acumen and political savvy have converged to impact South Florida. ("Robert 'Budd' Kneip: The Scholarly Business Activist. [Legends of South Florida]," Jennifer LeClaire, Oct. 1, 2005, *South Florida CEO*)

Forbidden fruit

Means: Someone or something desirable but prohibited

Biblical Text: *And out of the ground made the LORD God to grow every tree that is pleasant to the sight, and good for food; the tree of life also in the midst of the garden, and the tree of knowledge of good and evil. . . . And the LORD God took the man, and put him into the garden of Eden to dress it and to keep it. And the LORD God commanded the man, saying, Of every tree of the garden thou mayest freely eat: **But of the tree of the knowledge of good and evil, thou shalt not eat of it**: for in the day that thou eatest thereof thou shalt surely die* (Genesis 2:9, 15–17).

Example of Use: "He had, they said, tasted in succession all the apples of the tree of knowledge, and, whether from hunger or disgust, had ended by tasting **the forbidden fruit**." (Victor Hugo, *The Hunchback of Notre-Dame*)

Forefront of the hottest battle, At the

Means: A dangerous position, leaving one exposed to harm

Biblical Text: *And he wrote in the letter, saying, Set ye Uriah **in the forefront of the hottest battle**, and retire ye from him, that he may be smitten, and die* (2 Samuel 11:15).

Example of Use: In our modern version, the equivalent of the lovely Bathsheba is not a woman at all but the office of Prime Minister. Yet who is Uriah, and who David? In one version they are, respectively, Mr. Blair and Mr. Gordon Brown. It is, however, possible to construct an equally plausible framework of the future where it is Mr. Brown who is put into **the forefront of the hottest battle**. For the moment, let us assume it is Mr. Blair who is being placed in this dangerous position. ("He's Not Uriah Heep. He's Uriah the Hittite," Alan Watkins, May 15, 2005, *The Independent on Sunday*, London)

Forged lies

Means: Lies created with special cunning and purpose

Biblical Text: *But ye are **forgers of lies**, ye are all physicians of no value* (Job 13:4).

Example of Use: After visiting the various shrines so dear to his predecessor, on his last day, Sunday, May 28, Benedict visited the Nazi concentration camp of Auschwitz. . . . "The images beamed around the world," wrote Jan Fisher in the *New York Times* (May 29) "were striking: the pope in pristine white walking alone under the infamous **lie forged** in iron, promising freedom through work; two kisses on the cheeks of a Jewish survivor; dark rain that gave way to sun and then, somehow, a rainbow as he finished prayers." ("Pope's Visit to Poland a Further Step in Reconciliation," July 1, 2006, *Catholic Insight*)

Forget the things that are behind

Means: An exhortation not to let events of the past dictate one's conduct or attitude in the present

Biblical Text: *Brethren, I count not myself to have apprehended: but this one thing I do, **forgetting those things which are behind**, and reaching forth unto those things which are before, I press toward the mark for the prize of the high calling of God in Christ Jesus* (Philippians 3:13–14).

Example of Use: Let's face it, on Jan. 1st the old is gone, the new is now. We can either dwell on the past or **lay to rest those things which are behind** and reach forward to those things which are ahead. (*"Veronica's View: A Enjoying a New Season of Life,"* Veronica Hendrix, Jan. 7, 2004, *Los Angeles Sentinel*)

Forgive seventy times seven

Means: Forgive an unlimited number of times; forgive completely

Biblical Text: *Then came Peter to him, and said, Lord, how oft shall my brother sin against me, and I **forgive** him? till seven times? Jesus saith unto him, I say not unto thee, Until seven times: but, Until **seventy times seven**. Therefore is the kingdom of heaven likened unto a certain king, which would take account of his servants* (Matthew 18:21–23).

Example of Use: Some say there are crimes so horrific that there can be no rehabilitation, where an act of mercy might actually damage society by breaking down people's faith in order and justice. Others say there is always hope for redemption, as in the Gospel call to **forgive** not just once or even seven times, but "**seventy times seven**." Where should the line be drawn? ("A Murder in Britain," July 1, 2001, *The Record*, Bergen County, NJ)

Forgive them for they know not what they do

Means: A request to forgive someone who is ignorant of the ultimate negative effect of his action

Biblical Text: *Then said Jesus, Father, **forgive them; for they know not what they do**. And they parted his raiment, and cast lots* (Luke 23:34).

Example of Use: Declaring "**forgive them, for they know not what they do**" need not be an artificial, merely civilized pose, the temporary suspension of full-fledged human intercourse, as Strawson suggests. It may be an honest recognition of the human condition, the lamentable fact that we often preserve ourselves psychologically at others' expense. We forgive others more often than they know, and certainly more often than they ask us to. ("Determinism and Forbearance," Rony Guldmann, Jan. 1, 2006, *Social Theory and Practice*)

Former days

Means: The past, especially when romanticized or made to appear more pleasant than it actually was; the "good old days"

Biblical Text: *Say not thou, What is the cause that the **former days** were better than these? For thou dost not enquire wisely concerning this* (Ecclesiastes 7:10).

Example of Use: Basements have come a long way from their **former days** as musty storage for outdoor furniture and unpacked boxes. Now, Driflor joins the ranks of moisture-blocking products that keep underground spaces dry and warm. ("Panel Member," May 1, 2002, *Builder*, Washington, DC)

Forty days and forty nights

Means: An inordinately long period of time

F

Biblical Text: *In the six hundredth year of Noah's life, in the second month, the seventeenth day of the month, the same day were all the fountains of the great deep broken up, and the windows of heaven were opened. And the rain was upon the earth* ***forty days and forty nights*** *(Genesis 7:11).*

Example of Use: The weather has been playing fast and loose with us North Easterners (short bursts of brilliant, dazzling, equatorial sunshine alternating with long periods of torrential, gutter-swelling rain). In proper apocalyptic fashion, it feels like it's been stotting down for **forty days and forty nights**. ("Man & Boy," Dave Morton, July 10, 2004, *Evening Chronicle*, Newcastle, England)

Found wanting

Means: To fail, not meet expectations

Biblical Text: *Then was the part of the hand sent from him; and this writing was written. And this is the writing that was written, MENE, MENE, TEKEL, UPHARSIN. This is the interpretation of the thing: MENE; God hath numbered thy kingdom, and finished it. TEKEL; Thou art weighed in the balances, and art* ***found wanting***. *PERES; Thy kingdom is divided, and given to the Medes and Persians (Daniel 5:24–28).*

Example of Use: Like Diana, killed in her prime, the Queen Mum, who outlived the 20th century, was a one-off. Like the memory of Diana, the memory of the Queen Mum will be compared to the royals who go on living. They will be **found wanting**. ("Royals Will Be Measured by the Memory of the Queen Mum and Diana . . . They Will Be **Found Wanting**," Tony Parsons, Apr. 8, 2002, *The Mirror*, London)

Fountain of tears

Means: Much crying

Biblical Text: *Oh that my head were waters, and mine eyes a **fountain of tears**, that I might weep day and night for the slain of the daughter of my people!* (Jeremiah 9:1).

Example of Use: As the shots open up, we see that they are visiting ancient ruins from a long-gone Black Sea civilization. The once-mighty columns lay at the feet of Basar, the woman, and Isa, her middle-aged boyfriend. In case we miss the metaphor, Bahar wanders off to sit on a hillside. In a long, unbroken close-up, we see her placid, lovely face mutate into a **fountain of tears**. ("Climates," David Fellerath, Apr. 11, 2007, *The Independent Weekly*, Durham, NC)

Four Horsemen

Means: Someone or something personifying war, famine, pestilence, and death

Biblical Text: *And I saw when the Lamb opened one of the seals, and I heard, as it were the noise of thunder, one of the **four beasts** saying, Come and see. And I saw, and behold **a white horse**: and he that sat on him had a bow; and a crown was given unto him: and he went forth conquering, and to conquer. And when he had opened the second seal, I heard **the second beast** say, Come and see. And there went out **another horse that was red**: and power was given to him that sat thereon to take peace from the earth, and that they should kill one another: and there* *was given unto him a great sword. And when he had opened the third seal, I heard the third beast say, Come and see. And I beheld, and lo* **a black horse**; *and he that sat on him had a pair of balances in his hand. And I heard a voice in the midst of the* **four beasts** *say, A measure of wheat for a penny, and three measures of barley for a penny; and see thou hurt not the oil and the wine. And when he had opened the fourth seal, I heard the voice of* **the fourth beast** *say, Come and see. And I looked, and behold a pale horse: and his name that sat on him was Death, and Hell followed with him. And power was given unto them over the fourth part of the earth, to kill with sword, and with hunger, and with death, and with the beasts of the earth* (Revelation 6:1–8).

Example of Use: Middle Tennessee State University professor and current county commissioner Bob Bullen offered would-be politicians a look at behaviors he said they should try to avoid before their first elected office. . . . During the lecture, Bullen described what he calls the **four horsemen** of political destruction. "The problem with most politicians today is that they possess all or most of these qualities," he said. ("Middle Tennessee State U. Professor Outlines '**Four Horsemen** of Political Destruction,'" Tim Hill, Mar. 3, 2004, *University Wire*)

Foxes have holes, and the birds of the air have nests

Means: One's circumstances may provide no relief

Biblical Text: *And a certain scribe came, and said unto him, Master, I will follow thee whithersoever thou goest. And Jesus saith unto him, The* **foxes have holes, and the birds of the air have nests;** *but the Son of man hath not where to lay his head* (Matthew 8:19–20). See also Luke 9:57–58.

Example of use: It may seem a pity that George couldn't have enjoyed his Beatle memories more than he appeared to, but then how can any of us know what it must have been like to have lived for years at the centre of the worldwide storm of Beatlemania, where the only privacy the Beatles could find was in their bathrooms. As George said: **"Foxes have holes and birds have nests**, but Beatles have nowhere to lay their heads." ("The Reluctant Beatle: Overshadowed As a Songwriter by John and Paul, Harrison Was to Become Appalled by the Hysteria," Ray Connolly, Dec. 1, 2001, *The Daily Mail*, London)

F

Freely you have received, freely give

Means: An exhortation for one to be generous as other people have been generous to him

Biblical Text: *Heal the sick, cleanse the lepers, raise the dead, cast out devils: freely ye have received, freely give* (Matthew 10:8).

Example of Use: Pepperdine is an excellent academic institution, which also happens to be a vibrant community of faith. And Pepperdine students know that with your faith comes a calling. You know that those who are blessed with so much are called to give back—to feed the hungry, to comfort the mourning, lift up the weary, and heal the sick. This calling is spelled out in Scripture in your university's motto, and on Pepperdine's Seal: **"Freely you have received. Freely give."** ("Remarks by the First Lady [Laura Bush] at Pepperdine University Commencement Ceremony," Apr. 29, 2007, *Business Wire*)

From strength to strength, To go

Means: To become stronger

Biblical Text: *They go **from strength to strength**, every one of them in Zion appeareth before God* (Psalm 84:7).

Example of Use: Audi's A2 lightweight just goes **from strength to strength**. Sales are steadily climbing, the value for money is improving and it will become more practical next year when a bigger fuel tank is fitted. ("Lightweight Goes from Strength to Strength," Aug. 10, 2002, *The News Letter*, Belfast, Northern Ireland)

Fruit of one's labor

F

Means: Results of one's work

Biblical Text: *For to me to live is Christ, and to die is gain. But if I live in the flesh, this is **the fruit of my labour**: yet what I shall choose I wot not. For I am in a strait betwixt two, having a desire to depart, and to be with Christ; which is far better* (Philippians 1:21–23).

Example of Use: Several Minooka-area families are finally beginning to enjoy **the fruits of their labor** this summer, harvesting the summer crops of vegetables they planted last spring in Minooka Community High School FFA Community Garden. ("**Fruits of His Labor**: MCHS Student Establishes Community Garden," Jeanne Millsap, July 15, 2012, *Morris Daily Herald,* Morris, IL)

Fruit of one's loins

Means: One's offspring

Biblical Text: *Men and brethren, let me freely speak unto you of the patriarch David, that he is both dead and buried, and his sepulchre is with us unto this day. Therefore being a prophet, and knowing that God had sworn with an oath to him, that of **the fruit of his loins**, according to the flesh, he would raise up Christ to sit on his throne* (Acts 2:29–30). See also Gen. 35:11.

Example of Use: My wife is convinced that our son, now aged 16, is not **the fruit of our loins**. It's not that she believes that I am not the father. She is convinced that the wrong child was given to her after the caesarean operation. He doesn't look or behave like either of our families. I know that DNA tests are theoretically possible, but I think they might cause more problems than they would solve. What if they showed that she was right and he didn't belong to us? ("Health: A Question of Health," Dr. Fred Kavalier, July 17, 2002, *The Independent*, London)

Full of years (or days), Old and

Means: Old

Biblical Text: *Then Abraham gave up the ghost, and died in a good old age, an **old man, and full of years**; and was gathered to his people* (Genesis 25:8). See also Gen. 35:29.

Example of Use: When the curtain opens, Neil Young is standing onstage with a face **full of years**. Dressed in a gray western suit, with a plainsman's hat and a well-used acoustic guitar, he looks like an old-time cowboy crooner, but somehow scruffier. ("Tribute to Singer with a Face **Full of Years**," Manohla Dargis, Feb. 10, 2006, *International Herald Tribune*)

Fullness of time

Means: A time or an occasion especially suitable or propitious

Biblical Text: *But when the **fulness of the time** was come, God sent forth his Son, made of a woman, made under the law* (Galatians 4:4). See also Eph. 1:10.

Example of Use: As you know, our business model is to establish fixed margins with discrete customers based on credit judgment and location, and while our margins are generally realized in the **fulness of time** because of our hedging policy, the application of average costing can create anomalies from period to period. ("Q1 2007 World Fuel Services Corporation Earnings Conference Call—Final," May 11, 2007, *Fair Disclosure Wire*, Farmington Hills, MI)

RAISING CAIN

G

"GENERATION OF VIPERS"

Gabriel

Means: A messenger of God

Biblical Text: *And Zacharias said unto the angel, Whereby shall I know this? for I am an old man, and my wife well stricken in years. And the angel answering said unto him, I am **Gabriel**, that stand in the presence of God; and am sent to speak unto thee, and to shew thee these glad tidings* (Luke 1:18–19).

Example of Use: Billie Stein has been laid to rest, fully prepared for her next performance—with her beloved trumpet cradled in her left hand. "She always promised she'd have a gig with (the Angel) **Gabriel** one day, and the two of them would play 'When the Saints Go Marching In,'" said Gene Tepper, nephew of the lifelong musician. ("Trumpet in Hand, Music Pioneer Is Laid to Rest: Female Bandleader Had a Life Filled with Music, Volunteerism," Marc Shulgold, Aug. 22, 2002, *Rocky Mountain News*, Denver)

Gadarene rush

Means: Hasty, uncoordinated movement

Biblical Text: *And they came over unto the other side of the sea, into the country of the **Gadarenes**. And when he was come out of the ship, immediately there met him out of the tombs a man with an unclean spirit, Who had his dwelling among the tombs; and no man could bind him, no, not with chains: Because that he had been often bound with fetters and chains, and the chains had been plucked asunder by him, and the fetters broken in pieces: neither could any man tame him. And always, night and day, he was in the mountains, and in the tombs, crying, and cutting himself with stones. But when he saw Jesus afar off, he ran and worshipped him, And cried with a loud voice, and said, What have I to do with thee, Jesus, thou Son of the most high God? I adjure thee by*

God, that thou torment me not. For he said unto him, Come out of the man, thou unclean spirit. And he asked him, What is thy name? And he answered, saying, My name is Legion: for we are many. And he besought him much that he would not send them away out of the country. Now there was there nigh unto the mountains a great herd of swine feeding. And all the devils besought him, saying, Send us into the swine, that we may enter into them. And forthwith Jesus gave them leave. And the unclean spirits went out, and entered into the swine: and the **herd ran violently down a steep place into the sea,** *(they were about two thousand;) and were choked in the sea. And they that fed the swine fled, and told it in the city, and in the country. And they went out to see what it was that was done. And they come to Jesus, and see him that was possessed with the devil, and had the legion, sitting, and clothed, and in his right mind: and they were afraid. And they that saw it told them how it befell to him that was possessed with the devil, and also concerning the swine. And they began to pray him to depart out of their coasts* (Mark 5:1–17).

Example of Use: The most sensible investment for a fund with long-term liabilities is in shares (or property, their near neighbour) with a leavening of bonds when prices are low. The **Gadarene rush** into bonds at any price has looked foolish as share prices and dividends rose, but if it turns out the funds have bought junk, it will be really stupid. ("Who's the Mug at the Table?" Neil Collins, Sept. 8, 2007, *The Spectator*)

Gain the world and lose one's soul

Means: To achieve or acquire something useless or of only apparent value while failing to achieve or acquire something of real or greater value

Biblical Text: *Then said Jesus unto his disciples, If any man will come after me, let him deny himself, and take up his cross, and*

*follow me. For whosoever will save his life shall lose it: and who-soever will lose his life for my sake shall find it. For what is a man profited, if he shall **gain the whole world, and lose his own soul**? or what shall a man give in exchange for his soul?* (Matthew 16:24–26).

Example of Use: ABC correspondent Sam Donaldson, joining his news brethren March 18 for the annual awards dinner of the Radio & Television News Directors Foundation in D.C., was in his element, lambasting his bosses for essentially selling the news division's soul by looking to dump [Ted] Koppel's "Nightline" in favor of David Letterman. Donaldson suggested the net and parent Disney refer to the Bible, specifically, Matt. 16:26—For what is a man profited if he shall **gain the whole world and lose his soul**?" In other words, it's understandable that net toppers would want to boost ratings, but it's dangerous to sacrifice a sacrosanct news show such as "Nightline." ("Newsies Rally Koppel Cause at Kudos Dinner. ('Night' Depository). [Journalists Criticize ABC for Almost Cancelling 'Nightline']," Pamela McClintock, Mar. 18, 2002, *Variety*)

Gall and wormwood

Means: A bitter spirit or deep resentment

Biblical Text: *Lest there should be among you man, or woman, or family, or tribe, whose heart turned away this day from the* LORD *our God, to go and serve the gods of these nations; lest there should be among you a root that beareth **gall and wormwood*** (Deuteronomy 29:18). See also Jer. 9:15; 23:15; Lam. 3:19.

Example of Use: Auden wrote at incredible speed, and I marveled at his ability to do so, though there was a secret here, to be revealed only much later. His "lyrics" were stunning, rich in imagery, eloquent in language. But they were not lyrics. Some were poems. Some were diatribes, not against the world of

Cervantes but the world today. They made free use of anachronism (which I detested), and they tore at the fabric of the play. They were **gall-and-wormwood** attacks on the failings of an inimical society—our society, today. Some possessed inspired language—eloquent on the page but unsingable on stage. ("Auden in Autumn: What Would Man of La Mancha Be Like if the Poet W. H. Auden Had Written Lyrics for this Classical Musical?" Dale Wasserman, *American Theater*, Dec. 1, 2009)

Gamaliel

Means: A teacher, especially if religious

Biblical Text: *Then stood there up one in the council, a Pharisee, named **Gamaliel**, a doctor of the law, had in reputation among all the people, and commanded to put the apostles forth a little space; And said unto them, Ye men of Israel, take heed to yourselves what ye intend to do as touching these men. For before these days rose up Theudas, boasting himself to be somebody; to whom a number of men, about four hundred, joined themselves: who was slain; and all, as many as obeyed him, were scattered, and brought to nought. After this man rose up Judas of Galilee in the days of the taxing, and drew away much people after him: he also perished; and all, even as many as obeyed him, were dispersed. And now I say unto you, Refrain from these men, and let them alone: for if this counsel or this work be of men, it will come to nought: But if it be of God, ye cannot overthrow it; lest haply ye be found even to fight against God. And to him they agreed: and when they had called the apostles, and beaten them, they commanded that they should not speak in the name of Jesus, and let them go* (Acts 5:34–40).

Example of Use: [Concern existed about] a leaked memo [from publisher HarperCollins] that "we'll need to be able to give emphatic assurance that no attempt will be made to correlate the stories to Christian imagery/theology" [in C. S. Lewis's Narnia books that they planned to publish]. . . . [Y]ou suspect that Lewis would respond to the "threat" posed by this undertaking much as the great rabbi **Gamaliel** responded to the threat posed by Christianity. If this movement is not from God, said **Gamaliel**, then we don't need to worry about it. It will destroy itself. And if it is from God, then there's nothing we can do about it anyway. ("Orthodoxy; Christians Needn't Worry about the Narnia Deal—but Maybe HarperCollins Shareholders Should," June 25, 2001, *The Report Newsmagazine*)

G

Gehenna

Means: Hell or any extremely unpleasant place or conditions

Biblical Text: *Whoever shall say, Thou fool, shall be in danger of hell [Greek: **geenna**] fire* (Matthew 5:22c).

Example of Use: The Trans Canada Trail (TCT), if it is ever completed, will wind its way across the 10 provinces and three territories like a 10,000-mile network of blood vessels. It will be the longest such network in the world, offering a coast-to-coast path for hiking, biking, skiing and snowmobiles. Depending on whom you talk to, the TCT will be the last word in safe, sanitary family recreation, or a **Gehenna** of trash, excrement, fire and drunken fiends committing high-speed suicide on off-road vehicles. ("Trial of Fears," Golby Cosh, Dec. 4, 2000, *Alberta Report*)

Generation of vipers

Means: A group of people characterized by vicious malice

Biblical Text: *But when he saw many of the Pharisees and Saducees come to his baptism, he said unto them, O*

generation of vipers, who hath warned you to flee from the wrath to come? (Matthew 3:7).

Example of Use: [W]hy have we not done something with our own children in order to be certain we can sleep safely at night and know our children can go to and from school in relative safety. Why haven't we pulled them away from the TV baby-sitter and taught them life is sacred. Why have we not monitored their actions and taught them to respect the rights of others and property of others? Instead we have turned our collective backs on them and now we have truly created a **generation of vipers**. Snakes that will strike out at us and kill as soon as they get warm. . . . [W]e need for men to be men and take control of their homes and child. We need women to be mothers and to stop trying to be their child's "best friend." ("Kleaver's Klippins: When Do We Take Blinders from Our Eyes?," Feb. 5, 1997, *Los Angeles Sentinel*)

Get thee behind me

Means: An admonition for someone or something to depart and to stop doing a particular action, especially tempting one

Biblical Text: *And Jesus answered and said unto him [Satan], Get thee behind me, Satan: for it is written, Thou shalt worship the Lord thy God, and him only shalt thou serve* (Luke 4:8).

Example of Use: Only brown bread is now allowed in the house and I start the day with bran flakes, skimmed milk and a banana. Bacon, eggs and fried bread are but a distant memory. We have fruit and veg falling out of every cupboard and the only chocolate we buy is dark which is rich in antioxidants to help blood flow. Crisps? **Get thee behind me,** Satan. ("Sausages? Begone Temptation, Even Hot and Sizzling and Nestling in a Fresh Teacake with a Garnish of Tomato

Ketchup . . . the Diary," Denis Kilcommons, Mar. 16, 2006, *Huddersfield Daily Examiner*, England)

Gethsemane

Means: A place or condition of suffering and ordeal

Biblical Text: *Then cometh Jesus with them unto a place called* **Gethsemane**, *and saith unto the disciples, Sit ye here, while I go and pray yonder. And he took with him Peter and the two sons of Zebedee, and began to be sorrowful and very heavy. Then saith he unto them, My soul is exceeding sorrowful, even unto death: tarry ye here, and watch with me. And he went a little farther, and fell on his face, and prayed, saying, O my Father, if it be possible, let this cup pass from me: nevertheless not as I will, but as thou wilt* (Matthew 26:36–39). See also Mark 14:32–42.

Example of Use: Since I have suffered in my **Gethsemane** I can feel the touch of the deep anguish that is yours over the loss of your splendid son, Paul. So I am following the inclination of my heart and am writing to tell you of my sympathy. There is not one word in all the world to say in the face of the heart-breaking calamity which has befallen you. ("Mrs. Daisy Potter Viele Letters and Telegrams," Oct. 1, 2000, www.usgennet.org/usa)

Giants in the earth

Means: Heroes of a former age

Biblical Text: *There were* **giants in the earth** *in those days; and also after that, when the sons of God came in unto the daughters of men, and they bare children to them, the same became mighty men which were of old, men of renown* (Genesis 6:4).

Example of Use: What an Orwellian notion of honor. Since so many of our current American leaders seem to be motivated by greed and/or lust for power and/or a bizarre religious agenda, where is the honor for which they are to be honored? I have existed during an even dozen presidencies—starting with FDR, and then Truman, Eisenhower and Kennedy. There were **giants in the earth** in those days. ("Letters," Don Burt, May 10, 2005, *The Topeka Capital-Journal*)

Gideon

Means: A reluctant hero or champion

Biblical Text: *So **Gideon**, and the hundred men that were with him, came unto the outside of the camp in the beginning of the middle watch; and they had but newly set the watch: and they blew the trumpets, and brake the pitchers that were in their hands. And the three companies blew the trumpets, and brake the pitchers, and held the lamps in their left hands, and the trumpets in their right hands to blow withal: and they cried, The sword of the LORD, and of **Gideon**. And they stood every man in his place round about the camp: and all the host ran, and cried, and fled* (Judges 7:19–21). See also Judg. 6:11–14.

Example of Use: Microsoft did say that we are not going to be able to port VB5/6 projects directly to VB7. This is probably one of the reasons. VB5/6 transparently permeates COM in almost everything it does. Will it still qualify as a COM RAD tool? Can the average corporate developer handle object oriented programming? I have seen many examples of pure spaghetti developed in Powerbuilder because inheritance was used carelessly. These features may just be a **Gideon's** Sword. (Marc D'Aoust, Mar. 14, 2000, forums.devx.com)

Gideon's army

Means: True believers, able to conquer even when outnumbered; a group reduced in number yet still formidable

Biblical Text: *So **Gideon**, and **the hundred men** that were with him, came unto the outside of the camp in the beginning of the middle watch; and they had but newly set the watch: and they blew the trumpets, and brake the pitchers that were in their hands. And the three companies blew the trumpets, and brake the pitchers, and held the lamps in their left hands, and the trumpets in their right hands to blow withal: and they cried, The sword of the LORD, and of Gideon. And they stood every man in his place round about the camp: and all the host ran, and cried, and fled. And **the three hundred** blew the trumpets, and the LORD set every man's sword against his fellow, even throughout all the host: and the host fled to Beth-shittah in Zererath, and to the border of Abel-meholah, unto Tabbath. And **the men of Israel** gathered themselves together out of Naphtali, and out of Asher, and out of all Manasseh, and pursued after the Midianites* (Judges 7:19–23).

Example of Use: Saying that his proclamation of a "religious war" at the 1992 Republican National Convention was "understated," Mr. Buchanan called on an enthusiastic crowd to help him build a "**Gideon's army**" that will fight for conservative, populist values. ("Buchanan Calls for 'Army' to Fight for Populist Values," Carter Dougherty, Sept. 19, 2000, *The Washington Times*)

Gird one's loins

Means: To prepare for hard work, difficulty, or a journey

Biblical Text: *And the hand of the LORD was on Elijah; and he **girded up his loins**, and ran before Ahab to the entrance of Jezreel* (1 Kings 18:46).

Example of Use: Allergies are the modern consumption, felling strapping lasses and creating the perfect hook for well-bred ladies to hang their anxieties on. Is that runny nose a cold or a lactose intolerance? Is your fatigue the result of too many late nights or an auto-immune response? If you can't wait to join in, then check out the new Imutest range of home-testing kits, available for egg, milk, cat and house mite allergies, hay fever and general susceptibility. You'll need to **gird your loins**—the tests involve taking a blood sample from your finger—but the procedure is easy to follow. ("HealthShop," Aug. 26, 2001, *The Independent Sunday*, London)

Give up the ghost

Means: (1) To die; (2) in inanimate objects, to cease operation

Biblical Text: *And Jesus cried with a loud voice, and **gave up the ghost**. . . . And when the centurion, which stood over against him, saw that he so cried out, and **gave up the ghost**, he said, Truly this man was the Son of God* (Mark 15:37, 39).

Example of Use: The Patriot Act, enacted in a rush after the attacks of Sept. 11, 2001, to expand law-enforcement powers, could be broadened in coming months. But what if the president took over the selection of governors, judges and members of Congress? What if he took control of the media? There might be rioting in the streets. But don't look for riots in the streets of Moscow, where Russia's fledgling democracy is poised to **give up the ghost**—with the blessings of a shell-shocked citizenry. ("Russia Poised to **Give Up the Ghost**," Oct. 11, 2004, *The Post-Standard*, Syracuse, NY)

Give us this day our daily bread

Means: An exhortation to a provider, including God, to provide one's daily requirement of food

Biblical Text: *Give us this day our daily bread* (Matthew 6:11).

Example of Use: Since there are only about six of us left in the entire country who still eat bread, I probably shouldn't have been surprised about what happened when my wife and I went out to eat the other night. After we were seated, our server appeared with a basket of dinner rolls. "I don't know whether you still eat this stuff," she said, putting the basket on the table. Then she looked down at it the way you'd look at medical waste. Apparently, she figured us for two of the millions of diet zombies who have joined the low-carb cult. Or—even worse—for two who should join the low-carb cult. ("**Give Us This Day Our Daily Bread**—Including the Carbs," Kevin Cowherd, July 11, 2004, *The Milwaukee Journal Sentinel*)

Glory in the highest

Means: An exhortation to praise God or someone else

Biblical Text: *Saying, Blessed be the King that cometh in the name of the Lord: peace in heaven, and **glory in the highest*** (Luke 19:38).

Example of use: Wolves are currently heading wearily towards the purgatory of mid-table obscurity in the laugh-a-minute Championship, writes Paul Berry. Chelsea meanwhile, continue to despatch all-comers in their pursuit of **glory in the highest** echelons of competition at home and abroad, illustrated perfectly by that epic Champions League success against Barcelona. ("Football: Wolves News: Day Carr and the Mac Lads Ran Riot; Chelsea Are Massacred at Molineux," Paul Berry, Mar. 19, 2005, *Sports Argus,* Birmingham, England)

Glory is departed, One's

Means: One's former status has declined or disappeared.

Biblical Text: *And his daughter in law, Phinehas' wife, was with child, near to be delivered: and when she heard the tidings that the ark of God was taken, and that her father in law and her husband were dead, she bowed herself and travailed; for her pains came upon her. And about the time of her death the women that stood by her said unto her, Fear not; for thou hast borne a son. But she answered not, neither did she regard it. And she named the child Ichabod, saying, The **glory is departed** from Israel: because the ark of God was taken, and because of her father in law and her husband* (1 Samuel 4:19–21).

G

Example of Use: Old observers are elegiac about the Upper House. The spirit has gone already, they feel. First the life peers arrived, then the hereditaries were drummed out. The **glory is departed**. The place is full of phonies and cronies, of place-men, second-raters and superannuated hacks who stepped down from their constituency to allow some favoured son of Downing Street to be parachuted into the Commons. ("The Wonderful World of the House of Lords; It's the Magic Kingdom of British Politics: An Anachronistic Haven for the Eccentric, the Unbiddable and the Plain Mad. . . . ," Simon Carr, Nov. 7, 2001, *The Independent*, London)

Glory not

Means: Admonition to avoid taking comfort or pleasure in something, especially what is objectionable

Biblical Text: *But if ye have bitter envying and strife in your hearts, **glory not**, and lie not against the truth* (James 3:14).

Example of Use: The press corps (in the interests of news gathering and career preservation) jealously guard their right to maintain the confidentiality of sources. But in the Wilson scandal we already know that Novak wasn't the only journalist to whom the leak was made. A handful of other journalists were provided with the same information that they chose not to publish. Any one of them could now reveal the identity of their sources yet maintain their own anonymity. Is there among them a journalist with the courage to tell a great story yet **glory not** in the telling? ("There's a Time When Anonymity Is Called for—This Is It!" Paul Woodward, Oct. 1, 2003, warincontext.org)

Glory, In all one's

Means: One's best work or results on display or remembered

Biblical Text: *Consider the lilies of the field, how they grow; they toil not, neither do they spin: And yet I say unto you, That even Solomon **in all his glory** was not arrayed like one of these* (Matthew 6:28b–29). See also Luke 12:24–27.

Example of Use: There he was, **in all his glory**—Al Gore, slowly descending to Earth; his flight almost cancelled, due to his having but one wing . . . the left. ("Behold, the Second Coming of Al Gore Underwhelms," Oct. 26, 2007, *The Post-Standard*, Syracuse, NY)

Go and do thou likewise

Means: An exhortation to imitate another's behavior

Biblical Text: *And he said, He that shewed mercy on him. Then said Jesus unto him, **Go, and do thou likewise*** (Luke 10:37).

Example of Use: It's true that the Hutchinson City Council voted last week to abolish the pay for their positions, beginning after next April's election. They weren't really giving up all that much, though. They were only getting $100 a year. And it's true that school board members and people serving on lots of public boards and committees don't get paid. So, it's tempting to look to the Topeka City Council and say, "**Go, and do likewise**." Topeka

City Council members are paid $10,000 a year. ("Do Likewise," Aug. 7, 2006, *The Topeka Capital-Journal*)

Go and sin no more

Means: Discontinue wrongful practices

Biblical Text: *She said, No man, Lord. And Jesus said unto her, Neither do I condemn thee: go, and sin no more* (John 8:11).

Example of Use: It was a lot different world in 1994 when Microsoft agreed to be scolded and was told to **go and sin no more**. ("As Microsoft Case Evolved, Some Issues Stayed the Same," Bill Virgin, Mar. 29, 2000, *Seattle Post-Intelligencer*)

Go forth

Means: To go, usually with a specific purpose

Biblical Text: *The day following Jesus would go forth into Galilee, and findeth Philip, and saith unto him, Follow me* (John 1:43).

Example of Use: New Jerseyans, **go forth** and enjoy the holiday. ("Beaches, Barbecues Can't Be Beat," Giovanna Fabiano, July 2, 2006, *The Record*, Bergen County, NJ)

Go the way of all the earth

Means: To die or cease

BIblical Text: *And, behold, this day I am going the way of all the earth: and ye know in all your hearts and in all your souls, that not one thing hath failed of all the good things which the* LORD *your God spake concerning you; all are come to pass unto you, and not one thing hath failed thereof* (Joshua 23:14).

Example of Use: The largest growing age demographic is the senior citizen bracket. This means that more people are getting old than babies are being born. If this trend continues, once all these seniors **go the way of all the earth**, we will be facing a serious population drop. (In an online discussion of population control: "regfife," Apr. 6, 2009, www.newsvine.mobi)

God and mammon

Means: Contrast between devotion to God and the pursuit of money (mammon), not necessarily mutually exclusive goals

Biblical Text: *No man can serve two masters: for either he will hate the one, and love the other; or else he will hold to the one, and despise the other. Ye cannot serve **God and mammon*** (Matthew 6:24). See also Luke 16:1–13.

Example of Use: God and Mammon will join forces when the retiring Archbishop of Canterbury takes up a key post with one of the leading institutions of international capitalism. In a move that attempts to fuse religion with big business, Dr. George Carey will become chairman of a new religious leaders advisory council to the World Economic Forum (WEF). ("God and Mammon Will Join Forces When the Retiring Archbishop of Canterbury Takes Up a Key Post with One of the Leading Institutions of International Capitalism," Aug. 4, 2002, *Sunday Business,* London)

God is my witness

Means: A request by someone, asking God to corroborate his statement as true

Biblical Text: *For **God is my witness**, whom I serve with my spirit in the gospel of his Son, that without ceasing I make mention of you always in my prayers* (Romans 1:9).

Example of Use: I am up and on the treadmill by 6:05 a.m. According to my fuzzy pre-coffee calculations, I will be off the treadmill by 6:45 a.m., leaving me an hour and 15 minutes to get to work. This is ample time, even for someone like me. Today just might be the day I get to work by 8! And suddenly, I am Scarlett O'Hara: As **God is my witness**, this morning is not going to lick me. ("Oh, What a Middle-Aged Morning," Cathy Hamilton, Oct. 1, 2006, *Journal-World*, Lawrence, KS)

God forbid

Means: A request to God to prevent something; a strong affirmation that one will not do something

Biblical Text: *But **God forbid** that I should boast except in the cross of our Lord Jesus Christ, by whom the world has been crucified to me, and I to the world* (Galatians 6:14).

Example of Use: Is the United States planning to attack Iran in the near term? **God forbid**. Such a decision would exceed even the colossal blunder of intervening in Iraq. ("U.S. Attack Iran? Perish the Thought," John C. Bersia, Apr. 18, 2007, *Orlando Sentinel*)

God loves a cheerful giver

Means: God appreciates someone who gives freely to others

Biblical Text: *Every man according as he purposeth in his heart, so let him give; not grudgingly, or of necessity: for **God loveth a cheerful giver*** (2 Corinthian 9:7).

Example of Use: [President Bill Clinton:] But you know, when a great human being passes away, people search around in their minds for some part of the Scripture that captures that person. We talked about it a lot already today. Proverbs says, "A happy heart doeth good like medicine; but a broken spirit drieth the bone"; that **God loves a cheerful giver**—that's what Jack McAuliffe was. . . . Jack McAuliffe was **a cheerful giver**.

("William J. Clinton Delivers Remarks at Memorial Service for Jack McAuliffe," Jan. 4, 2001, Washington Transcript Service)

God save the king

Means: An exclamation expressing one's hope that God will provide the king a long reign and life

Biblical Text: *And Samuel said to all the people, See ye him whom the LORD hath chosen, that there is none like him among all the people? And all the people shouted, and said, **God save the king*** (1 Samuel 10:24).

Example of Use: Eventually, the kings were replaced with civil governments—that is, "**God save the King**" turned into "God save the State." ("Editorial: Hawaii Must Address Questions about Prisoner Treatment," Sept. 6, 2002, *University Wire*)

Godspeed

Means: A term usually used when leaving someone, expressing good wishes for the other

Biblical Text: *Whosoever transgresseth, and abideth not in the doctrine of Christ, hath not God. He that abideth in the doctrine of Christ, he hath both the Father and the Son. If there come any unto you, and bring not this doctrine, receive him not into your house, neither bid him **God speed**: For he that biddeth him **God speed** is partaker of his evil deeds* (2 John 9–11).

Example of Use: The latest vessels to bear the names **Godspeed** and Discovery are being built for the Jamestown Settlement living history museum in Virginia in time to take part in its 400th anniversary celebration next year. ("Setting Sail for a Date with the Past; New **Godspeed** Readies for Voyage to Virginia," Jerry Harkavy, Mar. 30, 2006, *The Washington Post*)

Gog and Magog

Means: Forces that threaten the safety of the world

Biblical Text: *And the word of the LORD came unto me, saying, Son of man, set thy face against **Gog**, the land of **Magog**, the chief prince of Meshech and Tubal, and prophesy against him* (Ezekiel 38:1–2). See also Ezek. 39:1–3; Rev. 20:7–9.

Example of Use: Due to the recent outbreaks across the Western Hemisphere of both mad cow and foot and mouth disease, the creative department of the Washington think tank **Gog and Magog** Enterprises has been put to the rather difficult task of creating new items for the McDonald's menu, so the restaurant can sell heretofore unpopular parts of its various slaughtered animals. ("Top 10 New Meals Coming to McDonald's: A Good Cow Is Hard to Find, but the Savvy Eatery Is on Top of Things. Think: McKnuckles," Al Astor, Apr. 4, 2001, salon.com)

Gold of Ophir

Means: Gold of the finest quality

Biblical Text: *Moreover, because I have set my affection to the house of my God, I have of mine own proper good, of gold and silver, which I have given to the house of my God, over and above all that I have prepared for the holy house, Even three thousand talents of gold, of the **gold of Ophir**, and seven thousand talents of refined silver, to overlay the walls of the houses withal* (1 Chronicles 29:3–4). See also 2 Chron. 9:10; Isa. 13:12.

Example of Use: University of Wisconsin-Platteville professor David M. Drury released his debut science fiction mystery novel *All the **Gold of Ophir*** on Nov. 22. The book's synopsis tells that the story is set in the middle of the 21st century on a space station orbiting Jupiter. Private detective Mike Flynn has been sent to investigate the deaths of two employees at the company that operates the station. He discovers the company is hiding something, and races to unravel the mystery before he becomes a victim. ("U. Wisconsin-Platteville Professor Publishes First Novel," J. R. Barnes, Jan. 3, 2006, *University Wire*)

Gold, frankincense, and myrrh

Means: Valuable gifts

Biblical Text: *And when they were come into the house, they saw the young child with Mary his mother, and fell down, and worshipped him: and when they had opened their treasures, they presented unto him gifts; **gold, and frankincense, and myrrh*** (Matthew 2:11).

Example of Use: My God-children really look out for me. I inherited a third one this Christmas. Kate was truly a gift from the Magi (tomorrow we celebrate Epiphany). **Gold and frankincense and myrrh** were all very fine in biblical times, but they aren't much use when you're trying to figure out a laptop computer, a fancy camera, and a computer phone. ("Lifestyle: Letter from America—White Christmas," Marsha Clarke, Jan. 5, 2005, *The News Letter,* Belfast, Northern Ireland)

Golden bowl

Means: Anything, especially life, that cannot be retained

Biblical Text: *Remember now thy Creator in the days of thy youth, while the evil days come not, nor the years draw nigh, when thou shalt say, I have no pleasure in them; . . . Or ever the silver cord be loosed, or the **golden bowl** be broken, or the pitcher be broken at the fountain, or the wheel broken at the cistern. Then shall the dust return to the earth as it was: and the spirit shall return unto God who gave it* (Ecclesiastes 12:1, 6–7).

Example of Use: "I have taken my **golden bowl** and foolishly and recklessly dashed it upon rocks of self-destruction," said Renehan, who has written six books. "I alone am responsible for this one great, indelible stain which now and forever disfigures a life I am otherwise proud of." ("Theft of Letters Nets Prison," Sept. 20, 2008, *Deseret News*, Salt Lake City)

Golden calf

G

Means: An inappropriate object of worship

Biblical Text: *And he [Aaron] received them at their hand, and fashioned it with a graving tool, after he had made it a **molten calf**: and they said, These be thy gods, O Israel, which brought thee up out of the land of Egypt* (Exodus 32:4).

Example of Use: Since 1995, the **golden calf** worshipped by golf fanatics is a video game know as Golden Tee. And since March 17, local Golden Tee golfers are flocking to catch the new 2004 courses, currently available in bars throughout the area. ("Bars Ace One with Golden Tee Fanatics Flocking to Pubs to Play Latest Edition," Kara Spak, Mar. 25, 2003, *Daily Herald*, Arlington Heights, IL)

Golden Rule, The

Means: A rule of ethical conduct based on the teaching, "Do unto others as you wish them to do to you"; any similar ethical rule

Biblical Text: *Therefore all things whatsoever ye would that men should do to you, do ye even so to them: for this is the law and the prophets* (Matthew 7:12).

Example of Use: The homespun ideals that underscore **The Golden Rule**—"Do unto others as you would have them do unto you"—gave birth to the retail empire known today as

J. C. Penney. Indeed, in naming his first store "**The Golden Rule**," John Cash Penney said four key words would define his new business: honor, confidence, service and cooperation. ("John Cash Penney, J. C. Penney; the Man Whose Name Is Made of Money Built a Company by Selling **The Golden Rule**," Barbara Thau, Nov. 27, 2000, *HFN The Weekly Newspaper for the Home Furnishing Network*)

Good cheer, Be of

G

Means: An exhortation to be happy and at ease

Biblical Text: *And, behold, they brought to him a man sick of the palsy, lying on a bed: and Jesus seeing their faith said unto the sick of the palsy; Son, **be of good cheer**; thy sins be forgiven thee* (Matthew 9:2).

Example of Use: Hannah Jennings makes a living through her company, Hannah Jennings Design, but her watercolor work through her other company, **Be of Good Cheer**, is her labor of love. "That's something I do to feed my soul," Jennings said. ("**Be of Good Cheer** through Watercolor," Chris Lafortune, July 23, 2009, *Oak Leaves*, Oak Park, IL)

Good conscience

Means: Good or pure motives; guileless

Biblical Text: *Pray for us: for we trust we have a **good conscience**, in all things willing to live honestly* (Hebrews 13:18).

Example of Use: "Management cannot in **good conscience** agree to add more than $1 million to the current budget year's projected deficit." ("RTA Board Rejects Finding; Director Says RTA 'Cannot in **Good Conscience**' Agree to Worker Pay Hikes," Joanne Huist Smith, May 7, 2010, *Dayton Daily News*)

Good for nothing

Means: Useless

Biblical Text: *This evil people, which refuse to hear my words, which walk in the imagination of their heart, and walk after other gods, to serve them, and to worship them, shall even be as this girdle, which is* **good for nothing** (Jeremiah 13:10).

Example of Use: The tug-of-war between work and marriage is not just a modern-day dilemma unique to BlackBerry-wielding, high-powered young women in search of it all. In *Stormy Weather*, a tale set in 1938 central Texas, that's basically what the story boils down to. Jeanine Stoddard is 20: Her drunken, **good-for-nothing** dad has died, leaving her to take charge of her mother and two sisters. ("Making It through 'Stormy Weather': Tale of 1930s Family's Struggles Rings Just As True Now," Ann Oldenburg, Aug. 5, 2007, *Chicago Sun-Times*)

Good measure

Means: Something that is extra; a little more to make sure that a sufficient amount of something is available

Biblical Text: *Judge not, and ye shall not be judged: condemn not, and ye shall not be condemned: forgive, and ye shall be forgiven: Give, and it shall be given unto you;* **good measure***, pressed down, and shaken together, and running over, shall men give into your bosom. For with the same measure that ye mete withal it shall be measured to you again* (Luke 6:37–38).

Example of Use: Smart chefs use this time-saving trick: measuring ingredients and stashing them in bowls before starting a recipe. By laying everything out first, you skip the start-and-stop delay of chopping as you go. Prep like a pro with Mario Batali's nested set of five melamine prep bowls (1/8 cup to

2 cups). $10 for set, amazon.com. ("For **Good Measure,**" Aug. 1, 2006, *Redbook*)

Good name, A

Means: A good reputation

Biblical Text: *A good name is rather to be chosen than great riches, and loving favour rather than silver and gold* (Proverbs 22:1). See also Eccl. 7:1.

Example of Use: Shakespeare wrote: "He that filches from me **my good name** . . . makes me poor indeed." In today's global society, amid billions of fellow human beings, **that good name** is not only a priceless asset, but vital. ("**Our Good Name** Is Invaluable," Feb. 21, 2002, *Daily Post*, Liverpool)

Good Samaritan

Means: One who helps others in need without seeking reward or acknowledgement

Biblical Text: *And Jesus answering said, A certain man went down from Jerusalem to Jericho, and fell among thieves, which stripped him of his raiment, and wounded him, and departed, leaving him half dead. And by chance there came down a certain priest that way: and when he saw him, he passed by on the other side. And likewise a Levite, when he was at the place, came and looked on him, and passed by on the other side. But a certain **Samaritan**, as he journeyed, came where he was: and when he saw him, he had compassion on him, And went to him, and bound up his wounds, pouring in oil and wine, and set him on his own beast, and brought him to an inn, and took care of him* (Luke 10:30–34).

Example of Use: Four bank robbers fleeing down a Miami expressway Friday threw out their stolen money when the dye pack exploded, and an honest man called police. The **Good Samaritan** then stood guard until the police arrived to pick up the money, *The Miami Herald* reported. The **Good Samaritan** said the thought of taking some of the money never entered his mind. "Nobody actually collected the money because he was holding the scene down until police arrived," said Robert Williams, Miami-Dade County Police spokesman. ("**Good Samaritan** Guards Stolen Cash," Apr. 9, 2004, United Press International)

Good Shepherd

Means: Someone who guides others, especially with great love and care

Biblical Text: *I am the **good shepherd**, and know my sheep, and am known of mine. As the Father knoweth me, even so know I the Father: and I lay down my life for the sheep* (John 10:14–15).

Example of Use: There's a saying in sheepdog circles that will, over the next three days, be put to the ultimate test. It goes: "There is no good flock without a **good shepherd**, and no **good shepherd** without a good dog." ("Ultimate Trial of Man and His Dog; The Welsh National Sheepdog Trials Demonstrate the Very Best Talents of Handlers and Charges," Andrew Forgrave, Aug. 3, 2006, *Daily Post*, Liverpool)

Good tidings of great joy

Means: Especially good news

Biblical Text: *And the angel said unto them, Fear not: for, behold, I bring you **good tidings of great joy**, which shall be to all people* (Luke 2:10).

Example of Use: The holidays are quickly approaching, bringing **good tidings of great joy**—and an immense deal of stress—for holiday hosts. ("Have Yourself a Merry [and Easy] Little Christmas Feast," Dec. 3, 2009, PR Newswire)

Good to begin well, better to end well

Means: Although beginning something well is important, a successful conclusion is even better.

Biblical Text: *Better is the end of a thing than the beginning thereof: and the patient in spirit is better than the proud in spirit* (Ecclesiastes 7:8).

Example of Use: "'It is good to begin well; it is better to end well,' comments Howard Shore. 'This simple phrase has come to mind often as I approach the end of this epic project'" [*The Lord of the Rings* film trilogy]. ("*The Lord of the Rings: The Return of the King* Soundtrack Features Music from Oscar Winner Howard Shore and a Special Song by Grammy Award Winner Annie Lennox . . . ," Oct. 29, 2003, PR Newswire)

Good works, Full of

Means: One who has a repertoire of good deeds done without seeking recognition or reward

Biblical Text: *Now there was at Joppa a certain disciple named Tabitha, which by interpretation is called Dorcas: this woman was full of good works and almsdeeds which she did* (Acts 9:36).

Example of Use: Miss Dixey spoke of what she had learned of the family following the discovery of Harold's letters. "I know from doing research in Malvern that Harold belonged to the Royal British Legion here and the King George Fund for Sailors. So he was **full of good works**." ("A Family at War: A Quirk of Fate Led to the Discovery of Letters Telling of How a God-Fearing Merseyside Family Faced Death, Tragedy and

Love As the Old World Died . . . ," David Charters, Jan. 8, 2004, *Daily Post*, Liverpool)

Good will toward men

Means: An expression indicating positive intentions for mankind

Biblical Text: *Glory to God in the highest, and on earth peace,* **good will toward men** (Luke 2:14).

Example of Use: 'Tis the season of peace and **good will toward men**. Here is what one city family, and a Dorchester activist, are doing for peace just down the block from where Isaura Mendes lost not one but two young sons to murder. In fact, as you enter the Grealish Boxing Club at night, you can see the single string of white Christmas lights on the porch of Mendes' home. ("Family-Run Boxing Club Keeps Kids Off Streets, Battles to Stay in Business," Margery Eagan, Dec. 24, 2006, *The Boston Herald*)

Goshen, Land of

Means: A fruitful and productive place

Biblical Text: *The land of Egypt is before thee; in the best of the land make thy father and brethren to dwell; in the* **land of Goshen** *let them dwell: and if thou knowest any men of activity among them, then make them rulers over my cattle* (Genesis 47:6).

Example of Use: "Oh my, yes," says Grace Snow, 91, an Indiana girl who's keen for greens of all flavors. "Just boil them up with some salt back or ham hock, and **Lands O' Goshen**—oooh, they're good!" ("Land O' Goshen Rarely Heard Today," *Palm Beach Post*, April 18, 2002)

Gospel (or Gospel truth)

Means: Something accepted as undisputed truth, guiding principle, or doctrine, not necessarily religious

Biblical Text: *And Jesus went about all Galilee, teaching in their synagogues, and preaching the **gospel** of the kingdom, and healing all manner of sickness and all manner of disease among the people* (Matthew 4:23).

Example of Use: Jobs has been dead for nearly a year, but the biography about him is still a best seller. Indeed, his life story has emerged as an odd sort of holy scripture for entrepreneurs—a **gospel** and an antigospel at the same time. To some, Jobs' life has revealed the importance of sticking firmly to one's vision and goals, no matter the psychic toll on employees or business associates. ("The Story of Steve Jobs: An Inspiration or a Cautionary Tale?" Ben Austen, *Wired*, July 23, 2012).

Grapes of wrath

Means: Imminent judgment

Biblical Text: *And the angel thrust in his sickle into the earth, and gathered the vine of the earth, and cast it into the great **winepress of the wrath of God*** (Revelation 14:19).

Example of Use: The **grapes of wrath** fermenting in the French wine industry boiled over into a mini-riot on the streets of Narbonne yesterday. A group of 50 young wine producers hurled Molotov cocktails, cobble stones, bottles and flares at riot police at the end of a turbulent but mostly peaceful demonstration by 10,000 growers from the French deep south. Joined by a sprinkling of local anarchists, the young wine-growers taunted and confronted the CRS riot police for nearly two hours across two bridges over a canal in the heart of the town. ("Violence As

10,000 Winegrowers Protest at French Overproduction," John Lichfield, Apr. 21, 2005, *The Independent*, London)

Graven image

Means: A carved image, usually of wood or stone, especially when used as an idol

Biblical Text: *Thou shalt not make unto thee any* **graven image**, *or any likeness of any thing that is in heaven above, or that is in the earth beneath, or that is in the water under the earth* (Exodus 20:4).

Example of Use: Although the contentious words "under God" were not added to the pledge until 1954, controversy over its compulsory recitation first arose in 1940, when two Jehovah's Witnesses in Pennsylvania were expelled for refusing to recite the pledge. They regarded the flag as a **graven image** and pledging to it was the same as worshipping it, which their religion forbade. The U.S. Supreme Court, however, sided with the school district. ("Courts Have Shot Down Mandatory Pledge Laws," Sunny Schubert, Oct. 13, 2001, *Wisconsin State Journal*, Madison)

Great men are not always wise

Means: A person's age or importance does not necessarily mean that he is wise

Biblical Text: *Great men are not always wise: neither do the aged understand judgment* (Job 32:9).

Example of Use: Knowledge is of no value unless you put it into practice.
Great men are not always wise. If you don't get a kick out of the job you're doing you'd better hunt for another one. ("The

Beauty of Stature Is the Only Beauty of Men," Secreto, June 4, 2007, segredando.blogspot.com)

Greater love has no man than this, that a man lay down his life for his friends

Means: The highest esteem one can show for another person is to give up his life for him.

Biblical Text: *Greater love hath no man than this, that a man lay down his life for his friends* (John 15:13).

Example of Use: He didn't have to go. Staff Sgt. John L. Hartman Jr. had done his duty in Iraq—twice. But when a buddy from his Army platoon, a new father, was given orders to ship out for a tour, Hartman volunteered to go in his place for a third tour to that violent country. He paid the ultimate price, dying with four other members of his unit when an improvised explosive device detonated near their Humvee in Baghdad last week. Sgt. Hartman's sacrifice brings to mind this verse from the Bible: "**Greater love has no one than this, than to lay down one's life for his friends.**" ("Editorial: Ultimate Sacrifice: Manatee County Loses Another Brave Soldier," Dec. 8, 2006, *Bradenton Herald,* FL)

Greatest of these is . . . , The

Means: An expression indicating the most important element of something

Biblical Text: *And now abide faith, hope, love, these three; but the greatest of these is love* (1 Corinthians 13:13).

Example of Use: And now head, hands, and heart abide, these three; and **the greatest of these is** heart. So sayeth PepsiCo Chairman Steve Reinemund. ("PepsiCo Chair Shares Thoughts on Business at Oklahoma City University Conference," Kelley Chambers, Apr. 13, 2007, *The Journal Record*, Oklahoma City)

Green bay tree, Flourish like a

Means: To develop vigorously

Biblical Text: *I have seen the wicked in great power, and spreading himself like a* **green bay tree**. *Yet he passed away, and, lo, he was not: yea, I sought him, but he could not be found* (Psalm 37:35–36).

Example of Use: I believe that one of the most deeply human, and humane, of these faculties is the power of imagination: so it is our pleasant duty, as librarians, or teachers, or parents, or writers, or simply as grownups, to encourage the development of that faculty of the imagination in our children, to encourage it to grow freely, to flourish like the **green bay tree**, by giving it the best, absolutely the best and purest, nourishment that it can absorb. ("Marxism and Science Fiction: A Celebration of the Work of Ursula K. Le Guin," Tony Burns, Dec. 22, 2004, *Capital & Class*)

Green pastures

Means: Very satisfactory conditions

Biblical Text: *The LORD is my shepherd; I shall not want. He maketh me to lie down in* **green pastures**: *he leadeth me beside the still waters* (Psalm 23:1–2).

Example of Use: When Jameer Nelson and Delonte West packed up their awards, records and talents for the **green pastures** of the NBA, the players left behind on the Saint Joseph's basketball team expected a learning curve. No one expected this. No one expected a team that each game finds a new way to lose. No one expected a team that looks woefully out of sync. No one expected a litany of questions and not a single readily available answer. ("Hawks Bring Losing Streak Home with Them: Fall at Fieldhouse for First Time Since March '03," Dana Pennett O'Neil, Dec. 29, 2004, *Philadelphia Daily News*)

Grind the faces of the poor

Means: To severely oppress poor and helpless people

Biblical Text: *What mean ye that ye beat my people to pieces, and **grind the faces of the poor**? saith the Lord GOD of hosts* (Isaiah 3:15).

Example of Use: From the White House itself, it is alleged, this conspiracy has been able to produce its most dangerous effect so far, namely, to **grind the faces of the poor** while driving the country into an illegitimate and unwinnable war in Iraq. (Decter, Midge, "Enemies Within?" Rev. of *The Theocons: Secular American Under Siege* by Damon Linker. *National Review*, Oct. 23, 2006.)

Guilty flee when no one pursues, The

Means: A person with a guilty conscience attempts escape even when unnecessary.

Biblical Text: *The wicked flee when no man pursueth: but the righteous are bold as a lion* (Proverbs 28:1).

Example of Use: The issue of whether the flight of a person, upon encountering law enforcement, constitutes an indicia of guilt or criminal activity, has long been the subject of much debate and litigation. Indeed, quite often you will find that when faced with the issue of how to interpret a person's flight upon the arrival of law enforcement, criminal justice scholars quickly split into two polarized factions: One faction will insist that it is an accepted axiom of criminal law that **"the wicked flee when**

no man pursueth," while the other faction will assert with equal fervor that "the righteous are as bold as a lion." ("'To Flee, or Not to Flee': The Implications of Illinois v. Wardlow on the Practice of Criminal Law in Florida. [U.S. Supreme Court]," Joseph G. Jarret, June 1, 2000, *Florida Bar Journal*)

G

RAISING CAIN

H

"HEAP COALS OF FIRE ON ONE'S HEAD"

Hairs of one's head are numbered, The very

Means: An expression indicating that God's care for mankind is commensurate with his minutely detailed understanding of them

Biblical Text: *And fear not them which kill the body, but are not able to kill the soul: but rather fear him which is able to destroy both soul and body in hell. Are not two sparrows sold for a farthing? and one of them shall not fall on the ground without your Father. But* **the very hairs of your head are all numbered** (Matthew 10:28–30).

Example of Use: Our preoccupation with our hair is nothing new. "**The very hairs of your head are all numbered,**" we learn in the Gospel of Matthew, and he was right: The average scalp sports about 100,000 hairs. And we want every one of them to do our bidding. ("How Celebs 'Do It'[;] We May Have Tangled Relationships with Our Hair, but the Stars Have Us Beat," Paige Wiser, May 17, 2004, *Chicago Sun-Times*)

Half was not told to me, The

Means: An expression indicating that someone was not informed sufficiently about a particular subject

Biblical Text: *Howbeit I believed not the words, until I came, and mine eyes had seen it: and, behold,* **the half was not told me***: thy wisdom and prosperity exceedeth the fame which I heard* (1 Kings 10:7).

Example of Use: Figures published by the ONS in the summer showed that non-whites now make up 33.5 percent of the population of London compared with 29 percent in 2001. And these figures show 70,000 Poles when the Government reckons

600,000+? "**The half was not told me.**" ("Things Fall Apart," Nov. 28, 2006, ukcommentators.blogspot.com)

Halt and blind

Means: People who are physically infirm

Biblical Text: *Go out quickly into the streets and lanes of the city, and bring in hither the poor, and the maimed, and **the halt, and the blind*** (Luke 14:21b). See also John 5:2–4.

Example of Use: Ah, January—that chilly, unforgiving season when the major studios flush their pipes and unleash their failed projects—the lame, **halt, and blind** of movies—upon an enervated public. ("You May Diss the Bride: Friends Become Enemies in a Chick Flick with a Mean Streak," Ty Burr, Jan. 9, 2009, *The Boston Globe*)

H

Hand of God

Means: The act or work of a supernatural power

Biblical Text: *There is nothing better for a man, than that he should eat and drink, and that he should make his soul enjoy good in his labour. This also I saw, that it was from the **hand of God*** (Ecclesiastes 2:24).

Example of Use: On this day 20 years ago Diego Maradona made three indelible marks on the World Cup, scoring its most infamous and then its most brilliant goal before providing its most memorable quote. Maradona's two goals in the space of four minutes for Argentina against England in the quarter-finals of the 1986 World Cup in Mexico and his "**Hand of God**" quote are the stuff of legend. . . . The Argentina captain described the goal [that he made, using his hand illegally but which the official did not notice] afterwards to reporters as "un poco con la cabeza de Maradona y otro poco con la mano de

Dios" (a little with the head of Maradona and a little with the **hand of God**), coining one of the most famous quotes in sport. ("SOC: Maradona's **'Hand of God'** Fooled More Than One," June 22, 2006, *AAP Sports News*, Australia)

Hand to the plow, Put one's

Means: To work earnestly; to get busy; to help; to start working

Biblical Text: *And Jesus said unto him, No man, **having put his hand to the plough**, and looking back, is fit for the kingdom of God* (Luke 9:62).

Example of Use: The first time Ravi Balaraman and Sunil Salve tried to help Sri Lanka, they almost started a riot.

The friends from Colorado Springs traveled to Sri Lanka in late January with little more than donated cash and a desire to help. . . . They teamed with Habitat for Humanity, which will provide the labor and split the costs of the homes. . . . "I'm glad we did something," Salve said. "I'm glad we **put our hand to the plow** and got it going." ("Experience Teaches Pair How to Help," Brian Newsome, June 6, 2005, *The Gazette*)

Hand, Give one's

Means: To make an unwritten agreement with someone, effecting a contract

Biblical Text: *And **they gave their hands** that they would put away their wives; and being guilty, they offered a ram of the flock for their trespass* (Ezra 10:19).

Example of Use: All that stuff about life style and changing leagues and DHing and ballpark dimensions, Clark never thought about any of it. You want to know why he **gave his hand** to the Yankees? They asked. ("Clark Puts on Pinstripes for

Greenbacks," Tony Kornheiser, Mar. 5, 1988, *The Washington Post*)

Hand, High (or High-handed)

Means: Arrogant; arbitrary or dictatorial in manner

Biblical Text: *And the LORD hardened the heart of Pharaoh king of Egypt, and he pursued after the children of Israel: and the children of Israel went out with an **high hand*** (Exodus 14:8).

Example of Use: In February, when this column called for the kind of homeland security restructuring that has now been proposed, President Bush was enjoying unparalleled political strength. Today, he's not playing with such a **high hand**. ("The Right Move," Timothy B. Clark, July 1, 2002, *Government Executive*)

Hands, Into one's

Means: To be received or controlled by someone

Biblical Text: *Jesus knowing that the Father had given all things **into his hands**, and that he was come from God, and went to God* (John 13:3).

Example of Use: The insurgent group al-Qaida in Iraq called Friday for the release of the kidnapped executive of the CARE charity, Margaret Hassan, and promised to free her if she fell **into their hands**. ("Iraqi Group Calls for Release of Hassan," Nadia Abou El-Magd, Nov. 5, 2004, AP Online)

Hands, Wash one's

Means: To end one's association with someone or something; to abandon or renounce responsibility for someone or something

Biblical Text: *When Pilate saw that he could prevail nothing, but that rather a tumult was made, he took water, and **washed his hands** before the multitude, saying, I am innocent of the blood of this just person: see ye to it* (Matthew 27:24).

Example of Use: Chicago aldermen gladly **washed their hands** of responsibility for the troubled Chicago Theater on Monday—and held out little hope of getting a 10 percent share of the profits after operating expenses. ("City Doesn't Expect Much Money from Theater Deal," Fran Spielman, Jan. 13, 2004, *Chicago Sun-Times*)

Hands, Work of one's

Means: The results or product of one's labor

Biblical Text: *And, Thou, Lord, in the beginning hast laid the foundation of the earth; and the heavens are the **works of thine hands*** (Hebrews 1:10).

Example of Use: "As an enslaved potter, Dave would want the **work of his hands** to be recognized and he did it in a very permanent way," said Juanita M. Holland, a professor of art history who teaches arts of the African diaspora at the University of Maryland. ("Part of Slave's Story Is Told in the Poetry Inscribed on His Pottery," Annette John-Hall, Mar. 9, 2000, Knight Ridder/Tribune News Service)

Hands on, Lay (1)

Means: To acquire or take something

Biblical Text: *Thou shouldest not have entered into the gate of my people in the day of their calamity; yea, thou shouldest not have looked on their affliction in the day of their calamity, nor have **laid hands on** their substance in the day of their calamity* (Obadiah 13). See also Esther 9:15–17.

Example of Use: Anyone wanting to **lay hands on** some of the millions—nay, billions—of dollars waiting to be made in the flowering capitalist democracy that the Bush administration promised in postwar Iraq would be advised to check the State Department's latest bulletin on travel there. ("Iraq's Reconstruction," July 2, 2004, *St. Louis Post-Dispatch*)

Hands on, Lay (2)

Means: To grab someone

Biblical Text: *And as soon as he was come, he [Judas] goeth straightway to him, and saith, Master, master; and kissed him. And they **laid their hands on** him, and took him* (Mark 14:45–46).

Example of Use: Avigliano said officers from Paterson, Passaic, Clifton, and the Passaic County Sheriff's Department, along with investigators from the Prosecutor's Office, kept up their search for Barris through the weekend. "We know he's still around, but we just can't **lay our hands on** him yet," he said. "I know we're going to get him. There's no question. It's just a matter of time." ("Suspect in Club Killings Eludes Cops," Douglass Crouse, Dec. 28, 2005, *The Record*, Bergen County, NJ)

Hands on, Lay (3)

Means: To harm someone

Biblical Text: *But Pharaoh shall not hearken unto you, that I may **lay my hand upon** Egypt, and bring forth mine armies, and my people the children of Israel, out of the land of Egypt by great judgments* (Exodus 7:4).

Example of Use: Let's just say that whoever did the crime is lucky Mr. Bad Manners didn't **get his hands on** him. ("A Right Good Christmas Knees-Up with Buster," Dec. 16, 2006, *Hull Daily Mail*, UK)

Hands on, Lay (4)

Means: (1) To show personal approval of a person or a thing by a particular act, sometimes by physically putting one's hands on another person; (2) to bring about healing, success, or victory by the symbolic act of placing one's hands on someone or something

Biblical Text: *And Joseph took them both, Ephraim in his right hand toward Israel's left hand, and Manasseh in **his left hand** toward Israel's **right hand**, and brought them near unto him. And Israel stretched out **his right hand**, and **laid it upon** Ephraim's head, who was the younger, and his **left hand** upon Manasseh's head, guiding his hands wittingly; for Manasseh was the firstborn* (Genesis 48:13–14).

Example of Use: Ron Torda and his boss, Allen "Swede" Peterson, were christened into the religion of fly-fishing by older deacons of that esoteric calling. Ron was, aptly enough, fishing in Alaskan waters when an older fellow introduced him to fly-fishing in a sort of **laying-on of hands**. Swede fished almost since infancy with his father in the Northwest, "and one day, he took away my spinning rod and gave me a fly rod and said, 'This is the way you will fish,'" he recalled. ("Fly-Fishing Hooks a Devout Follower," Jon Hahn, Feb. 25, 2003, *Seattle Post-Intelligencer*)

Hang one as high as Haman

Means: To suffer a punishment that one has prepared for another

Biblical Text: *And Harbonah, one of the chamberlains, said before the king, Behold also, the gallows fifty cubits high, which Haman had made for Mordecai, who had spoken good for the king, standeth in the house of Haman. Then the king said, Hang him thereon. So **they hanged Haman on the gallows** that he* *had prepared for Mordecai. Then was the king's wrath pacified* (Esther 7:9–10).

Example of Use: Since that fateful day Dwight Eisenhower named Earl Warren chief justice, the U.S. Supreme Court has been engineering a social revolution. Seizing legislative power, the court legalized pornography, declared abortion a constitutional right, abolished the death penalty for a generation and prohibited a once-Christian people from paying public homage to their God. Yet, Americans have not rebelled. Why not? Because they were raised to believe the court was the final judge of what the Constitution says, and to defy it is to dishonor the Founding Fathers. Andy Jackson **would have hanged** judges like Warren, Brennan, Blackmun and Douglas **as high as Haman**. ("Exclusive Commentary Moses and Judge Moore vs. Morris Dees," Patrick J. Buchanan, Nov. 25, 2002, *World Net Daily*)

Hang one's harps on the willows

Means: To be inconsolably sad

Biblical Text: *By the rivers of Babylon, there we sat down, yea, we wept, when we remembered Zion.* **We hanged our harps upon the willows** *in the midst thereof* (Psalm 137:1–2).

Example of Use: "They may steal your vote, but don't let them steal your joy. Don't let them steal your joy. **Don't hang your harps on the willows.** ("The Reverend Jesse Jackson Delivers Remarks at Florida Rally," Dec. 13, 2000, Washington Transcript Service)

Hard-hearted

Means: To be extremely unkind or unsympathetic

Biblical Text: *And when he had looked round about on them with anger, being grieved for **the hardness of their hearts**, he saith unto the man, Stretch forth thine hand. And he stretched it out: and his hand was restored whole as the other* (Mark 3:5).

Example of Use: In this city of neighborhoods, that mind-set raises a serious question: Which neighborhoods are willing to care for the homeless? Which neighborhoods will care? It's a question that goes to the heart of who we are as a community, and I'm afraid the answer—not many neighborhoods—would suggest we're becoming collectively more **hard-hearted**. ("Are We More **Hard-Hearted** These Days?" Mark Brown, *Chicago Sun-Times*, Oct. 5, 2008)

H

Harmless as doves, As

Means: To be innocent or guileless

Biblical Text: *Behold, I send you forth as sheep in the midst of wolves: be ye therefore wise as serpents, and **harmless as doves*** (Matthew 10:16).

Example of Use: You know you're getting old when you spot a surly-looking group of teenagers congregating in a shopping centre and the first reaction is to hide your wallet. . . . On closer inspection, these weren't brainless thugs perpetually on the brink of an ASBO, but acne-ridden, awkward-looking students who look like they spend most of their free time indoors. At least, that's what the pale skin and obvious signs of vitamin D deficiency suggested. They were video game enthusiasts—"gamers," to use the parlance—and as **harmless as doves**. ("No Need for Panic over the Effects of Video Gaming," Graeme Demianyk, Nov. 13, 2010, *Western Morning News*, The Plymouth, UK)

Have found favor, To

Means: To have pleased someone

Biblical Text: *Then Esther the queen answered and said, **If I have found favour in thy sight**, O king, and if it please the king, let my life be given me at my petition, and my people at my request* (Esther 7:3).

Example of Use: Glitzy and glamorous, Jimmy Choo shoes exude star appeal—no wonder they **have found favour** with a raft of young Hollywood actresses including Brittany Murphy, Kirsten Dunst and Keira Knightley. ("That's Shoebusiness! From the Grandaddies of Sole to the Up-and-Coming Young Guns, Here's Our Shoe's Who Guide," Deborah Arthurs, Oct. 31, 2005, *The Daily Mail*, London)

H

Have I none, Something

Means: A statement meaning that one has nothing of what another person wants.

Biblical Text: *Then Peter said, **Silver and gold have I none**; but such as I have give I thee: In the name of Jesus Christ of Nazareth rise up and walk* (Acts 3:6).

Example of Use: Answers **have I none**, but let me conclude with some questions. ("Now We Deport Canadian Citizens on the Basis of Mere Guesswork—and This We Call Justice?" Ian Hunter, July 24, 2000, *Alberta Report*, Canada)

He that is not with me is against me

Means: One is either a foe or a friend but cannot be both.

Biblical Text: ***He that is not with me is against me**; and he that gathereth not with me scattereth abroad* (Matthew 12:30).

Examples of use: Bush darkly warned: "Every nation in every region now has a decision to make: **Either you are with us, or you are with the terrorists.**" ("Will U.S. Action Damage the Indo-Pak Repose?" Mana Ranjan Josse, Sept. 1, 2001, *World Paper*)

Head on a platter, Bring one's

Means: To cause someone's downfall, especially if in death

H

Biblical Text: *And he [Herod] sent, and beheaded John in the prison. And **his head was brought in a charger**, and given to the damsel: and she brought it to her mother. And his disciples came, and took up the body, and buried it, and went and told Jesus* (Matthew 14:10–12). See also Mark 6:26–28.

Example of Use: While Wall Street wizards weren't clamoring for former Ford Motor Co. chief executive Jacques Nasser's **head on a platter**, news of William Clay Ford Jr.'s, decision to take over the top spot at the Dearborn automaker was greeted with some relief by analysts on Tuesday. ("Wall Street Analysts Choose to Wait and See on Ford Changes," Alejandro Bodipo-Memba, Oct. 30, 2001, Knight Ridder/Tribune News Service)

Head, On one's

Means: One's responsibility or fault

Biblical Text: *His mischief shall return **upon his own head**, and his violent dealing shall come down upon his own pate* (Psalm 7:16).

Example of Use: A mentally ill man who fled the Bede Wing and had a history of self-harm died just hours after failing to be sectioned, an inquest heard. Minutes after Malcolm Walker walked away from police, his life-long friend Martin Barry angrily told officers: "If he kills himself tonight, **on your head**

be it." The next day, Mr. Barry received a phone call to say he was dead. ("'If He Kills Himself Tonight, **on Your Head** Be It,'" June 18, 2008, *Shields Gazette*, South Shields, England)

Head, To be a (or the)

Means: To be the leader or the one responsible for someone or something

Biblical Text: *And he is **the head** of the body, the church: who is the beginning, the firstborn from the dead; that in all things he might have the preeminence* (Colossians 1:18).

H

Example of Use: James Jolis grew up in Paris and studied 18th-century British poetry at Stanford, then spent a decade on the road as a backup singer for Barry Manilow. It was a nice life, and he got to see the world, but, Mr. Jolis said, there comes a point where you just can't sing "Copacabana" anymore. He spoke a few languages, so on the advice of an uncle, he applied to be a concierge and has been doing it for 20 years. Now he's the **head** concierge at the Michelangelo on West 51st Street. ("In the City, It's Super: The Power to Suggest," Campbell Robertson, Mar. 27, 2007, *The New York Times*)

Heap coals of fire on one's head

Means: To be kind or helpful to someone who has done wrong to one, so that he is ashamed

Biblical Text: *If thine enemy be hungry, give him bread to eat; and if he be thirsty, give him water to drink: For thou shalt **heap coals of fire upon his head**, and the LORD shall reward thee* (Proverbs 25:21–22). See also Rom. 12:20.

Example of Use: A Frenchman does not offer close friendship easily, but once given it is never withdrawn, however foul the weather. A Frenchwoman who loves you will defend you till death. The French are sometimes quixotically forgiving and **heap coals of fire on your head**. I have experienced this twice in recent years. ("Stop This Frog-Bashing! They Can Teach Us a Thing or Two," Paul Johnson, June 20, 1998, *The Spectator*)

Heart melts, One's

Means: To (1) lose one's strength, resolve, morale, or courage due to apparently insurmountable opposition; (2) be sympathetically inclined toward someone or something; (3) experience emotional relief

Biblical Text: *She is empty, and void, and waste: and **the heart melteth**, and the knees smite together, and much pain is in all loins, and the faces of them all gather blackness* (Nahum 2:10).

Example of Use: Amity's dad and I got married when Amity was 13, following her wishes to the letter. She specified a church wedding at which she would wear a white dress and walk down the aisle with her dad. The camera caught Amity crying as she hugged her dad fiercely—her first, her own true love. **My heart melted** as I swore to myself to be the very best stepmother ever, so happy that this bright little spirit had come into my life. ("The Daughter I Never Had: At the Wedding, Amity Cried and Hugged Her Father Fiercely. **My Heart Melted** as I Swore to Be the Best Stepmom Ever," Lee Smith, Oct. 1, 2006, *Good Housekeeping*)

Heart of stone (or Heart, Stony)

Means: To be cruel or to have no sympathy for someone

Biblical Text: *Yea, they made their **hearts as an adamant stone**, lest they should hear the law, and the words which the LORD of hosts hath sent in his spirit by the former prophets: therefore came a great wrath from the LORD of hosts* (Zechariah 7:12).

Example of Use: It doesn't have a Christmas tree that grows. It doesn't have a crotchety miser who finds Christmas after years of showing a **stony heart**. That doesn't make "Oliver!" any less a holiday confection. ("'Oliver!' Is a Holiday Favorite," Joan E. Vadeboncoeur, Dec. 4, 2001, *The Post-Standard*, Syracuse, NY)

Heart on something, To set one's

Means: To determine to get or do something greatly desired or expected

Biblical Text: *Now **set your heart** and your soul to seek the* LORD *your God* (1 Chronicles 22:19).

H

Example of Use: I'd **set my heart on** a school for her that was progressive, egalitarian and only three blocks from our house. How could they have rejected her? Was she not smart enough? Not cute enough? Or was it me? ("Letter from New York; Survival of the Richest," Katherine Stewart, July 25, 2005, *Newsweek International*)

Heart, After one's own

Means: To conform to one's inmost feelings, beliefs, or desires

Biblical Text: *I have found David the son of Jesse, a man **after mine own heart**, which shall fulfil all my will* (Acts 13:22).

Example of Use: This is also a story about and with great music. It's by someone with a truly trashy punk rock hillbilly heart. A director who loves bar bands and vinyl hissing from cheap record players. A woman **after my own heart**. ("She's an Artist, She Don't Look Back," Zilpah Feiser, May 19, 2004, *Colorado Daily*, Boulder, CO)

Heart, Hate in one's

Means: The presence of hate toward someone or something

Biblical Text: *Thou shalt not **hate thy brother in thine heart**: thou shalt in any wise rebuke thy neighbour, and not suffer sin upon him* (Leviticus 19:17). See also Ps. 105:25.

Example of Use: Harboring anger and **hate in one's heart** can certainly prove to be detrimental to one's covenant union. Sometimes, it is pretty difficult to display love when you don't feel like it. But, it is absolutely essential to exercise longsuffering and to love your wife as Christ loved the church. ("Today, Loose Bitterness from Your Marriage," Anthony Jerrod, Sept. 13, 2011, ThyBlackMan.com)

Heart, Heavy

Means: A feeling of sadness

Biblical Text: *As he that taketh away a garment in cold weather, and as vinegar upon nitre, so is he that singeth songs to an **heavy heart*** (Proverbs 25:20).

Example of Use: Buck played well, limiting Caldwell, scoring 11 points and grabbing seven rebounds in A-B's 82–69 victory. However, it was how Buck put together the performance that was the story of the day.

For he did so with a very **heavy heart**. See, Buck's brother, Chris, was killed Saturday night within the Washington Beltway loop. ("**Heavy Heart** Puts Other Stories on Back Burner," Mitch Vingle, Mar. 5, 2010, *Charleston Gazette*, WV)

Heart, Humble

Means: Accurately unpretentious measure of oneself

Biblical Text: *And thou his son, O Belshazzar, hast not **humbled thine heart**, though thou knewest all this* (Daniel 5:22).

Example of Use: Sohn said that he felt the voters "yearning for change" during the campaign. "I threw myself into the campaign . . . and I will wait for the results with the **humble heart** that I had during the campaign," he said after balloting. ("South Koreans Vote in Parliamentary, Local By-Elections," Apr. 27, 2011, *AsiaPulse News*)

Heart, In (or On) one's

Means: In one's innermost nature or deepest feelings

Biblical Text: *For as he thinketh **in his heart**, so is he* (Proverbs 23:7).

H

Example of Use: "Obesity: Whose Fault? **In Your Heart**, You May Know You're Right but in Court, You Could Be Wrong. Retailers Have an Opportunity (and Added Risk) in Their Private Label Programs," Warren Thayer, Mar. 1, 2004, *Private Label Buyer*

Heart, Love with all one's

Means: To love someone or something with complete devotion or affection

Biblical Text: *And thou shalt love the Lord thy God **with all thy heart**, and with all thy soul, and with all thy mind, and with all thy strength: this is the first commandment* (Mark 12:30).

Example of Use: He's 33 now, her only son, "a wonderful young man who I love **with all my heart** and soul." ("A Mother Shares Anguish over Son's Battle with Demons," Joe Fitzgerald, July 18, 2005, *The Boston Herald*)

Heart, One

Means: To be united; unity

Biblical Text: *And the multitude of them that believed were of **one heart** and of one soul: neither said any of them that ought of*

the things which he possessed was his own; but they had all things common (Acts 4:32).

Example of Use: Differences of opinion were voiced but eventually the group would come to one opinion to achieve the state of being of "**one heart**" before decisions could be put into effect. ("Being of '**One Heart**': Power and Politics among the Iraqw of Tanzania," Katherine A. Snyder, Jan. 1, 2001, *Africa*)

Heart, One's

Means: (1) One's essential nature or character; the source and center of one's emotions; (2) one's capacity for courage and determination; (3) one's mood or mental state; (4) the distinctive, significant, and characteristic center of something

Biblical Text: *For the LORD seeth not as man seeth; for man looketh on the outward appearance, but the LORD looketh on the heart* (1 Samuel 16:7).

Example of Use: You know how every morning, I put on my shoes and coat, kiss you good-bye, and walk out the door? Well, just as I'm leaving, I feel something in **my heart**. I look inside, and what do you think I find? You! Right here in my **heart**! ("Molly Bang: In **My Heart**," Martha V. Parravano, Mar. 1, 2006, *The Horn Book Magazine*)

Heart, Pure

Means: Innocence or goodness

Biblical Text: *Flee also youthful lusts: but follow righteousness, faith, charity, peace, with them that call on the Lord out of a pure heart* (2 Timothy 2:22).

Example of Use: Hornets coach Paul Silas says Jamaal Magloire plays "with a **pure heart**." Wednesday, Magloire had a pure game to match. ("Hornets Move up the Ladder with Win,"

Rick Bonnell, Mar. 27, 2002, Knight Ridder/Tribune News Service)

Heart, Soft

Means: A sympathetic, lenient, or compassionate nature, especially to a degree perceived as excessive

Biblical Text: *Therefore am I troubled at his presence: when I consider, I am afraid of him. For God maketh my **heart soft**, and the Almighty troubleth me: Because I was not cut off before the darkness, neither hath he covered the darkness from my face* (Job 23:15–17). See also Ezek. 11:19.

H

Example of Use: "You, Sir Bob, Your Rock Friend Bono and Politicians Such As Tony Blair and Gordon Brown Display a **Soft Heart** to Africa. But a **Soft Heart** Will Not Cure the Hard Situation in Africa," Moeletsi Mbeki, July 3, 2005, *The Mail on Sunday*, London

Heart, Take something to

Means: To consider something seriously and personally

Biblical Text: *Now therefore let not my lord the king **take the thing to his heart**, to think that all the king's sons are dead: for Amnon only is dead* (2 Samuel 13:33).

Example of Use: When it premiered at the Cannes Film Festival earlier this year, *Marie Antoinette* drew boos from French critics. Kirsten Dunst, who plays Antoinette in the movie, has a laid-back attitude about it.

"I didn't **take it to heart**," Dunst says in an interview in the latest issue of *Entertainment Weekly*. "How would we feel about the French doing a movie about George Washington with French actors?" ("Dunst Understands Boos for Her Character," Oct. 5, 2006, Associated Press/AP Online)

Heart, Tender

Means: Quick to feel sympathetic, compassionate, or kind

Biblical Text: *Because thine **heart was tender**, and thou didst humble thyself before God, when thou heardest his words against this place, and against the inhabitants thereof, and humbledst thyself before me, and didst rend thy clothes, and weep before me; I have even heard thee also, saith the LORD (2 Chronicles 34:27).*

Example of Use: "He Once Walked in Trees: Logger Calvin 'Red' Lewis Was Known for His **Tender Heart**," Jim Steinberg, Oct. 11, 2006, *Fresno Bee*, Fresno, CA

Heart, Understanding

Means: An attitude of tolerance and sympathy

Biblical Text: *Give therefore thy servant an **understanding heart** to judge thy people, that I may discern between good and bad: for who is able to judge this thy so great a people? (1 Kings 3:9).*

Example of Use: Indeed, Dowdell admits there is a "distinct possibility" that his tendency toward personal involvement has contributed to his woes. "Sometimes people don't know who to turn to," he said. "They need a listening ear and an **understanding heart**. I care about people, and therein lies my problem." ("Belle Glade Divided on Police Department's Leader and Future of His Force," Mike Clary, June 11, 2006, *South Florida Sun-Sentinel*, Fort Lauderdale, FL)

Heart, Written in one's

Means: Remembered with special emotion

Biblical Text: *For when the Gentiles, which have not the law, do by nature the things contained in the law, these, having not the law, are a law unto themselves: Which shew the work of the law **written in their hearts**, their conscience also bearing witness, and their thoughts the mean while accusing or else excusing one another* (Romans 2:14–15). See also 2 Cor. 3:2–3.

Example of Use: During my term as President, I have had many opportunities to talk, connect, and reflect with our members worldwide in person, via e-mail, by telephone, or via interactive two-way audio and video. . . . Many highlights can only be **written on my heart** and stored in my special memory files. ("Serving As President: Opportunities, Discoveries, Insights, and Requests," Jacqueline Blackwell, Jan. 1, 2005, *Childhood Education*)

Hearts and minds

Means: Complete support

Biblical Text: *Be careful for nothing; but in every thing by prayer and supplication with thanksgiving let your requests be made known unto God. And the peace of God, which passeth all understanding, shall keep your **hearts and minds** through Christ Jesus* (Philippians 4:6–7).

Example of Use: The thing that struck me was his revelation when he said: "This was not the way to conduct operations if you want to win the **hearts and minds** of the population." ("Winning **Hearts and Minds** of People," Mej-Jen Datuk Nordin Yusof, Mar. 16, 2006, *New Straits Times*, Kuala Lumpur, Malaysia)

Heaven

Means: Paradise, an ideal place or situation

Biblical Text: *After this I looked, and, behold, a door was opened in* **heaven** (Revelation 4:1).

Example of Use: VAS Cardiff City's season threatens to fall apart, owner Sam Hammam has pointed out that his club are only in the third year of a 20-year plan towards greatness. "Everybody wants to go to **heaven** but nobody wants to die," he said, explaining why fans should take the rough with the smooth. "We are not going to reach **our heaven** at the top of the Premiership without many more heartbreaks and defeats along the way." ("Football: The Sweeper," Nick Harris, Apr. 26, 2003, *The Independent,* London)

Heaven's gate

Means: The entrance to heaven

Biblical Text: *How dreadful is this place! this is none other but the house of God, and* **this is the gate of heaven** (Genesis 28:17).

Example of Use: "Blues Clueless: PBS Strikes Again Listening to Scorsese's Whispered Narration for His 'Blues' Contribution, 'Feel Like Going Home,' You May Think He's the Voice on the Intercom at **Heaven's Gate**," Lloyd Sachs, Sept. 28, 2003, *Chicago Sun-Times*

Hell

Means: A situation or place of evil, misery, or destruction

Biblical Text: *And fear not them which kill the body, but are not able to kill the soul: but rather fear him which is able to destroy both soul and body in* **hell** (Matt. 10:28).

Example of Use: War is **hell**. And, as a high-ranking member of the IDF General Staff said on April 9, "This is a war." A full-fledged war, being waged by Palestinians against the Jewish state and a war being waged by Israel against Palestinian terrorism. ("War Is **Hell**," Liat Collins, Apr. 14, 2006, *Jerusalem Post*)

Hellfire

Means: Torment

Biblical Text: *Whosoever shall say, Thou fool, shall be in danger of **hell fire*** (Matthew 5:22c).

Example of Use: **Hellfire** I/II missiles are the USA's preferred aerial anti-armor missile, and are widely deployed with America's allies. . . . Range is officially listed as 9 km/5.6 miles. (http://www.defenseindustrydaily.com/US-**Hellfire**-Missile-Orders -FY-2011–2014–07019)

Helpmeet (or helpmate)

Means: One's spouse or mate

Biblical Text: *And the LORD God said, It is not good that the man should be alone; I will make him an **help meet** for him* (Genesis 2:18).

Example of Use: The widow of a former bishop of Coventry has died, aged 89. ("Bishop's Widow and **Helpmate** Dies at 89," Jan. 5, 2002, *Coventry Evening Telegraph*, England)

Hem of one's garment, Touch the

Means: To show great respect or reverence for someone

Biblical Text: *For she said within herself, **If I may but touch his garment**, I shall be whole. But Jesus turned him about, and when he saw her, he said, Daughter, be of good comfort; thy faith* *hath made thee whole. And the woman was made whole from that hour* (Matthew 9:21–22).

Example of Use: My first contact with Rosa Parks came in 1988, when, advanced in age and rather frail, she crisscrossed the country to encourage people, especially young people, to become involved in civic life.

Out in Brooklyn, the Rev. Herbert Daughtry's House of the Lord Church was jam-packed for what was ostensibly a voter-registration drive, but was actually an opportunity for black folks to **touch the hem of the garment** of an icon. ("Her Eyes Were on a Bigger Prize," E. R. Shipp, Nov. 1, 2005, *New York Daily News*)

Here am I

Means: A statement expressing one's presence or availability to another

Biblical Text: *And the angel of God spake unto me in a dream, saying, Jacob: And I said, **Here am I*** (Genesis 31:11).

Example of Use: [George David, Chairman & CEO, UTX:] I've been coming down here for a long time and it's nice to be back with all of you. And I always note you've got sand in your shoes when that happens and **here am I** all tricked out with my tie and suit, but that's okay. ("United Technologies at Electrical Products Group Annual Spring Conference—Final," May 22, 2007, *Fair Disclosure Wire*)

Here am I, send me

Means: An expression stating one's readiness to serve someone

Biblical Text: *Also I heard the voice of the Lord, saying, Whom shall I send, and who will go for us? Then said I, **Here am I; send me*** (Isaiah 6:8).

Example of Use: I have never been more proud to be an American. When I see Iraqi children as young as 7 and 8 being set free from prison my heart swells. When I see old Iraqi men giving the thumbs up sign I am celebrating with them. When I see Iraqi troops receiving medical attention and food I am struck by the compassion of our country. However, the thing that makes me most grateful is to see how the men and women of our military have, with honor, represented the United States. In courage and conviction they answered the call, "Who will stand up for those who cannot stand up for themselves?" They answered, **"Here am I, send me!"** ("Letters," Kim Whitlock Apr. 19, 2003, *Rocky Mountain News,* Denver)

H

Hewers of wood and drawers of water

Means: People who do difficult and essential work, often of a demeaning nature or with relatively little compensation or recognition

Biblical Text: *And the princes said unto them, Let them live; but let them be **hewers of wood and drawers of water** unto all the congregation; as the princes had promised them* (Joshua 9:21).

Example of Use: Establishing a Canadian identity is notoriously difficult. . . . Take for instance, a simple phrase from Harold Innis, who once indicated that we are a nation of **"hewers of wood, and drawers of water."** It is part of his staples theory, in which Canada's cultural, political, and economic history and status can be traced to the extraction and exploitation of resources, including timber, lumber and water, but also beaver fur, cod fish, wheat, and metals. . . . Innis was developing these ideas mid 20th century, but I suspect that in these more secular times, most people don't realize it's a biblical turn of phrase (from Joshua 9), well worn before the question of Canadian identity might even have appeared, and really not all that positive. In Joshua, to be **a hewer of wood or drawer of water** (a woodcutter or water carrier) is to be a slave to the community. (Blog posted by Scott Campbell, University of Waterloo, Centre for Society, Technology and Values, http://cstv.uwaterloo.ca/2011/07/hewers-of-wood-drawers-of-water-bloggers-of.html, July 20, 2011)

Highways and hedges

Means: Places where people are likely to be

Biblical Text: *And the lord said unto the servant, Go out into the **highways and hedges**, and compel them to come in, that my house may be filled* (Luke 14:23).

Example of Use: "If it wasn't [sic] for the City Union Mission, hundreds of thousands of homeless would be somewhere. They would be on the streets, under the bridges, **highways and hedges**, and that costs a whole lot more than rehabilitation." ("City Union Mission Launches Fund Drive to Meet Growing Demands from Homeless: Hoping to Help KC's Neediest," Debra Skodack, Mar. 23, 2006, *The Kansas City Star*)

Hoary head

Means: (1) Someone's hair that is gray or white with age; (2) someone who possesses wisdom by virtue of age as reflected by gray or white hair

Biblical Text: *The **hoary head** is a crown of glory, if it be found in the way of righteousness* (Proverbs 16:31). See also Lev. 19:32.

Example of Use: How much more time do you need? This year marks the 400th anniversary of *Don Quixote*, and you still haven't read it. Harold Bloom is shaking his **hoary head**: "Where shall wisdom be found, indeed!" And don't even bother trying to hum *The Impossible Dream*. A few diverting hours with *Man of La Mancha* are no substitute for working through 1,000 pages of the world's first novel. ("Writers," Ron Charles, Feb. 22, 2005, *The Christian Science Monitor*)

Holier than thou

Means: An attitude in which one believes that he is morally superior to other people

Biblical Text: *Stand by thyself, come not near to me; for I am **holier than thou**. These are a smoke in my nose, a fire that burneth all the day* (Isaiah 65:5).

Example of Use: "Still Waters Run Deep, So They Say, and That's Certainly True of Canada, Which Sometimes Errs into **Holier-Than-Thou** Territory When It Comes to Its Warmongering, Rapacious, Intolerant Neighbor to the South," May 23, 2005, *National Review*

Holy of holies

Means: An inviolably private place; a special place, especially one that is private or accessible to only an elite group

Biblical Text: *And thou shalt put the mercy seat upon the ark of the testimony in the **most holy place*** (Exodus 26:34).

Example of Use: "To the practitioners of the circus arts this Museum is our **holy of holies**, filled with treasured heirlooms of past master showmen, great performers and legendary circuses."—George Cahill, Ringmaster for Circus Sarasota. ("The Circus Is Coming to Town!" Oct. 1, 2005, *Sarasota Magazine*)

Holy Writ

Means: Sacred writings of a religion, especially the Bible, or any document presumed to hold unquestioned authority

Biblical Text: *All scripture is given by inspiration of God, and is profitable for doctrine, for reproof, for correction, for instruction in righteousness: That the man of God may be perfect, throughly furnished unto all good works* (2 Timothy 3:16–17).

Example of Use: Keeping in mind that what is said at this stage in the campaign can't be taken as **holy writ**, and that even with the best of intentions candidates often change positions, his [Rudy Giuliani] viewpoint is refreshingly frank and astute. ("No Time for a Terrorist State," Anonymous, Aug. 24, 2007, *Chicago Jewish Star*)

Hope deferred makes the heart sick

Means: Waiting for some desired end makes one miserable

Biblical Text: *Hope deferred maketh the heart sick: but when the desire cometh, it is a tree of life* (Proverbs 13:12).

Example of use: Now don't get me wrong, there is nothing wrong with hope. It's a good thing. Losing hope is a bad thing. **Hope deferred makes the heart sick.** It's just that too many of us only hope things will change, get better, etc., and then that is all we do. Faith may move mountains, but you had better bring a shovel. We hope, but we don't do anything, we don't decide. ("Have Hope, but Decide to Do Whatever It Takes," Jeff Herring, Mar. 8, 2004, *Tallahassee Democrat*, Tallahassee, FL)

Horns of the altar

Means: A means of protection

Biblical Text: *And Adonijah feared because of Solomon, and arose, and went, and caught hold on the **horns of the altar*** (1 Kings 1:50).

Example of Use: Furthermore, that resignation was not a manipulation aimed at clinging to the **horns of the altar**, but the humble, remorseful and unequivocal relinquishing of power, which took him 15 years to restore. ("The Resignation That Wasn't," Amotz Asa-El, Dec. 15, 2000, *Jerusalem Post*)

Hot nor cold, Neither

Means: To be without strong convictions on a subject

Biblical Text: *I know thy works, that thou art **neither cold nor hot**: I would thou wert cold or hot. So then because thou art lukewarm, and **neither cold nor hot**, I will spue thee out of my mouth* (Revelation 3:15–16).

Example of Use: Zuckerman writes with the moribund even-handedness of someone worried that he might not be invited back to A-list dinner parties. Which is curious, since he hosts about one-half of them. On Israel, I'd much rather read Marty Peretz from the right or Eric Alterman from the left. To paraphrase the Book of Revelations [sic], Zuckerman on the Middle East is **neither hot nor cold**; I spew him out. ("Breaking out the Wooden Prose-o-Meter," Alex Beam, Aug. 6, 2007, *The Boston Globe*)

House divided against itself cannot stand, A

Means: Division within an organization will destroy it

Biblical Text: *And Jesus knew their thoughts, and said unto them, Every kingdom divided against itself is brought to desolation; and **every city or house divided against itself shall not stand*** (Matthew 12:25). See also Mark 3:25.

Example of Use: On Friday night, the Cougars, the other residents of the stadium, christened the new house with a 24–21 win in the annual Hula Bowl. **A house divided against itself cannot stand**, but the SM North District Stadium rocked when an estimated 6,000 fans from both schools filled the stands. ("SM Northwest Feels at Home: Cougars' Last-Minute Touchdown Sinks SM North in First Game at North District Stadium," Candace Buckner, Sept. 2, 2006, *Kansas City Star*)

House not made with hands

Means: Heaven, or a heavenly place

Biblical Text: *For we know that if our earthly house of this tabernacle were dissolved, we have a building of God, **an house not made with hands**, eternal in the heavens* (2 Corinthians 5:1).

Example of Use: These trials have also reminded us that we are often stronger than we know, with the help of grace and one another. They remind us of a hope beyond all pain and death, a God who welcomes the lost to **a house not made with hands**. And they remind us that we are tied together in this life, in this nation, and that the despair of any touches us all. ("Text of President Bush's Address," Sept. 16, 2005, AP Online)

House of God

Means: A place or worship

Biblical Text: *And he was afraid, and said, How dreadful is this place! this is none other but the **house of God**, and this is the gate of heaven* (Genesis 28:17).

Example of Use: Just keeping [Chester Cathedral] open costs around pounds 6 a minute. Like Chester itself, the **house of God** has adapted to circumstances in suitably down-to-earth, pragmatic ways. ("Rain Won't Dampen Your Spirits Given the Right Hotel and Lots of Easy-to-Reach Attractions, Chester Is Ideal for a Short Break Whatever the Weather," James English, Sept. 22, 2002, *The Sunday Telegraph,* London)

House with many mansions

Means: A vast place or situation, especially one with great potential

Biblical Text: *In my Father's house are many mansions: if it were not so, I would have told you* (John 14:2).

Example of Use: According to the most recent census, in 2001, Newham is 39% white, 33% Asian and 22% black, and its residents rub along together pretty well. Trouble, when there is any, tends to come from outside. ("A House with **Many Mansions**," Feb. 3, 2007, *The Economist*)

How are the mighty fallen

Means: The previously powerful are now reduced

Biblical Text: *The beauty of Israel is slain upon thy high places: how are the mighty fallen!* (2 Samuel 1:19).

Example of Use: How are the mighty fallen! Shares of ICI fell 7p to a 19-year low of 183p as brokers continued to fret over prospects for the group following the disclosure yesterday of flat profits and a whopping hole in its pension fund. ("ICI Falls to 19-year Low As Brokers Fret over Figures," Michael Clark, Feb. 7, 2003, *Evening Standard,* London)

How long, O Lord?

Means: A lament, asking God why he has not yet brought relief

Biblical Text: *Then the angel of the LORD answered and said, **O LORD of hosts, how long** wilt thou not have mercy on Jerusalem and on the cities of Judah, against which thou hast had indignation these threescore and ten years?* (Zechariah 1:12).

Example of Use: For remaining Orioles fans, the ones who screech "O!" during the national anthem and pray that someday another Brooks, Frank or Cal will come to the rescue, the only possible mantra is: **How long, O Lord, how long?** ("Angelos, Bonds a Perfect Couple," Dick Heller, June 7, 2006, *The Washington Times*)

H

RAISING CAIN

I

"IRON SHARPENS IRON"

I shall not be moved

Means: A statement affirming one's determination not to change his convictions

Biblical Text: *I have set the LORD always before me: because he is at my right hand,* **I shall not be moved** (Psalm 16:8).

Example of Use: If players had theme music, [Kendrick] Perkins' would be "**I Shall Not Be Moved**." ("Perk up for Tough Job; Work Centers on Punishing Howard," Ron Borges, May 18, 2010, *The Boston Herald*)

Ichabod

Means: Something or someone (or a symbol for either) that is not as glorious as it once was

Biblical Text: *And she [Phinehas' wife] named the child* **Ichabod**, *saying,* **The glory is departed from Israel**: *because the ark of God was taken, and because of her father in law and her husband. And she said, The glory is departed from Israel: for the ark of God is taken* (1 Samuel 4:21–22).

Example of Use: If balletgoers have a family motto it is surely 'Ichabod' and most are happy to bore for Britain with tales of departed glories, but today's company looks in very good shape. ("Dance Spring Is Sprung New York City Ballet," Louise Levene, Mar. 23, 2008, *The Sunday Telegraph*, London)

If God be for us, who can be against us?

Means: A statement of confidence in God

Biblical Text: *What shall we then say to these things?* **If God be for us, who can be against us?** (Romans 8:31).

Example of Use: Who deserves the NBA title more—Dallas or Miami? With the finals getting revved up here tomorrow, we offer a decidedly biased list of 10 answers to the question. . . . 1. **If David Hasselhoff is for us, who can be against us?** ("Editorial: Superiority Complex: Top 10 Reasons Dallas Deserves the NBA Trophy," June 7, 2006, *Dallas Morning News*)

If you beat him with the rod, he shall not die

Means: Corporal punishment, when properly administered, will not harm a child and may even save him from a worse fate later in life

Biblical Text: *Withhold not correction from the child: for **if thou beatest him with the rod, he shall not die. Thou shalt beat him with the rod**, and shalt deliver his soul from hell* (Proverbs 23:13–14).

Example of Use: Allen argued that the Bible supports the use of corporal punishment. One of the passages he cited was Proverbs 23:13, which says: "Withhold not correction from the child; for if **thou beatest him with the rod, he shall not die.** Thou shalt beat him with the rod, and shalt deliver his soul from hell." ("Georgia Pastor Convicted of Child Abuse," Oct. 17, 2002, United Press International)

In the beginning

Means: An expression indicating the start of something

Biblical Text: *In the beginning God created the heaven and the earth* (Genesis 1:1).

Example of Use: [Maureen Dowd, quoted from her new book, *Are Men Necessary?*] "The irony for me is that **in the beginning** you had to conform to the whole feminist ethos. If you wore high heels you didn't fit in. There was no room for originality within feminist codes of dress, so you were conforming to the whole cheesecloth shirt and no make-up thing. Now women seem to be striving for the same face and body, so there's just as much conformity at one end of the scale as there is at the other." ("In the Beginning There Was This Dame . . . : The Saturday Interview with Maureen Dowd," Caroline Foulkes, Apr. 1, 2006, *Birmingham Post*, England)

In the beginning was . . .

Means: Something existed initially

Biblical Text: *In the beginning was the Word, and the Word was with God, and the Word was God* (John 1:1).

Example of Use: Paul Cronin's mesmerizing docu[mentary,] ***In the Beginning Was** the Image: Conversations with Peter Whitehead*[,] is a long, continually surprising film about a remarkable Englishman who turned his back on film. ("**In the Beginning** Was the Image: Conversations with Peter Whitehead," Lisa Nesselson, Dec. 18, 2006, *Variety*)

Inherit the wind

Means: To be unable to keep and enjoy what one gets because of carelessness or wickedness

Biblical Text: *He that troubleth his own house shall **inherit the wind**: and the fool shall be servant to the wise of heart* (Proverbs 11:29).

Example of Use: For the last few years, the international trade community in Miami has lived by the adage that what doesn't kill you makes you stronger. With economies in most of the Americas sputtering since 2001, companies have weathered the downturn by honing operations. Now they are about to

inherit the wind, or at least a stiff breeze of relief. ("The Return of Latin Markets; Say What You Will about Diversity, and Expanding into New Markets. When It Comes to International Trade and Services in Miami, Nothing Beats the Healthy Latin America Predicted for 2004," J. P. Faber, Jan. 1, 2004, *South Florida CEO*)

Inner man, The

Means: One's emotions, spirit, or mind; the core of one's character

Biblical Text: *Though our outward man perish, yet the **inward man** is renewed day by day* (2 Corinthians 4:16b).

Example of Use: "Martial arts teach you that **the inner man** is always stronger than the outer man," says Smith, now 44. "I figured if I got back into martial arts, it would give me the strength I needed." Smith figured right. ("Soldier On: War Veteran Overcomes Personal Tragedy to Continue a Life of Service," Tamara E. Holmes, Apr. 1, 2011, *Black Enterprise*)

Innocent blood

Means: A symbol of an innocent person

Biblical Text: *Moreover Manasseh shed **innocent blood** very much, till he had filled Jerusalem from one end to another; beside his sin wherewith he made Judah to sin, in doing that which was evil in the sight of the LORD* (2 Kings 21:16).

Example of Use: Life and death were honored Friday on sacred ground where cultures once clashed and **innocent blood** once spilled along the frozen banks of the Washita River. ("'What Happened Here . . . Was a Massacre': Washita Battlefield Center Marks Dark Day in U.S. History," Ron Jackson, Apr. 21, 2007, *Daily Oklahoman*, Oklahoma City, OK)

Iron sharpens iron

Means: Constructive interaction among people makes them more effective

Biblical Text: *Iron sharpeneth iron; so a man sharpeneth the countenance of his friend* (Proverbs 27:17).

Example of Use: Catcher Michael Barrett said playing the Sox should bring out the best in the Cubs. "Like I said last year, **iron sharpens iron**." ("Baker Denies Rooting against Sox— Again," Paul Sullivan, May 19, 2006, *Chicago Tribune*)

Ishmael

Means: A social outcast

Biblical Text: *And the angel of the LORD said unto her, Behold, thou art with child, and shalt bear a son, and shalt call his name Ishmael; because the LORD hath heard thy affliction* (Genesis 16:11).

Example of Use: "'A Chinese **Ishmael**': Sui Sin Far, Writing, and Exile," Joy M. Leighton, Sept. 22, 2001, *MELUS the Journal*

It is not good for man to be alone

Means: A person living in isolation will not enjoy personal fulfillment as he would in a relationship with another

Biblical Text: *And the LORD God said, It is not good that the man should be alone; I will make him an help meet for him* (Genesis 2:18).

Example of use: This would represent a significant evolution from the mindset of "the nation that stands alone" to a new mindset of **"it is not good that a man should be alone."** ("Headline: Israel's Atlantic Dimension," Ron Prosor, Feb. 24, 2005, *Jerusalem Post*)

RAISING CAIN

J

"JONAH"

Jacob's ladder

Means: A ladder of rope used to climb aboard a ship or other structure

Biblical Text: *And **Jacob** went out from Beersheba, and went toward Haran. And he lighted upon a certain place, and tarried there all night, because the sun was set; and he took of the stones of that place, and put them for his pillows, and lay down in that place to sleep. And he dreamed, and behold **a ladder set up on the earth**, and the top of it reached to heaven: and behold the angels of God ascending and descending on it* (Genesis 28:10–12).

Example of Use: Just as **Jacob's Ladder** offers adults the skills to climb the ladder to self-sufficiency, this young agency is climbing its own ladder toward greater service to the community. ("Robert Miller Column," Dec. 22, 2002, *The Dallas Morning News*)

Jael

Means: A deadly woman

Biblical Text: *But Barak pursued after the chariots, and after the host, unto Harosheth of the Gentiles: and all the host of Sisera fell upon the edge of the sword; and there was not a man left. Howbeit Sisera fled away on his feet to the tent of **Jael** the wife of Heber the Kenite: for there was peace between Jabin the king of Hazor and the house of Heber the Kenite. . . . He [Sisera] said unto her, Stand in the door of the tent, and it shall be, when any man doth come and inquire of thee, and say, Is there any man here? that thou shalt say, No. Then **Jael** Heber's wife took a nail of the tent, and took an hammer in her hand, and went softly unto him, and smote the nail into his temples, and fastened it into the ground: for he was fast asleep and weary. So he died* (Judges 4:16–17, 20–21).

Example of Use: Sibylle is a compassionately viewed victim, at least as much as she is a femme fatale, a Salome or a **Jael** or a Medusa. ("From a Sad Affair," Wolfgang Koeppen, 2007, www. granta.com/books)

Jawbone of an ass

Means: A simple weapon that proves especially effective

Biblical Text: *And he found a new **jawbone of an ass**, and put forth his hand, and took it, and slew a thousand men therewith* (Judges 15:15).

Example of Use: Representatives for gun rights groups argued that without the convenience of gun shows, criminals will resort to organizing swap meets at McDonald's restaurants. They noted that without access to firearms, mentally deranged people will resort to making napalm bombs, igniting gasoline and using box cutters and maybe even **"the jawbone of an ass"** when they go on killing sprees. ("Reason Fails in the Gun Debate," Feb. 7, 2011, *The Virginian-Pilot,* Norfolk, VA)

Jealous god

Means: Someone or something that is intolerant of disloyalty or infidelity

Biblical Text: *And Joshua said unto the people, Ye cannot serve the LORD: for he is an holy God; he is a **jealous God**; he will not forgive your transgressions nor your sins* (Joshua 24:19).

Example of Use: The very idea that markets are imperfect at some things may come as a shock—or even sacrilege—to true believers in the cult of the market god. According to this cult, the market is like an all-wise and all-good but **jealous god** which becomes exceedingly wrathful when interfered with by things like coal mine or workplace safety laws, minimum wage protections, or taxes that pay for health, education or other services. Its ways are not our ways, nor are its thoughts our thoughts. And if it demands an occasional human sacrifice, we just have to deal with it. ("Real World Markets Act Differently," Rick Wilson, Oct. 21, 2007, *Sunday Gazette-Mail*, Charleston, WV)

Jehu, Drive like

Means: To drive a vehicle fast

Biblical Text: *And Jehu answered, What hast thou to do with peace? turn thee behind me. And the watchman told, saying, He came even unto them, and cometh not again: and **the driving is like the driving of Jehu** the son of Nimshi; for he driveth furiously. And Joram said, Make ready. And his chariot was made ready. And Joram king of Israel and Ahaziah king of Judah went out, each in his chariot, and they went out against Jehu, and met him in the portion of Naboth the Jezreelite* (2 Kings 9:19b–21).

Example of Use: At the time of my birth, my family was living in South Carolina. However, my mother, a native of North Carolina, didn't want me born a Palmetto. So when she went into labor, she and Dad **drove like Jehu** to Concord, North Carolina, so I could be born a Tarheel. One more bump and I would have been a Palmetto after all. (Stan Banker, 2007, barclaypress.com/writers)

Jephthah

Means: Someone who makes a hasty vow with tragic results

Biblical Text: *And **Jephthah** vowed a vow unto the LORD, and said, If thou shalt without fail deliver the children of Ammon into mine hands, Then it shall be, that whatsoever cometh forth of the doors of my house to meet me, when I return in peace from*

the children of Ammon, shall surely be the LORD's, and I will offer it up for a burnt offering (Judges 11:30–31).

Example of Use: Not engaged on either side; unbiased; impartial. "The next person who talks is going to be in big trouble." Two seconds after you issue your ultimatum, a class angel slips and speaks. You then have a choice: allow the angel to have another chance, or stick to your word and issue discipline. You have put yourself into a "**Jephthah's**" corner. ("Classroom Common Sense," 2007, www.aacs.org)

Jewel of gold in a swine's snout, A

Means: Something important or attractive that fails to improve that to which it is added

Biblical Text: *As **a jewel of gold in a swine's snout**, so is a fair woman which is without discretion* (Proverbs 11:22).

Example of Use: "To my thought," he [Wallace Nutting] confided to William Sumrier Appleton (1874–1947), the founder and corresponding secretary of the Society for the Preservation of New England Antiquities, "antique furniture in a modem house is like **a jewel of gold in a swine's snout**." ("Wallace Nutting and the Intention of Old America," Trina Evarts Bowman, May 1, 2003, *The Magazine Antiques*)

Jezebel

Means: A shameless, immoral woman, especially one who schemes to lead others into immorality

Biblical Text: *And of **Jezebel** also spake the LORD, saying, The dogs shall eat **Jezebel** by the wall of Jezreel. Him that dieth of Ahab in the city the dogs shall eat; and him that dieth in the field shall the fowls of the air eat. But there was none like unto Ahab,* *which did sell himself to work wickedness in the sight of the* Lord, *whom* **Jezebel** *his wife stirred up* (1 Kings 21:23).

Example of Use: A boss accused of banning short skirts was a religious fundamentalist who once called a female lawyer **a Jezebel**, it has been claimed. Sean Kehoe is accused of enforcing an "archaic" dress code for women at his Staffordshire firm. ("I Got the Sack over Short Skirt; Lawyer Suing Firm over 'Archaic' Dress Code," Jeanette Oldham, May 2, 2004, *Sunday Mercury,* Birmingham, England)

Job, Patience of

J

Means: Real or apparent patience in facing suffering or great difficulties, sometimes used in jest

Biblical Text: *Ye have heard of the* **patience of Job**, *and have seen the end of the Lord; that the Lord is very pitiful, and of tender mercy* (James 5:11).

Example of Use: Curtis Coleman must have **the patience of Job**. The president and CEO of Safe Foods Corp. of North Little Rock admits he and the company have had "a tough year." Actually, one could say it has been a tough six years, but this year and much of 2004 were particularly frustrating. ("Safe Foods Prepares for Growth: Russian Roadblock Removed, Company Plans to Make up Lost Time," John Henry, Dec. 19, 2005, *Arkansas Business*)

Job's comforters

Means: Someone who tries to comfort another but, by so doing, adds to the person's misery

Biblical Text: *Now when* **Job's three friends** *heard of all this evil that was come upon him, they came every one from his own place; Eliphaz the Temanite, and Bildad the Shuhite, and Zophar*

the Naamathite: for they had made an appointment together to come to mourn with him and to comfort him (Job 2:11).

Example of Use: Nor had he through all this been lacking in **Job's comforters** in the conservative community to instruct him in the many different ways he had brought it all upon himself, forgetting that it was his strength for which he was being punished and not his weakness (weakness being something that members of Congress were by tradition only too willing to forgive in one another). ("Comeback Kid? [Newt Gingrich])," Midge Decter, Dec. 7, 1998, *National Review*)

Job's wife

Means: A woman who offers advice that is unsound and could be destructive

Biblical Text: *Then said **his** [Job's] **wife** unto him, Dost thou still retain thine integrity? curse God, and die* (Job 2:9).

Example of Use: Studies of successful professional women confirm that they, like Sophia or **Job's wife**, use "creative aggression" in furthering their aims. ("What Is Success?" Gail Carr Feldman, 2006, www.gailfeldman.com)

John the Baptist

Means: A forerunner

Biblical Text: *In those days came **John the Baptist**, preaching in the wilderness of Judaea, And saying, Repent ye: for the kingdom of heaven is at hand. For this is he that was spoken of by the prophet Esaias, saying, The voice of one crying in the wilderness, Prepare ye the way of the Lord, make his paths straight* (Matthew 3:1–3).

Example of Use: He [William Dyce] played a **John the Baptist** role in the Pre-Raphaelite movement but is hardly as celebrated as its star artists. ("Chaste and Symbolic: William Dyce's Bicentenary Exhibition in His Native Aberdeen Reveals a Painter Very Different in Character from the Pre-Raphaelites, Whose Precursor He Is Often Said to Be," Simon Poe, Nov. 1, 2006, *Apollo*)

Jonah

Means: Someone who causes misfortune for others

Biblical Text: *Now the LORD had prepared a great fish to swallow up **Jonah**. And **Jonah** was in the belly of the fish three days and three nights* (Jonah 1:17).

Example of Use: It has been a **Jonah**-like year for Crenshaw Corp. "We've had easier-to-swallow growth," said Robert W. Ashby Jr., president and chief executive officer of the truck repair and customizing business in South Richmond. ("Rising 25: Ashby's Inc./Crenshaw Corp.," Chip Jones, Jan. 22, 2007, *Richmond Times-Dispatch*)

Joram

Means: A large bowl for drinking

Biblical Text: *And **Joram** brought with him vessels of silver, and vessels of gold, and vessels of brass: Which also king David did dedicate unto the LORD, with the silver and gold that he had dedicated of all nations which he subdued* (2 Samuel 8:10b–11).

Example of Use: Gyles Brandreth, founder of the championship, presented the winner with the Gyles Brandreth shield, which Mr. Willis last won 10 years ago, and everyone yode for a **joram** (went for a big drink). ("The AA to ZO of Scrabble's Spell," William Hartston, Nov. 21, 1994, *The Independent*, London)

Jordan, Cross the (or Jordan, Pass over)

Means: (1) To make a transition into a new situation that is one's ultimate goal; (2) to die and go to heaven

Biblical Text: *And the LORD spake unto Moses in the plains of Moab by **Jordan** near Jericho, saying, Speak unto the children of Israel, and say unto them, When ye are **passed over Jordan** into the land of Canaan; Then ye shall drive out all the inhabitants of the land from before you, and destroy all their pictures, and destroy all their molten images, and quite pluck down all their high places* (Numbers 33:50–52).

Example of Use: Disfranchised and economically vulnerable, African American women believed the Republican Party's suggestion that a Hampton victory would mean a return to slavery. Thus, black women willingly shamed black men who had "**crossed Jordan**" to the Democratic cause. ("Religion, Gender, and the Lost Cause in South Carolina's 1876 Governor's Race: 'Hampton or Hell!,'" W. Scott Poole, Aug. 1, 2002, *Journal of Southern History*)

Joseph

Means: Someone who wears a colorful garment

Biblical Text: *Now Israel loved **Joseph** more than all his children, because he was the son of his old age: and he made him a coat of many colours* (Genesis 37:3).

Example of Use: Like **Joseph's** coat of many colors, so are the children and staff members at the Free to Be Child Care Center at Crest View Community complex in Columbia Heights. ("Helping Out; Serving the Global at the Local Level; North Metro Child Care Center Caters to Immigrants with Varied Services," Karen Gail Jostad, July 6, 2002, *Star Tribune*, Minneapolis, MN)

Joseph, To know not

Means: To fail to recognize the value of someone or something that has a history of value to a group or organization

Biblical Text: *Now there arose up a new king over Egypt, which **knew not Joseph**. And he said unto his people, Behold, the people of the children of Israel are more and mightier than we: Come on, let us deal wisely with them; lest they multiply, and it come to pass, that, when there falleth out any war, they join also unto our enemies, and fight against us, and so get them up out of the land* (Exodus 1:8–10).

Example of Use: Retired Army Col. Harry Lindauer had a favorite expression: "A new Pharaoh arose **who knew not Joseph**." What he meant by that, his wife Thea explained, is that a man can be honored for many things, but as generations follow generations eventually the man is forgotten. But a man who lived a life like Col. Lindauer's would be hard to forget, family and friends say. And what he'll be remembered for depends on who is asked. ("Retired Col. Will Be 'Hard to Forget,'" Heather Rawlyk and Lori Phelan, Dec. 17, 2006, *Capital*, Annapolis, MD)

Jot or tittle

Means: A tiny amount, especially if relatively insignificant

Biblical Text: *For verily I say unto you, Till heaven and earth pass, one **jot or one tittle** shall in no wise pass from the law, till all be fulfilled* (Matthew 5:18).

Example of Use: Common Cause, the League of Women Voters and all those who want to limit free speech by limiting political spending are back once more—with a vengeance. . . .

This time their initiative is an amendment to the state constitution that they seek to put on the November ballot. If it passes, not a **jot or tittle** can be changed without a subsequent vote of the people. ("Elections: Another Misguided Spending Initiative[.] The Issue: Another Campaign 'Reform' Proposal[.] Our View: Another Lawyers' Relief Act," May 25, 2002, *Rocky Mountain News*, Denver, CO)

Joy comes in the morning

Means: Better conditions will eventually come after a period of difficulty

Biblical Text: *Sing unto the* Lord, *O ye saints of his, and give thanks at the remembrance of his holiness. For his anger endureth but a moment; in his favour is life: weeping may endure for a night, but* **joy cometh in the morning** (Psalm 30:4–5).

Example of Use: "Katrina Has Wrought Sore Weeping in the Night . . . but **Joy Comes in the Morning**," Sybil C. Mitchell, Sept. 28, 2005, *Tri-State Defender*, Memphis, TN

Jubilee

Means: A fiftieth anniversary

Biblical Text: *In the year of the* **jubilee** *the field shall return unto him of whom it was bought, even to him to whom the possession of the land did belong* (Leviticus 27:24).

Example of Use: **Jubilee** 2000 is an initiative for cancellation of Third World debt, inspired by the tradition of the **Jubilee**. ("Born to Shop—Born to Debt: **Jubilee** 2000—Bringing Third World Debt to a Store Near You," Stephen Ames, June 1, 1999, *Arena Magazine*)

Judas

Means: Someone who betrays another under the guise of friendship

Biblical Text: *Then one of the twelve, called **Judas** Iscariot, went unto the chief priests, And said unto them, What will ye give me, and I will deliver him unto you? And they covenanted with him for thirty pieces of silver. **And from that time he sought opportunity to betray him**. . . . And while he yet spake, lo, **Judas**, one of the twelve, came, and with him a great multitude with swords and staves, from the chief priests and elders of the people. Now he that betrayed him gave them a sign, saying, Whomsoever I shall kiss, that same is he: hold him fast. And forthwith he came to Jesus, and said, Hail, master; and kissed him* (Matthew 26:14–15).

Example of Use: Died Nov. 9, 1997. Murdered by cowards, betrayed by a **Judas**, one of the three best sons. Deeply missed and loved by his Mum and Dad. Remembering you is easy, we do it every day, missing you is the heartache, it never goes away, no matter how our lives have changed or whatever we may do, we won't forget the precious years, the ones we shared with you. ("Raymond Christopher McCord," Nov. 9, 2007, *Belfast Telegraph*)

Judge not, that ye be not judged

Means: A proverb advising one to not be critical of others unless one is prepared to accept the same form of criticism oneself

Biblical Text: *Judge not, that ye be not judged* (Matthew 7:1).

Example of use: A corollary to this was Carter's opposition to imposing democracy or any other form of government on other peoples. Carter explained that God forbids judging, **"Judge not, that ye be not judged"** (Pippert 1978, 101). Instead, the United States should become an evangelist of democracy. But such evangelism was not to be by words alone. Rather, the United States was to be the democratic model or light to the world. ("Jimmy Carter and George W. Bush: Faith, Foreign Policy, and an Evangelical Presidential Style," D. Jason Berggren and Nicol C. Rae, Dec. 1, 2006, *Presidential Studies Quarterly*)

Judged by one's own words, To be

Means: To be judged by one's record, particularly by what one says or writes

Biblical Text: *And he saith unto him, **Out of thine own mouth will I judge thee**, thou wicked servant. Thou knewest that I was an austere man, taking up that I laid not down, and reaping that I did not sow* (Luke 19:22).

Example of Use: But Tony Blair must be **judged by his own words**. "We have the chance to make things happen—we are the party of the many not the few . . . fairness and social justice . . . liberty and equality of opportunity . . . solidarity and responsibility to others . . . we will never sacrifice those principles." ("Stotty on Sunday: Striking the Wrong Tone," Richard Stott, Sept. 25, 2005, *Sunday Mirror*, London)

Judgment Day

Means: A time when a matter of importance will be decided or resolved

Biblical Text: *But the heavens and the earth, which are now, by the same word are kept in store, reserved unto fire against the **day of judgment** and perdition of ungodly men* (2 Peter 3:7).

Example of Use: Talk about your **day of judgment**. Minutes after Marin Alsop and the Baltimore Symphony Orchestra wrapped up a high-octane gala program Saturday night—a program that included the fire-and-brimstone *Dies Irae* from Giuseppe Verdi's *Requiem*—a propane tank exploded alongside the party tent across the street from Meyerhoff Hall, interrupting the dessert reception for patrons. Luckily, a timely warning got everyone out before the eruption. ("BSO's Gala Features Fiery Moments and an Eclectic Lineup," Tim Smith, Sept. 17, 2007, *Baltimore Sun*)

J

RAISING CAIN

K

"KISS OF DEATH"

Kedar's tents

Means: Kedar was the second son of Ishmael and grandson of Abraham. The word means "mighty," swarthy," or "black."

Biblical Text: *Sharp arrows of the mighty, with coals of juniper. Woe is me, that I sojourn in Mesech, that I dwell in the **tents of Kedar**! My soul hath long dwelt with him that hateth peace* (Psalm 120:4–6). See also Gen. 25:13; Song 1:5.

Example of Use: Deep in the night he comes to her, the young woman, dark and lost. She is sleeping. He stands above her and watches her breathe. Comely, he thinks, as the **tents of Kedar**, as the curtains of Solomon. Her face is dark against the white cloth. ("Ackerman in Eden," Donald Hays, Sept. 22, 2004, *The Southern Review*)

K

Keep the faith

Means: An exhortation to remain strong and faithful to a cause or ideal

Biblical Text: *I have fought a good fight, I have finished my course, **I have kept the faith*** (2 Timothy 4:7).

Example of Use: Despite two shock defeats in the four-nation tournament in India, the Australian women's cricket team are refusing to give up hope of reaching the final. ("Crik: Australians **Keep the Faith** in India," Feb. 26, 2007, *AAP Sports News*, Australia)

Keys of the kingdom

Means: Great authority for something

Biblical Text: *And I say also unto thee, That thou art Peter, and upon this rock I will build my church; and the gates of hell shall not prevail against it. And I will give unto thee the **keys of the***

kingdom of heaven: and whatsoever thou shalt bind on earth shall be bound in heaven: and whatsoever thou shalt loose on earth shall be loosed in heaven (Matthew 16:18–19).

Example of Use: State Rep. John Millner, a Carol Stream Republican, said he voted the way his constituents wanted. "The people said 'absolutely not,'" Millner said. "I received literally hundreds of e-mails and phone calls from members of our district saying that they don't know why we're providing the **keys of the kingdom**, in other words, driver's licenses, to people who are considered illegal." ("Driver's License Legislation Rejected," Sara Hooker, Apr. 1, 2004, *Daily Herald*, Arlington Heights, IL)

Kick against the pricks

Means: To hurt oneself by useless resistance or protest against a particular authority

Biblical Text: *And he fell to the earth, and heard a voice saying unto him, Saul, Saul, why persecutest thou me? And he said, Who art thou, Lord? And the Lord said, I am Jesus whom thou persecutest: it is hard for thee to kick against the pricks. And he trembling and astonished said, Lord, what wilt thou have me to do? And the Lord said unto him, Arise, and go into the city, and it shall be told thee what thou must do* (Acts 9:4–5).

Example of Use: "A rebel is different from a revolutionary," argues Hodson. "A revolutionary believes that society is perfectible, something no society really truly wants. Rebels are people we need to **kick against the pricks** of authority. ("Rebels with a Cause," Liz Hoggard, Aug. 20, 2006, *The Independent on Sunday*, London)

King of kings

Means: An extremely powerful king or other authority

Biblical Text: *That thou keep this commandment without spot, unrebukable, until the appearing of our Lord Jesus Christ: Which in his times he shall shew, who is the blessed and only Potentate, the **King of kings**, and Lord of lords* (1 Timothy 6:14–15).

Example of Use: "Nadal the **King of Kings** in Clay/Grass Battle," May 3, 2007, *The Independent,* London

Kingdom come

Means: A statement of affirmation concerning the beginning of one's reign or authority

Biblical Text: *Thy **kingdom come**. Thy will be done in earth, as it is in heaven* (Matthew 6:10).

Example of use: A friend of mine was recently writing to me about his fear of being blown to **kingdom come** by some power station not far from where he lives. He added that he'd better go to the other world in a more comfortable way. I wrote him back saying that, never mind this power station, "he had probably walked by the door of **Kingdom come** more than once," given the potential hazards we encounter in daily life. (Wordreference.com, Mar. 30, 2012)

Kingdom of, Of such is the

Means: A reference to the particular nature of a sphere of dominion

Biblical Text: *But Jesus called them unto him, and said, Suffer little children to come unto me, and forbid them not: for **of such is the kingdom of God*** (Luke 18:16).

Example of Use: It is a foregone conclusion that population shifts revealed in the new census data will increase the clout of urban areas in the Kansas Legislature. **Of such is the Kingdom**

of Kansas. ("More Conservative," Jim McLean, Mar. 19, 2001, *The Topeka Capital-Journal*, KS)

Kiss of death

Means: An act of betrayal expressed as an act of friendship, whether with knowledge or not

Biblical Text: *And while he yet spake, behold a multitude, and he that was called **Judas**, one of the twelve, went before them, and drew near unto Jesus to kiss him. But Jesus said unto him, Judas, **betrayest thou the Son of man with a kiss?*** (Luke 22:47–48).

Example of Use: "Lockheed, Boeing in High-Stakes Race if Pentagon Drops One As Rocket Builder, It Could Be '**Kiss of Death**,'" Heather Draper, Jan. 30, 2003, *Rocky Mountain News*, Denver

K

Knock and it shall be opened

Means: An exhortation to pursue an opportunity

Biblical Text: *And I say unto you, Ask, and it shall be given you; seek, and ye shall find; **knock, and it shall be opened** unto you* (Luke 11:9). See also Matt. 7:7.

Example of Use: Besides his son's felt-material animal art-work, large sheets of paper containing business concepts are hung on the wall in front of him. One shows a "business tri-angle" that indicates the importance of communication, mis-sion, product, cash flow and leadership. Another contains words of inspiration for businesses or individuals: Givers get. Clarity is power. **Knock and it shall be opened**. It all starts with a dream. Changing your reality is a snap. ("Omahan Left a Quadriplegic in Iraq Will Soon Move into a New Home," Rick Ruggles, May 5, 2007, *Omaha World-Herald*, NB)

RAISING CAIN

L

"LEAP FOR JOY"

Labor is not in vain, One's

Means: One's work is important and worthwhile

Biblical Text: *Therefore, my beloved brethren, be ye stedfast, unmoveable, always abounding in the work of the Lord, forasmuch as ye know that **your labour is not in vain** in the Lord* (1 Corinthians 15:58).

Example of Use: To the workers on this Labor Day, I say: Thanks, and do not despair. **Your labor is not in vain**, you are important and it is your hand that turns the wheel. ("Letters to the Editor," Donald Lane, Sept. 4, 2006, *The Virginian-Pilot*, Norfolk, VA)

Labor of love

Means: Productive work performed without regard for material reward or compensation

Biblical Text: *For God is not unrighteous to forget your work and **labour of love**, which ye have shewed toward his name, in that ye have ministered to the saints, and do minister* (Hebrews 6:10).

Example of Use: "**Labor of Love** Needs Room to Grow," Bill Nemitz, Dec. 15, 2004, *Portland Press Herald*, ME

Laborer is worthy of his hire, A

Means: A good worker is worth the pay he receives.

Biblical Text: *For the scripture saith, Thou shalt not muzzle the ox that treadeth out the corn. And, **The labourer is worthy of his reward*** (1 Timothy 5:18). See also Luke 10:7.

Example of Use: While it is true that "**the laborer is worthy of his hire**" and that the individual who has taken the pains to equip himself for the practice of the healing art should receive remuneration in proportion to the expense and self-sacrifice which the acquisition of the necessary knowledge and skill may have entailed upon him, we have no hesitation in saying that the individual who makes dollars and cents the great desideratum is utterly unworthy to be found in the ranks of this grand and glorious profession. ("Broad-Scope and Proud of It," James Winterstein, Aug. 13, 2001, *Dynamic Chiropractic*)

Lake of fire

Means: An expansive fire or, figuratively, severely difficult conditions

Biblical Text: *And the devil that deceived them was cast into the **lake of fire** and brimstone, where the beast and the false prophet are, and shall be tormented day and night for ever and ever* (Revelation 20:10). See also Rev. 19:19–21.

L

Example of Use: Chrisy Castillo, who was convicted Wednesday of recklessly causing serious bodily injury to her 23-month-old disabled son, angrily denied ever harming the toddler. She told state District Judge Mark Kent Ellis he would someday be in "the **lake of fire**" before a bailiff escorted her from the courtroom. ("Mom Lashes Out at Judge during Sentencing," Peggy O'Hare, May 11, 2006, *Houston Chronicle*)

Lamb brought to slaughter

Means: Someone or something sacrificed for another, especially if defenseless

Biblical Text: *He was oppressed, and he was afflicted, yet he opened not his mouth: he is brought **as a lamb to the slaughter**, and as a sheep before her shearers is dumb, so he openeth not his mouth* (Isaiah 53:7). See also Acts 8:32; 1 Pet. 1:19.

Example of Use: "I Felt like a **Lamb to the Slaughter**, said Diana: Intimate Tapes Reveal the Princess's Thoughts on Her Wedding and Camilla," Mar. 5, 2004, *The Daily Mail,* London

Lamb of God

Means: Reference to Jesus, the Lamb of God in the NT; sometimes an especially respected and revered person

Biblical Text: *The next day John seeth Jesus coming unto him, and saith, Behold the **Lamb of God**, which taketh away the sin of the world* (John 1:29).

Example of Use: According to Donna Lehrer, the mother of two teenagers at **Lamb of God** Farm in Big Rock near Rockford, "A trip to the farm helps your children put together the process of growing dinner. That makes meal times memorable." ("Trip to the Farm Introduces Kids to Food Chain," Aug. 11, 2004, *Daily Herald,* Arlington Heights, IL)

Lamb, Sacrificial

Means: Someone or something that is sacrificed for the sake of others or in the place of others

Biblical Text: *And it shall be, when he [a "soul"] shall be guilty in one of these things, that he shall confess that he hath sinned in that thing: And he shall bring his trespass offering unto the LORD for his sin which he hath sinned, a female from the flock, **a lamb** or a kid of the goats, **for a sin offering**; and the priest shall make an atonement for him concerning his sin* (Leviticus 5:5–6).

Example of Use: Lawmakers were preparing Thursday night to vote on a $145 billion state budget, and there were growing signs that public transit funding would be a **sacrificial lamb** of negotiations as Democrats and Republicans moved toward a deal. ("Lawmakers Aim for Vote Today on State Budget," Mike Zapler, July 20, 2007, *Oakland Tribune*)

Land of Nod

Means: Reference to the Land of Nod in the book of Genesis; Sometimes, the state of sleep (whimsical)

Biblical Text: *And Cain went out from the presence of the Lord, and dwelt in the **land of Nod**, on the east of Eden* (Genesis 4:16).

Example of Use: Whatever the reason, Gordon Brown briefly left the House of Commons yesterday for the **Land of Nod**. The Chancellor's eyes drooped and he slumped forward in his front-bench seat as Tony Blair addressed MPs. But, luckily for him, the TV microphones failed to pick up any evidence of a snore. ("First Minister in the Land of Nod," Apr. 15, 2003, *The Daily Mail*, London)

L

Land of the living, In the

Means: In a place where people and other living things are; in normal circumstances

Biblical Text: *But where shall wisdom be found? and where is the place of understanding? Man knoweth not the price thereof; neither is it found **in the land of the living*** (Job 28:12–13).

Example of Use: They may no longer be **in the land of the living** but that is clearly a minor impediment in their eternal attempts to amass a fortune. Yesterday, a somewhat macabre list detailing the highest earning dead celebrities in the past year was unveiled. King of the posthumous earners was Elvis Presley, who has not allowed his death 27 years ago to prevent a healthy inflation of his bank account. His annual income last year, based on admissions to Graceland, licencing and merchandising, was cited as pounds 21.8m. ("Elvis Tops List of

Posthumous Earners," Danielle Demetriou, Oct. 26, 2004, *The Independent*, London)

Laodicean

Means: Indifferent, half-hearted

Biblical Text: *And unto the angel of the church of the **Laodiceans** write; These things saith the Amen, the faithful and true witness, the beginning of the creation of God; I know thy works, that thou art neither cold nor hot: I would thou wert cold or hot. So then because thou art lukewarm, and neither cold nor hot, I will spue thee out of my mouth* (Revelation 3:14–16).

Example of Use: The commissioners are latter-day **Laodiceans**, whom the Book of Revelation describes as "neither cold nor hot . . . (but) lukewarm." As a result, most of the report hits stratospheric heights of banality. ("Iraq Study Group Report[:] Is It a Bipartisan Blueprint for the Future or Lukewarm Tripe? It's War, Not a Political Problem to Be Haggled," Jonah Greenberg, Dec. 10, 2006, *Wisconsin State Journal*, Madison)

Last days

Means: The ultimate end of something

Biblical Text: *And it shall come to pass in the **last days**, saith God, I will pour out of my Spirit upon all flesh: and your sons and your daughters shall prophesy, and your young men shall see visions, and your old men shall dream dreams* (Acts 2:17).

Example of Use: The **Last Days** of Democracy: How Big Media and Power-Hungry Government Are Turning America into a Dictatorship [Elliot D. Cohen and Bruce W. Fraser, Prometheus Books] surveys how Constitutional promises and premises are being eroded by both private and federal special interests.

("*The **Last Days** of Democracy*" (Book Review), Sept. 1, 2007, *Internet Bookwatch*)

Last Supper

Means: A last meal before an ordeal or a climactic event

Biblical Text: *And he took bread, and gave thanks, and brake it, and gave unto them, saying, This is my body which is given for you: this do in remembrance of me. Likewise also the cup after supper, saying, This cup is the new testament in my blood, which is shed for you. But, behold, the hand of him that betrayeth me is with me on the table. And truly the Son of man goeth, as it was determined: but woe unto that man by whom he is betrayed! And they began to inquire among themselves, which of them it was that should do this thing* (Luke 22:19–23).

Example of Use: George Harrison enjoyed an emotional **Last Supper** with fellow Beatles Sir Paul McCartney and Ringo Starr just days before he lost his tragic battle with cancer, the Sunday *People* can reveal today. . . . A source close to Paul said last night: "They knew this was their **last supper**. It was really emotional. ("George Harrison Born 1943—Died 2001: Macca and Ringo's Secret Beatles **Last Supper** with Deathbed George," Dec. 2, 2001, *The People,* London)

Last trump

Means: Reference to the announcement by God of the world's end and the beginning of Christ's reign; a signal for the ultimate end of something

Biblical Text: *Behold, I shew you a mystery; We shall not all sleep, but we shall all be changed, In a moment, in the twinkling of an eye, at the **last trump**: for the trumpet shall sound, and the*

dead shall be raised incorruptible, and we shall be changed. (1 Corinthians 15:51–52). See also Matt. 24:31.

Example of Use: Arrrgghh! If ever there were a time to become a Luddite, this is it. This is what our parents warned us about, when the computer revolution started around 1980. This is the Death of the Book, the end of printed text and old-style reading, as predicted thousands of times in the past decade. This is, more shockingly, the **Last Trump** of the Private Library. ("Tales of the City," John Walsh, Nov. 27, 2007, *The Independent*, London)

Laugh one to scorn

Means: To ridicule or deride someone severely

Biblical Text: *All they that see me **laugh me to scorn**: they shoot out the lip, they shake the head, saying, He trusted on the LORD that he would deliver him: let him deliver him, seeing he delighted in him* (Psalm 22:7–8).

L

Example of Use: One question should never have to be asked in this mature democracy. One doubt should be utterly unthinkable as the nation goes to the polls. But the issue is now inescapable: can voters have any real confidence in the honesty, fairness or integrity of the result on May 5? Time was when the merest suggestion of something wrong and rotten in our democratic process would have been **laughed to scorn**. ("The Scandal of Postal Votes and the Question: Can We Trust This Election," Apr. 6, 2005, *The Daily Mail*, London)

Law of the Medes and the Persians, According to the

Means: A rule or practice so strict that it cannot be changed

Biblical Text: *Now, O king, establish the decree, and sign the writing, that it be not changed, **according to the law of the Medes and Persians**, which altereth not* (Daniel 6:8).

Example of Use: To insiders and outsiders alike, the tobacco economy as it existed from the 1930s to very recently sometimes seemed as "traditional" and permanent as **the law of the Medes and the Persians**. ("Front Porch," Harry L. Watson, Sept. 22, 2003, *Southern Cultures*)

Law unto oneself, A

Means: One who is totally independent, especially one who ignores established rules and procedures

Biblical Text: *For when the Gentiles, which have not the law, do by nature the things contained in the law, these, having not the law, are **a law unto themselves*** (Romans 2:14).

Example of Use: They came "out of the sea" . . . and terrorized Hampton Roads. . . . They were **a law unto themselves**, sailing where they would and taking whatever they wanted . . . until Virginia's colonial governor declared war on them. ("Report to Readers: The Real Pirates of Local History," Marvin Lake, Aug. 6, 2006, *The Virginian Pilot,* Hampton Roads, VA)

Law, The letter of the

Means: Strict interpretation of laws and regulations, often ignoring their basic principles

Biblical Text: *But he is a Jew, which is one inwardly; and circumcision is that of the heart, in the spirit, and **not in the letter**; whose praise is not of men, but of God* (Romans 2:29).

Example of Use: "**Letter of the Law** Must Be Followed in Transparency Rule[;] Oxfam Calls on Securities and Exchange

Commission to Bring Life to Oil, Gas and Mining Transparency Law," Feb. 23, 2011, States News Service

Lay down one's life, To

Means: To sacrifice oneself for another, especially to die

Biblical Text: *This is my commandment, That ye love one another, as I have loved you. Greater love hath no man than this, that a man lay down his life for his friends* (John 15:12–13).

Example of Use: As this Thanksgiving Day nears, Oregonians across the state should pause to think of Robert Charles Hanners, Randall Carpenter and Jeffery Edward Common— and the hundreds of men and women like them across the state—who every day stand prepared to **lay down their lives for their communities. For their friends.** ("The Greatest Sacrifice," Nov. 27, 2002, *The Register-Guard*, Eugene, OR)

Lazarus

Means: Someone who reemerges after being considered no longer to be vital

Biblical Text: *Then said Jesus unto them plainly,* **Lazarus** *is dead. . . . And when he thus had spoken, he cried with a loud voice,* **Lazarus, come forth. And he that was dead came forth,** *bound hand and foot with graveclothes: and his face was bound about with a napkin. Jesus saith unto them, Loose him, and let him go* (John 11:14, 43–44).

Example of Use: The apparent resurrections of the coelacanth and other long-missing species have led scientists to give such living fossils another name: **Lazarus** taxa, after the beggar who was raised from the dead in a biblical parable [sic]. ("Back from the Dead? 'Resurrections' of Long-Missing Species Lead to Revelations," Sid Perkins, Nov. 17, 2007, *Science News*)

Lead us not into temptation

Means: A request not to be placed into a situation in which one is tempted

Biblical Text: *And **lead us not into temptation**, but deliver us from evil: For thine is the kingdom, and the power, and the glory, for ever. Amen* (Matthew 6:13). See also Luke 11:4.

Example of Use: Having been elected by practicing the typical politician's pledge of benefits with sacrifice, the governor now looks for money by capitalizing on vain games of chance wherein the devil is the winner. . . . To which I say, **lead us not into temptation** but deliver us from [Governor] Deval. ("Letters to the Editor," Daniel Hamilton, Sept. 27, 2007, *The Boston Herald*)

Leap for joy

Means: To rejoice or be glad, especially when expressed physically through dance or other movement

Biblical Text: *Blessed are ye, when men shall hate you, and when they shall separate you from their company, and shall reproach you, and cast out your name as evil, for the Son of man's sake. Rejoice ye in that day, and **leap for joy**: for, behold, your reward is great in heaven: for in the like manner did their fathers unto the prophets* (Luke 6:22–23).

Example of Use: Firefighter Stephen Johnson **leaped for joy** and did a high-stepping dance in the street when the "Extreme Makeover: Home Edition" bus rolled away and he and his five children first saw their new home. ("'God Opens a Window and Pours out a Blessing': An Extremely Sweet Homecoming," Mará Rose, Apr. 7, 2005, *The Kansas City Star*)

Leaven the lump

Means: To affect something greatly by adding only a relatively small element or amount of something

Biblical Text: *Know ye not that a little leaven **leaveneth the whole lump**? Purge out therefore the old leaven, that ye may be a new lump, as ye are unleavened. For even Christ our passover is sacrificed for us: Therefore let us keep the feast, not with old leaven, neither with the leaven of malice and wickedness; but with the unleavened bread of sincerity and truth* (1 Corinthians 5:6b–8).

Example of Use: When I first started working on newspapers, there wasn't much fashion in them and it wasn't fabulous. Fashion coverage was a weekly dole, usually on a Monday, to "brighten up" the paper as the working week began. You brighten up a paper by putting pictures of women in it, in order to **leaven the lump** of men-in-suits droning on about the economy. ("By the End of This Week, Even the Least Fashionable among Us Will Know Who This Woman Is. Here's Why . . . ," Vicki Woods, Sept. 16, 2007, *The Independent on Sunday*, London)

Left hand know what your right hand is doing, Don't let your

Means: An exhortation to be discreet about one's interests

Biblical Text: *But when you give to the poor, **do not let your left hand know what your right hand is doing**, That thine alms may be in secret: and thy Father which seeth in secret himself shall reward thee openly* (Matthew 6:3–4).

Example of Use: Get rid of all of those unnecessary things and stuff, the more stuff you have and brag about, the more your so-called friends secretly resent you and talk about you behind your back. We're living in the days where **you can't let your**

left hand know what your right hand has. Get busy and start tracking your money; call me if you need some help. ("Your Money; Understanding Cash Flow," Robert Henderson, Oct. 18, 2005, *Miami Times*)

Legion, My name is

Means: A statement meaning "there are many like me"

Biblical Text: *And he asked him, What is thy name? And he answered, saying, **My name is Legion**: for we are many* (Mark 5:9). See also Luke 8:30.

Example of Use: My name is legion, for we are many. Mobile phones are changing politics faster than academics can follow. ("Mobiles, Protests and Pundits; Liberation Technology: Mobiles Phones Are Empowering the Powerless, So Far in Mostly Benign Ways," Oct. 28, 2006, *The Economist*)

Legion, We are

Means: A statement meaning "we are many in number"

Biblical Text: *And he asked him, What is thy name? And he answered, saying, **My name is Legion**: for we are many. . . . And they come to Jesus, and see him that was possessed with the devil, and had the **legion**, sitting, and clothed, and in his right mind: and they were afraid* (Mark 5:9, 15). See also Luke 8:30.

Example of Use: Mourners for the State of the TV sitcom— and **we are legion**—occasionally take solace in the classics. Watching "Cheers," "Newhart" and anything else from the glory days in the '70s and '80s can be an alternately uplifting and depressing experience. ("Devito Rounds out 'Always Sunny' Cast," Melanie McFarland, June 29, 2006, *Seattle Post-Intelligencer*)

Length and breadth of something, The

Means: The full extent or area of something

Biblical Text: *Arise, walk through the land in the **length of it and in the breadth of it;** for I will give it unto thee* (Genesis 13:17).

Example of Use: The Historic Bethlehem Partnership, a consortium of museums and historic sites in the city, recognizes the importance of preserving what has made Bethlehem special through the decades.

That includes **the length and breadth** of the municipality—not just its downtown district, but also Bethlehem Steel's former blast furnaces and Machine Shop No. 2. In fact, national recognition for the entire city's historic significance has come twice from the prestigious Smithsonian Institution. ("Valley Should Support Historical Projects **the Length and Breadth** of Bethlehem; Historic Preservation," Sept. 28, 2003, *The Morning Call*, Allentown, PA)

Leopard change its spots?, Can the

Means: A question implying that changing aspects of one's nature is difficult

Biblical Text: ***Can the** Ethiopian **change** his skin, or the **leopard his spots**? Then may ye also do good, that are accustomed to do evil* (Jeremiah 13:23).

Example of Use: The notion that things cannot change their innate nature. Those and other incidents build a convincing case against Busch. So what must Busch do to win fans? Can he change? "Why should he?" Kyle Petty asked. "**Why should a leopard change his spots** or a tiger change his (stripes)? That's what makes him Kurt Busch." ("Polarizing Personality,"

Dustin Long, Feb. 19, 2006, *The News & Record*, Piedmont Triad, NC)

Let my people go

Means: A plea for freedom from servitude

Biblical Text: *And afterward Moses and Aaron went in, and told Pharaoh, Thus saith the* Lord *God of Israel,* **Let my people go,** *that they may hold a feast unto me in the wilderness* (Exodus 5:1).

Example of Use: "My relationship with the CPA [Coalition Provisional Authority] now is non-existent. . . . My message to the CPA is **let my people go**, let my people be free. We are grateful to President Bush for liberating Iraq but it is time for the Iraqi people to run their affairs," Chalabi said at a Baghdad press conference. ("Chalabi's New Tune: '**Let My People Go**,'" Geraldine Sealey, May 20, 2004, www.salon.com)

Let my right hand forget its cunning

Means: A self-exhortation to experience calamity if certain conditions are not met

Biblical Text: *If I forget thee, O Jerusalem,* **let my right hand forget her cunning** (Psalm 137:5).

Example of Use: Heeding the pledge of the psalmist, "**If I forget thee, O Jerusalem, let my right hand forget her cunning** [. . .] let my tongue cleave to the roof of my mouth," electronic composer Random Inc (aka Sebastian Meissner) has devoted two consecutive projects to the embattled holy city. For "Walking," he assembles sound fragments from Jerusalem and the music of a host of collaborators into textured melodies of truncated notes and spliced snippets. ("Walking in Jerusalem," Stephen Weiss, Dec. 13, 2002, dir.salon.com)

Let not the sun go down upon your wrath

Means: An exhortation to be forgiving and not to remain angry

Biblical Text: *Be ye angry, and sin not: **let not the sun go down upon your wrath*** (Ephesians 4:26).

Example of Use: The time for patients to modulate their hostile attitudes is now, rather than waiting for the occurrence of a frustrating event when plaque has been present for years. And we all have plaque from mid-to-late childhood on. "**Let not the sun go down on your wrath**." ("Anger and Myocardial Infarction. [Psychoneuroimmunoendocrinology Review and Commentary])," Robert A. Anderson, Aug. 1, 2004, *Townsend Letter for Doctors and Patients*)

Let not your heart be troubled

Means: An exhortation to avoid worry

Biblical Text: *Let not your heart be troubled: ye believe in God, believe also in me* (John 14:1). See also John 14:27.

Example of Use: Florida nipped Tampa Bay 11–4. The loss dropped the Devil Rays 10 games behind the Yankees, but **let not your heart be troubled**. They usually trail by 83 games at this point in the season. ("Devil Rays Just Might Begin to Pester Steinbrenner," David Whitley, June 28, 2004, *The Orlando Sentinel*)

Let the dead bury the dead

Means: An exhortation to deal with important issues while ignoring less important matters

Biblical Text: *And another of his disciples said unto him, Lord, suffer me first to go and bury my father. But Jesus said unto him, Follow me; and **let the dead bury their dead*** (Matthew 8:21–22).

Example of Use: It seems blindingly obvious to me that Ruth Kelly is being assassinated by the Downing Street machine, which wants to sacrifice her because her Education Bill has fallen apart. This will ensure that the sacred figure of Princess Tony is not harmed when the Bill is amended out of all recognition. That's one reason why I won't join in this ridiculous frenzy. **Let the dead bury their dead**, I say. ("They Killed Off Respect and a Kind Old Lady Too," Peter Hitchens, Jan. 15, 2006, *Mail on Sunday,* London)

Let there be light

Means: A statement calling for light to replace dark

Biblical Text: *And God said, **Let there be light**: and there was light* (Genesis 1:3).

Example of Use: With lucent leathers, gleaming satins and flashes of decoration, Italy's menswear has come up with a new mantra: **Let there be light!** From Alexander McQueen's powerful show pitting the rebellious street against royal tailoring, through Fendi's exceptional inspiration from the paintings of the 16th-century painter Caravaggio, light and shade are playing as strong a role as cut and silhouette. ("The New Mantra: **Let There Be Light**!" Suzy Menkes, Jan. 21, 2005, *International Herald Tribune*)

Let this cup pass from me

Means: A plea to be spared from suffering

Biblical Text: *And he went a little farther, and fell on his face, and prayed, saying, O my Father, if it be possible, **let this cup pass from me**: nevertheless not as I will, but as thou wilt* (Matthew 26:39). See also Mark 14:36.

Example of Use: Democracy, as Jesus puts it—a reference George W. Bush would surely enjoy but which, you should know, at the moment comes from a Jew—is saying, in the direction of that which we would not wish to happen: "Oh, my electorate, if it is possible, **let this cup pass from me**: nevertheless not as I will it, but as thou wilt." (Slightly modified from Matthew 26:39.) When we allow things like choice and freedom, we allow that those choices may not always be the ones that we, individually, would make. ("Column: My Country, Bush or Kerry," Andrew Tobolowsky, Nov. 5, 2004, *University Wire*)

Let us reason together, Come

Means: A plea for mutual understanding or agreement among parties

Biblical Text: *Come now, and **let us reason together**, saith the* LORD: *though your sins be as scarlet, they shall be as white as snow; though they be red like crimson, they shall be as wool* (Isaiah 1:18).

L

Example of Use: So in addition to Matt and Emily and their ongoing tiff, you have the conflict between the **let-us-reason-together** side and the blast-them-back-to-the-Stone-Age school of thought. Yawn. It's hard to imagine a civilized audience of any significant size wanting to sit through these trumped-up conflicts and lazy-daisy crises week after week. ("Bombs Away: Fox Drops a Big One," Tom Shales, Sept. 5, 2006, *The Washington Post*)

Let your words be few

Means: A request for one to be concise in one's speech

Biblical Text: *God is in heaven, and thou upon earth: therefore **let thy words be few*** (Ecclesiastes 5:2b).

Example of Use: When sharing with someone else who is grieving, words often fail you. Do talk. That person needs to hear from you, but **let your words be few** and specific. ("Day 337—Words of Comfort," 2007, www.griefshare.org)

Let your yes be yes and your no be no

Means: An exhortation to say what one means, speaking the truth

Biblical Text: *But **let your communication be, Yea, yea; Nay, nay**: for whatsoever is more than these cometh of evil* (Matthew 5:37).

Example of Use: Religion can be very po-faced about this. **Let your Yes be Yes, and your No be No**, as the Bible has it. And some secular philosophers have taken just as hard a line. Lying, Kant said in his *The Metaphysics of Morals*, is "the greatest violation of a human being's duty to himself." The principle of truthfulness must be upheld whatever is at stake. ("Faith & Reason: What Spike Milligan Has to Say to Stephen Byers; There Are Interesting Parallels between Laughter and Lying. Both Subvert the Truth and Are Infectious. So How Does One Liberate and the Other Stultify?" Mar. 2, 2002, *The Independent*, London)

Letter kills but the Spirit gives life, The

Means: The "letter," or, the strict implementation of the law, is sometimes harmful, especially to the innocent, but leniency often provides needed second chances.

Biblical Text: *Who also hath made us able ministers of the new testament; not of the letter, but of the spirit: **for the letter killeth, but the spirit giveth life*** (2 Corinthians 3:6).

Example of Use: Is **Letter Kills** a good band? Yes. Do they bring emotion and intensity? Yes. . . . I would go out of my way to see the **Letter Kills** live, anyone should. ("CD Review: Music for Happy, Hyper, Local Folks," Joe Franklin, Aug. 31, 2004, *University Wire*)

Leviathan

Means: An intimidating, powerful force or thing, not easily subdued

Biblical Text: *In that day the LORD with his sore and great and strong sword shall punish **leviathan** the piercing serpent, even leviathan that crooked serpent; and he shall slay the dragon that is in the sea* (Isaiah 27:1). See also Job 41:1; Pss. 74:14; 104:26.

Example of Use: Florida homes have taken the design party outside. Lavishly appointed and **leviathan** in scope, outdoor living spaces now boast a world of comforts, as any tour of the region's luxury model homes will show. ("Rooms without Walls: Luxury Living Expands with Lavish Outdoor Space," Mary Alice Collins, Dec. 1, 2003, *Sarasota Magazine*)

Lie in wait

Means: To wait in ambush

Biblical Text: *But their **laying await** was known of Saul. And they watched the gates day and night to kill him* (Acts 9:24).

Example of Use: Gardai were last night hunting for a brutal attacker who repeatedly stabbed a pretty French student and left her for dead on the doorstep of her flat. Officers believe the 23-year-old woman may have known her attacker who **lay in wait** for her as she returned home from college on Tuesday night. ("Attacker **Lay in Wait** for Student at Door to Her Home; Knife Victim Fights for Life," Aine Hegarty and Michael Doyle, May 12, 2005, *The Mirror,* London)

Light of the world

Means: Someone who considers himself to be extremely attractive, talented, or special in some way

Biblical Text: *Then spake Jesus again unto them, saying, I am **the light of the world**: he that followeth me shall not walk in darkness, but shall have the light of life* (John 8:12).

Example of Use: "A **light of the world** to his generation" was how Ralph Usherwood once described the graphic artist Eric Fraser. ("Obituary: Ralph Usherwood," Nicholas Usherwood, Jan. 26, 2000, *The Independent,* London)

Light under a bushel, To hide one's

Means: To display excessive modesty about one's abilities

Biblical Text: *Neither do men **light a candle, and put it under a bushel**, but on a candlestick; and it giveth light unto all that are in the house. Let your light so shine before men, that they may see your good works, and glorify your Father which is in heaven* (Matthew 5:15–16). See also Mark 4:21; Luke 11:33.

Example of Use: Grant Humphreys **kept his light under a bushel** when his father, Kirk, was Oklahoma City mayor from 1998–2003.

It was legal for him to pursue investments and to carry on his own business, but the younger Humphreys knew the mere appearance of impropriety was enough to bring trouble to his business, to his dad's work at City Hall—and to the family name. So he stayed out of the limelight as much as possible, and stepped away from some business deals that he had every right to pursue. ("Businessman Sees Downtown Growing," Richard Mize, Sept. 11, 2005, *Daily Oklahoman*, Oklahoma City, OK)

Like people, like priest

Means: As the people conduct themselves, their leaders imitate them

Biblical Text: *And there shall be,* **like people, like priest**: *and I will punish them for their ways, and reward them their doings* (Hosea 4:9).

Example of Use: Thomas Carlyle once said, "In the long run every Government is the exact symbol of its People, with their wisdom and unwisdom; we have to say, **Like People like Government**." ("A Disconnect between Leaders, Citizenry," Marilou Johanek, Jan. 6, 2006, *Blade,* Toledo, OH)

Lilies of the field

Means: Someone or something that is inconsequential; someone who does no work, often used in jest

Biblical Text: *And why take ye thought for raiment? Consider the* **lilies of the field**, *how they grow; they toil not, neither do they spin: And yet I say unto you, That even Solomon in all his glory was not arrayed like one of these* (Matthew 6:28–29).

Example of Use: A week ago last Thursday—on the morning of March 15—there were 64 NCAA Division I teams eligible to win the men's basketball tournament. Today there are four. . . . In a span of 250 hours, the **lilies of the field** were systematically uprooted—here's looking at you, Niagara, Albany, Holy Cross and Old Dominion—and the survivors were pared to a quartet. ("Coach Carousel Should Stop until NCAA Ride Ends," John McGrath, Mar. 26, 2007, *News Tribune*, Tacoma, WA)

Lily among thorns

Means: Someone or something that is superior to other people or things with which it is associated or compared

Biblical Text: *As the **lily among thorns**, so is my love among the daughters* (Song of Solomon 2:2).

Example of Use: "Story 11: A **Lily among Thorns**, True Stories about Couples Who Have Met on the Internet," May 2007, cyberlove101:com

Lily of the valley

Means: Low-growing perennial plant

Biblical Text: *I am the rose of Sharon, and the **lily of the valleys**. As the lily among thorns, so is my love among the daughters* (Song of Solomon 2:1–2).

Example of Use: Shiseido launched Zen with notes of grapefruit, bergamot, peach, pineapple, blue rose, freesia, gardenia, red apple, violet, **lily of the valley**, hyacinth, rose lotus flower, patchouli, cedar, musk, white musk, amber, incense and marine plant. A version of the scent was launched in 1964 and 2000. ("Floral Relaunch. [Fragrance Focus: News about the Fragrance Industry]," Oct. 1, 2007, *Global Cosmetic Industry*)

Lion in the way

Means: A contrived excuse, especially when made by a lazy person

Biblical Text: *The slothful man saith, There is **a lion in the way**; a lion is in the streets* (Proverbs 26:13).

Example of Use: Visiting E.U. Trade Commissioner Peter Mandelson spoke in Beijing on Nov. 10, saying that more focus will probably be placed on climate change, including proposing levying even lower tariffs on "climate-friendly" products in future WTO negotiations. Once carried out, the measures will be another "**lion in the way**" of Chinese enterprises that are already locked in by "environmental barriers." China is undoubtedly the chief target for this round of talks. ("Washington Observer Weekly," Yan Li, Nov. 29, 2006, www.washingtonobserver.org)

Lions' den, To be in the (or To be thrown into the)

Means: To be in grave danger

Biblical Text: *Then the king commanded, and they brought Daniel, and cast him into the **den of lions**. Now the king spake and said unto Daniel, Thy God whom thou servest continually, he will deliver thee* (Daniel 6:16).

Example of Use: Scotland enter the "**lion's den**" today determined to find the strength and spirit to pull off an historic win over South Africa. ("Ultimate Test Lam Sure Scots Can Defy Odds and History to Win in South African '**Lion's Den**,'" Niall Aitcheson, June 14, 2003, *Daily Mail*, London)

Little bird told me, A

Means: One has been provided information by an unnamed person

Biblical Text: *Curse not the king, no not in thy thought; and curse not the rich in thy bedchamber: for **a bird of the air shall carry the voice**, and that which hath wings shall tell the matter* (Ecclesiastes 10:20).

Example of Use: A little bird told me that the *Connecticut Sun* are working to finalize plans to come back to the Arena at Harbor Yard for another exhibition game next May. ("Chris

Elsberry Column," Chris Elsberry, Dec. 3, 2006, *Connecticut Post*, Bridgeport)

Little foxes

Means: Small matters and details that affect larger, more important matters

Biblical Text: *Take us the foxes, the **little foxes**, that spoil the vines: for our vines have tender grapes. My beloved is mine, and I am his: he feedeth among the lilies* (Song of Songs 2:15–16).

Example of Use: When it comes to automatic data flow, the adage ["]It's the **little foxes** that ruin the vineyard["] is most appropriate. In this case, the **little foxes** are bar code labels. Printing labels is easy. Getting them correct is something else. ("On the Importance of Being Right," Clyde E. Witt, June 1, 2000, *Material Handling Management*)

L

Live and move and have one's being

Means: To live

Biblical Text: *For in him we live, and move, and have our being; as certain also of your own poets have said, For we are also his offspring* (Acts 17:28).

Example of Use: All humans dwell in two [worlds]. One is the world of nature that we share with minerals, plants, and animals, namely, the everyday physical world. The other is the world of culture and, in a very real sense, the truly and exclusive human world. It is the place **in which we live and breathe and have our being**. ("The Creative Human Mind: Parting Thoughts," Gerald F. Kreyche, Sept. 1, 2004, *USA Today*)

Live by the sword, die by the sword

Means: One shall be defeated by the same means by which he defeats others.

Biblical Text: *Then said Jesus unto him, Put up again thy sword into his place: for all **they that take the sword shall perish with the sword*** (Matthew 26:52). See also Rev. 13:10.

Example of Use: Hatton said: "**I live by the sword and die by the sword** and that's why people come and watch my fights. It's never been about just winning for me, it means a lot what the fans think." ("Boxing: Educated Hatton Is Ready for Real War," Mark Staniforth, June 23, 2007, *Daily Post*, Liverpool)

Living dog is better than a dead lion, A

Means: Being alive is preferable to being brave and dead.

Biblical Text: *For to him that is joined to all the living there is hope: for **a living dog is better than a dead lion*** (Ecclesiastes 9:4).

Example of Use: As if on cue, our author proceeds to address this concern for human dignity in his ongoing quest for meaning while life remains. . . . "But for him who is joined to all the living there is hope, for **a living dog is better than a dead lion**." ("The Debate on Assisted Suicide—Redefining Morally Appropriate Care for People with Intractable Suffering," James Reitman, Dec. 22, 1995, *Issues in Law & Medicine*)

Loaves and fishes

Means: Something small in quantity or quality that is able to provide far more effect or value than warranted by its size or quality

Biblical Text: *One of his disciples, Andrew, Simon Peter's brother, saith unto him, There is a lad here, which hath **five barley loaves, and two small fishes**: but what are they among so*

many? And Jesus said, Make the men sit down. Now there was much grass in the place. So the men sat down, in number about five thousand. And Jesus took the loaves; and when he had given thanks, he distributed to the disciples, and the disciples to them that were set down; and likewise of the fishes as much as they would. When they were filled, he said unto his disciples, Gather up the fragments that remain, that nothing be lost. Therefore they gathered them together, and filled twelve baskets with the fragments of the five barley loaves, which remained over and above unto them that had eaten (John 6:8–13).

Example of Use: The rich are always with us. And they do a good job spreading it around. They called it the trickle-down effect in the 1980s—the idea of selfless rich people as "wealth-creators" who'd create something miraculously new out of a few old **loaves and fishes** and then leak it over the rest of us like a lot of amiable champagne fountains. ("Worried, Rich or Just Wet? Hiscox Has a Question for You," Leigh Coleman, Sept. 2, 2007, *The Independent on Sunday,* London)

Locusts and wild honey

Means: Something unappetizing or little desired

Biblical Text: *And the same John had his raiment of camel's hair, and a leathern girdle about his loins; and his meat was locusts and wild honey* (Matthew 3:4). See also Mark 1:6.

Example of Use: Conservative pundits have spent so many years playing John the Baptist—feeding on the **locusts and wild honey** of liberal piety—that it's time someone broke the news to them: They're no longer crying in the wilderness. ("Vice and Easy: Author Seeks out Sin," Louis Bayard, Nov. 15, 2002, *Rocky Mountain News,* Denver)

Loose the bands of Orion

Means: Do what seems impossible

Biblical Text: *Canst thou bind the sweet influences of Pleiades, or **loose the bands of Orion?*** (Job 38:31).

Example of Use: Finally, we will discover, as we always have, that however much we know, there is always more still to learn, and more that will never be learned. **We can understand the bands of Orion, not loose them.** ("The Week. Continuing Controversy over President Bush's Proposed Tax Cuts," Mar. 5, 2001, *National Review*)

Lord gives and the Lord takes away, The

Means: God is at work in the vicissitudes of life.

Biblical Text: *And said, Naked came I out of my mother's womb, and naked shall I return thither: **the Lord gave, and the Lord hath taken away**; blessed be the name of the Lord* (Job 1:21).

Example of Use: For those years, with only a poignant September reminder, the words on the page seemed little more than philosophical abstracts to be discussed in class and referenced in papers. But as events unfolded in Blacksburg, Va., it was never more true and never more real that **the Lord giveth, and the Lord taketh away**. ("Column: The Lord Giveth, and the Lord Taketh Away," Andrew Kaplun, Apr. 19, 2007, *University Wire*)

Lord is my shepherd, The

Means: God cares for those who love and live for him.

Biblical Text: *The **Lord is my shepherd**; I shall not want* (Psalm 23:1).

Example of Use: The hoplophobes [those who have an irrational fear of guns] running Virginia Tech are attempting to impose their own religion on their students, in violation of both the First and Fourteenth amendments. They even have their own version of the 23rd Psalm, which starts with "**The government is my shepherd**, I shall not fear . . . ," and ends with ". . . and I will dwell in a fool's paradise forever." ("Unbalanced Reporting," Andy Breglia, May 5, 2007, *Oakland Tribune*, CA)

Lord over

Means: Behave in a superior manner to someone, exercising authority

Biblical Text: *And when the ten heard it, they began to be much displeased with James and John. But Jesus called them to him, and saith unto them, Ye know that they which are accounted to rule over the Gentiles **exercise lordship over them**; and their great ones exercise authority upon them. But so shall it not be among you: but whosoever will be great among you, shall be your minister: And whosoever of you will be the chiefest, shall be servant of all* (Mark 10:41–44). See also Luke 22:24–27.

Example of Use: This is the season when New Englanders get to **lord it over** Americans who live in warm climates. We may not be able to bake our bones in the sun year-round like Californians, or bask in the beauty of blossoming flora in December like south Floridians, but we know how to glory in the arrival of spring. ("Editorial: A Season of Hope," Apr. 16, 2006, *Hartford Courant*, Hartford, CT)

Lord's Prayer

Means: A prayer Jesus taught his disciples, expressing the need for humility and unity with God and others

Biblical Text: *After this manner therefore pray ye: Our Father which art in heaven, Hallowed be thy name. Thy kingdom come. Thy will be done in earth, as it is in heaven. Give us this day our daily bread. And forgive us our debts, as we forgive our debtors. And lead us not into temptation, but deliver us from evil: For thine is the kingdom, and the power, and the glory, for ever. Amen* (Matthew 6:9–13). See also Luke 11:1–4.

Example of Use: With his final words, [he] begged the forgiveness of the family of the woman he had raped and murdered. Then, as he mouthed the words to the **Lord's Prayer**, the poison began to flow into his veins. It took less than 10 minutes early this morning to end the life of one of four Britons on America's death row. ("The **Lord's Prayer**, Then a Dying Gasp. Atlanta Has Justice," James Langton, Mar. 13, 2002, *Evening Standard,* London)

L

Lost sheep

Means: Someone who has left a group and is no longer part of it

Biblical Text: *My people hath been **lost sheep**: their shepherds have caused them to go astray, they have turned them away on the mountains: they have gone from mountain to hill, they have forgotten their restingplace* (Jeremiah 50:6).

Example of Use: Can Detroit's new cars bring in the **lost sheep**? Can the foreigners prosper at 90 yen to the dollar and $1.50 to the euro? This is a year to test possibilities. ("Hold That Line!" Jerry Flint, Jan. 1, 2005, *Ward's Auto World*)

Lot's wife

Means: Reference to the woman in Genesis 19 who looked back at Sodom and then turned to salt.

Biblical Text: *But his **wife [Lot's]** looked back from behind him, and she became a pillar of salt* (Genesis 19:26).

Example of Use: A developing fetus hangs submerged in it. **Lot's wife** became entombed in it. A grain placed on the tongue of an infant causes obvious displeasure, yet many manufacturers add it to jars of baby food. A component of rocks and oceans and found in religious traditions and pagan customs, sodium is a necessary, element of our lives from gestation to the grave. ("Sodium: How Much Is Too Much?" D. M. Flynn, Mar. 1, 2006, *Vibrant Life*)

Love of money is the root of all evil, The

Means: Greed is the basis of all evil

Biblical Text: *For **the love of money is the root of all evil**: which while some coveted after, they have erred from the faith, and pierced themselves through with many sorrows* (1 Timothy 6:10).

Example of Use: They say **the love of money is the root of all evil**. Given what's been happening lately from Chicago to Springfield and in the halls of Congress and City Hall, they're right. Of all things that have happened in this adult's lifetime of watching politicians, the saddest, the most worrisome is the slow decline of electoral politics at every level into a grubby grab for campaign cash, in which everyone and everything is or seems to be for sale. ("Cash Corrupts; Recent Political Scandals Stem from Candidates' Desperate Need for Money," Greg Hinz, Oct. 10, 2005, *Crain's Chicago Business*)

Love your enemies

Means: Love those who don't love you.

Biblical Text: *Ye have heard that it hath been said, Thou shalt love thy neighbour, and hate thine enemy. But I say unto you, **Love***

your enemies, *bless them that curse you, do good to them that hate you, and pray for them which despitefully use you, and persecute you; That ye may be the children of your Father which is in heaven: for he maketh his sun to rise on the evil and on the good, and sendeth rain on the just and on the unjust* (Matthew 5:43–45).

Example of Use: We have tried Bush's way. It does not work, and now the war is spreading. Isn't it time we try a different Christian way? It is easiest to fight back when attacked. It is hard work to turn your cheek and **love your enemies**. But peace and love are the only ways to get us out of the cycle of aggression, retaliation and revenge that we are mired in. ("Letters in the Editor's Mailbag," July 24, 2006, *The Register-Guard*, Eugene, OR)

Love your neighbor as yourself

L

Means: An exhortation to love other people as one would oneself

Biblical Text: *Thou shalt not avenge, nor bear any grudge against the children of thy people, but thou shalt **love thy neighbour as thyself**: I am the LORD* (Leviticus 19:18).

Example of Use: During slavery and segregation most [S]outhern churches blessed the existing order. Now they are sorry they did. This about-face was traumatic for many, but easy to justify scripturally. Attempts to find biblical backing for separate lunch counters always required a bit of reading between the lines, whereas "**Love thy neighbour as thyself**" is unambiguous. ("Doing It by the Book," Mar. 3, 2007, *The Economist*)

RAISING CAIN

M

"MUZZLE THE OX"

Make a joyful noise

Means: Celebrate with exuberance

Biblical Text: *Make a joyful noise unto the LORD, all ye lands. Serve the LORD with gladness: come before his presence with singing* (Psalm 100:1–2). See also Pss. 66:1; 81:1; 95:1–2; 98:4, 6.

Example of Use: Each school operates independently and in a variety of ways, but all share one common bond: they provide musical opportunities for students who otherwise may never get the chance to simply **make a joyful noise**. ("Play On," Jaclyn C. Stevenson, Jan. 22, 2007, *BusinessWest*)

Make light of

Means: Treat a major situation as of little consequence

Biblical Text: *Behold, I have prepared my dinner: my oxen and my fatlings are killed, and all things are ready: come unto the marriage. But they **made light of it**, and went their ways, one to his farm, another to his merchandise: And the remnant took his servants, and entreated them spitefully, and slew them* (Matthew 22:4–6).

Example of Use: "Retailer Pulls T-Shirts That **Make Light of** Violence against Women," Leslie Brody, June 23, 2004, *The Record*, Bergen County, NJ

Make peace

Means: Create peace in a situation in which it does not exist, especially peace that is permanent or long-lasting

Biblical Text: *And the fruit of righteousness is sown in peace of them that **make peace*** (James 3:18). See also Isa. 27:5; 45:7.

Example of Use: "Tribes, States Clash over Gaming; Lawmakers Rally to **Make Peace**," Bunty Anquoe, Apr. 27, 1994, *Lakota Country Times*, SD

Make whole

Means: To complete or make something as it should be

Biblical Text: *And, behold, a woman, which was diseased with an issue of blood twelve years, came behind him, and touched the hem of his garment: For she said within herself, If I may but touch his garment, I shall* **be whole***. But Jesus turned him about, and when he saw her, he said, Daughter, be of good comfort; thy faith hath* **made thee whole***. And the woman was made whole from that hour* (Matthew 9:20–22).

Example of Use: "Ugly Budget Battle Means 'Nobody's **Made Whole**,'" Elisabeth J. Beardsley, May 12, 2002, *The Boston Herald*

Make the crooked straight

Means: Make difficult tasks easier

Biblical Text: *Every valley shall be filled, and every mountain and hill shall be brought low; and* **the crooked shall be made straight***, and the rough ways shall be made smooth* (Luke 3:5).

Example of Use: The afternoon's soloist was the Siberian violinist Vadim Repin, who gave a dazzling account of Prokofiev's First Violin Concerto. The composer would have expected more roughage, but Repin's silky virtuosity didn't make the mistake of **making the crooked straight**, the rough places plain, and when Prokofiev spun a lyric line or set trills to shimmering like fireflies, Repin came into his element. ("Masters Take Stage and Podium, and Masterpieces Result," Richard Dyer, Aug. 15, 2000, *The Boston Globe*)

Mammon

Means: Money or other material wealth

Biblical Text: *No man can serve two masters: for either he will hate the one, and love the other; or else he will hold to the one, and despise the other. Ye cannot serve God and **mammon*** (Matthew 6:24). See also Luke 16:1–13.

Example of Use: Our civilization is a canvas that holds the sum of our actions. It is well-gilt, dotted with MasterCard logos, gold bullion and garnished with all the currencies of the Earth. . . . And Lord **Mammon** sits atop it all, his visage encrusted with diamonds and rubies. ("**Mammon's** the Man," Josh Fredman, Mar. 29, 2001, *University Wire*)

Man born of woman

Means: Any person

Biblical Text: *How then can man be justified with God? or how can he be clean that is **born of a woman**?* (Job 25:4).

Example of Use: In Shakespeare's "Macbeth," you will remember, there is a scene in which the king goes off to see the witches for further advice on his prospects. They say he is safe from **man born of woman** and "until Great Birnam wood to high Dunsinane hill shall come." He goes away, cheered. Silly boy: a few scenes later he is killed by Macduff, who turns out to have been untimely ripped from his mother's womb, and who got to Dunsinane behind boughs torn from the Birnam woods. ("Wanted: A Suitable Boy," Sukhraj Randhawa, Aug. 3, 2003, *The Sunday Telegraph*, London)

Man shall not live by bread alone

Means: Because mankind's spiritual needs are great, one cannot live a full life on physical nourishment alone; one needs more than basic elements with which to enjoy life.

Biblical Text: *And he humbled thee, and suffered thee to hunger, and fed thee with manna, which thou knewest not, neither did thy fathers know; that he might make thee know that **man doth not live by bread only**, but by every word that proceedeth out of the mouth of the LORD doth man live* (Deuteronomy 8:3).

Example of Use: Bakers may not like to admit it, but **man cannot live by bread alone**. As bakery cafe chains, such as Panera Bread Co. and Atlanta Bread Co., usher in a new model of bakery, complete with built in synergies between baked products and foodservice, retail bakeries are looking beyond traditional lines of bread, cakes and pastries to generate revenue. ("Extras Buoy the Bottom Line," Matthew Reynolds, June 1, 2007, *Modern Baking*)

M

Man that thou art mindful of him?, What is

Means: Mankind is small in comparison to all the world around him, making God's attention to him something to ponder

Biblical Text: *What is man, that thou art mindful of him? and the son of man, that thou visitest him?* (Psalm 8:4).

Example of Use: "The Earth Is Your Mother" is ecobabble. The Eighth Psalm gets a lot closer to the truth: "**What is man that thou art mindful of him** ... ? Thou madest him to have dominion over the works of thy hands. . . ." Just so. We're not here to be cowed by the environment. ("Us 'n' Nature. [Happy Warrior]," Mark Steyn, Jan. 31, 2005, *National Review*)

Manna

Means: An unexpected but welcome source of relief

Biblical Text: *And when the children of Israel saw it, they said one to another, It is* **manna**: *for they wist not what it was* (Exodus 16:15).

Example of Use: Chemotherapy never hurt his appetite, said Rice, 42, but he was "so exhausted I didn't have the strength to make a sandwich." **Manna** took meals to Rice for nine months: "All I had to do was pop them in the oven." Rice is in remission, and **Manna** now has 150 cancer patients among its 800 clients in Philadelphia, the Pennsylvania suburbs, South Jersey and northern Delaware who get three balanced meals five days a week—for free. ("**Manna** Reaches Out to Serve a Wider Need," Joseph A. Slobodzian, Mar. 9, 2007, *Philadelphia Inquirer*)

Mantle

Means: A position of authority or responsibility

Biblical Text: *So he departed thence, and found Elisha the son of Shaphat, who was plowing with twelve yoke of oxen before him, and he with the twelfth: and Elijah passed by him, and cast his* **mantle** *upon him* (1 Kings 19:19). See also 2 Kings 2:8.

Example of Use: Let him go, he's ours. To whom does William Wilberforce—the best-known figure in the British campaign to end slavery—belong? As with many historical figures, his **mantle** is contested by devotees of different political hues. ("A New Tug of War: A Contested **Mantle**. (An Abolitionist's Heritage Is Claimed by Left and Right Alike)," Feb. 24, 2007, *The Economist*)

Many are called but few are chosen

Means: While many people pursue their hopes and dreams, only a minority succeed; while many are considered for an enterprise, only few are often selected.

Biblical Text: *So the last shall be first, and the first last: for **many be called, but few chosen*** (Matthew 20:16).

Example of Use: But, no, trade shows are an extremely profitable business, but much like restaurants and Broadway shows and movies, very few make it, **many are called but few are chosen**. Hopefully we still have some skills over here to create shows that nobody else has thought of. ("Q1 2007 Jupitermedia Corporation Earnings Conference Call—Final," May 10, 2007, *Fair Disclosure Wire*)

Mark of the beast

M

Means: A physical mark indicating someone's association with evil

Biblical Text: *And the **beast** was taken, and with him the false prophet that wrought miracles before him, with which he deceived them that had received the **mark of the beast**, and them that worshipped his image. These both were cast alive into a lake of fire burning with brimstone* (Revelation 19:20).

Example of Use: A group of Christian conservatives is urging Gov. Joe Manchin to reject a federally mandated digitized driver's license law, comparing the bar-coded national ID program to the "**mark of the beast**." ("'**Mark of the Beast**' Seen in National ID," Eric Eyre, Apr. 16, 2006, *Charleston Gazette*, West Virginia)

Measure for measure

Means: The same in kind or degree

Biblical Text: *Judge not, that ye be not judged. For with what judgment ye judge, ye shall be judged: and with what **measure ye mete, it shall be measured to you again*** (Matthew 7:1–2).

Example of Use: Restaurant chefs have always prized vanilla bean paste for an intense flavor you just can't get with extract. Now the paste is available to home cooks as well. Use it **measure for measure** in place of the liquid. ("Not Just Plain Vanilla. [Front Burner: What's New, What's Hot, What's Cooking]. [Vanilla Bean Paste for Cooking]," Feb. 1, 2002, *Good Housekeeping*)

Meek shall inherit the earth, The

Means: A quality of gentleness and humility that God will vindicate

Biblical Text: *Blessed are **the meek**: for they **shall inherit the earth*** (Matthew 5:5).

Example of Use: The geek shall inherit the earth. The science-club presidents with the bowl haircuts are laughing all the way to the bank (with the trophy blonde sitting in the passenger seat of a tricked-out Porsche). Bill Gates and the dot-com boom brought unimaginable credibility, fabulous wealth and enormous power to the pocket-protector set. ("Nerds Make Calculated Leap to Top," Greg Morago, May 6, 2007, *The Record*, Bergen County, NJ)

Melchizedek

Means: A person greatly admired; A mysterious king of the OT

Biblical Text: *And **Melchizedek** king of Salem brought forth bread and wine: and he was the priest of the most high God. And he blessed him, and said, Blessed be Abram of the most high God, possessor of heaven and earth: And blessed be the most high God, which hath delivered thine enemies into thy hand. And he gave him tithes of all* (Genesis 14:18–20).

Example of Use: Melchizedek is a virtual nation set up in 1990. (The name comes from the Old Testament's "king of righteousness," who blessed Abraham.) ("Answer Man: In Search of Virtual Countries," John Kelly, Apr. 9, 2006, *The Washington Post*)

Mene, mene, tekel, upharsin

Means: A warning of impending doom

Biblical Text: *Then was the part of the hand sent from him; and this writing was written. And this is the writing that was written, **MENE, MENE, TEKEL, UPHARSIN**. This is the interpretation of the thing: MENE; God hath numbered thy kingdom, and finished it. TEKEL; Thou art weighed in the balances, and art found wanting. PERES; Thy kingdom is divided, and given to the Medes and Persians* (Daniel 5:24–28).

Example of Use: Hirst is not a genius; Hirst is a bloke of low cunning and high vanity who, having had the good fortune to become a multimillionaire, has sycophantic courtiers who encourage him to indulge every whim, whether or not within his aesthetic capacity—and this gigantic figure was not. No doubt these minions greet him with "Oh King, Live for ever," as did Belshazzar's, but I would like to be the critic who writes "**Mene, mene, tekel, upharsin**" upon his bathroom wall, wryly translated into English for King James as ". . . art weighed in the balances and art found wanting." ("The Royal Academy

Sells Its Soul," Brian Sewell, June 9, 2006, *The Evening Standard*, London)

Merry heart is good medicine, A

Means: A positive, happy attitude helps to keep one healthy in mind and body

Biblical Text: *A merry heart doeth good like a medicine: but a broken spirit drieth the bones* (Proverbs 17:22).

Example of Use: Cheer up. Researchers have confirmed what a Bible proverb set forth long ago: **A merry heart doeth good like a medicine.** Higher levels of optimism can cut the risk of cardiovascular death in half, said a Dutch study published yesterday in the *Archives of Internal Medicine*, a journal of the American Medical Association. ("Cheers to Expectations and Heart Health; Dutch Study Finds Optimism Can Halve Risk of Cardiovascular Death," Mar. 1, 2006, *The Washington Times*)

Mess of pottage

Means: An item of relatively little value exchanged for something of greater value

Biblical Text: *And Jacob said, Swear to me this day; and he sware unto him: and he sold his birthright unto Jacob. Then Jacob gave Esau bread and **pottage** of lentiles; and he did eat and drink, and rose up, and went his way: thus Esau despised his birthright* (Genesis 25:31–34).

Example of Use: Lew Perkins and The Suits on Mount Oread stirred up a **mess of pottage** when they shifted the Nov. 24 Kansas-Missouri football game from the KU campus to Kansas City. That's supposed to dump a million bucks or so into the Jayhawk cash drawer. ("KU-MU Moved Before," Bill Mayer, July 27, 2007, *Journal-World,* Lawrence, KS)

Messiah

Means: One who is anticipated as, regarded as, or professes to be a deliverer, savior, or liberator

Biblical Text: *But Jesus held his peace. And the high priest answered and said unto him, I adjure thee by the living God, that thou tell us whether thou be the **Christ** (**Messiah**), the Son of God. Jesus saith unto him, Thou hast said* (Matthew 26:63–64b).

Example of Use: This is no ordinary man but a **messiah** for the missing children of Pakistan. Anwar Khokhar, who served as a barber to then Pakistani prime minister Zulfikar Ali Bhutto, has reunited over 8,500 children with their parents since he took up the cause two decades ago. ("Pakistani Man a **Messiah** for Missing Kids," Dec. 31, 2010, *Hindustan Times*, New Delhi, India)

M

Methuselah

Means: Reference to the oldest man in the Bible

Biblical Text: *And all the days of **Methuselah** were nine hundred sixty and nine years: and he died* (Genesis 5:27).

Example of Use: Then came the men's combined, the downhill-and-slalom contest that determines the best all-around skier in the world. The story line was the battle between two likable, slightly grizzled Norwegian comrades who have dominated the sport for years, Lasse Kjus and Kjetil Andre Aamodt, vs. an upstart American, Bode Miller—with a creaking, **old-as-Methuselah**, 35-year-old Swiss guy named Accola thrown in to preserve the pathetic, the-older-I-get-the-faster-I-was delusions of middle-aged male spectators. ("Flight of the Wonder Boy: If Ski Jump Hero Simon Ammann Never Grows Up, We Won't Mind," Gary Kamiya, Feb. 14, 2002, salon.com)

Milk

Means: Elementary instruction, as contrasted to more sophisticated instruction

Biblical Text: *For when for the time ye ought to be teachers, ye have need that one teach you again which be the first principles of the oracles of God; and are become such as have need of **milk**, and not of strong meat. For every one that useth **milk** is unskilful in the word of righteousness: for he is a babe* (Hebrews 5:12–13).

Example of Use: About ten years ago an anchor man had received a 16 mm color film of the motorcade with a fuzzy view of the famous window where Oswald supposedly fired. Yes, it was fuzzy, but it appeared there were two men in white shirts moving around up there as the motorcade turned in front of the building. The anchor man was giddy with this legacy and was going to rush the film to Washington D.C. the next morning—and soon as he got the results we would get an immediate update on that incredible finding. He's still around, but have heard nothing more about that film. ("We Have Been Fed with **Milk, Not Meat**," By "Ff—150," Sept. 23, 2003, www.freerepublic.com)

Milk and honey

Means: Abundance, especially of life's necessities

Biblical Text: *And I am come down to deliver them out of the hand of the Egyptians, and to bring them up out of that land unto a good land and a large, unto a land flowing with **milk and honey*** (Exodus 3:8).

Example of Use: Can any soul out there in **milk and honey** land, please try to explain to my humble self why our overpaid, self opinionated politicians can't manage on pounds 61,000, plus high expenses and extra housing freebies, a year? ("Time to Wake Up," June 30, 2008, *Grimsby Telegraph*, UK)

Millstone around one's neck, A

Means: Any heavy mental or emotional burden

Biblical Text: *But whoso shall offend one of these little ones which believe in me, it were better for him that **a millstone were hanged about his neck**, and that he were drowned in the depth of the sea* (Matthew 18:6).

Example of Use: Mortgages have traditionally been regarded as a 25-year **millstone around the neck** of homeowners. ("Personal Finance: Here's Why the Mortgage **Millstone** Is Just a Myth," John Cranage, May 15, 2004, *The Birmingham Post*, England)

Mind, Come into (or Enter one's)

Means: To become aware; to occur to one

Biblical Text: *But they set their abominations in the house, which is called by my name, to defile it. And they built the high places of Baal, which are in the valley of the son of Hinnom, to cause their sons and their daughters to pass through the fire unto Molech; which I commanded them not, neither **came it into my mind**, that they should do this abomination, to cause Judah to sin* (Jeremiah 32:34–35). See also Jer. 19:5.

Example of Use: With the pressure building around him, University of Miami coach Larry Coker stayed upbeat and remained resolute Monday that he is the right coach for the Hurricanes, he will respect what the administration decides about his future and he will remain coach unless someone tells him otherwise. "That's never **entered my mind**, to resign," Coker said. "I don't do that." ("Coker Will Not Resign," Nov. 21, 2006, *Miami Herald*)

Molech

Means: Reference to an OT god to whom adherents sacrificed their children in worship

Biblical Text: *And thou shalt not let any of thy seed pass through the fire to **Molech**, neither shalt thou profane the name of thy God: I am the L*ORD (Leviticus 18:21).

Example of Use: Unless drastic action is taken with the ruling party at the forefront, South Africa will continue to sacrifice its children to **Molech**. ("The AIDS Orphans of South Africa," Carol Landman, Nov. 1, 2002, *Contemporary Review*)

Money changers

Means: People who deal with money illegally or immorally

Biblical Text: *Jesus went into the temple, and began to cast out them that sold and bought in the temple, and overthrew the tables of the **moneychangers**, and the seats of them that sold doves* (Mark 11:15).

Example of Use: "Fighting Bob" La Follette lives in all of us who call Wisconsin home. Fighting Bob and his allies threw the **money changers** out of the people's temple. ("What 'Fighting Bob' Means Today," Mike McCabe, June 14, 2005, *The Capital Times*, Madison, WI)

More blessed to give than to receive, It is

Means: Giving to others brings more blessing than does receiving.

Biblical Text: *I have shewed you all things, how that so labouring ye ought to support the weak, and to remember the words of the Lord God, how he said, **It is more blessed to give than to receive*** (Acts 20:35).

M

Example of Use: Syracuse University professor Arthur C. Brooks said he has the data to prove the biblical adage: "**It is more blessed to give than to receive.**" "Perhaps it's not so profound, but it's kind of nice when social science backs up Scripture," [said] Brooks, director of the Nonprofit Studies Program at Syracuse University's Maxwell School of Citizenship and Public Affairs. . . . Brooks said charitable giving—both in money and time—helps the economy, increases the giver's happiness and can lead to a healthier and longer life. ("Giving Boosts the Economy and Giver," Mariam Jukaku, Mar. 23, 2007, *The Post-Standard*, Syracuse, NY)

More precious than rubies

Means: To be more valuable than earthly wealth

Biblical Text: *Happy is the man that findeth wisdom, and the man that getteth understanding. For the merchandise of it is better than the merchandise of silver, and the gain thereof than fine gold. She is **more precious than rubies**: and all the things thou canst desire are not to be compared unto her* (Proverbs 3:13–15).

Example of Use: I am well aware that there are social workers, particularly in the field of mental health, who work tirelessly to help the most disadvantaged members of the community. They are to be **prized above rubies**, even when they have to do things we may not like. But too often the wishes of some of their colleagues seem to be rubber-stamped by courts which are supposed to weigh evidence. ("Bureaucratic Cruelty That Has Pulled Apart a Loving Couple," Denise Robertson, June 13, 2006, *The Journal*, Newcastle, England)

Moses

Means: Someone who is a great leader

Biblical Text: *And the child grew, and she brought him unto Pharaoh's daughter, and he became her son. And she called his name **Moses**: and she said, Because I drew him out of the water* (Exodus 2:10).

Example of Use: For 38 years conservatives have been wandering in the desert, looking for a **Moses**. ("A **Moses** for GOP Conservatives State Sen. Patrick O'Malley Is True to Right's Agenda," Thomas Roeser, Jan. 19, 2002, *Chicago Sun-Times*)

Moses basket

Means: A basket made for carrying a baby

Biblical Text: *And when she could not longer hide him, she took for him an **ark of bulrushes**, and daubed it with slime and with pitch, and put the child [Moses] therein; and she laid it in the flags by the river's brink* (Exodus 2:3).

Example of Use: On the kitchen table in Annabelle Bond's Kensington home is a gingham-lined **Moses basket**. Lying inside is the adventure woman's daughter Isabella, born three weeks ago at London's Portland Hospital. ("I'm Going It Alone; Climber Annabelle Bond Talks for the First Time . . . ," Sophie Goodchild, Oct. 2, 2007, *Evening Standard*, London)

Moses' rod

Means: A powerful tool, similar to Moses' rod that he used to perform miracles in the OT

Biblical Text: *And the LORD said unto **Moses**, Wherefore criest thou unto me? speak unto the children of Israel, that they go forward: lift thou up thy **rod**, and stretch out thine hand over the*

sea, and divide it: and the children of Israel shall go on dry ground through the midst of the sea (Exodus 14:15–16).

Example of Use: Vouchers, I know, have become the **Moses' rod** of politics: capable of dividing the electorate as efficiently as Moses parted the Red Sea. Democrats and the institutions that support them—labor, teachers, civil rights organizations—are overwhelmingly anti-voucher. ("Give Poor Students a Choice," William Raspberry, Sept. 15, 2003, *The Washington Post*)

Mote in one's eye, A

Means: A small fault in someone else as perceived by one with even greater faults who is unaware of them or who chooses to ignore them

Biblical Text: *And why beholdest thou* **the mote that is in thy brother's eye**, *but considerest not the beam that is in thine own eye?* (Matthew 7:3).

M

Example of Use: An important element of what the world calls evil is our failure to see an aspect of ourselves in others' behavior, especially in their bad behavior. **The mote in his eye** is the beam in mine, and to acknowledge that fact is essential to achieving ordinary human goodness. ("Serial Killers, Evil, and Us," Robert I. Simon, Sept. 22, 2000, *National Forum*)

Moth and rust

Means: The natural effect of decay that destroys something or makes it worthless

Biblical Text: *Lay not up for yourselves treasures upon earth, where* **moth and rust** *doth corrupt, and where thieves break through and steal: But lay up for yourselves treasures in heaven, where neither* **moth nor rust** *doth corrupt, and where thieves do not break through nor steal* (Matthew 6:19–20).

Example of Use: As unfortunate events recently revealed, structures don't last—mere bad weather can ruin a house. True history should be and is always organic, evidenced when cultures empower their storytellers. That is a foundation worth building on—one that **moth and rust** cannot destroy. ("St. Charles Homeowner's Rights Are Important," Tony Myles, Sept. 2, 2007, *Daily Herald,* Arlington Heights, IL)

Mount Sinai

Means: Reference to the mountain on which Moses and God communicated in the OT

Biblical Text: *In the third month, when the children of Israel were gone forth out of the land of Egypt, the same day came they into the wilderness of **Sinai*** (Exodus 19:1).

Example of Use: Sinai Hospital is celebrating the second anniversary of its CyberKnife Center on a very successful note. ("CyberKnife® Center at **Sinai** Hospital Celebrates Second Anniversary; Strong Growth in Radiosurgery Treatments Sparked by Dramatic Expansion in Extracranial Procedures," June 29, 2005, PR Newswire)

Much learning makes you mad

Means: Excessive study causes one to become wildly excited or irrational

Biblical Text: *And as he thus spake for himself, Festus said with a loud voice, Paul, thou art beside thyself; **much learning doth make thee mad*** (Acts 26:24).

Example of Use: Much education doth make one mad, I said. Uncle Gates sucked his teeth while considering this. You botched it, he said after a while. You misappropriated that from the New Testament. **Much learning doth make thee**

mad. ("Lost in Uttar Pradesh," Evan S. Connell, Dec. 1, 2005, *Harper's Magazine*)

Much study is a weariness of the flesh

Means: Excessive study is marked by physical tiredness

Biblical Text: *And further, by these, my son, be admonished: of making many books there is no end; and* **much study is a weariness of the flesh** (Ecclesiastes 12:12).

Example of Use: Of the making of many books about Abraham Lincoln there is no end. But the rest of this updated proverb from Ecclesiastes may be inapplicable: **Much study of these books is not necessarily a weariness of the flesh**. New research, new perspectives, new questions and new answers to old questions about this complex and endlessly fascinating man continue to inspire books that are a stimulation of the mind, if not also of the flesh. ("Top Gun" [a review of three recent books on Abraham Lincoln: *Lincoln's War: The Untold Story of America's Greatest President as Commander in Chief*; *Lincoln's Emancipation Proclamation: The End of Slavery in America*; *Lincoln's Last Months*], James M. McPherson, June 14, 2004, *The Nation*)

Multitude of sins, Hide a

Means: Conceal many bad deeds or wickedness

Biblical Text: *But the end of all things is at hand: be ye therefore sober, and watch unto prayer. And above all things have fervent charity among yourselves: for charity shall* **cover the multitude of sins** (1 Peter 4:7–8). See also James 5:20.

Example of Use: What other appeal does the tie have? According to Jon Snow, they can be both the focal point of an outfit and **hide a multitude of sins**. An extravagant tie draws attention away from a below-standard suit and solves the problem of the unsightly male neck. ("Is the Tie Still a Necessary Sartorial and Professional Statement? The Big Question," Michael Savage, July 10, 2007, *The Independent,* London)

Mustard seed

Means: A small thing capable of great development or growth

Biblical Text: *And he said, Whereunto shall we liken the king-dom of God? or with what comparison shall we compare it? It is like **a grain of mustard seed**, which, when it is sown in the earth, is less than all the seeds that be in the earth: But when it is sown, it groweth up, and becometh greater than all herbs, and shooteth out great branches; so that the fowls of the air may lodge under the shadow of it* (Mark 4:30–32).

Example of Use: It's true: I've become something of a spiritual couch potato in the last few years. The only time I can muster a **mustard seed** of discipline is during Lent. Then it's right back to the couch. ("Confessions of a Spiritual Couch Potato," Jim Loney, July 3, 2005, *Catholic New Times*)

Mustard seed, Faith the size of a

Means: A small amount of faith, especially when compared to the task to which it relates

Biblical Text: *And Jesus said unto them, Because of your unbe-lief: for verily I say unto you, If ye have **faith as a grain of mus-tard seed**, ye shall say unto this mountain, Remove hence to yonder place; and it shall remove; and nothing shall be impossi-ble unto you* (Matthew 17:20). See also Luke 17:6.

Example of Use: An entrepreneur needs a passion for owning a piece of the American dream and **faith "the size of a mus-tard seed."** ("All You Need Is **Faith the Size of a Mustard Seed:**

M

The Franchise Community Can Attract More Minority and Women Entrepreneurs by Using Faith—Focus, Anticipation, Initiative, Time and Harmony," Robert Wallace, Nov. 1, 2001, *Franchising World*)

Muzzle the ox

Means: Not to pay for work that is done or not to reward someone appropriately; to expect that someone will work for nothing

Biblical Text: *For the scripture saith, **thou shalt not muzzle the ox** that treadeth out the corn. And, The labourer is worthy of his reward* (1 Timothy 5:18). See also Deut. 25:4; 1 Cor. 9:9.

Example of Use: "**Don't muzzle the ox** that treads the corn" advises the Old Testament, yet Congress and the President have refused to return even a small portion of the excess taxation (budget surplus) to those who have created it through their hard work and creativity. ("IPI Asks: Budget Balanced Even without Social Security—What Excuse Remains to Delay Tax Cuts?" Oct. 15, 1999, *US Newswire*)

M

RAISING CAIN

N

"NINTH PLAGUE OF EGYPT"

Naboth's vineyard

Means: A particularly fruitful ground, especially if coveted by someone other than its owner

Scripture Reference: *And the word of the Lord came to Elijah the Tishbite, saying, Arise, go down to meet Ahab king of Israel, which is in Samaria: behold, he is in the **vineyard of Naboth**, whither he is gone down to possess it. And thou shalt speak unto him, saying, Thus saith the Lord, Hast thou killed, and also taken possession? And thou shalt speak unto him, saying, Thus saith the Lord, In the place where dogs licked the blood of **Naboth** shall dogs lick thy blood, even thine* (1 Kings 21:17–19).

Example of Use: Although Rupert did not get Arley Cottage, he did successfully bid for a couple of smaller lots, including a second arboretum called **Naboth's Vineyard** which he hopes to renovate and open to the public. ("How I Had to Bid against My Own Nephew to Keep Our Family Home. Three Sisters Opted to Share Their Mother's Cottage, but the Decision Led 16 Years Later to a Battle in the High Court and an Agonising Auction," Ross Clark, Aug. 24, 2003, *Mail on Sunday*, London)

Naked I came, naked I go

Means: Just as one enters the world with nothing, one will die with nothing.

Biblical Text: *Then Job arose, and rent his mantle, and shaved his head, and fell down upon the ground, and worshipped, And said, **Naked came I out of my mother's womb, and naked shall I return thither**: the Lord gave, and the Lord hath taken away; blessed be the name of the Lord* (Job 1:20–21). See also Eccl. 5:15.

Example of Use: During three years of occupation by the Wehrmacht troops, seventeen thousand Jews in Uman would lie down under the bullets, filling the neighboring ravines and gullies with their bodies. Why would they calmly undress while the rifles were loaded? Why would they accept their death without murmur? Would they really come to realize the justice of Ecclesiastes's words: "**As he came forth of his mother's womb, naked shall he return to go as he came**"? But I don't want to get ahead of myself. ("No Kith, No Kin," Emil Draitser, Jan. 1, 2003, *Partisan Review*)

Name for oneself, Make a

Means: Achieve distinction, become prominent or well known

Biblical Text: *And they said, Go to, let us build us a city and a tower, whose top may reach unto heaven; and **let us make us a name**, lest we be scattered abroad upon the face of the whole earth* (Genesis 11:4).

Example of Use: Far from the television studios of New York and the cauldron of political ambition that is the U.S. Senate, Illinois Gov. Rod Blagojevich is trying to **make a name for himself** as an innovative, against-the-grain, values-minded Midwestern governor, sometimes angering his own family and his Democratic Party in the process. ("Governor Positions Himself for Possible Presidential Run: Blagojevich Is Trying to **Make a Name for Himself**," Steven Thomma, May 9, 2005, *Belleville News-Democrat*, IL)

Name in vain, Take one's

Means: To use someone's name lightly or profanely; to use a name in making flippant or dishonest oaths; to use someone's name in a way that shows a lack of respect

Biblical Text: *Thou shalt not take the name of the Lord thy God in vain; for the Lord will not hold him guiltless that **taketh his name in vain*** (Exodus 20:7).

Example of Use: Ol' Roy took Kansas to four Final Fours in 14 seasons there. . . . Then he left for North Carolina, his alma mater, after saying three years earlier he planned to finish his career at Kansas. They still **take his name in vain** in Kansas for leaving them with no national titles and a trail of tears. ("Time for Ol' Roy to Make Last Cut," John Feinstein, Apr. 3, 2005, *The Washington Post*)

Name is better than riches, A good

Means: A good reputation is far more valuable than tangible wealth

Biblical Text: *A good name is more desirable than great riches; to be esteemed is better than silver or gold* (Proverbs 22:1).

Example of Use: We believe our company now has a good name in two senses. First, we have developed a good new name—Sparta WoodWorks. Second, we have built a good name for more than a century. And that is what is really most important to us. As a wise man once said, "**A good name is more desirable than great riches**." ("Changing Your Name for All the Right Reasons: Perhaps the Only Thing Harder than Settling on a Name for a Company Is Having to Change It after It's Become Well Established," R. Les Tubb, June 1, 2004, *Wood & Wood Products*)

Narrow way

Means: A way of life exemplified by high standards and moral behavior, especially a pattern of living conducted by relatively few people

Biblical Text: *Enter ye at the strait gate: for wide is the gate, and broad is the way, that leadeth to destruction, and many there be which go in thereat: Because strait is the gate, and **narrow is the***

way, which leadeth unto life, and few there be that find it (Matthew 7:13–14).

Example of Use: Scribes of this order not only get stuck writing year-end, top-10 compilations, they also must predict key happenings for the coming year. Well, as a young cat (or cad, if you prefer) I studied palm reading informally decades ago as a way to talk with girls. In an effort to better myself, I later abandoned that practice and others to walk a more **narrow way**. ("Agricultural Forecasts for 2007 Are Ripe for the Picking," Jan. 3, 2007, *The Topeka Capital-Journal*, KS)

Nathan

Means: Someone who confronts another with news or information about him, especially if it relates to the person's sin or misconduct

Biblical Text: *And* **Nathan** *said to David, Thou art the man. . . . And David said unto Nathan, I have sinned against the Lord. And* **Nathan** *said unto David, The Lord also hath put away thy sin; thou shalt not die. Howbeit, because by this deed thou hast given great occasion to the enemies of the Lord to blaspheme, the child also that is born unto thee shall surely die* (2 Samuel 12:7, 13–14).

Example of Use: Most obviously, Joseph Lieberman's devout practice of Judaism has caught the attention of voters and powerbrokers alike. Though Lieberman makes some politicos nervous with his public views on matters moral and religious, most everybody recognizes him as the guy who rebuked Bill Clinton for sexual promiscuity, much as the biblical prophet **Nathan** once chided King David. ("Morals, Religion Return to Political Arena," Frederick Niedner, Sept. 24, 2000, *Post-Tribune*, IN)

Nazarite

Means: Sometimes who keeps a sacred vow, especially to refrain from drinking alcohol and having one's hair cut

Biblical Text: *Speak unto the children of Israel, and say unto them, When either man or woman shall separate themselves to vow a vow of a* **Nazarite**, *to separate themselves unto the Lord: All the days of the vow of his separation there shall no razor come upon his head: until the days be fulfilled, in the which he separateth himself unto the Lord, he shall be holy, and shall let the locks of the hair of his head grow* (Numbers 6:2, 5).

Example of Use: Bowden alleged religious discrimination after the department refused to allow him to wear his hair in dreadlocks, which he said was part of his **Nazarite** beliefs. Bowden was suspended by the police department in March 2007; he was never fired and currently works in the police department's check fraud section, Hoffman wrote. ("Baltimore Police Dept. Settles with 2 Officers," Danny Jacobs, Sept. 3, 2009, *The Daily Record*, Baltimore)

New Jerusalem

Means: Reference to the new earthly city to be made by God when he triumphs over Satan at the end of time; a new community, especially if it displays high ideals, standards, or glory

Biblical Text: *And I saw a new heaven and a new earth: for the first heaven and the first earth were passed away; and there was no more sea. And I John saw the holy city,* **new Jerusalem**, *coming down from God out of heaven, prepared as a bride adorned for her husband* (Revelation 21:1–2). See also Rev. 3:12.

Example of Use: As [Rob] Andrew moved into Twickenham, head coach Andy Robinson promised him that he was building a **new Jerusalem** for English rugby. ("England Expects

Andrew to Make Toughest Decision; Elite Rugby Director Must Wield the Axe for Nation's Sake," Malcolm Folley, Nov. 26, 2006, *The Mail on Sunday,* London)

New song

Means: A fresh awareness of confidence or hope

Biblical Text: *And he hath put a **new song** in my mouth, even praise unto our God: many shall see it, and fear, and shall trust in the Lord* (Psalm 40:3).

Example of Use: "The urban woman facing these kinds of pressures deserves a **new song**—a song of hope," said Parker. ("Island/Def Jam Rap Song Advocates Violence against Pregnant Women: Urban Women Deserve a **New Song**, Care Net Says," July 1, 2004, *US Newswire*)

New wine into old bottles

Means: Something new or innovative added to an existing system or organization

Biblical Text: *And no man putteth **new wine into old bottles**: else the new wine doth burst the bottles, and the wine is spilled, and the bottles will be marred: but new wine must be put into new bottles* (Mark 2:22). See also Matt. 9:17; Luke 5:37.

Example of Use: However, without a hard look at the actors in the system and the incentives facing those actors, these fads will prove the educational equivalent of pouring **new wine into old bottles**. ("Fixing Teacher Professional Development: A Broken System of Professional Learning Requires Decisive Action in Order to Ensure Wise Expenditure of Limited Resources," Heather C. Hill, Mar. 1, 2009, *Phi Delta Kappan*)

Nimrod, a mighty hunter

Means: An adept hunter

Biblical Text: *And Cush begat **Nimrod**: he began to be **a mighty one** in the earth* (Genesis 10:8).

Example of Use: The first RAF **Nimrod** to return from operational duties around Afghanistan touched down safely yesterday. The hunt and kill aircraft was involved in unspecified duties for five weeks in the continuing war against terrorism. ("War on Terror: Home of the 'Mighty Hunter' for a Safe Christmas away from the War; Winging In: **Nimrod** Crews Reunited with Families after Afghan Action," Dec. 21, 2001, *The Birmingham Post*, England)

Ninth plague of Egypt

Means: Darkness, literally or figuratively

N

Biblical Text: *And Moses stretched forth his hand toward heaven; and there was **a thick darkness in all the land of Egypt** three days* (Exodus 10:22).

Example of Use: It was like the **ninth plague** of Egypt on Friday night for thousands of observant residents in Jerusalem's Har Nof and Givat Shaul neighborhoods, when a high-power line malfunctioned, leaving them without electricity for nearly two hours. ("News in Brief," Marilyn Henry, Judy Siegel, and Danna Harman, Nov. 22, 1998, *Jerusalem Post*)

No man can serve two masters

Means: One cannot give full and satisfactory allegiance to more than one authority

Biblical Text: ***No man can serve two masters**: for either he will hate the one, and love the other; or else he will hold to the one,* *and despise the other. Ye cannot serve God and mammon* (Matthew 6:24). See also Luke 16:13.

Example of Use: Rami Zur recognizes it's a difficult concept for people to grasp. You know, **no man can serve two masters**. Still, one of the world's best flat-water kayakers wants you to understand something: Just because he competed for Israel at the 2000 Olympics doesn't make him any less loyal to the team he will represent this August at the Athens Games. He was, after all, born in Berkeley, Calif., 27 years ago. So what if his parents moved with him back to Israel when he was three weeks old? ("Kayaker Proud to Represent Two Countries," Mike Berardino, June 12, 2004, *South Florida Sun-Sentinel*, Fort Lauderdale)

No respecter of persons

Means: Someone who treats everyone the same, without being influenced by factors such as social status or wealth

Biblical Text: *Then Peter opened his mouth, and said, Of a truth I perceive that God is **no respecter of persons*** (Acts 10:34).

Example of Use: The rain has proven once again that it is indeed **no respecter of persons**, be they rich or poor. How else to explain why a steady drizzle intensified into a pouring rain during the very half-hour of Donald J. Trump's visit to downtown White Plains, where he celebrated the rising of a 35-story, 212-condominium tower that bears his name within the City Center complex? ("Trump Puts on the Glitz in White Plains. [Fly on the Wall]," Aug. 23, 2004, *Westchester County Business Journal*, NY)

No rest for the wicked

Means: The wicked will experience many woes because of their wickedness and will be unable to rest; Often used in a jocular, self-deprecating way, implying that one is wicked and, therefore, is too busy to rest

Biblical Text: *There is **no peace**, saith my God, **to the wicked*** (Isaiah 57:21).

Example of Use: There's no rest for the wicked—or, thankfully, for those of us in Sarasota who love theater. The 2006–2007 theater season was the most jam-packed yet, with close to 60 productions on our main stages, and just weeks after it finished, several theater groups began staging summer productions. ("Critic's Choice: Kay Kipling Picks the Best of Our Busiest-Ever Theater Season," Kay Kipling, June 22, 2007, *Sarasota Magazine*)

N

Noah's ark

Means: A place or thing holding many animals

Biblical Text: *And God said unto **Noah**, The end of all flesh is come before me; for the earth is filled with violence through them; and, behold, I will destroy them with the earth. Make thee an ark of gopher wood; rooms shalt thou make in the **ark**, and shalt pitch it within and without with pitch. And of every living thing of all flesh, two of every sort shalt thou bring into the **ark**, to keep them alive with thee; they shall be male and female. Of fowls after their kind, and of cattle after their kind, of every creeping thing of the earth after his kind, two of every sort shall come unto thee, to keep them alive* (Genesis 6:13–14, 19–20).

Example of Use: Dr. Fisher's *Life on the Ark* is the autobiographical story of Lester E. Fisher and his adventures (and misadventures) arising from his responsibilities of being the director of the famous Lincoln Park Zoo. ("Dr. Fisher's *Life on the Ark*," Sept. 1, 2004, *Wisconsin Bookwatch*)

Noah's wife

Means: Reference to the wife of Noah in the OT, whose name is unknown

Biblical Text: *In the selfsame day entered Noah, and Shem, and Ham, and Japheth, the sons of Noah, and* **Noah's wife**, *and the three wives of his sons with them, into the ark* (Genesis 7:13).

Example of Use: Ten percent of Americans think Joan of Arc was **Noah's wife**. (For the record, I'm not one of them.) ("America by the Numbers," Jim Shea, Dec. 4, 2007, *The Virginian Pilot*)

Noonday demon

Means: Acedia, or despondency

Biblical Text: *Thou shalt not be afraid for the terror by night; nor for the arrow that flieth by day; Nor for the pestilence that walketh in darkness; nor for* **the destruction that wasteth at noonday**. *A thousand shall fall at thy side, and ten thousand at thy right hand; but it shall not come nigh thee* (Psalm 91:5–7).

Example of Use: This persistent restlessness is not a new experience. Sixteen hundred years ago, the Christian monks of the Egyptian desert noticed a similar phenomenon. When they were at work, they felt drawn to prayer; when they prayed, they felt drawn to work; when they settled in one monastery, they became convinced that true spirituality could be found only in the monastery down the road. Because such feelings struck hardest in the middle of the day, monks associated them with the "**noonday demon**" in Ps. 91. The monk's task was not to flee from this demon, but to stay put and wrestle with it. ("Called to the Everyday," Amy Carr, July 1, 1999, *Sojourners*)

Not done in a corner

Means: Not done secretly

Biblical Text: *For the king knoweth of these things, before whom also I speak freely: for I am persuaded that none of these things are hidden from him; for this thing was **not done in a corner*** (Acts 26:26).

Example of Use: For now, it is enough to take note of the awesome scale of these demonstrations, especially in Britain, Spain and Italy—the three European governments that have been most supportive of current U.S. policy and to consider, as the Book of Acts in the New Testament pithily puts it, "This thing was **not done in a corner.**" ("Millions March but War Will Come," Feb. 17, 2003, United Press International)

Not worthy to untie one's shoes

Means: An expression of profound humility

Biblical Text: *John answered, saying unto them all, I indeed baptize you with water; but one mightier than I cometh, **the latchet of whose shoes I am not worthy to unloose**: he shall baptize you with the Holy Ghost and with fire* (Luke 3:16).

Example of Use: In my opinion, Philip Chard is an educated fool who doesn't have the intestinal fortitude to tell it like it is but writes smooth things to make his readers feel good about themselves. His June 20 column did not please me. He's **not worthy to tie Dr. Laura's shoelaces.** His psyche needs to be tuned into what real truth is. ("Dr. Laura Has Faithful Following," June 26, 2000, *The Milwaukee Journal Sentinel*)

Nothing new under the sun, There is

Means: Everything we experience has happened to people who lived before us.

Biblical Text: *The thing that hath been, it is that which shall be; and that which is done is that which shall be done: and there is **no new thing under the sun*** (Ecclesiastes 1:9).

Example of Use: Most new insights all link back to these basic principles and it seems that **there really is nothing new under the sun**—technology might change slightly, we refine our technique and new jargon is introduced like new packaging. However the basic product is the same. ("Nothing New under the Sun," Laura Overton, July 1, 2006, *E.learning Age*)

Number of the beast (666)

Means: A satanic symbol

Biblical Text: *Here is wisdom. Let him that hath understanding count the number of the beast: for it is the number of a man; and his number is **Six hundred threescore and six*** (Revelation 13:18).

Example of Use: According to court documents, Duran's aliases were listed as Satan, Lucifer, Morning Star, Satan's Son, Anti-Jesus and **666**. He sports a tattoo on his forehead that reads "**666**." ("Self-Professed Satanist Faces Charge As Habitual Criminal," Audry Olmsted, Sept. 29, 2004, *El Defensor Chieftain*, Socorro County, New Mexico)

RAISING CAIN

O

"OUT OF THE MOUTH OF BABES"

O ye, of little faith

Means: A declaration to one who expresses doubt; sometimes used in a jocular fashion

Biblical Text: *And when he was entered into a ship, his disciples followed him. And, behold, there arose a great tempest in the sea, insomuch that the ship was covered with the waves: but he was asleep. And his disciples came to him, and awoke him, saying, Lord, save us: we perish. And he saith unto them, Why are ye fearful,* **O ye of little faith?** *Then he arose, and rebuked the winds and the sea; and there was a great calm. But the men marvelled, saying, What manner of man is this, that even the winds and the sea obey him!* (Matthew 8:23–27).

Example of Use: During recent years we oft heard that "there are only three or four carriers insuring general aviation—obviously, the market ain't working." **Oh, ye of little faith.** The market is alive and well in the insurance business, and is proving it. ("Insurance 101," Ralph Hood, Apr. 1, 2007, *Airport Business*)

O, that my adversary had written a book!

O

Means: A declaration stating that one wishes that his opponent had a written record that he could use against him

Biblical Text: *Oh that one would hear me! behold, my desire is, that the Almighty would answer me, and* **that mine adversary had written a book** (Job 31:35).

Example of Use: If only I knew of what I am accused! I am told he was asked if he had read my book, *The Tempting of America: The Political Seduction of the Law*, and he said, well, he had bought it. Of the two, that's the one I prefer. The absence of a paper trail may have been one the White House found attractive about John Roberts. I should have known, as the Bible has it in the Book of Job, "**Oh, that mine adversary had written a book**."

And the last thing you want to do is write a book. ("Former Supreme Court Nominee Robert Bork Delivers Remarks at the National Press Club," Robert Bork, Sept. 6, 2005, Washington Transcript Service)

Old men shall dream dreams

Means: People have hopes and dreams for the future, especially older ones

Biblical Text: *And it shall come to pass afterward, that I will pour out my spirit upon all flesh; and your sons and your daughters shall prophesy, your **old men shall dream dreams**, your young men shall see visions* (Joel 2:28). See also Acts 2:17.

Example of Use: This wonderful forum brought people together across generations, gender and life experience. It was never more passionate than when the old mentioned sea rights, or the young cited Biblical prophecy that **the old shall dream dreams** and the young see visions. ("Decolonisation, from the Sea-Grass Roots," Peter Jull, Dec. 1, 2003, *Arena Magazine*)

Old wives' tale

Means: Lore or myth passed on informally by word of mouth, often believed to be true

Biblical Text: *But refuse profane and **old wives' fables**, and exercise thyself rather unto godliness* (1 Timothy 4:7).

Example of Use: Frustrated couples often find themselves bombarded with **old wives' tales** and urban legends promising increased odds of fertility. ("Urban Legend? Old Wives' Tale?" Howard Ludwig, Sept. 21, 2008, *Post-Tribune*, IN)

Olive branch

Means: An emblem of peace

Biblical Text: *And the dove came in to him in the evening; and, lo, in her mouth was an **olive leaf** pluckt off: so Noah knew that the waters were abated from off the earth* (Genesis 8:11).

Example of Use: Libyan leader Moammar Gadhafi, once considered one of the world's most dangerous men, came to Europe for the first time in 15 years Tuesday, offering business deals and an **olive branch**—along with a veiled threat to return to the "days of explosive belts" if provoked by "evil" from the West. ("Gadhafi Offers an **Olive Branch**," Paul Geitner, Apr. 28, 2004, *The Milwaukee Journal Sentinel*)

On earth peace

Means: An expression of hope for peace in the world

Biblical Text: *Glory to God in the highest, and **on earth peace**, good will toward men* (Luke 2:14).

Example of Use: This Holiday Season, we need to step up to the plate and really Occupy **"Peace on Earth,** Goodwill to Men." (Sherry L. Ackerman, Ph.D., "Occupy **peace on earth**, good will to men," http://www.naturalnews.com/034473_peace_on_Earth_good_will_world.html#ixzz2AVkSMuf4, Dec. 24,2011)

Once for all

Means: Conclusively; for the last time

Biblical Text: *By the which will we are sanctified through the offering of the body of Jesus Christ **once for all*** (Hebrews 10:10).

Example of Use: German Chancellor Gerhard Schroeder said that the difference over the Iraq war was "over **once for all**." The remark came before a planned visit to Germany by U.S. President George W. Bush. ("Schroeder Says Difference over Iraq War Finally Over," Feb. 22, 2005, Xinhua News Agency)

One voice, With

Means: Unanimously, in complete agreement

Biblical Text: *And Moses came and told the people all the words of the LORD, and all the judgments: and all the people answered* **with one voice***, and said, All the words which the LORD hath said will we do* (Exodus 24:3). See also Acts 19:34; 24:21.

Example of Use: "Speak **with one voice**." That is Rule No. 1 for anyone asking for anything from any legislative body. It applies doubly to regions asking for money from a state government. (Journalism's Champions Must Speak **with One Voice**," Geneva Overholser, Jan. 1, 2002, *Columbia Journalism Review*)

Original sin

Means: The innate corruptness of human nature; an example of such corruption

Biblical Text: *As it is written,* **There is none righteous***, no, not one: There is none that understandeth,* **there is none that seeketh after God***. They are all gone out of the way, they are together become unprofitable;* **there is none that doeth good***, no, not one* (Romans 3:10–12).

Example of Use: A racial divide, once lived, dwells in the deepest parts of the psyche. This is what was captured by Barack Obama's pitch-perfect speech on race. Slavery was indeed America's "**original sin**." Of course "the brutal legacy of slavery and Jim Crow" lives on in forms of African-American humiliation and anger that smolder in ways incommunicable to whites. ("Beyond American **Original Sin**," Roger Cohen, Mar. 20, 2008, *International Herald Tribune*)

Our Father, who art in heaven

Means: The opening words of Jesus' model prayer he taught to his disciples

Biblical Text: *And he said unto them, When ye pray, say, **Our Father which art in heaven**, Hallowed be thy name. Thy kingdom come. Thy will be done, as in heaven, so in earth* (Luke 11:2). See also Matt. 6:9.

Example of Use: Our Father, who art in Washington. Mixing religion and development raises soul-searching questions. ("Keeping the Faith; World Bank. [Religion and Development]," Aug. 19, 2006, *The Economist*)

Out of the mouths of babes

Means: An expression used when a child makes a statement that seems unusually mature for his young age

Biblical Text: *O LORD, our Lord, how excellent is thy name in all the earth! who hast set thy glory above the heavens. **Out of the mouth of babes** and sucklings hast thou ordained strength because of thine enemies, that thou mightest still the enemy and the avenger* (Psalm 8:1–2). See also Matt. 21:15–16.

Example of Use: Out of the mouth of babes comes the wisdom of the ages. Samantha is all of 11 years old and is one of the leads in the production [the dance musical, "Hot Feet"], which features the terpsichorean talents of 19-year-old Vivian Nixon, who got her early training at Washington's Kirov Academy of Ballet. ("Talented beyond Their Years," Ann Geracimos, Mar. 31, 2006, *The Washington Times*)

Outer darkness

Means: Oblivion; a situation with few good prospects for improvement or advancement

Biblical Text: *For unto every one that hath shall be given, and he shall have abundance: but from him that hath not shall be taken away even that which he hath. And cast ye the unprofitable servant into* **outer darkness**: *there shall be weeping and gnashing of teeth* (Matthew 25:29–30). See also Matt. 8:11–12; 22:13.

Example of Use: Trent Lott, of course, had to go. That is fairly clear. This isn't: Precisely what are the transgressions for which Lott was cast into the **outer darkness**? The proximate sin, of course, was his statement made at Strom Thurmond's birthday bash that America would have been better off if that centenarian had been elected president when he ran on a segregationist platform in 1948: The response from his party was extraordinary. ("Sins of the Stone Throwers," William Raspberry, Dec. 23, 2002, *The Washington Post*)

Out-Herod Herod, To

Means: To be more vicious and murderous than even Herod the Great, as described in the Nativity story

Biblical Text: *Then* **Herod**, *when he saw that he was mocked of the wise men, was exceeding wroth, and sent forth, and* **slew all the children that were in Bethlehem, and in all the coasts thereof, from two years old and under,** *according to the time which he had diligently enquired of the wise men* (Matthew 2:16).

Example of Use: Hudson said the words of "Coventry Carol" came to him while watching Al Gore and Sen. Bill Bradley debating during the Democratic primaries, both "arguing over who was more committed to taking innocent life . . . attempting to '**out-Herod Herod**.'" ("NRL Convention Speakers Focus on Humanizing the Vulnerable," Liz Townsend, July 1, 2000, *National Right to Life News*)

Ox out of the pit, Pull one's

Means: To improve or rectify a situation, especially one of trouble

Biblical Text: *Which of you shall have an ass or an ox fallen into a pit, and will not straightway pull him out on the sabbath day? And they could not answer him again to these things* (Luke 14:5–6).

Example of Use: "As the mayor said, 'We're going to **get the ox out of the ditch.**'"("Donations Arriving, but Charleston Symphony Orchestra Goal Not Met," Dec. 5, 2006, *The Post and Courier*, Charleston, SC)

O

RAISING CAIN

P

"PILLAR OF SALT"

Painted woman

Means: A prostitute or a woman who dresses like a prostitute

Biblical Text: *And when Jehu was come to Jezreel, Jezebel heard of it; and **she painted her face**, and tired her head, and looked out at a window* (2 Kings 9:30).

Example of Use: An irony of a different sort is that makeup was traditionally a part of an upper-class Japanese woman's toilette, whereas in America in the early 20th century, manufacturers had to overcome the negative stereotype of a "**painted**" **woman** to sell their product to the masses. ("From Geisha to Grunge," Janet Koplos, Feb. 1, 2001, *Art in America*)

Pale horse, Behold a

Means: An expression signifying imminent death

Biblical Text: *And I looked, and **behold a pale horse**: and his name that sat on him was Death, and Hell followed with him. And power was given unto them over the fourth part of the earth, to kill with sword, and with hunger, and with death, and with the beasts of the earth* (Revelation 6:8).

P

Example of Use: That's right, my fellow man, our **pale horse** has arrived in the form of "irritable-male syndrome." The days of pre-menstrual syndrome have come to an end. We do not have cramps, but let the truth be revealed—we have feelings too. Researchers in Edinburgh, Scotland—once the stomping grounds of William Wallace—have found reason to believe that hormonal imbalances might lead to symptoms resembling the dreaded monster known as PMS. ("Column: Women's Ace Gets Trumped," Bill Bender, May 9, 2002, *University Wire*)

Parable of the talents

Means: A story Jesus told about using one's talents or abilities to the fullest extent

Biblical Text: *For the kingdom of heaven is as a man travelling into a far country, who called his own servants, and delivered unto them his goods. And unto one he gave five **talents**, to another two, and to another one; to every man according to his several ability; and straightway took his journey. Then he that had received the five **talents** went and traded with the same, and made them other five **talents**. And likewise he that had received two, he also gained other two. But he that had received one went and digged in the earth, and hid his lord's money. After a long time the lord of those servants cometh, and reckoneth with them. And so he that had received five **talents** came and brought other five **talents**, saying, Lord, thou deliveredst unto me five **talents**: behold, I have gained beside them five **talents** more. His lord said unto him, Well done, thou good and faithful servant: thou hast been faithful over a few things, I will make thee ruler over many things: enter thou into the joy of thy lord. He also that had received two **talents** came and said, Lord, thou deliveredst unto me two **talents**: behold, I have gained two other **talents** beside them. His lord said unto him, Well done, good and faithful servant; thou hast been faithful over a few things, I will make thee ruler over many things: enter thou into the joy of thy lord. Then he which had received the one **talent** came and said, Lord, I knew thee that thou art an hard man, reaping where thou hast not sown, and gathering where thou hast not strawed: And I was afraid, and went and hid thy **talent** in the earth: lo, there thou hast that is thine. His lord answered and said unto him, Thou wicked and slothful servant, thou knewest that I reap where I sowed not, and gather where I have not strawed: Thou oughtest therefore to have put my money to the exchangers, and then at*

P

*my coming I should have received mine own with usury. Take therefore the **talent** from him, and give it unto him which hath ten **talents**. For unto every one that hath shall be given, and he shall have abundance: but from him that hath not shall be taken away even that which he hath. And cast ye the unprofitable servant into outer darkness: there shall be weeping and gnashing of teeth* (Matthew 25:14–30).

Example of Use: Stewardship Partners will manage someone's money for a start-up fee of $100,000 (or more). The company has more than 600 clients. One of its teachings, based on the **Parable of the Talents**, is this: Fear not. In that parable from Matthew, one man buried his treasure, but because he did, his money didn't grow in value. Another man doubled his income. The preferred way is to double income, Leonard said. ("Rusty Leonard Monitors Values of Companies for Investors, Holds Nonprofits Accountable," Allison Kennedy, Sept. 29, 2007, *Columbus Ledger-Enquirer*, Columbus, GA)

Paradise

Means: Any place of complete bliss, delight and peace

Biblical Text: *I knew such a man, (whether in the body, or out of the body, I cannot tell: God knoweth;) How that he was caught up into **paradise**, and heard unspeakable words, which it is not lawful for a man to utter* (2 Corinthians 12:3–4).

Example of Use: A director of the Simon Wiesenthal Centre has described Austria as a "**paradise** for Nazi war criminals" and bitterly criticised its government and legal authorities for failing to bring suspected Holocaust perpetrators to justice. ("Nazi Hunter Denounces Austria as a 'Paradise for War Criminals,'" Tony Paterson, Feb. 2, 2006, *The Independent*, London)

Part the waters (or the sea)

Means: To make possible what seems impossible

Biblical Text: *Moses stretched out his hand over the sea; and the Lord caused the sea to go back by a strong east wind all that night, and made the sea dry land, and **the waters were divided*** (Exodus 14:21).

Example of Use: A judge **parted the waters** Thursday for a grocer's move to Towers Shopping Center, where Kroger is the dominant anchor. ("Judge Clears Way for Grocer to Move into Roanoke, Va., Retail Center," Jenny Kincaid, Dec. 10, 2004, *Roanoke Times,* VA)

Pass all understanding, To

Means: To exceed one's knowledge or comprehension of something

Biblical Text: *Be careful for nothing; but in every thing by prayer and supplication with thanksgiving let your requests be made known unto God. And the peace of God, which **passeth all understanding**, shall keep your hearts and minds through Christ Jesus* (Philippians 4:6–7).

Example of Use: [Announcement about lutefisk dinners:] Wednesday, Dec. 1: St. Olaf's Church, County O at Roosevelt Road, Dodge County, town of Ashippun. 3:30 to 8 p.m. or when the fish runs out. Adults $14, kids 5 to 10 $8, under 5 free. Lutefisk (or the cod that **passes all understanding**, as they call it), lefse, meatballs, rutabagas, cranberry salad, flatbrod and many cookies. Bake Sale and Third World Craft Shop from Milwaukee. ("Election? Packers? No, Lutefisk!!" Mike Miller, Oct. 14, 2004, *The Capital Times,* Madison, WI)

P

Pass by on the other side

Means: Ignore or avoid someone or something, especially when one is responsible, either explicitly or implicitly

Biblical Text: *And Jesus answering said, A certain man went down from Jerusalem to Jericho, and fell among thieves, which stripped him of his raiment, and wounded him, and departed, leaving him half dead. And by chance there came down a certain priest that way: and when he saw him, he **passed by on the other side*** (Luke 10:30–31).

Example of Use: It's inconceivable that a country as rich as ours should have so many needy and homeless people. But being good Samaritans, we don't **pass by on the other side**. Universal caring and sharing should end homelessness and poverty, bringing about peace and good will for all men all of the time. ("Peace Vigil Today," Maggie Peters, Dec. 24, 2004, *Wisconsin State Journal*, Madison, WI)

Pass on or away

Means: To cease to exist; to perish, disappear, or be dissolved

Biblical Text: *Heaven and earth shall **pass away**, but my words shall not pass away* (Matthew 24:35).

Example of Use: An estimated 565,000 U.S. veterans will **pass away** this year. This number will grow to 620,000 per year in 2008 before it starts to decline. ("A Wake-Up Call for Veterans. (Veterans Should Have a Right to Have Taps Played at Their Funerals)," Marilyn Moores, Jan. 1, 2001, *Saturday Evening Post*)

Pass under the rod

Means: To be closely scrutinized

Biblical Text: *And that which cometh into your mind shall not be at all, that ye say, We will be as the heathen, as the families of the countries, to serve wood and stone. As I live, saith the Lord GOD, surely with a mighty hand, and with a stretched out arm, and with fury poured out, will I rule over you: And I will bring you out from the people, and will gather you out of the countries wherein ye are scattered, with a mighty hand, and with a stretched out arm, and with fury poured out. And I will bring you into the wilderness of the people, and there will I plead with you face to face. Like as I pleaded with your fathers in the wilderness of the land of Egypt, so will I plead with you, saith the Lord GOD. And I will cause you to* **pass under the rod***, and I will bring you into the bond of the covenant: And I will purge out from among you the rebels, and them that transgress against me: I will bring them forth out of the country where they sojourn, and they shall not enter into the land of Israel: and ye shall know that I am the LORD* (Ezekiel 20:32–38).

Example of Use: I lived on the north end of the barracks close to the entrance, so I was among the first to **"pass under the rod."** The men ahead of me were taken by surprise and were fleeced right and left. While Nagatomi raked the money into a paper bag, his sidekick wrote a receipt for the valuables confiscated and insultingly handed it to the victim. When my turn came, I turned my pockets inside out to show I had nothing to contribute. (*Under the Shadow of the Rising Sun: The True Story of a Missionary Family's Survival and Faith*, Donald Ernest Mansell, Vesta West Mansell, 2003, Pacific Press Publishing, page 98)

Peace on earth

Means: An expression of desire for worldwide peace

Biblical Text: *And suddenly there was with the angel a multitude of the heavenly host praising God, and saying, Glory to God in the highest, and **on earth peace**, good will toward men* (Luke 2:13–14).

Example of Use: "In Pursuit of Finding True Happiness and **Peace on Earth** for Dilbert and Dilbert-like Individuals across the Globe, Cartoonist and Visionary Scott Adams Embarked on a Journey to Create 'Dilbert's Ultimate House' (DUH)," Sept. 27, 2004, PRNews

Peace, peace, when there is no peace

Means: Talk intended to deceive; a shallow prediction or proclamation intended to mislead or mollify

Biblical Text: *They have healed also the hurt of the daughter of my people slightly, saying, **Peace, peace; when there is no peace*** (Jeremiah 6:14).

Example of Use: At 10:30 the mob dragged the two bodies to Al-Manara Square, the town center, where an impromptu victory celebration began. Palestinian police then tried to remove film of the attack from reporters. **Peace, peace, when there is no peace**. ("Spending Blood on the Folly of Fools," Wesley Pruden, Oct. 13, 2000, *The Washington Times*)

Pearl of great price

Means: Something of great value, not necessarily monetarily

Biblical Text: *Again, the kingdom of heaven is like unto a merchant man, seeking goodly pearls: Who, when he had found one **pearl of great price**, went and sold all that he had, and bought it* (Matthew 13:45–46).

Example of Use: In 1990 my wife Patricia and I decided to get away from it all. The Eighties had been both easy and hard on us, as they had been on a lot of people. We had acquired much of what we had dreamed of having and worked to have, but we had lost more. Both of our fathers had died, along with my brother-in-law and one of my most beloved friends. A business I had no business starting had failed, as had both my hip joints. And, somewhere, Patricia and I had lost the cohesive, protective intimacy of the family life we had begun in 1964 with the birth of our first child, and which had been our ballast, our nourishment, our **pearl of great price** ever since. For a while there in the Eighties we even lost each other. ("A Simple Summer Place: Summer Home in Nova Scotia," Charles Gaines, Aug. 1, 1997, *Town & Country*)

Pearls before swine, To cast

Means: To offer something of value to someone incapable of appreciating it

Biblical Text: *Give not that which is holy unto the dogs, **neither cast ye your pearls before swine**, lest they trample them under their feet, and turn again and rend you* (Matthew 7:6).

Example of Use: Accounting challenged as I am, I do know this much about business: There is no quick fix and there certainly is no free lunch. So when you download Office Accounting Express 2007 at IdeaWins.com you are in for some pretty persuasive sales pitches aimed at getting you to shell out for the $149.95 Office Accounting 2007 Professional. In one of the most blatant incidents in the history of **casting pearls before swine**, Microsoft made both products available for me to review. ("Microsoft Makes Basic Tools of Accounting Free for Taking," James Coates, Mar. 7, 2007, *Chicago Tribune*)

Pearly gates

Means: Heaven, especially when used in a whimsical manner

Biblical Text: *And **the twelve gates were twelve pearls**; every several gate was of one pearl: and the street of the city was pure gold, as it were transparent glass* (Revelation 21:21).

Example of Use: Al, played by James Craven, has collected the requisite masterpieces by Rembrandt, Van Gogh and Picasso. But when he gets to the **pearly gates**, he finds that not even that is enough to admit him into "the land of the free," a stand-in for heaven. He is given a fatal task. ("A Debate at the **Pearly Gates**; Penumbra Theatre's 'On the Open Road' Probes 'The Tensions between the Material and the Spiritual,'" Rohan Preston, May 30, 2004, *Star Tribune*, Minneapolis, MN)

Pharisee

Means: Someone with a zealous concern for keeping rules or laws, especially if his zeal for persons fails to match; someone with a self-righteous attitude

Biblical Text: *Then spake Jesus to the multitude, and to his disciples, Saying, The scribes and the **Pharisees** sit in Moses' seat: All therefore whatsoever they bid you observe, that observe and do; but do not ye after their works: for they say, and do not. For they bind heavy burdens and grievous to be borne, and lay them on men's shoulders; but they themselves will not move them with one of their fingers. But all their works they do for to be seen of men: they make broad their phylacteries, and enlarge the borders of their garments, And love the uppermost rooms at feasts, and the chief seats in the synagogues, And greetings in the markets, and to be called of men, Rabbi, Rabbi* (Matthew 23:1–6).

Example of Use: The New Rifkind was an acolyte of the flame; a Thatcherite of the Thatcherites; touching the law, a **Pharisee**. And by the year's end he was, with vim and relish, proceeding to impose the poll tax over his Scottish subjects, against the incensed opposition of the mass of Scots MPs and almost

P

every local authority in the country. ("It's New! And Improved! It's Sir Malcolm! As a Top Scots Tory Attempts a Comeback Down South," John Macleod, Sept. 4, 2003, *Daily Mail,* London)

Philistine

Means: Someone who is ignorant and uncultured

Biblical Text: *And Saul and the men of Israel were gathered together, and pitched by the valley of Elah, and set the battle in array against the* **Philistines***. And the Philistines stood on a mountain on the one side, and Israel stood on a mountain on the other side: and there was a valley between them* (1 Samuel 17:2–3).

Example of Use: The war of words over political interference in the arts intensified yesterday after opposition parties branded Culture Minister Alun Pugh a '**philistine**' over his handling of the Arts Council. ("You're a **Philistine**, Mr. Arts Minister," Tomos Livingstone and Catrin Pascoe, Jan. 11, 2006, *Western Mail,* Cardiff, Wales)

Physician, heal thyself

Means: An admonition to attend to one's own faults instead of commenting on the faults of others

Biblical Text: *And he said unto them, Ye will surely say unto me this proverb,* **Physician, heal thyself***: whatsoever we have heard done in Capernaum, do also here in thy country* (Luke 4:23).

Example of Use: A survey of primary-care physicians several years ago found that doctors who regularly get aerobic exercise are more likely to counsel their patients about its benefits. We wouldn't want it any other way. Fair or not, people still hold doctors to high standards. Maybe it goes back to "**physician, heal thyself**": if you are going to tell me what to do, for goodness' sake, you'd better do it yourself. ("What the Doctors Do; They Know What's Best for Us When It Comes to Exercise, but Do They Follow Their Own Advice? Read All about It," Anthony L. Komaroff and Peter Wehrwein, Mar. 26, 2007, *Newsweek*)

Physicians of no value

Means: People, not necessarily physicians, whose abilities are inadequate or inferior to a normal standard

Biblical Text: *But ye are forgers of lies, ye are all **physicians of no value*** (Job 13:4).

Example of Use: A 51 year-old attorney specializing in medical negligence was enraged when his many complaints were ultimately diagnosed as multiple sclerosis. Known for his flashy wardrobe and courtroom pyrotechnics, he roamed from doctor to doctor, refusing to understand the nature of his illness and threatening to sue the previous "bastard" who had tried to help him. He was like Job (xiii:4), who raged, "ye are forgers of lies, ye are all **physicians of no value**." He adamantly refused treatment and demanded more and more tests and consultations. Eventually, his doctors did not return his calls for appointments and were frightened and depressed about him. ("Taking Care of the Hateful Patient," James E. Groves, Apr. 20, 1978, *New England Medical Journal*)

Pilate's wife

Means: A woman who warns someone, especially her husband, of some danger

Biblical Text: *When he was set down on the judgment seat, his [Pilate's] **wife** sent unto him, saying, Have thou nothing to do with that just man: for I have suffered many things this day in a dream because of him* (Matthew 27:19).

Example of Use: Fusing formal ingenuity and social concern in insightful, exuberant dramatic monologues, Duffy explores contemporary and historical scenes from surprising and unexpected viewpoints. Written from the perspective of the wives of famous and often infamous men (Mrs. Midas, Mrs. Aesop, **Pilate's Wife**, Mrs. Faust, Mrs. Darwin, and Queen Kong, among others appearing here), *The World's Wife* is the perfect showcase for Duffy's masterful subversions of myth and history. (Satterfield, Jane, "The World's Wife." Rev. of *The World's Wife* by Carol Ann Duffy, Faber & Faber, The Antioch Review, Jan. 1, 2001)

Pillar or Pillar of the church

Means: One who occupies a central or responsible position; a prominent supporter or member

Biblical Text: *And when James, Cephas, and John, who seemed to be **pillars**, perceived the grace that was given unto me, they gave to me and Barnabas the right hands of fellowship; that we should go unto the heathen, and they unto the circumcision* (Galatians 2:9). See also 1 Tim. 3:15; Rev. 3:12.

Example of Use: Rubinstein was thus under enormous pressure to quietly shelve the case. But, unlike his opponents, he grasped from the start which **pillar** of democracy was really at stake: not freedom of the press, but public trust in the legal system. ("That **Pillar** of Democracy," Evelyn Gordon, May 20, 2003, *Jerusalem Post*)

Pillar of salt

Means: Reference to Lot's wife in the OT

Biblical Text: *But his wife looked back from behind him, and she became **a pillar of salt*** (Genesis 19:26).

Example of Use: In a fascinating memoir, the American award-winning and once blacklisted film writer, Walter Bernstein, warns about the dangers of looking back by reminding us of what happened to Lot's wife: she turned into a **pillar of salt**. So, if perchance that happens to me, all I can ask is that you throw a little of that salt over your left shoulder. ("Red in Winnipeg's North End," Emma Goldman, Sept. 1, 2007, *Canadian Dimension*)

Plague of locusts

Means: A horrible condition, especially if greater than can be coped with

Biblical Text: *Else, if thou refuse to let my people go, behold, tomorrow will I bring the **locusts** into thy coast: And they shall cover the face of the earth, that one cannot be able to see the earth: and they shall eat the residue of that which is escaped, which remaineth unto you from the hail, and shall eat every tree which groweth for you out of the field: And they shall fill thy houses, and the houses of all thy servants, and the houses of all the Egyptians; which neither thy fathers, nor thy fathers' fathers have seen, since the day that they were upon the earth unto this day. And he turned himself, and went out from Pharaoh. . . . And the LORD said unto Moses, Stretch out thine hand over the land of Egypt for the **locusts**, that they may come up upon the land of Egypt, and eat every herb of the land, even all that the hail hath left. And Moses stretched forth his rod over the land of Egypt, and the LORD brought an east wind upon the land all that day, and all that night; and when it was morning, the east wind brought the **locusts**. And the **locusts** went up over all the land of Egypt, and rested in all the coasts of Egypt: very grievous were they; before them there were no such locusts as they, neither after them shall be such. For they covered the face of the whole earth, so that the land was darkened; and they did eat every herb of the*

P

land, and all the fruit of the trees which the hail had left: and there remained not any green thing in the trees, or in the herbs of the field, through all the land of Egypt (Exodus 10:4–6, 12–15).

Example of Use: He developed a steady sheen of sweat as the session dragged on, fuelled by a vocal minority. One shareholder even brandished Tesco's growth as "creeping megalomania." "I'm concerned about the rise and rise of Tesco. Everywhere you go you see an Express or a Metro and it's a **plague of locusts** actually," he said. It was all too much for those who were there to hear about the company's financial performance, who resorted to openly heckling and jeering the rebels in their midst. ("Tesco Chiefs Fend off a **Plague of Locusts**: The Tesco Shareholders' Meeting Offered a Chance for Protestors to Ambush Management," Beth Brooks, July 2, 2005, *Grocer*)

Plagues (or Plagues of Egypt)

Means: Undesirable conditions of horrendous proportions

Biblical Text: *For I will at this time send all my **plagues** upon thine heart, and upon thy servants, and upon thy people; that thou mayest know that there is none like me in all the earth* (Exodus 9:14).

Example of Use: A **plague** of flies of biblical proportions has descended on a town in New York state after chicken farmer Mark Adams spread 200 tons of manure over his 18-acre farm. Hundreds of millions of houseflies hatched from the manure and some residents of the 1,200-population town of Naples have fled as the insects entered houses and cars. "You wake up with flies crawling on your face," said one. Officials have declared part of the town a health hazard and some residents are threatening to sue Mr. Adams. ("Residents Flee U.S. Town Hit by a **Plague** of Flies," June 22, 2000, *Evening Standard,* London)

Plowshares

Means: Humanitarian or other irenic acts, resources, or purposes, especially in place of war or weapons

Biblical Text: *And he shall judge among many people, and rebuke strong nations afar off; and they shall beat their swords into **plowshares**, and their spears into pruninghooks: nation shall not lift up a sword against nation, neither shall they learn war any more* (Micah 4:3). See also Isa. 2:2–4; Joel 3:10.

Example of Use: On May 6, 2011 Practising Law Institute (PLI), the nation's largest producer of continuing legal education, in collaboration with The State Bar of California and Swords to **Plowshares**, will present Advocating for Veterans—the Basics on Benefits, Discharge Upgrades and Cultural Competency, a full-day program designed to increase the number of pro bono attorneys and advocates available to represent veterans before the Department of Veterans Affairs to get the benefits that they deserve. ("Practising Law Institute to Present Advocating for Veterans—the Basics on Benefits, Discharge Upgrades and Cultural Competency," May 14, 2011, *Investment Weekly News*)

Plumb line

Means: A means or test used to determine conformity to a certain standard, especially if of a moral or spiritual nature

Biblical Text: *Thus he shewed me: and, behold, the LORD stood upon a wall made by a plumbline, with a **plumbline** in his hand. And the LORD said unto me, Amos, what seest thou? And I said, A plumbline. Then said the LORD, Behold, I will set a **plumbline** in the midst of my people Israel: I will not again pass by them any more* (Amos 7:7–8).

Example of Use: "If one steps back from examining the procedures provision by provision, and instead drops a **plumb line** down through the center of them all, we believe that most people will find that taken together, they are fair and balanced and that justice will be served in their application," Defense Secretary Donald Rumsfeld told reporters at the Pentagon Thursday. ("Military Court Would Not Allow Appeals," Mar. 21, 2002, United Press International)

Point of death

Means: The time when one dies or immediately before someone could die

Biblical Text: *And besought him greatly, saying, My little daughter lieth at the **point of death**: I pray thee, come and lay thy hands on her, that she may be healed; and she shall live* (Mark 5:23). See also John 4:47.

Example of Use: The oil-covered penguins appeared in early September, thin, exhausted and at the **point of death**. ("Foreign Journal; Pollution Reaches Penguin Rookery," Eugene Robinson, Oct. 7, 1991, *The Washington Post*)

Pontius Pilate

Means: Someone who serves as judge over another, especially if the one being judged is more virtuous than he; one who tries to remove his responsibility for such judgment

Biblical Text: *When **Pilate** saw that he could prevail nothing, but that rather a tumult was made, he took water, and washed his hands before the multitude, saying, I am innocent of the blood of this just person: see ye to it* (Matthew 27:24).

Example of Use: Prime Minister John Howard had done a **Pontius Pilate** and washed his hands of Iraq, Opposition

Foreign Affairs spokesman Kevin Rudd said today. ("QLD: Howard's Done a '**Pontius Pilate**': Rudd," Nov. 10, 2003, *AAP General News,* Australia)

Poor will be with you always, The

Means: Poverty will continue always.

Biblical Text: *For ye have the poor with you always, and whensoever ye will ye may do them good: but me ye have not always* (Mark 14:7). See also Matt. 26:11.

Example of Use: Crop Walks to raise money for the fight against hunger take place Sunday across Oswego County. The walks also remind people that many of the less fortunate must walk to find water and food.

"We **always have the poor with us**, so we need to support them. We walk because they walk," said Bonnie Fauler, recruiter for the Fulton Crop Walk committee, which holds its 17th annual walk Sunday. "The Crop Walk is a gathering of people who are fighting hunger." ("Fulton's 17th Annual Crop Walk Comes Sunday; Churches in Pulaski, Mexico and Hannibal Also to Hold Fund-Raising Walks," Rebecca Madden, Oct. 2, 2004, *The Post-Standard,* Syracuse, NY)

P

Potiphar's wife

Means: A woman who tries to seduce a man

Biblical Text: *And the Midianites sold him into Egypt unto **Potiphar**, an officer of Pharaoh's, and captain of the guard. . . . And it came to pass after these things, that **his master's** [Potiphar's] **wife** cast her eyes upon Joseph; and she said, Lie with me. But he refused, and said unto his master's wife, Behold, my master wotteth not what is with me in the house, and he hath committed all that he hath to my hand; There is none greater in this house* *than I; neither hath he kept back any thing from me but thee, because thou art his wife: how then can I do this great wickedness, and sin against God? And it came to pass, as she spake to Joseph day by day, that he hearkened not unto her, to lie by her, or to be with her. And it came to pass about this time, that Joseph went into the house to do his business; and there was none of the men of the house there within. And she caught him by his garment, saying, Lie with me: and he left his garment in her hand, and fled, and got him out. And it came to pass, when she saw that he had left his garment in her hand, and was fled forth, That she called unto the men of her house, and spake unto them, saying, See, he hath brought in an Hebrew unto us to mock us; he came in unto me to lie with me, and I cried with a loud voice: And it came to pass, when he heard that I lifted up my voice and cried, that he left his garment with me, and fled, and got him out. And she laid up his garment by her, until his lord came home. And she spake unto him according to these words, saying, The Hebrew servant, which thou hast brought unto us, came in unto me to mock me: And it came to pass, as I lifted up my voice and cried, that he left his garment with me, and fled out. And it came to pass, when his master heard the words of **his wife**, which she spake unto him, saying, After this manner did thy servant to me; that his wrath was kindled. And Joseph's master took him, and put him into the prison, a place where the king's prisoners were bound: and he was there in the prison* (Genesis 37:36; 39:7–20).

Example of Use: Another more emphatically Baroque ivory relief [among carved figures on display] shows Joseph with **Potiphar's wife**, who is trying to seduce him. Joseph's hair and garments, blowing sideways, suggest the speed with which he retreats from the naked woman, but the real actors in the scene are the roiled bed linens and especially the canopy's swirling drapes, which reach toward Joseph like surrogate arms. ("Small

White Wonders and Other Delicacies," Roberta Smith, Mar. 16, 2007, *The New York Times*)

Potter's field

Means: A place for the burial of unknown or indigent persons

Biblical Text: *And they took counsel, and bought with them the **potter's field**, to bury strangers in. Wherefore that field was called, The field of blood, unto this day. Then was fulfilled that which was spoken by Jeremy the prophet, saying, And they took the thirty pieces of silver, the price of him that was valued, whom they of the children of Israel did value; And gave them for the **potter's field**, as the Lord appointed me* (Matthew 27:7–10).

Example of Use: Dedication of the Read-Dunning Memorial Park, as it has been named, should come by summer. "We are talking about a historic memorial project here," said the Rev. William Brauer, retired pastor of nearby Portage Park Presbyterian Church. It is a park unlike others. It sits on what was Chicago's first **potter's field**, where tens of thousands of indigent were laid to rest in unmarked graves more than a century ago. ("Dead of **Potter's Field** Finally Honored," Janet Rausa Fuller, May 28, 2002, *Chicago Sun-Times*)

P

Powers that be

Means: Persons or institutions in authority

Biblical Text: *Let every soul be subject unto the higher powers. For there is no power but of God: The **powers that be** are ordained of God* (Romans 13:1).

Example of Use: He had dreamed of seeing thousands of Black parents in a united front, waving a sea of banners, defying the **powers that be** and standing up like proud and responsible parents for their children at the Mar. 31 demonstration at

Camden Yards. ("Fighting the **Powers That Be** for Education," Earl Byrd, Apr. 11, 2003, *Baltimore Afro-American*)

Preach the gospel

Means: To tout someone or something with enthusiasm

Biblical Text: *And he said unto them, Go ye into all the world, and **preach the gospel** to every creature* (Mark 16:15).

Example of Use: A woman who once considered herself "just a mom" is traveling to far corners of the globe to **preach the gospel** of women's health issues. For Kathy Mueller, of Fort Mitchell, Ky., talking to audiences and individuals about breast cancer, osteoporosis and heart health is her way of giving back. ("Trotting Globe for Women's Health," Jack Hicks, Sept. 27, 2007, *The Cincinnati Post*)

Price of wisdom is beyond rubies, The

Means: Wisdom is of more earthly and eternal value than tangible possessions, no matter how valuable.

Biblical Text: *No mention shall be made of coral, or of pearls: for **the price of wisdom is above rubies*** (Job 28:18).

Example of Use: In the second section, "The Problem Resolved in Principle," Gould defines and defends NOMA. He writes that since the two realms of science and religion cannot fuse, each of us must integrate them into a coherent view of life with the result of something "**more precious than rubies**"—wisdom. ("Gould's Separate 'Magisteria': Two Views," Mark W. Durm and Massimo Pigliucci, Nov. 1, 1999, *Skeptical Inquirer*)

Pride goes before destruction

Means: Self-pride is a prelude to failure and loss

Biblical Text: *Pride goeth before destruction, and an haughty spirit before a fall* (Proverbs 16:18).

Example of Use: As it is performed by all and sundry—even down to the very young children—we are seeing the manifestation of these very same forces around us in everyday life. The abuse, rage, and rebellion affect all society, and all age-groups. We appear to be reaping the results of our sowing. It is well said that **pride goes before destruction**. ("Joke on Us," Glywn McInnes, Jan. 31, 2001, *Waikato Times*, New Zealand)

Principalities and powers

Means: Persons or institutions with great power or authority

Biblical Text: *For I am persuaded, that neither death, nor life, nor angels, nor **principalities**, nor **powers**, nor things present, nor things to come, Nor height, nor depth, nor any other creature, shall be able to separate us from the love of God, which is in Christ Jesus our Lord* (Romans 8:38–39).

Example of Use: A Los Angeles-based expert on peacemaking said Saturday the community is so traumatized by the Klan-Nazi killings of Nov. 3, 1979, it has taken refuge in denial and cover-up. . . . But victims maintain there was a conspiracy to cover up the events, including the role of local police. Dr. Marty Nathan, whose husband Mike Nathan was killed that day, said Saturday her husband and friends were targeted for confronting the power structure. "They were hated, all of us were, for what we were doing," she said. "If you are in-your-face about deep, deep injustice . . . those **principalities and powers** are not going to like you." ("Sessions Address Shootings' Aftermath; Many Issues Surrounding the 1979 Shootings Remain Unresolved, Speakers Say," Margaret Moffett Banks, Nov. 2, 2003, *The News & Record*, Piedmont Triad, NC)

P

Proclaim it from the housetops

Means: Announce something loudly; make something widely known

Biblical Text: *Therefore whatsoever ye have spoken in darkness shall be heard in the light; and that which ye have spoken in the ear in closets shall be **proclaimed upon the housetops*** (Luke 12:3).

Example of Use: Music touches people in different ways. Even the most hard-core metal fan has a softer side—who says that he or she doesn't enjoy some Kenny G while getting his or her groove on? . . . Don't shut yourself in a room and listen to your tunes in shame. Why not **proclaim it from the rooftops**? Go ahead, Metallica fan, it's perfectly fine to shout, "I love Mariah Carey's music" out to the world. I'm sure it will make you feel much better about yourself. ("Commentary: 'Mmmbop,' You Got a Problem?" Sarah Butchin, Mar. 24, 2004, *University Wire*)

Prodigal son

Means: A person, especially a young man, who wastes his assets or potential

Biblical Text: *And he said, A certain man had two sons: And **the younger of them** said to his father, Father, give me the portion of goods that falleth to me. And he divided unto them his living. And not many days after the **younger son** gathered all together, and took his journey into a far country, and **there wasted his substance** with riotous living* (Luke 15:11–13).

Example of Use: Anwar Ibrahim, the **prodigal son** of Malaysian politics, has this advice to opposition leaders who campaigned for his release from jail: "Move with the times to ensure your political survival." ("Politics-Malaysia: '**Prodigal Son**' Anwar Returns to His Power Base," Anil Netto, Nov. 9, 2004, Inter Press Service English News Wire)

Promised Land

Means: A place, literal or figurative, offering excellent prospects

Biblical Text: *Now the LORD had said unto Abram, **Get thee out of thy country**, and from thy kindred, and from thy father's house, **unto a land** that I will show thee: And I will make of thee a great nation, and I will bless thee, and make thy name great; and thou shalt be a blessing: . . . And Abram took Sarai his wife, and Lot his brother's son, and all their substance that they had gathered, and the souls that they had gotten in Haran; and they went forth to go into the land of Canaan; and **into the land of Canaan they came**. And Abram passed through the land unto the place of Sichem, unto the plain of Moreh. And the Canaanite was then in the land. And the LORD appeared unto Abram, and said, **Unto thy seed will I give this land**: and there builded he an altar unto the LORD, who appeared unto him* (Genesis 12:1–2, 5–7).

Example of Use: Yes, I must call it a **promised land** because at one time I was dreaming, almost every night, of trips to Asia. Up to the doomsday, I think I can't understand why Asia was my choice in those days when U.S., Europe and the Arab world were choice of most of my friends. ("Memory of the **Promised Land**," May 7, 2007, *All Africa Global Media*)

Prophet is not without honor . . . , A

Means: One receives more respect among people who know him less well than those who know him well

Biblical Text: *But Jesus, said unto them, **A prophet is not without honour**, but in his own country, and among his own kin, and in his own house* (Mark 6:4). See also Matt. 13:57.

Example of Use: "I really don't think [Chicagoans] appreciate her," Stedman told the normally sunny David Novarro and Jan Jeffcoat. "**A prophet does not have any honor in its own town.**"

P

If this sounds like a Messianic description of Oprah, that's because Stedman was quoting another charismatic personality known mainly by a first name. In the Gospel of Mark, Jesus says, **"A prophet is not without honor except in his native place."** This analogy is not entirely fair to Oprah, since Jesus wasn't a billionaire and did not have his own magazine, but Stedman's point stands. ("Forgive Me Stedman, for I Know Not What She's Done for Me," June 10, 2010, *Chicago Sun-Times*)

Pure, all things are pure, To the

Means: One's innocent nature generates wholesome behavior, something that law or other outside forces cannot create

Biblical Text: *Unto the pure all things are pure: but unto them that are defiled and unbelieving is nothing pure; but even their mind and conscience is defiled* (Titus 1:15).

Example of Use: If one keeps in mind Belloc's three rules, one may read the op-ed pages—and even watch political talk shows—without fearing the forces of darkness: **To the pure, all things are pure**. ("Shelf Life," Michael Potemra, Mar. 25, 2002, *National Review*)

Put not your faith in princes

Means: Do not trust in people who will disappoint you

Biblical Text: *While I live will I praise the LORD: I will sing praises unto my God while I have any being. **Put not your trust in princes**, nor in the son of man, in whom there is no help. His breath goeth forth, he returneth to his earth; in that very day his thoughts perish* (Psalm 146:2–4).

Example of Use: Lord Radice reveals that Mr. Blair promised a ministerial job on July 27, 1994, shortly after he became leader, and again on Nov. 8, 1995, at Mr. Blair's Islington home.

Lord Radice writes: "He says once again that he would like me to be in his Government." But on May 4, 1997, as Mr. Blair starts to hand out the ministerial jobs, he records what he called "a classic wait by the telephone (unsuccessful as it turns out)." Lord Radice writes: "I have to face the fact that, despite all my years in Parliament and my contribution to getting Labour back to power, I shall never be a minister. It is clear that Tony has failed to deliver on his promise to make me a minister (**Put not your trust in princes**, as Psalm 146 puts it.)" ("Blair Broke Pledge to Me, Says Lord Radice," Paul Linford, Sept. 30, 2004, *The Journal*, Newcastle, England)

P

RAISING CAIN

Q

"QUEEN OF SHEBA"

Queen of Sheba

Means: A woman who considers herself of a higher status than is warranted

Biblical Text: *And when the* **queen of Sheba** *heard of the fame of Solomon concerning the name of the* Lord, *she came to prove him with hard questions. And she came to Jerusalem with a very great train, with camels that bare spices, and very much gold, and precious stones: and when she was come to Solomon, she communed with him of all that was in her heart. And Solomon told her all her questions: there was not any thing hid from the king, which he told her not. And when the* **queen of Sheba** *had seen all Solomon's wisdom, and the house that he had built, And the meat of his table, and the sitting of his servants, and the attendance of his ministers, and their apparel, and his cupbearers, and his ascent by which he went up unto the house of the* Lord; *there was no more spirit in her. . . . And king Solomon gave unto the* **queen of Sheba** *all her desire, whatsoever she asked, beside that which Solomon gave her of his royal bounty. So she turned and went to her own country, she and her servants* (1 Kings 10:1–5, 13).

Example of Use: My history teacher, who later wrote a book called *Uncommon People: A Study of England's Elite*, was contemptuous of convention. He brought his bicycle into the classroom and wore his pajamas under his coat. He bears at least some responsibility for my difficulty with history and with change, since he eventually threw me out of his class for behaving like the **Queen of Sheba**. ("All Changes Great and Small," Jane Miller, May 1, 2011, *In These Times*)

Question, Call into

Means: Challenge the accuracy, probity, or propriety of something

Biblical Text: *For we are in danger to be **called in question** for this day's uproar, there being no cause whereby we may give an account of this concourse* (Acts 19:40).

Example of Use: A lawyer for a Sept. 11 charity that has raised nearly $2 million has received more than $500,000 in legal fees while doling out just $73,000 to potential recipients, a published report has said. ("Fees to 9/11 Fund's Lawyer Are **Called into Question**," Mar. 16, 2004, *The Record*, Bergen County, NJ)

Quick and the dead, The

Means: The living and the dead

Biblical Text: *I charge thee therefore before God, and the Lord Jesus Christ, who shall judge **the quick and the dead** at his appearing and his kingdom* (2 Timothy 4:1).

Example of Use: It is the dramatic instant when the mystical bull, described in an accompanying article, shifts the earth from one horn to the other. For magical seconds, the Manichean world of opposites—good and evil, light and darkness, **the quick and the dead**, the worlds of irreconcilable opposites—stand together. ("There's Also a Deeper Meaning," Mar. 18, 2011, *Iran Times International*, Washington, DC)

RAISING CAIN

R

"RAIN FALLS ON THE JUST AND UNJUST"

Race is not to the swift, nor the battle to the strong, The

Means: Success or victory in life is not always achieved by strength or speed alone but by other, less-expected factors

Biblical Text: *I returned, and saw under the sun, that **the race is not to the swift, nor the battle to the strong**, neither yet bread to the wise, nor yet riches to men of understanding, nor yet favour to men of skill; but time and chance happeneth to them all* (Ecclesiastes 9:11).

Example of Use: The race is not to the swift, nor the battle to the strong, Ecclesiastes' author wrote from a press box many years ago. Of course, few Old Testament teams had to tackle Adrian Peterson or block Rufus Alexander. Which brings us to Boise State's Fiesta Bowl dilemma Monday night. The Oklahoma football Sooners are bigger, stronger, faster. No one really argues otherwise. "It's the Big 12; they get the blue-chip player," said Boise State center Jadon Dailey. ("Boise Has a Chance, but It Won't Be Easy," Berry Tramel, Dec. 31, 2006, *Daily Oklahoman*, Oklahoma City)

Rachel weeping for her children

Means: Someone, especially a woman, who laments the loss of others, especially children, whether her own or someone else's

Biblical Text: *Thus saith the LORD; A voice was heard in Ramah, lamentation, and bitter weeping; **Rahel** [an alternate form of "Rachel"] **weeping** for her children refused to be comforted for her children, because they were not. Thus saith the LORD; Refrain thy voice from weeping, and thine eyes from tears: for thy work shall be rewarded, saith the LORD; and they shall come again from the land of the enemy. And there is hope in* *thine end, saith the* LORD, *that thy children shall come again to their own border* (Jeremiah 31:15–17).

Example of Use: What is this? Replicants are not supposed to have feelings. Has she somehow transcended replicant-being to join human-being? Deckard, recognizing at one point that he cannot kill her because she has helped to save him when one of the horrifically violent renegade replicants was preparing to gouge his eyes out and because he has fallen in love with her, plunges into dark self-doubt. What about Rachel? **Rachel weeping, weeping** not for her children but for her own nonchildhood, her nonhuman-being. (*Who Are We? Critical Reflections and Hopeful Possibilities* [Chapter 1: "How Far Have We Fallen?"], Jean Bethke Elshtain, William B. Eerdmans Publishing Company, 2000)

Rain falls on the just and the unjust, The

Means: Good things happen to good people as well as bad

Biblical Text: *That ye may be the children of your Father which is in heaven: for he maketh his sun to rise on the evil and on the good, and **sendeth rain on the just and on the unjust*** (Matthew 5:45).

Example of Use: We all know about Noah and the flood, but there are numerous references in the Bible to God's power over the weather. . . . Lest we become too fearful, recall that Matthew 5:45 reminds us God "**sendeth rain on the just and on the unjust.**" But, as a ditty goes, "mostly on the just because the unjust steals the just's umbrella." ("What Did We Do to Deserve This?" Stephanie Schorow, June 23, 2003, *The Boston Herald*)

Rain forty days and forty nights

Means: To rain for an unusually long period

Biblical Text: *For yet seven days, and I will cause it to* **rain upon the earth forty days and forty nights***; and every living substance that I have made will I destroy from off the face of the earth. And Noah did according unto all that the LORD commanded him* (Genesis 7:4–5). See also Gen. 7:11.

Example of Use: Have you ever had one of those winters where it seems like it's been **raining for forty days and forty nights** and you can't remember exactly when it was you last saw the sun and you just freaked out at the ghostly white visage staring back at you in the bathroom mirror and then you discovered fuzzy green stuff growing between your toes and you looked outside and it's started to sleet and you're sick and tired of it all and you just want to scream? ("9 Top Baja Sea Kayak Getaways," Mike Everitt, May 1, 2000, *Paddler*)

Raise Cain

Means: To create a disturbance. One sense of *raise* in old English is to conjure up. To raise Cain is to bring up or express the spirit of Cain.

Biblical Text: *But unto* **Cain** *and to his offering he had not respect. And Cain was very wroth, and his countenance fell. And the LORD said unto* **Cain, Why art thou wroth? and why is thy countenance fallen?** *If thou doest well, shalt thou not be accepted? and if thou doest not well, sin lieth at the door. And unto thee shall be his desire, and thou shalt rule over him* (Genesis 4:5–7).

Example of Use: Not long afterward, that same editor changed the term "Canada goose" to "Canadian goose." That's a fairly common mistake, so I didn't **raise Cain** about it. I did, however, offer him a way to remember the difference. ("The Words We Write Can Bite Us," John McCoy, Apr. 3, 2011, *Sunday Gazette-Mail*)

Raise from the dead

Means: To bring back into practice, notice, or use something that has not been expected to be used again

Biblical Text: *But for us also, to whom it shall be imputed, if we believe on him that* **raised** *up Jesus our Lord* **from the dead***; Who was delivered for our offences, and was raised again for our justification* (Romans 4:24–25).

Example of Use: You almost never see a Lazarus story in the television universe. Once a show has been canceled—not just sentenced to death, but actually executed—networks do not **raise it from the dead**. "Family Guy" is an exception. ("An Amazing Comeback Cartoon," Virginia Rohan, May 1, 2005, *The Record*, Bergen County, NJ)

Ravening wolves

Means: People who are excessively greedy and grasping, especially for power or possessions; excessively angry or vindictive

Biblical Text: *Beware of false prophets, which come to you in sheep's clothing, but inwardly they are* **ravening wolves** (Matthew 7:15). See also Ezek. 22:27.

R

Example of Use: The commission's work was met with resistance, especially from the local real estate community. Predicting backlash, the commission was stacked with high-profile professionals from a variety of backgrounds, Cassin said. "There were those in the community, amazingly, who referred to this very prestigious group of people as a group of '**ravening wolves**,'" she said. These meetings drew crowds in the hundreds, many opposed to a fair housing law. ("Making History," John Huston, Mar. 26, 2008, *Oak Leaves*, Oak Park, IL)

Reap the whirlwind

Means: To suffer penalties for one's misdeeds

Biblical Text: *For they have sown the wind, and they shall reap the whirlwind: it hath no stalk; the bud shall yield no meal: if so be it yield, the strangers shall swallow it up* (Hosea 8:7).

Example of Use: The al Qaedaists of the Middle East know . . . well what they're doing: They want to sabotage the region's economies, disconnecting them from the world, and **reap the whirlwind** of social distress. ("Should Dubai Buy Part of the NASDAQ?" James Pethokoukis, Sept. 21, 2007, *U.S. News & World Report*)

Reap what you sow, You

Means: One will eventually receive according to how he has lived, good for good, bad for bad

Biblical Text: *Be not deceived; God is not mocked: for **whatsoever a man soweth, that shall he also reap.** For he that soweth to his flesh shall of the flesh reap corruption; but he that soweth to the Spirit shall of the Spirit reap life everlasting. And let us not be weary in well doing: for in due season we shall reap, if we faint not* (Galatians 6:7–9).

Example of Use: Pride comes before the fall. **You reap what you sow**. Those two hard truths are in the harvest stage for us who once believed in the basic integrity of sport. NBA commissioner David Stern's increasing arrogance through the years—especially toward those of us who dared, even casually, to question the integrity of his referees—has come back to haunt him and his enterprise like a plague of locusts. ("Not Your Dad's Sports Page; Referee Scandal, Steroid Allegations and Dog Fighting Indictment Show Fairness, Decency and

Trustworthiness Are All out the Window," Rick Telander, July 25, 2007, *Chicago Sun-Times*)

Rechabite

Means: Someone who does not drink alcohol

Biblical Text: *The word which came unto Jeremiah from the* LORD *in the days of Jehoiakim the son of Josiah king of Judah, saying, Go unto the house of the **Rechabites**, and speak unto them, and bring them into the house of the* LORD, *into one of the chambers, and give them wine to drink. Then I took Jaazaniah the son of Jeremiah, the son of Habaziniah, and his brethren, and all his sons, and the whole house of the **Rechabites**; And I brought them into the house of the* LORD, *into the chamber of the sons of Hanan, the son of Igdaliah, a man of God, which was by the chamber of the princes, which was above the chamber of Maaseiah the son of Shallum, the keeper of the door: And I set before the sons of the house of the **Rechabites** pots full of wine, and cups, and I said unto them, Drink ye wine. But they said, We will drink no wine: for Jonadab the son of Rechab our father commanded us, saying, Ye shall drink no wine, neither ye, nor your sons for ever* (Jeremiah 35:1–6).

Example of Use: The **Rechabite** Friendly Society has more than 25,000 members—all of them teetotal and all entitled to a low 6 per cent rate on variable rate mortgages. That is a sobering 0.85 per cent less than the cost of a mortgage with one of the major lenders. The only catch is you have to promise not to drink. If you do, you can also take out the **Rechabite's** funeral plans and child saving bonds. ("Home and Dry: Cheaper Loans for Teetotallers," Anna Day, Aug. 18, 1999, *The Mirror*, London)

R

Red sky at night is sailor's delight

Means: A red sky at sunset usually indicates that the next day will bring fair weather.

Biblical Text: *The Pharisees also with the Sadducees came, and tempting desired him that he would show them a sign from heaven. He answered and said unto them,* **When it is evening, ye say, It will be fair weather: for the sky is red.** *And in the morning, It will be foul weather to day: for the sky is red and lowering. O ye hypocrites, ye can discern the face of the sky; but can ye not discern the signs of the times?* (Matthew 16:1–3).

Example of Use: Sherry Trabert, of Baltimore, asks if there is truth to the adage her father, a Navy vet, repeated: "**Red sky at night, sailor's delight**; red sky at morning, sailors take warning." This ancient wisdom has Biblical roots (Matthew 16:2–3). It's often true in mid-latitudes where weather moves generally west to east. Red at sunset means the sun is setting in clear, stable air to the west, its light filtered through dust and water vapor. At sunrise, red signals the clear weather has moved east, and rain may follow. ("The Weather Page," Jan. 12, 2007, *Baltimore Sun*)

Redeem the time

R

Means: An exhortation to use one's time wisely

Biblical Text: *See then that ye walk circumspectly, not as fools, but as wise,* **Redeeming the time,** *because the days are evil* (Ephesians 5:15–16). See also Col. 4:5.

Example of Use: Our city leaders have made the wrong choice again. They have a chance to **redeem the time** and do the right thing by discontinuing annexation. Involuntary annexation is legal, but not ethical. ("Involuntary Annexations Are Violations of Freedoms," June 22, 2003, *The News & Record*, Piedmont Triad, NC)

Rehoboam

Means: Reference to the final king of Israel, the son of Solomon; a large wine bottle, used especially for champagne, equivalent to about five quarts

Biblical Text: *And Solomon slept with his fathers, and was buried in the city of David his father: and **Rehoboam** his son reigned in his stead* (1 Kings 11:43).

Example of use: Mr. Brown treated Stephen Pound yesterday in an inexplicably stupid way. Everyone likes Mr. Pound. Well, not everyone. He asked Mr. Brown a relatively respectable patsy question, asking him whether it was morally right or legally possible for one person to fund a political party. Mr. Brown mumbled "It should not happen" and sat down. A wholesale lack of pastoral care of his back bench is not a brilliant idea just now.

Two years ago, I suggested Mr. Brown would recall **Rehoboam's** coronation speech: "You have been chastised with whips; I shall chastise you with scorpions!" But I was joking. ("The Iron Fist Needs All of Its Rivets Tightening," Simon Carr, Nov. 15, 2007, *The Independent*, London)

Remnant (or Saving Remnant)

R

Means: A small, remaining number of a formerly larger number; a trace or vestige of a former body

Biblical Text: *And this shall be a sign unto thee, Ye shall eat this year such things as grow of themselves, and in the second year that which springeth of the same; and in the third year sow ye, and reap, and plant vineyards, and eat the fruits thereof. And the remnant that is escaped of the house of Judah shall yet again take root downward, and bear fruit upward. For out of Jerusalem shall go forth a **remnant**, and they that escape out of mount*

Zion: the zeal of the LORD *of hosts shall do this* (2 Kings 19:29–31).

Example of Use: Stay informed, of course. But more importantly, we must become active. When schools invest more in stadiums than libraries, speak up. When township leaders prefer sprawl to smart growth, call them on it. When politicians insult your intelligence, vote them out! It's not up to the person down the street. It's up to you.

"If there's any way to resist the worst aspects of our culture today . . . ," Jacoby advised, "it can only be created one family at a time, one individual at a time, by parents and citizens determined to preserve the saving **remnant** of those who prize memory and learning above all else." ("There's a Smart Way to Show We're Not Stupid; We're to Blame Cultural Conservation," Jeff Hawkes, Oct. 14, 2008, *Intelligencer Journal,* Lancaster, PA)

Remove the beam from your own eye . . .

Means: An admonition to rectify one's own sins before commenting on the sins of others

Biblical Text: *And why beholdest thou the mote that is in thy brother's eye, but considerest not the beam that is in thine own eye? Or how wilt thou say to thy brother, Let me pull out the mote out of thine eye; and, behold, a beam is in thine own eye? Thou hypocrite, **first cast out the beam out of thine own eye**; and then shalt thou see clearly to cast out the mote out of thy brother's eye* (Matthew 7:5).

Example of Use: It is totally unprofessional for Education MEC Cameron Dugmore to launch such a scathing and personal attack on Terence Klassen, the principal of Fairmount High School in Grassy Park. . . . Terence Klassen is a person of integrity who has not only the interests of his pupils, but also those of education as a whole, at heart. I suggest the MEC **remove the beam** from his own eye before looking for a possible splinter in the eye of another. ("Play the Ball, Not the Man, Dugmore," Roy Erfort, Jan. 25, 2007, *Cape Argus*, South Africa)

Render unto Caesar what is Caesar's

Means: Pay the government what it requires

Biblical Text: *And they sent out unto him their disciples with the Herodians, saying, Master, we know that thou art true, and teachest the way of God in truth, neither carest thou for any man: for thou regardest not the person of men. Tell us therefore, What thinkest thou? Is it lawful to give tribute unto Caesar, or not? But Jesus perceived their wickedness, and said, Why tempt ye me, ye hypocrites? Shew me the tribute money. And they brought unto him a penny. And he saith unto them, Whose is this image and superscription? They say unto him, Caesar's. Then saith he unto them, **Render therefore unto Caesar the things which are Caesar's**; and unto God the things that are God's. When they had heard these words, they marvelled, and left him, and went their way* (Matthew 22:16–22).

Example of Use: The Florida law that shifted about $7.8 billion in property taxes from homesteaders to all other property owners this year is "even-handed" and not discriminatory, a Tallahassee judge ruled Monday.

Circuit Judge John C. Cooper dismissed a suit filed by Alabama citizens who say they're paying an unconstitutional amount of taxes for second homes in the Panhandle. . . . "Who knows?" he [the plaintiffs' attorney] said. "Somewhere on the road to Damascus the Florida Supreme Court may have an epiphany." Meantime, the Alabamans will have to **render unto**

R

Caesar in Florida. ("Judge Upholds Save Our Homes Law," Marc Caputo, Aug. 7, 2007, *Miami Herald*)

Return to one's own vomit

Means: Return to one's bad habits, misdeeds, or mistakes

Biblical Text: *As a dog returneth to his vomit, so a fool returneth to his folly* (Proverbs 26:11). See also 2 Pet. 2:22.

Example of Use: "When the Ninth Circuit Court of Appeals delivered the craziest ruling in American history by striking down the Pledge of Allegiance three years ago, the U.S. Supreme Court stepped in and stopped the insanity," said Randy Thomasson, president of Campaign for Children and Families, a religious liberties group. "The lower court's striking down the Pledge again is like a dog **returning to its vomit**." ("Judge Rules against Pledge," Maura Dolan, Sept. 15, 2005, *The Cincinnati* Post, OH)

Right hand

Means: Someone who is especially helpful or reliable

Biblical Text: *Thy **right hand**, O LORD, is become glorious in power: thy right hand, O LORD, hath dashed in pieces the enemy* (Exodus 15:6).

Example of Use: Choosing the perfect **right-hand** man is a bit like choosing the perfect suit. You want him tailored to your specifications, you want to be able to breathe and be comfortable when he is around you, and when you need him to make you look good, you want to know you can rely on his quality and polish. ("Picking a **Right-Hand** Man," Mr. Mafioso, May 13, 2005, www.askmen.com)

R

Right hand of fellowship

Means: A sign of welcome, goodwill, and cooperation

Biblical Text: *And when James, Cephas, and John, who seemed to be pillars, perceived the grace that was given unto me, they gave to me and Barnabas the **right hands of fellowship**; that we should go unto the heathen, and they unto the circumcision* (Galatians 2:9).

Example of Use: Having jumped on a re-elected President Bush to extend **the right hand of fellowship**, now let me leap on Democrats. The president has started making strategic calls to Democratic legislators, even having some down to the White House. If he keeps offering his hand, will any of you accept it? Let's hope so. ("Are Democrats Going to Accept Bush's **Right Hand**?" William McKenzie, Nov. 28, 2004, *Sunday Gazette-Mail*)

Riotous living

Means: An extravagant, indulgent lifestyle

Biblical Text: *And not many days after the younger son gathered all together, and took his journey into a far country, and there wasted his substance with **riotous living*** (Luke 15:13).

Example of Use: A prudent and responsible parent will use his capital sparingly in order to pass on to his children as much as possible of his inheritance. A selfish and irresponsible parent will squander it in **riotous living** and care not one whit how his offspring will fare. ("Mystery Cassandra," Andrew Leonard, Dec. 5, 2006, salon.com)

Rock, A

Means: Someone who does not waver in providing support for another or a body

Biblical Text: *Bow down thine ear to me; deliver me speedily: be thou **my strong rock**, for an house of defence to save me. For thou art **my rock** and my fortress; therefore for thy name's sake lead me, and guide me* (Psalm 31:2–3).

Example of Use: Andy Reid is religiously stoic, deliberately dispassionate. "He's a **rock**, man," said Philadelphia Eagles linebacker Shawn Barber. "He's as solid as they come." ("Reid Needs to Make Team Accountable," Jerry Reimenschneider, Oct. 26, 2006, *Reading Eagle*, Reading, PA)

Rod and rebuke give wisdom, but a child left to himself brings his mother to shame, The

Means: Discipline helps a child mature responsibly whereas a lack of discipline causes humiliation and disgrace.

Biblical Text: *The rod and reproof give wisdom: but a child left to himself bringeth his mother to shame* (Proverbs 29:15).

Example of Use: The studies of corporal punishment combined don't give as much sound advice to parents as the ancient book of Proverbs. In it we learn of the need for balanced discipline. "**The rod and reproof give wisdom, but a child who gets his own way** (i.e., an undisciplined child) **brings shame to his mother**" (Proverbs 29:15). We are also guided to be diligent in our discipline. ("How to Raise a Juvenile Delinquent," Steve Cornell, Aug. 11, 2002, *Sunday News*, Lancaster, PA)

Roof of one's mouth, The

Means: The palate of the mouth

Biblical Text: *The nobles held their peace, and their tongue cleaved to **the roof of their mouth*** (Job 29:10).

Example of Use: Toads catch their food with a sticky tongue and sink their eyes into the **roof of their mouth** to help swallow. ("Gardening: Five Facts on Toads," Nov. 20, 2005, *The People*, London)

Root of all evil

Means: A pervasive cause of something negative or evil

Biblical Text: *For the love of money is the **root of all evil**: which while some coveted after, they have erred from the faith, and pierced themselves through with many sorrows* (1 Timothy 6:10).

Example of Use: The public mood was that it was just too much trouble to keep the monarchy. The Maoists had portrayed the monarchy as **the root of all evil**, and promised things would get better with a republic. Three years later, most Nepalis feel the abolition of the monarchy hasn't made much of a difference. ("A Sad Ending," May 27, 2011, *The Nepali Times*, Kathmandu, Nepal)

R

Root of bitterness

Means: The source of a bitter attitude, resentment, or acrimony

Biblical Text: *Looking diligently lest any man fail of the grace of God; lest any **root of bitterness** springing up trouble you, and thereby many be defiled; Lest there be any fornicator, or profane person, as Esau, who for one morsel of meat sold his birthright. For ye know how that afterward, when he would have inherited* *the blessing, he was rejected: for he found no place of repentance, though he sought it carefully with tears* (Hebrews 12:15–17).

Example of Use: I was most amazed by this guy's happy optimism. There is not a **root of bitterness**, grumpiness, or anger in him—despite living through a century of societal and personal turmoil. I asked him his secret and he replied, "Love yourself to love others." For a fairly unremarkable day, I'm grateful to have met quite a remarkable man. ("2083," Nov. 3, 2006, forzaitalia99.blogspot.com)

Root of the matter, The

Means: The essential part or cause of something

Biblical Text: *For I know that my redeemer liveth, and that he shall stand at the latter day upon the earth: And though after my skin worms destroy this body, yet in my flesh shall I see God: Whom I shall see for myself, and mine eyes shall behold, and not another; though my reins be consumed within me. But ye should say, Why persecute we him, seeing **the root of the matter** is found in me? Be ye afraid of the sword: for wrath bringeth the punishments of the sword, that ye may know there is a judgment* (Job 19:25–29).

Example of Use: FMC Corp. captures the **root of the matter** in a spot for Capture, an insecticide. "Why don't we give our corn to the rootworm?" asks a voiceover. "Well, why don't we give our ice cream to the flies? Our sidewalk to the gum? Why don't we just give our planet to the apes?" ("Landmarks," Jan. 8, 2001, *Advertising Age*)

Rose of Sharon

Means: Reference to the rose of Sharon cited in Song of Solomon 2:1; a plant, Hibiscus syriacus, having showy white, red, or purple flowers

Biblical Text: *I am the **rose of Sharon**, and the lily of the valleys* (Song of Solomon 2:1).

Example of Use: One of the most glorious hot-weather plants is the **rose of Sharon**. It is only because of our deep-seated prejudice toward deciduous plants that we do not see more of it. ("Gardening **Rose of Sharon** a Terrific Summer-Blooming Treasure," Joshua Siskin, July 15, 2000, *Daily News*, Los Angeles)

Rule with a rod of iron

Means: To control a group with absolute power

Biblical Text: *And out of his mouth goeth a sharp sword, that with it he should smite the nations: and he shall **rule them with a rod of iron**: and he treadeth the winepress of the fierceness and wrath of Almighty God* (Revelation 19:15). See also Rev. 2:27; 12:5.

Example of Use: Once we had matrons who **ruled** the wards **with a rod of iron** but, since their demise, the basics of care have been overlooked and standards have fallen to a woeful low. ("NHS Bugbear," Oct. 31, 2007, *The Daily Mail*, London)

R

Run the race

Means: To pursue or persevere for something, especially an important goal

Biblical Text: *Wherefore seeing we also are compassed about with so great a cloud of witnesses, let us lay aside every weight, and the sin which doth so easily beset us, and let us **run** with patience **the race** that is set before us* (Hebrews 12:1).

Example of Use: In any race, inspiration, endurance and models are needed. I am not speaking of a ROLE model but a REAL model, someone who has **run the race** and fought the battles and WON! ("**Run the Race** . . . It's Yours to Run. (Perseverance as Key to Success)," Calvin Mackie, Apr. 1, 1996, *The Black Collegian*)

Ruth

Means: Reference to a Gentile woman of the OT who was an ancestor of Jesus

Biblical Text: *And **Ruth** said, Intreat me not to leave thee, or to return from following after thee: for whither thou goest, I will go; and where thou lodgest, I will lodge: thy people shall be my people, and thy God my God* (Ruth 1:16).

Example of Use: Often, mother-in-law and daughter-in-law relationships are rewarding. But sometimes they are very painful and, for better or worse, the effects of this relationship can affect the extended family. In most cultures, this relationship is expected to be full of tension, and folk sayings and jokes reflect the expected hostility between a daughter-in-law and her mother-in-law. In contrast, however, is the mother-daughter-in-law relationship described in the Bible's Book of **Ruth**—a model of an ideal in-law relationship. ("Women Examine Special In-Law Relationship: Their Book Reflects Experiences of In-Laws," Pam Griffin, Apr. 14, 2007, *Destin Log*, Destin, FL)

RAISING CAIN

S

"STUMBLING BLOCK"

Sabbath

Means: A period of rest; any special day of prayer or rest resembling the Sabbath

Biblical Text: *Remember the **sabbath** day, to keep it holy. Six days shalt thou labour, and do all thy work: But the seventh day is the **sabbath** of the LORD thy God: in it thou shalt not do any work, thou, nor thy son, nor thy daughter, thy manservant, nor thy maidservant, nor thy cattle, nor thy stranger that is within thy gates: For in six days the LORD made heaven and earth, the sea, and all that in them is, and rested the seventh day: wherefore the LORD blessed the sabbath day, and hallowed it* (Exodus 20:8–11).

Example of Use: Even in subtropical Los Angeles, there is a down time for plants. Despite balmy late-November weather, the shortened days and colder nights signal to plants that dormancy is at hand. For the next eight weeks, plants will grow scarcely, if at all. For gardeners, this is a precious time, a **Sabbath** season. No need to worry about doing anything, no need to assess whether it is too late to prune or too early to plant. If you plant now, what you put in the ground will just sit there; it may as well be in a pot. ("Nice Landscape Doable in Cold," Joshua Siskin, Dec. 2, 2000, *Daily News,* Los Angeles)

Sackcloth and ashes

Means: A sign of humility and contrition

Biblical Text: *When Mordecai perceived all that was done, Mordecai rent his clothes, and put on sackcloth with ashes, and went out into the midst of the city, and cried with a loud and a bitter cry; And came even before the king's gate: for none might enter into the king's gate clothed with sackcloth. And in every province, whithersoever the king's commandment and his decree* *came, there was great mourning among the Jews, and fasting, and weeping, and wailing; and many lay in **sackcloth and ashes*** (Esther 4:1–3).

Example of Use: No word has less meaning or says as much about what has become of education. It is easy—and fashionable—to dismiss it as a personal pet peeve (a pedagogical hypersensitivity,) a verbal tic (like Tourette's, a disability that, though embarrassing, calls for accommodation, not correction), or a sophomoric affliction akin to acne—soon to be outgrown and impolite to point out. It amuses others as an endearing aspect of the ingénue who texts through class and surfaces now and again, with hand raised, bursting with earnestness to volunteer that "like, when I, like, think about this, I, like. . . . " ("Thank you, Heather," says the instructor, grateful for any relief from his or her own monotonous monologue.) Then there are those who are merely disdainful, content to ridicule the afflicted, and take it on as part of **the sackcloth and ashes** that goes with being a teacher. The collective response of the academy: feigned deafness. ("Diss 'Like,'" Ted Gup, *The Chronicle of Higher Education*, Jan. 8, 2012)

Sadducees

Means: An elite, priestly group in the NT that did not believe in bodily resurrection

Biblical Text: *Then came to him [Jesus] certain of the **Sadducees**, which deny that there is any resurrection and they asked him, Saying, Master, Moses wrote unto us, If any man's brother die, having a wife, and he die without children, that his brother should take his wife, and raise up seed unto his brother. There were therefore seven brethren: and the first took a wife, and died without children. And the second took her to wife, and he died childless. And the third took her; and in like manner the seven also: and* *they left no children, and died. Last of all the woman died also. Therefore in the resurrection whose wife of them is she? for seven had her to wife* (Luke 20:27–33).

Example of Use: Ian Paisley goes on the offensive over the IRA. Firstly he suggests that John de Chastellaine was "misinformed" as to the extent of IRA weaponry, and goes on to demand that the IRA must be packed away for good before his party will deal with Sinn Fein. As for an inclusive Executive: "It is buried in a **Sadducee**'s grave from which there is no resurrection," as the *Irish News* has it (subs needed). Then he accuses Tony Blair of encouraging IRA criminality by his government's offer to restore expenses to Sinn Fein, in the wake of the latest IMC report. ("Paisley: Executive Buried in a **Sadducee**'s Grave," Mick Fealty, Feb. 6, 2006, www.sluggerotoole.com)

Safety in numbers, There's

Means: A group can sometimes make better decisions than individuals alone and can help conceal one's responsibility for a poor decision or action

Biblical Text: *Where no counsel is, the people fall: but **in the multitude of counsellors there is safety*** (Proverbs 11:14).

Example of Use: Don't be afraid or embarrassed to ask others for help. Seek counsel in all aspects of life, even in the areas of your expertise. Others may be able to sharpen your ideas or add an insight that elevates your thoughts or work to a higher level. Most people are glad to give advice in areas where they are knowledgeable. In the same way, be open to helping others. ("**In the Multitude of Counselors: Safety in Sound Advice**," Ken Faulkenberry, arborinvestmentplanner.com)

S

Salt of the earth

Means: Any person or group of people who are guileless, uncomplicated, innocent, good, or of admirable character; among the best or noblest members of society

Biblical Text: *Ye are the **salt of the earth**: but if the salt have lost his savour, wherewith shall it be salted? It is thenceforth good for nothing, but to be cast out, and to be trodden under foot of men* (Matthew 5:13).

Example of Use: We are the **salt of the earth** here. Not as fancy as some places, not as rundown as others. We are salt, bread, and wine—the basic elements on a table, the elemental fruits of life. We are capable of extraordinary things here; in literacy, in fellowship, and in leadership. Let's make it happen. ("The **Salt of the Earth**; A Vision of Literature and Literacy in 'The Heart of New York,'" Laurie Halse Anderson, Apr. 2, 2006, *The Post-Standard*, Syracuse, NY)

Salt, Season with

Means: To add zest, interest, or liveliness to something

Biblical Text: *Let your speech be always with grace, **seasoned with salt**, that ye may know how ye ought to answer every man* (Colossians 4:6).

Example of Use: Yes, I would answer the same. I hope that all my answers are "**seasoned with salt**" and presentable enough for my mother. Actually, I fear some of the answers that my mother might give on this site. She can be pretty tough! (By Perryman, Jan. 3, 2007, www.answerbag.com)

Samaritan

Means: An inhabitant of Samaria; A reference to the "Good Samaritan" in the NT; Someone who is compassionate and helpful to another in distress

Biblical Text: *But a certain **Samaritan**, as he journeyed, came where he was: and when he saw him, he had compassion on him* (Luke 10:33).

Example of Use: Under the good **samaritan** laws which grant immunity, if the good **samaritan** makes an error while rendering emergency medical care, he or she cannot be held legally liable for damages in court. However, two conditions usually must be met; 1) the aid must be given at the scene of the emergency, and, 2) if the volunteer" has other motives, such as the hope of being paid a fee or reward, then the law will not apply. (uslegal.com)

Same calling

Means: The same occupation as someone else

Biblical Text: *Let every man abide in the **same calling** wherein he was called* (1 Corinthians 7:20).

Example of Use: While her mother has been an inspiration to her, Lopez said her desire to also become an educator came from a strong inner passion to promote lifelong learning in young children. "My mother said she had a calling, and I felt the **same calling**." ("Mother-Daughter Teachers to Earn Master's Degrees in Education," May 16, 2008, U.S. Fed News Service)

Samson

Means: A man of unusual strength or with long hair

Biblical Text: *And she [Delilah] said unto him [**Samson**], How canst thou say, I love thee, when thine heart is not with me? thou*

*hast mocked me these three times, and hast not told me wherein thy great strength lieth. And it came to pass, when she pressed him daily with her words, and urged him, so that his soul was vexed unto death; That he told her all his heart, and said unto her, There hath not come a razor upon mine head; for I have been a Nazarite unto God from my mother's womb: if I be shaven, then my strength will go from me, and I shall become weak, and be like any other man. And when Delilah saw that he had told her all his heart, she sent and called for the lords of the Philistines, saying, Come up this once, for he hath shewed me all his heart. Then the lords of the Philistines came up unto her, and brought money in their hand. And she made him [**Samson**] sleep upon her knees; and she called for a man, and she caused him to shave off the seven locks of his head; and she began to afflict him, and his strength went from him* (Judges 16:15–19).

Example of Use: There aren't many actual mullets in the majors anymore, now that Randy Johnson has shed his. But flowing locks haven't hurt a certain ex-Sox. Magglio Ordonez is having an MVP kind of year for the Detroit Tigers. His curls look nearly twice as long as a Tiger than when they blew through the Windy City. "I think he's crazy and he needs to cut it," Mets bench coach and former Sox manager Jerry Manuel said recently. "But he probably feels it's a **Samson** thing right now." **Samson**'s haircut . . . Elvis Presley's when he joined the Army . . . John Edwards' $400 one on the presidential campaign trail . . . throughout time there have been a lot of trims. ("Chicago Has Always Had Its Share of Head Cases," July 1, 2007, *Chicago Tribune*)

Samson, As strong as

Means: To be unusually strong (as was Samson of the OT)

Biblical Text: *And it came to pass, when their hearts were merry, that they said, Call for* **Samson**, *that he may make us sport. And they called for* **Samson** *out of the prison house; and he made them sport: and they set him between the pillars. And* **Samson** *said unto the lad that held him by the hand, Suffer me that I may feel the pillars whereupon the house standeth, that I may lean upon them. Now the house was full of men and women; and all the lords of the Philistines were there; and there were upon the roof about three thousand men and women, that beheld while* **Samson** *made sport. And Samson called unto the* LORD, *and said, O Lord God, remember me, I pray thee, and strengthen me, I pray thee, only this once, O God, that I may be at once avenged of the Philistines for my two eyes. And* **Samson** *took hold of the two middle pillars upon which the house stood, and on which it was borne up, of the one with his right hand, and of the other with his left. And* **Samson** *said, Let me die with the Philistines. And he bowed himself with all his might; and the house fell upon the lords, and upon all the people that were therein. So the dead which he slew at his death were more than they which he slew in his life* (Judges 16:25–30).

Example of Use: But what diet is best? The debate is still **as strong as Samson** on anabolic steroids and will likely never be settled. It all depends on who you ask, what you believe, and what you think you can stick to. All I can offer is good sense and my own personal experience. ("I'm Not Lovin' It: Choose," Apr. 25, 2007, progressivewednesday.com)

Sanctum, Inner

Means: An inviolably private place; a special place, especially one that is private or accessible to only an elite group (based on the most restricted place in the Jewish temple, accessible only by the high priest once a year)

Biblical Text: *The vail shall divide unto you between the holy place and the most holy: And thou shalt put the mercy seat upon the ark of the testimony in **the most holy place*** (Exodus 26:33–34).

Example of Use: The paneling opens to a hidden room that Mr. Rogers' staff calls his **"inner sanctum,"** the place where he gets the real work done. Inside is a cluttered desk. ("The **Inner Sanctum,**" May 23, 2005, *Crain's Chicago Business*)

Sand, Build on

Means: To base something on an unstable foundation

Biblical Text: *And every one that heareth these sayings of mine, and doeth them not, shall be likened unto a foolish man, which **built** his house **upon the sand**: And the rain descended, and the floods came, and the winds blew, and beat upon that house; and it fell: and great was the fall of it* (Matthew 7:26–27).

Example of Use: Mike Holmes believes in doing a job right the first time. He shows how the botched job should have been completed, fixes the project thoroughly, and educates the owners on future decisions. It's all about building it right the first time. So what does this have to do with your writing career? Plenty. I believe that if you build your writing career right the first time, you'll set yourself up for a lifetime of success. The key is *a solid foundation.* ("Is Your **House Built on Sand** or Stone?" Steve Roller, American Writers and Artists Inc., http:// www.awaionline.com)

Satan

Means: God's archenemy; someone fiercely opposed to God or his people

Biblical Text: *But he turned, and said unto Peter, Get thee behind me, Satan: thou art an offence unto me: for thou savourest not the things that be of God, but those that be of men* (Matthew 16:23).

Example of Use: Inducing man to postpone has been the most successful weapon of **Satan**. "Don't Worry, there is enough time" has been the most effective and favorite sentence of **Satan**. ("Satan's Favorite Sentence," Paulose Varkis, http://voices.yahoo.com/satans-favorite-sentence-6250254.html)

Satyr

Means: A strange, goat-like creature; a lascivious man

Biblical Text: *The wild beasts of the desert shall also meet with the wild beasts of the island, and the satyr shall cry to his fellow; the screech owl also shall rest there, and find for herself a place of rest* (Isaiah 34:14).

Example of Use: Few Broadway stars can boast that their own soap-and-perfume line is for sale in the theater lobby. This retail coup has, though, been wrangled by Alan Cumming, the compulsively watchable **satyr** of an actor who headlines in the Roundabout Theater Company's The Threepenny Opera. ("Now, a Word from Our Sponsors: 'The Threepenny Opera,'" Celia Wren, May 19, 2006, *Commonweal*)

Saul (OT)

Means: Reference to the first king of Israel in the OT

Biblical Text: *And all the people went to Gilgal; and there they made Saul king before the LORD in Gilgal; and there they sacrificed sacrifices of peace offerings before the LORD; and there Saul and all the men of Israel rejoiced greatly* (1 Samuel 11:15).

Example of Use: When [King] **Saul** is compelled to confront the evidence of his sin, the "bleating sheep," he must change course. His contrition and pleas are too late. God knows **Saul's** contrition is not genuine, that his request for forgiveness is not sincere. His initial defiance is the emblem of his character. **Saul**, unlike David, loses his throne. The White House desperately wants a deal with Congress to resolve the scandal, but Mr. Clinton, like King **Saul**, continues to shade and evade the truth. ("David, **Saul** and Bill," Suzanne Fields, Sept. 28, 1998, *The Washington Times*)

Saul (NT)

Means: Reference to Saul, or Paul, in the NT

Biblical Text: *And **Saul**, yet breathing out threatenings and slaughter against the disciples of the Lord, went unto the high priest, And desired of him letters to Damascus to the synagogues, that if he found any of this way, whether they were men or women, he might bring them bound unto Jerusalem. And as he journeyed, he came near Damascus: and suddenly there shined round about him a light from heaven: And he fell to the earth, and heard a voice saying unto him, **Saul, Saul**, why persecutest thou me? And he said, Who art thou, Lord? And the Lord said, I am Jesus whom thou persecutest: it is hard for thee to kick against the pricks. And he trembling and astonished said, Lord, what wilt thou have me to do? And the Lord said unto him, Arise, and go into the city, and it shall be told thee what thou must do. And the men which journeyed with him stood speechless, hearing a voice, but seeing no man. And **Saul** arose from the earth; and when his eyes were opened, he saw no man: but they led him by the hand, and brought him into Damascus. And he was three days without sight, and neither did eat nor drink (Acts 9:1–22).*

S

Example of Use: As New Year's miracles go, this one is very much incomplete. Jerry Bush's transformation from drug dealer to community asset is a work in progress. Still, I walk away from a visit with this 22-year-old, 270-pound teddy bear of a guy with the feeling that he just might make it. And if he does, then dozens—no thousands—of young people we are too quick to dismiss as lawbreakers and thugs have a shot at making it.

It's easy enough to get excited about people who, like **Saul** on the road to Damascus, turn their lives completely around. But **Saul** was an expert in both his lives. Jerry Bush never was that good as a drug dealer. ("Big Jerry Turns His Life Around; A Former Drug Dealer Learns His Life Can Have Meaning," Dec. 30, 1999, *The News & Record*, Piedmont Triad, NC)

Scales fall from one's eyes

Means: To be no longer deceived as a truth is revealed

Biblical Text: *And Ananias went his way, and entered into the house; and putting his hands on him said, Brother Saul, the Lord, even Jesus, that appeared unto thee in the way as thou camest, hath sent me, that thou mightest receive thy sight, and be filled with the Holy Ghost. And immediately **there fell from his eyes as it had been scales**: and he received sight forthwith, and arose, and was baptized. And when he had received meat, he was strengthened. Then was Saul certain days with the disciples which were at Damascus* (Acts 9:17–19).

Example of Use: Suddenly as I looked around the room, the **scales fell from my eyes**. They had picked the solution that offered an acceptable failure. No one would lose their jobs from picking this solution, and, if the department did shut down due to that failure, no one would blame them individually, so it would not interfere with their chances of getting other jobs. ("Lessons of a Searcher's Life," July 1, 2002, *Searcher*)

Scapegoat

Means: Someone made to bear the punishment for others or to take their blame

Biblical Text: *And Aaron shall cast lots upon the two goats; one lot for the LORD, and the other lot for the **scapegoat**. And Aaron shall bring the goat upon which the LORD's lot fell, and offer him for a sin offering. But the goat, on which the lot fell to be the **scapegoat**, shall be presented alive before the LORD, to make an atonement with him, and to let him go for a **scapegoat** into the wilderness* (Leviticus 16:8–10). See also Lev. 16:26–27.

Example of Use: Dan Rather filed a $70 million lawsuit against CBS on Wednesday, alleging that the network made him a "**scapegoat**" for a discredited story about President Bush's National Guard service. Rather, 75, whose final months were clouded by controversy over the report, says the complaint stems from "CBS' intentional mishandling" of the aftermath of the story. ("Rather Sues, Says CBS Made Him 'Scapegoat,'" Samuel Maull, Sept. 20, 2007, *The Virginian Pilot*)

Scarlet woman

Means: A sexually promiscuous woman, especially a prostitute or an adulteress

Biblical Text: *And there came one of the seven angels which had the seven vials, and talked with me, saying unto me, Come hither; I will shew unto thee the judgment of the great whore that sitteth upon many waters: With whom the kings of the earth have committed fornication, and the inhabitants of the earth have been made drunk with the wine of her fornication. So he carried me away in the spirit into the wilderness: and I saw a woman sit upon a scarlet coloured beast, full of names of blasphemy, having seven heads and ten horns. **And the woman was***

arrayed in purple and scarlet colour, and decked with gold and precious stones and pearls, having a golden cup in her hand full of abominations and filthiness of her fornication: And upon her forehead was a name written, MYSTERY, BABYLON THE GREAT, THE MOTHER OF HARLOTS AND ABOMINATIONS OF THE EARTH. And I saw the woman drunken with the blood of the saints, and with the blood of the martyrs of Jesus: and when I saw her, I wondered with great admiration (Revelation 17:1–6).

Example of Use: If you want to blend in, wear black. If you want to stand out, red's your surefire route. Red is the colour of love, sex, passion, power, dynamism, notoriety, excitement, joy and danger. . . . But red can also be the colour of hate and war. And it has the association with the **scarlet woman**, a woman of ill repute. This is where red in fashion gets dangerous. ("Lady in Red," Eva Friede, Dec. 2006, www.canada.com)

Scorpions, To chastise with

Means: To punish someone by excessive means

Biblical Text: *And now whereas my father [Solomon] did lade you with a heavy yoke, I will add to your yoke: my father hath chastised you with whips, but I [Rehoboam] **will chastise you with scorpions**. So Jeroboam and all the people came to Rehoboam the third day, as the king had appointed, saying, Come to me again the third day. And the king answered the people roughly, and forsook the old men's counsel that they gave him; And spake to them after the counsel of the young men, saying, My father made your yoke heavy, and I will add to your yoke: my father also chastised you with whips, but I will **chastise you with scorpions**. Wherefore the king hearkened not unto the people; for the cause was from the* LORD, *that he might perform*

S

his saying, which the LORD spake by Ahijah the Shilonite unto Jeroboam the son of Nebat (1 Kings 12:11–15).

Example of Use: From 1911 through part of 1913, he [Ludwig Wittgenstein] worked with Russell on mathematics and logic, and met G. E. Moore, whose chair in philosophy at Cambridge he'd inherit in 1939. They found him brilliant, ferociously impatient, ill-mannered and intimidating. He retired for a year to a Norwegian mountain cabin, there to **chastise himself with scorpions** for impurities. He fought during the war for the Austro-Hungarian Empire, on the Russian front. ("A Philosophical Investigation," John Leonard, June 7, 1993, *The Nation*)

Seat of the scornful

Means: A group or conditions despised by those who seek the good

Biblical Text: *Blessed is the man that walketh not in the counsel of the ungodly, nor standeth in the way of sinners, nor sitteth in the **seat of the scornful*** (Psalm 1:1).

Example of Use: He eloquently described Congressman Ford through the words of the Psalmist, as a man who does not walk in the counsel of the ungodly, nor sit in the **seat of the scornful**. ("The Men of Fourth Street Observes Annual Celebration," Natasha David, Aug. 1, 2000, *Columbus Times*)

Second Coming

Means: The unexpected reappearance of someone in an especially climactic event

Biblical Text: *For as the lightning cometh out of the east, and shineth even unto the west; **so shall also the coming of the Son of man be*** (Matthew 24:27).

Example of Use: The man who unleashed *Chainsaw* believes the **second coming** of the thunderous bull will strike fear into the hearts of riders at this weekend's Mount Isa rodeo. ("*Chainsaw's* **Second Coming** to Strike Fear into Riders," Aug. 11, 2006, *AAP General News,* Australia)

Second mile, Go the

Means: To do more than what is required, especially as a kind gesture

Biblical Text: *And whosoever shall compel thee to go a mile,* ***go with him twain*** (Matthew 5:41).

Example of Use: "Our staff is on the front line in the fight to give children the best start in life possible," said Paula Tolson, manager of the Communications Office for the state Department of Human Resources, for which the county OCSE is a field office. "Our people are willing to **go the second mile** to help make the future brighter for families in need, even though they are dealing with furloughs and cutbacks." ("Workers Honored for Making a Difference," May 4, 2011, *Maryland Gazette*)

See eye to eye

Means: To agree with someone

Biblical Text: *Thy watchmen shall lift up the voice; with the voice together shall they sing: for they shall* ***see eye to eye****, when the* LORD *shall bring again Zion* (Isaiah 52:8).

Example of Use: Speaking publicly for the first time since his decision to leave Kansas State, [basketball] guard Fred Peete said Tuesday his ill will toward coach Jim Wooldridge and the program kept building during last season. Peete, a sophomore junior-college transfer, thought he should be playing more point guard, among other things. "We just didn't **see eye to**

eye," Peete said. "More than Coach, it was just the program. I just didn't like the direction the program was going." ("Peete: We Didn't **See Eye to Eye**: The Former Kansas State Guard Said He Is Transferring to New Mexico State," Jeffrey Parson, May 4, 2005, *The Wichita Eagle*, KS)

See the light (See also "Damascus road experience" and "Scales fall from one's eyes")

Means: To understand or begin to understand something

Biblical Text: *And Saul, yet breathing out threatenings and slaughter against the disciples of the Lord, went unto the high priest, And desired of him letters to Damascus to the synagogues, that if he found any of this way, whether they were men or women, he might bring them bound unto Jerusalem. And as he journeyed, he came near Damascus: **and suddenly there shined round about him a light from heaven**: And he fell to the earth, and heard a voice saying unto him, Saul, Saul, why persecutest thou me? And he said, Who art thou, Lord? And the Lord said, I am Jesus whom thou persecutest: it is hard for thee to kick against the pricks. And he trembling and astonished said, Lord, what wilt thou have me to do? And the Lord said unto him, Arise, and go into the city, and it shall be told thee what thou must do* (Acts 9:1–6). See also Rom. 2:18–20; 2 Pet. 1:19.

S

Example of use: There was less session work in the late '80s, but Gold was on Cher's multi-million selling Heart Of Stone (1989). In 1992, the UK band, Undercover, had a Top 10 with a revival of "Never Let Her Slip Away," and he wrote a US country hit for Wynonna Judd, "I **Saw The Light**." A torch song, "Try Me Again," that he and Ronstadt had written for Hasten Down The Wind, was revived by Trisha Yearwood and was also a country success. ("Andrew Gold," Spencer Leigh, June 8, 2011, *The Independent*, London)

See through a glass darkly

Means: To have an obscure or imperfect vision or understanding of something

Biblical Text: *For now we **see through a glass, darkly**; but then face to face: now I know in part; but then shall I know even as also I am known* (1 Corinthians 13:12).

Example of Use: Here on planet earth, the obfuscation is relentless. We squint by day as the firmament pours down on us in blinding waves, veiling the mysteries of space. By night the stars twinkle, twinkle, hiding in plain sight behind that pulsing mirage. We **see through a glass darkly**. . . . The earth's atmosphere is the culprit, of course, scattering blue light all day and making the stars flicker at night, to the profound frustration of astronomers. ("Big Freakin' Laser Beams in Space: By Shining a Light on Atmospheric Turbulence, the Air Force's Starfire Optical Range Has Taken the Twinkle out of Stars—and Dramatically Improved Our Vision of All That Is Above Us," Bucky McMahon, Dec. 1, 2006, *Esquire*)

Seek and you shall find

Means: An effort by one is required in order to reach one's goal

Biblical Text: *And I say unto you, Ask, and it shall be given you; **seek, and ye shall find**; knock, and it shall be opened unto you* (Luke 11:9).

Example of Use: "It's written, 'seek and ye shall find.'" But first, 'imagine what you seek.' Otherwise, you will end up searching everything everywhere forever." (Toba Beta, "My Ancestor was an Ancient Astronaut," http://www.goodreads.com/quotes/268821)

Separate the sheep from the goats

Means: Divide people or things into superior and inferior or favored and unfavored groups

Biblical Text: *[The Son of man] shall separate them one from another, as a shepherd **divideth his sheep from the goats: And he shall set the sheep on his right hand, but the goats on the left*** (Matthew 25:31–34).

Example of Use: They cut off any cluster of grapes that might produce inferior wine by virtue of being under-ripe, unevenly ripe, over-ripe, sunburned or somehow anemic. Only the fittest survive, less [sic] than half the clusters, and only the fittest of those highly flavored grapes go into the limited bottling of Harlan Estate cabernet. "We **separate the sheep from the goats**," says Weaver. The goats go into the cheap stuff, Harlan's second label, the Maiden—which sells at about $100 a bottle. ("Two Hundred Buck Chuck," Stephen Yafa, Nov. 7, 2006, salon.com)

Separate the wheat from the chaff

Means: Select what is useful or valuable and reject what is useless or worthless

Biblical Text: *The ungodly are . . . like **the chaff which the wind driveth away*** (Psalm 1:4).

Example of Use: "Only new hiring policies that effectively **separate the wheat from the chaff** can transform the teaching profession." ("**Separating the Wheat from the Chaff**: School Choice Can Transform the Teaching Profession, Study Finds," Sept. 25, 2006, *US Newswire*)

Seraphic

Means: A sweet nature befitting an angel or cherub

Biblical Text: *In the year that king Uzziah died I saw also the Lord sitting upon a throne, high and lifted up, and his train filled the temple. Above it stood the **seraphims**: each one had six wings; with twain he covered his face, and with twain he covered his feet, and with twain he did fly. And one cried unto another, and said, Holy, holy, holy, is the LORD of hosts: the whole earth is full of his glory. And the posts of the door moved at the voice of him that cried, and the house was filled with smoke. Then said I, Woe is me! for I am undone; because I am a man of unclean lips, and I dwell in the midst of a people of unclean lips: for mine eyes have seen the King, the LORD of hosts. Then flew one of the **seraphims** unto me, having a live coal in his hand, which he had taken with the tongs from off the altar: And he laid it upon my mouth, and said, Lo, this hath touched thy lips; and thine iniquity is taken away, and thy sin purged* (Isaiah 6:1–7).

Example of Use: Is there any more **seraphic** jangle in the world than the riot of melodies, scales and sonorities that tumble out of a conservatory's open windows on a fine spring day? A young woman on the second floor is singing Puccini; a pianist is making his way through Beethoven's "Hammerklavier" sonata; an orchestra is preparing "Carmina Burana" in stops and starts—and the industrious chaos leaves a listener cheerfully overwhelmed. ("Ah, the Glorious Strains of Everyday Life at Peabody; Music Fills the Air at Updated Conservatory," Tim Page, Apr. 26, 2004, *The Washington Post*)

Serpent

Means: The serpent in the Creation story in the OT; a subtle, sly, or treacherous person

Biblical Text: *Now **the serpent** was more subtil than any beast of the field which the LORD God had made. And he said unto the*

woman, Yea, hath God said, Ye shall not eat of every tree of the garden? (Genesis 3:1).

Example of Use: "We have a character named Cyrus, he's a **serpent** and the antagonist. We've had children come up to Cyrus and hit him and try to help us out. They hit him in the belly or tell him he's bad. ("Breathing Fire into Dragon Tales Children Encouraged to Go Along on Fun-Filled 'Journey to Crystal Cave,'" Jen Mulson, Jan. 16, 2004, *The Gazette*)

Set one's face against

Means: To strongly disapprove of or oppose someone or something

Biblical Text: *And I will **set my face against** that man, and will cut him off from among his people; because he hath given of his seed unto Molech, to defile my sanctuary, and to profane my holy name.... Then I will **set my face against** that man, and against his family, and will cut him off, and all that go a whoring after him, to commit whoredom with Molech, from among their people. And the soul that turneth after such as have familiar spirits, and after wizards, to go a whoring after them, I will even **set my face against** that soul, and will cut him off from among his people.... And I will **set my face against** you, and ye shall be slain before your enemies: they that hate you shall reign over you; and ye shall flee when none pursueth you* (Leviticus 20:3, 5–6; 26:17).

Example of Use: From his parents and church, he [Ken Starr] had learned to "**set your face against** the popular mood." ("1998 and All That—the Lewinsky Affair Nailed—at Last," Jay Nordlinger, May 22, 2000, *National Review*)

Set one's teeth on edge

Means: To cause someone to feel intense discomfort or irritation

Biblical Text: *In those days they shall say no more, The fathers have eaten a sour grape, and the children's **teeth are set on edge**.* (Jeremiah 31:29). See also Ezek. 18:2.

Example of Use: I hear what you're saying, but, to be honest, basically, at the end of the day, it's, like, literally not rocket science. Could this be the most irritating sentence ever? A study today reveals the words and phrases that most **set our teeth on edge**. From American imports "awesome" and "24/7," to bosses who refer to staff as "crack troops," the report lists the clichés we cannot stand. ("It's Not Rocket Science . . . like, Just Shut Up," Scott Duggan, Mar. 24, 2004, *Evening Standard*, London)

Seven last words

Means: Reference to Jesus' seven last statements made from the cross; any final statements made by someone

Biblical Text: *And about the ninth hour Jesus cried with a loud voice, saying, **Eli, Eli, lama sabachthani?** that is to say, My God, my God, why hast thou forsaken me?* (Matthew 27:46).

*Then said Jesus, **Father, forgive them; for they know not what they do**. And they parted his raiment, and cast lots* (Luke 23:34).

*And Jesus said unto him, **Verily I say unto thee, To day shalt thou be with me in paradise*** (Luke 23:43).

*And when Jesus had cried with a loud voice, he said, **Father, into thy hands I commend my spirit**: and having said thus, he gave up the ghost* (Luke 23:46).

*When Jesus therefore saw his mother, and the disciple standing by, whom he loved, he saith unto his mother, **Woman, behold thy son!** Then saith he to the disciple, **Behold thy mother!** And*

from that hour that disciple took her unto his own home. After this, Jesus knowing that all things were now accomplished, that the scripture might be fulfilled, saith, **I thirst**. . . . *When Jesus therefore had received the vinegar, he said,* **It is finished**: *and he bowed his head, and gave up the ghost* (John 19:26–28, 30).

Example of Use: Law of Creativity: The **seven last words** of most organizations, businesses and families are "we've always done it that way before." Creativity is simply looking at something that has always been there (the need to balance family and career) and seeing something that has never been seen before (your own unique ways to do this balance thing). Use your creativity and experiment to find what works for you. ("Be Creative in Balancing Work, Family," Jeff Herring, Sept. 11, 2000, Knight Ridder/Tribune News Service)

Seven pillars of wisdom

Means: Wise maxims

Biblical Text: *Wisdom hath builded her house, she hath hewn out her seven pillars* (Proverbs 9:1).

Example of Use: The report recommended that health messages be communicated to consumers "on a sustained, continuous basis." It laid down '**seven pillars of wisdom**' for retailers and processors to take account of in their marketing. ("Potato Industry 'Must Pull in Young People,'" Richard Ford, Jan. 31, 2009, *Grocer*)

Seven years of plenty

Means: A period of good fortune or abundance

Biblical Text: *And it came to pass at the end of two full years, that Pharaoh dreamed: and, behold, he stood by the river. And, behold, there came up out of the river seven wellfavoured kine*

S

*and fatfleshed; and they fed in a meadow. And, behold, seven other kine came up after them out of the river, ill favoured and leanfleshed; and stood by the other kine upon the brink of the river. And the ill favoured and leanfleshed kine did eat up the seven wellfavoured and fat kine. So Pharaoh awoke. And he slept and dreamed the second time: and, behold, seven ears of corn came up upon one stalk, rank and good. And, behold, seven thin ears and blasted with the east wind sprung up after them. And the seven thin ears devoured the seven rank and full ears. And Pharaoh awoke, and, behold, it was a dream. And it came to pass in the morning that his spirit was troubled; and he sent and called for all the magicians of Egypt, and all the wise men thereof: and Pharaoh told them his dream; but there was none that could interpret them unto Pharaoh. . . . And Joseph said unto Pharaoh, The dream of Pharaoh is one: God hath shown Pharaoh what he is about to do. The **seven good kine are seven years; and the seven good ears are seven years**: the dream is one. And the seven thin and ill favoured kine that came up after them are seven years; and the seven empty ears blasted with the east wind shall be seven years of famine. This is the thing which I have spoken unto Pharaoh: What God is about to do he showeth unto Pharaoh. Behold, there come **seven years of great plenty** throughout all the land of Egypt: And there shall arise after them seven years of famine; and all the plenty shall be forgotten in the land of Egypt; and the famine shall consume the land; And the plenty shall not be known in the land by reason of that famine following; for it shall be very grievous. And for that the dream was doubled unto Pharaoh twice; it is because the thing is established by God, and God will shortly bring it to pass* (Genesis 41:1–7, 25–32).

Example of Use: From surplus to deficit: suddenly America's states find that their finances are ailing. Revenues have plunged. Costs, particularly medical costs, are spiraling. In

California, the worst afflicted state of all, the budget office predicts deficits for the next five years if tax rates are not raised or spending cut. Harsh choices must be made. America's least fortunate are the likely victims. This is the unhappy end to **seven years of plenty**. ("Analysis: Cal. Leads States' Fiscal Mess," Sept. 12, 2002, United Press International)

Shadow of death

Means: A situation of intense gloom or peril; sorrow and fear associated with approaching death

Biblical Text: *Yea, though I walk through the valley of the **shadow of death**, I will fear no evil: for thou art with me; thy rod and thy staff they comfort me* (Psalm 23:4).

Example of Use: Prime Minister Gordon Brown has stolen his [David Cameron's] thunder by lifting the **shadow of death** duties from more than 2.4m homeowners with immediate effect. ("Your Money: Will to Win; Brown Scored a Victory over Cameron on Inheritance Tax—but Are the Reforms As Good for You As They Are for the PM?" John Husband, Oct. 10, 2007, *The Mirror*, London)

Shambles

Means: (1) A place in severe disarray; (2) a place where meat and other kinds of food are sold

Biblical Text: *Whatsoever is sold in the **shambles**, that eat, asking no question for conscience sake: For the earth is the Lord's, and the fulness thereof* (1 Corinthians 10:25–26).

Example of Use: The launch in Wales this week of a new "super commission" covering equality issues has been described as an "absolute **shambles**." ("Equality Commission

Launch Labelled 'Absolute **Shambles**,'" Martin Shipton, Oct. 3, 2007, *Western Mail*, Cardiff, Wales)

Sharp tongue

Means: A manner of speaking intended to criticize or hurt someone

Biblical Text: *My soul is among lions: and I lie even among them that are set on fire, even the sons of men, whose teeth are spears and arrows, and their **tongue** a **sharp** sword* (Psalm 57:4).

Example of Use: Even ministers can't escape Ms. Bennett's fast, **sharp tongue** when she fumes and fusses about "a cadre of people" who are capable of doing much more to help the less fortunate but don't. ("Bennett's **Sharp Tongue** and Soft Heart Aid Less-Fortunate," Adrienne T. Washington, Mar. 23, 2001, *The Washington Times*)

Sheep without a shepherd, Like

Means: A condition in which a group has no leader, especially one who is sympathetic to them

Biblical Text: *And Jesus went about all the cities and villages, teaching in their synagogues, and preaching the gospel of the kingdom, and healing every sickness and every disease among the people. But when he saw the multitudes, he was moved with compassion on them, because they fainted, and were scattered abroad, **as sheep having no shepherd*** (Matthew 9:35–36).

Example of Use: "You can't have a country of between 140 and 150 million people with nobody effectively in charge," said Richard Joseph, a political science professor who studies Africa at Northwestern University. "Something has got to happen." That question has risen a number of times in Nigerian newspapers, which splayed bold headlines across archive

S

photographs of their missing president. "We are 150 million **sheep without a shepherd**," said an editorial in the Nigerian newspaper NEXT. ("Nigeria's Future, President's Power in Question," Jon Gambrell, Dec. 18, 2009, AP Worldstream)

Shepherd, To

Means: To guard or guide in the manner of a shepherd

Biblical Text: *And I will set up **shepherds** over them which shall feed them: and they shall fear no more, nor be dismayed, neither shall they be lacking, saith the LORD* (Jeremiah 23:4).

Example of Use: As election night wore on and the tears started to flow, Nativo Lopez knew he had lost his seat on the school board. Arms outstretched, he turned to his followers like a **shepherd** to his flock and urged them to keep fighting for their rights, including bilingual education. Misuari was like a **shepherd** who led his flock, not to safety, but to the slaughter. The blood of his people are on his hands. And why did he lead his followers to a massacre? All because of pique. ("Santa Ana, Calif., Bilingual Education Advocate Ousted from School Board," Maria Sacchetti, Feb. 9, 2003, *The Orange County Register*, CA)

Shibboleth

Means: A word, custom, or practice used to reveal one as an outsider

Biblical Text: *Then said they unto him, Say now **Shibboleth**: and he said Sibboleth: for he could not frame to pronounce it right. Then they took him, and slew him at the passages of Jordan: and there fell at that time of the Ephraimites forty and two thousand* (Judges 12:6).

Example of Use: My father, who is an eminent and respected man of words, has informed me that the word Ibiza is a **shibboleth**, which basically means that the way you pronounce it indicates whether or not you're part of the smarty-pants in-crowd that knows about these sort of things. Apparently, the correct way to say it is "I-beetza," while I say "I-beetha," which therefore means that I'm a commoner who knows nowt. Thanks, dad. Fascinating stuff, eh? ("Get Lost in Ibiza: Mention Ibiza and People Often Think of Drunken Brits and Clubbers," Ettrick Scott, June 18, 2006, *Sunday Mercury,* Birmingham, England)

Shining light

Means: An exemplary person or leader

Biblical Text: *But the path of the just is as the **shining light**, that shineth more and more unto the perfect day: The way of the wicked is as darkness: they know not at what they stumble* (Proverbs 4:18–19).

Example of Use: The former British School, a **shining light** of the early 19th century, is in line for a new lease of life—against all the odds. Only two years ago, it was feared that this worthy old collection of buildings, in the shadow of the preened and revamped Mailbox, would simply succumb to years of neglect. ("A **Shining Light** of 19th Century," Marsya Lennox, Nov. 25, 2005, *Birmingham Post*)

Shulamite

Means: An epithet meaning "princess"

Biblical Text: *Return, return, O **Shulamite**; return, return, that we may look upon thee. What will ye see in the **Shulamite**? As it were the company of two armies* (Song of Solomon 6:13).

Example of Use: Indeed. I felt a little naughty listening to it in the newsroom, frankly. Kept looking over my shoulder as if . . . trying to read it before an editor sneaked up on me. "Let him kiss me with the kisses of his mouth," a woman's voice on the CD begins. This is "the beloved" (also known as "the **Shulamite** woman"), the female character in the Song of Solomon. "Your love is more delightful than wine. Mmmmmm, pleasing is the fragrance of your perfumes. No wonder the maidens love you." ("Sex and the Bible—and You Can Sing Along with It," Cathleen Falsani, Feb. 10, 2006, *Chicago Sun-Times*)

Sign of the times

Means: Something that shows how society is different than it was in the past

Biblical Text: *And in the morning, It will be foul weather to day: for the sky is red and lowring. O ye hypocrites, ye can discern the face of the sky; but can ye not discern the **signs of the times**? A wicked and adulterous generation seeketh after a sign; and there shall no sign be given unto it, but the sign of the prophet Jonas. And he left them, and departed. And when his disciples were come to the other side, they had forgotten to take bread* (Matthew 16:3–5).

S

Example of Use: Is domestic violence a **sign of the times**? We have heard many individuals say that some of the things happening today are a **sign of the times**. Domestic violence is physical, emotional or sexual abuse. The figures estimate 90 percent of the perpetrators are men and 10 percent are women. ("Domestic Violence, **A Sign of the Times?**" May 12, 2004, *Columbus Times*, GA)

Simony

Means: Making a profit from the sale of precious things

Biblical Text: *But there was a certain man, called **Simon**, which beforetime in the same city used sorcery, and bewitched the people of Samaria, giving out that himself was some great one: To whom they all gave heed, from the least to the greatest, saying, This man is the great power of God. And to him they had regard, because that of long time **he had bewitched them with sorceries**. But when they believed Philip preaching the things concerning the kingdom of God, and the name of Jesus Christ, they were baptized, both men and women. Then Simon himself believed also: and when he was baptized, he continued with Philip, and wondered, beholding the miracles and signs which were done. Now when the apostles which were at Jerusalem heard that Samaria had received the word of God, they sent unto them Peter and John: Who, when they were come down, prayed for them, that they might receive the Holy Ghost: (For as yet he was fallen upon none of them: only they were baptized in the name of the Lord Jesus.) Then laid they their hands on them, and they received the Holy Ghost. And when **Simon** saw that through laying on of the apostles' hands the Holy Ghost was given, **he offered them money**, Saying, Give me also this power, that on whomsoever I lay hands, he may receive the Holy Ghost. But Peter said unto him, Thy money perish with thee, because thou hast thought that the gift of God may be purchased with money. Thou hast neither part nor lot in this matter: for thy heart is not right in the sight of God. Repent therefore of this thy wickedness, and pray God, if perhaps the thought of thine heart may be forgiven thee. For I perceive that thou art in the gall of bitterness, and in the bond of iniquity. Then answered **Simon**, and said, Pray ye to the Lord for me, that none of these things which ye have spoken come upon me (Acts 8:9–24).*

Example of Use: A long time ago, the man who named "cybernetics," Norbert Wiener, warned about its corruptions. He denounced the "gadget-worshippers," who were committing the sin of "**simony**," selling their precious knowledge for money. ("Outsmarting Turing," J. R. Ravetz, Sept. 1, 2003, *Futures*)

Sins as scarlet

Means: Especially offensive sins or misdeeds

Biblical Text: *Come now, and let us reason together, saith the* LORD: ***though your sins be as scarlet,*** *they shall be as white as snow; though they be red like crimson, they shall be as wool* (Isaiah 1:18).

Example of Use: Time was, presidential nominations were dispensed by kingmakers in smoke-filled rooms. Today smoking is a **scarlet sin** and the democratization of the nominating process supposedly has made kingmakers extinct. Not quite. Meet Gerald McEntee. ("Union Chief Aims to Be Democrat Presidential Kingmaker[.] Leader Gerald McEntee Says AFSCME Will Endorse a Candidate 'by Late September, Early October,'" George Will, June 12, 2003, *Chicago Sun-Times*)

Sins of the fathers

Means: Misdeeds of a previous generation, especially when the present generation is punished for those sins

Biblical Text: *O* LORD, *according to all thy righteousness, I beseech thee, let thine anger and thy fury be turned away from thy city Jerusalem, thy holy mountain: because for our sins, and for the **iniquities of our fathers,** Jerusalem and thy people are become a reproach to all that are about us* (Daniel 9:16).

Example of Use: Are we repeating **the sins of our fathers**? When it comes to growth and development in Guilford

County, the answer, sadly, seems to be yes. As new subdivisions sprout like wildflowers, the once under-built east is starting more and more to resemble its overgrown cousin to the west: overwrought and underplanned. ("Been There, Done That," Mar. 5, 2006, *The News & Record*, Piedmont Triad, NC)

Sit at the feet of someone

Means: To be a student, disciple, or follower of someone, especially showing admiration

Biblical Text: *And she had a sister called Mary, which also **sat at Jesus' feet**, and heard his word* (Luke 10:39).

Example of Use: I sought out all the books and I read them all. At this point, he was pretty much completely out of print. So it was sort of an eccentric commitment to make. This was when, I should say—you know, Dick was still alive and I sort of had this chance that I blew to rush out to California and you know, **sit at the feet of** my master. And I never quite managed to do it. He died in '82, just as I was starting college, and so I sort of lost my chance to go and try to become his official protégé. ("Philip K. Dick Collection Aimed at New Generation," Jacki Lyden, July 29, 2007, *NPR Weekend All Things Considered*, National Public Radio)

Skin of one's teeth, By the

Means: Barely; a narrow escape

Biblical Text: *My bone cleaveth to my skin and to my flesh, and I am escaped **with the skin of my teeth*** (Job 19:20).

Example of Use: We won—**by the skin of our teeth**, but we won. A 4–4 tie at the Supreme Court in December (Justice Anthony M. Kennedy abstained) meant that a developer who destroyed wetlands on his property had to pay a $500,000 fine and restore some of what he had ruined. ("Drain Stopper," Mar. 22, 2003, *OnEarth*)

Slippery places

Means: Conditions conducive to lapses in ethics or personal commitment

Biblical Text: *Surely thou didst set them in **slippery places**: thou castedst them down into destruction* (Psalm 73:17).

Example of Use: As I sopped up the steak pieces and looked around the table at my sober buddies, it was with a sense of real wonder. Ten of us. Started with three hard-core, degenerate boozers 20 years ago, stuck together, helped each other over the **slippery places**, stayed sober, got bigger. The "youngest" member of the group has been 12 years sober. We like each other. We're loyal together. Still we keep a wary eye on each other, looking for dangerous attitudes. ("A Murderous Beast: When the Black Dog Gets You, the Odds of Permanent Escape Are Slim," Denny Boyd, Mar. 1, 2002, *BC Business*)

Slow to anger

Means: Long-suffering; patient when provoked

Biblical Text: *And rend your heart, and not your garments, and turn unto the LORD your God: for he is gracious and merciful, **slow to anger**, and of great kindness, and repenteth him of the evil* (Joel 2:13).

Example of Use: I'd been talking on the phone for a few minutes with Alex Biscaro, spokesman for the Swiss Embassy, when I finally had to ask: Look, aren't Americans just a bunch of stupid idiots? "I would never say that," Alex said, neutrally. That's the Swiss for you: even-keeled, **slow to anger**, reluctant to take offense. I'd wanted to start an international incident, and I'd picked the wrong country. ("Flying the Colors, but All Crossed Up," John Kelly, Sept. 16, 2004, *The Washington Post*)

Smite hip and thigh

Means: To strike an enemy, especially with a weapon, in order to inflict serious injury or death; to strike unsparingly with overwhelming blows or slaughter

Biblical Text: *And Samson said unto them, Though ye have done this, yet will I be avenged of you, and after that I will cease. And he* **smote them hip and thigh** *with a great slaughter: and he went down and dwelt in the top of the rock Etam* (Judges 15:7–8).

Example of Use: Rule No.1 for teams attempting to **smite** prestigious enemies **hip and thigh** is, don't give them anything. The Terps ignored this sensible dictum in the first half and paid for it through their derrieres. Four of Florida State's first five scores followed a blocked field goal attempt, a 28-yard punt, a lost fumble and an interception, which should have been frustrating enough to make the newer, slimmer Fridge snarf a few Twinkies on the sideline. ("Bowden's Boys Needed No Help, but Got It," Sept. 15, 2002, *The Washington Times*)

Sodom and Gomorrah

S

Means: Any place of such immoral standards to resemble Sodom and Gomorrah of the OT

Biblical Text: *Then the* LORD *rained upon* **Sodom and upon Gomorrah** *brimstone and fire from the* LORD *out of heaven. . . . And he looked toward* **Sodom and Gomorrah,** *and toward all the land of the plain, and beheld, and, lo, the smoke of the country went up as the smoke of a furnace* (Genesis 19:24, 28).

Example of Use: Have no doubt, the real reason is to support the profitability of the "entertainments" industry, especially the drinks industry and now the USA gambling fraternity. **Sodom and Gomorrah** has arrived, courtesy of your ruling Labour party, which has engineered this anti-social step in the wrong direction for society. A policy for sickness and not health! ("Letter: Road to **Sodom and Gomorrah**," K. Armstrong-Braun, Oct. 27, 2004, *Daily Post*, Liverpool)

Soft answer turns away wrath, A

Means: A calm response to an angry assault will reduce tension and help eliminate further agitation or harm

Biblical Text: *A soft answer turneth away wrath: but grievous words stir up anger* (Proverbs 15:1).

Example of Use: Gov. Jon Huntsman, 45, is a seventh-generation Utahan. A former diplomat, he believes what the proverb asserts, that "**a soft answer turneth away wrath**." He says, tactfully, that perhaps Margaret Spellings, the U.S. secretary of education, "has not had time to read our legislation." ("In Utah, No Right Left Behind," George F. Will, Nov. 11, 2005, *The Washington Post*)

Solomon

Means: An unusually wise person

Biblical Text: *And God gave **Solomon** wisdom and understanding exceeding much, and largeness of heart, even as the sand that is on the sea shore. And **Solomon's** wisdom excelled the wisdom of all the children of the east country, and all the wisdom of Egypt. . . . And there came of all people to hear the wisdom of **Solomon**, from all kings of the earth, which had heard of his wisdom* (1 Kings 4:29–30, 34).

Example of Use: City officials in Fort Collins, Colo., have devised a **Solomon**-like solution to a dispute on whether

S

Christian music should be played on public buses. Last month city officials banned such music after a passenger complained. Drivers are allowed to listen to radio music, which is piped throughout the buses. [. . .] Now officials say they will install switches in all city buses to enable drivers to play a radio station throughout the buses, or if someone objects, only near the driver's seat. ("Christian Music Dispute," Jan. 26, 1991, *The Washington Post*)

Sons of Belial

Means: Especially wicked people

Biblical Text: *Now as they were making their hearts merry, behold, the men of the city, certain* **sons of Belial**, *beset the house round about, and beat at the door, and spake to the master of the house, the old man, saying, Bring forth the man that came into thine house, that we may know him. . . . Now therefore deliver us the men, the* **children of Belial**, *which are in Gibeah, that we may put them to death, and put away evil from Israel. But the children of Benjamin would not hearken to the voice of their brethren the children of Israel* (Judges 19:22; 20:13).

Example of Use: And when night darkens the streets, then wander forth the **sons of Belial**, flown with insolence and wine. ("Poeta As Vezes, Mesmo!" Rachel Mendes, May 14, 2007, rachelmendes.blogspot.com)

Sounding brass or a tinkling cymbal

Means: Noisy but with little significance

Biblical Text: *Though I speak with the tongues of men and of angels, and have not charity, I am become as* **sounding brass, or a tinkling cymbal** (1 Corinthians 13:1).

S

Example of Use: "We risk the entrenchment of these global disparities," the Summit acknowledged, "and unless we act in a manner that fundamentally changes their lives, the poor of the world may lose confidence in their representatives and the democratic systems to which we remain committed, seeing their representatives as nothing more than **sounding brass or tinkling cymbals**." ("Undoing the Damage We Have Caused. [Ensuring Environmental Sustainability]. [World Summit on Sustainable Development]," Horst Rutsch, Dec. 1, 2002, *UN Chronicle*)

Sow the wind, reap the whirlwind

Means: Minor misdeeds or other actions can sometimes lead to far more serious consequences

Biblical Text: *For they have sown the wind, and they shall reap the whirlwind: it hath no stalk: the bud shall yield no meal: if so be it yield, the strangers shall swallow it up* (Hosea 8:7).

Example of Use: DaimlerChrysler is threatening the job cuts unless workers will agree to reduced shift premiums and less paid break time. . . . Worker signs read, "**Sow the wind, reap the whirlwind**," and "Take away our break, we'll take away your peace." ("DaimlerChrysler Workers Protest Proposed Cost Cuts," July 15, 2004, AP Worldstream)

Spare the rod, spoil the child

Means: A failure to discipline a child will lead him to ruin and bad behavior.

Biblical Text: *He that spareth his rod hateth his son: but he that loveth him chasteneth him betimes* (Proverbs 13:24).

Example of Use: Philosophies have shifted in the past several decades, from the biblical "**spare the rod, spoil the child**" ethos to today's emphasis, by doctors and parenting experts, on developmentally appropriate discipline that balances positive reinforcement with firm guidance. But check out online discussion boards on the topic, and it's not so neatly limned. (**"Spare the Rod, Spoil the Debate?"** Jackie Burrell, Mar. 5, 2007, *Oakland Tribune*)

Sparrow's fall

Means: A relatively insignificant event

Biblical Text: *Are not two **sparrows** sold for a farthing? and one of them shall not **fall on the ground** without your Father. But the very hairs of your head are all numbered. Fear ye not therefore, ye are of more value than many sparrows* (Matthew 10:29–31).

Example of Use: At all events, sparrow numbers in London alone have dropped by 70 percent between 1994 and 2001. So who counted them? The British Trust for Ornithology, that's who. No mean task, given that we are talking about six to seven million pairs of the little perishers. And forever on the flitter-fluttering move. But is this the time to worry about the **fall of a sparrow**? ("Requiem for the **Fall of a Sparrow**," Keith Waterhouse, Mar. 13, 2003, *The Daily Mail*, London)

Speak to the earth, and it shall teach thee

S

Means: Interaction with nature can teach mankind about the world

Biblical Text: *But ask now the beasts, and they shall teach thee; and the fowls of the air, and they shall tell thee: Or **speak to the earth, and it shall teach thee**: and the fishes of the sea shall declare unto thee. Who knoweth not in all these that the hand of the LORD hath wrought this?* (Job 12:7–9).

Example of Use: In 1905, Columbia University built a magnificent brick and limestone palace of science, Schermerhorn

Hall, for its new and expanding departments of geology, botany, and zoology. Carved on its facade is the inscription **"Speak to the Earth and it will teach you."** To someone who has studied the Bible, whether the Jewish Tanakh or the Christian Old Testament, this line from the Book of Job is clearly not the motto of science that it appears to be. It is Job himself, in pain, telling his friends that neither he nor they can possibly understand the ways of Heaven and that he therefore wants to die (Job 12:8). ("Attending to the Pain of the Dying: An Agenda for Science," Robert Pollack, June 22, 2006, *CrossCurrents—The Journal of Addiction and Mental Health*)

Spirit is willing but the flesh is weak, The

Means: Although one's mind may be strong in avoiding temptation, one's bodily desires are often greater

Biblical Text: *Watch and pray, that ye enter not into temptation: the spirit indeed is willing, but the flesh is weak* (Matthew 26:41). See also Mark 14:38.

Example of Use: Sleeper's "home" ensemble plays well here, under the direction of colleague Zoe Zeniodi. The fly in the ointment (a small one) is tenor John Duykers, who made his professional debut some 45 years ago. **The spirit is willing, but the flesh is, if not weak, then at least a little well seasoned.** Still, this is not a love story (not in the usual sense, anyway), so if Duykers is more a character tenor than a romantic lead at this point, it doesn't min [sic] the music. Some of his high notes are nevertheless more penetrating than appealing. ("Sleeper Symphony No. 1(1). Xenia2. 6 Arias for Cello and Orchestra3," Raymond Tuttle, Jan. 1, 2011, *Fanfare*)

S

Spread one's net

Means: To set a trap for someone; to seek someone or something over a wide area

Biblical Text: *The proud have hid a snare for me, and cords; they have spread a net by the wayside; they have set gins for me. Selah* (Psalm 140:5).

Example of Use: Evesham United manager Phil Mullen **spread his net** far and wide this week when bringing in two new signings. Mullen has snapped up Bristol-based left-back Chris Sage, who previously played for Bilston Town and Bloxwich United. ("Football: Mullen Lands Double Boost," Feb. 1, 2003, *Sports Argus*, Birmingham, England)

Spy out the land

Means: To observe a new place one has never entered for the purpose of gaining intelligence about it

Biblical Text: *These are the names of the men which Moses sent to **spy out the land.** And Moses called Oshea the son of Nun Jehoshua. And **Moses sent them to spy out the land** of Canaan, and said unto them, Get you up this way southward, and go up into the mountain: And see the land, what it is, and the people that dwelleth therein, whether they be strong or weak, few or many* (Numbers 13:16–18).

Example of Use: Julius Caesar's first visit to Britain, or Albion as the Romans called this island, was in 55 BC It was a reconnaissance trip, to **spy out the land**. He came again a year later, this time with 800 ships, carrying five legions and 2,000 cavalry. ("The Coming of Foes from Afar," John Harper, Sept. 23, 2010, *The Tamworth Herald*)

Staff of life

Means: A staple or necessary food, especially bread

Biblical Text: *Son of man, when the land sinneth against me by trespassing grievously, then will I stretch out mine hand upon it, and will break the **staff of the bread** thereof, and will send famine upon it, and will cut off man and beast from it* (Ezekiel 14:13).

Example of Use: But gone are the days when bread was seen as a mystery or even, as Jonathan Swift famously wrote, "the **staff of life**." In the past 50 years, the West's ability to produce food has grown exponentially; here in America, virtually no one lives by bread alone. With so many inexpensive sources of calories, it's possible for the first time in history for humans to forgo bread. And that has bakers worried. ("Breaking Bread / Low-Carb Craze Challenges the Staff of Life," Erica Marcus, Feb. 23, 2004, *Newsday*, New York City)

Stand

Means: To continue in existence, endure; to remain firm, sure, or steadfast

Biblical Text: *The grass withereth, the flower fadeth: but the word of our God shall **stand** for ever* (Isaiah 40:8). See also Dan. 2:44.

Example of Use: It would be easy for anyone who was part of it to cling to and defend such an auspicious run. Some members of the Miami Dolphins' undefeated 1972 team, for example, actively root for their record to **stand** forever. ("Patriots Can Bring Back the Dynasty; Free Agency, Salary Cap Make Task More Difficult," Bob Cohn, Jan. 27, 2005, *The Washington Times*)

Stand for

Means: Represent

Biblical Text: *And in that day there shall be a root of Jesse, which shall **stand for** an ensign of the people; to it shall the Gentiles seek: and his rest shall be glorious* (Isaiah 11:10).

Example of Use: I'm only 22, but have already become completely disillusioned with men. I loathe everything they seem to **stand for**. Everything I read about them and their needs leaves me with a bad taste. They seem to leave women hurt and broken when they feel slightly misunderstood and it seems a woman can put everything into a relationship, but men will still be likely to up and leave when they find a replacement. ("I Now Loathe Men and Everything They **Stand For**. Will I Ever Get Over It?" Bel Mooney, Sept. 20, 2008, *Daily Mail*, London)

Stars in their courses

Means: Stars as observed from the Earth

Biblical Text: *They fought from heaven; **the stars in their courses** fought against Sisera* (Judges 5:20).

Example of Use: The semi-documentary drama] *Frost/Nixon* captures the excitement of trying to make a historic TV programme and the struggle to discover how to beat a politician at his own game. The play shows the process by which, three years after his enforced resignation, President Nixon is coaxed onto a four-hour TV interview. Nixon's aim is to revive his ruined reputation by submitting to questions from a young television chat show host, that oleaginous admirer of **stars in their courses**, David Frost. ("Chilling Account of Nixon's Trial by Television," Nicholas de Jongh, Aug. 22, 2006, *The Evening Standard*, London)

Stiff-necked

Means: Obstinate; stubborn

Biblical Text: *For the* L<small>ORD</small> *had said unto Moses, Say unto the children of Israel, Ye are a* **stiffnecked** *people* (Exodus 33:5).

Example of Use: As U.S. attorney general, John Ashcroft came across as a model of moral rectitude, both to the conservatives who embraced his values and to detractors who saw him as a **stiff-necked** moralist. ("Ex-Attorney General Turns into a Lobbyist. Ashcroft Begins Selling His Know-How," Leslie Wayne, Mar. 17, 2006, *International Herald Tribune*)

Still small voice

Means: One's conscience, God, or another source that presents to one a soft impulse or motivation

Biblical Text: *And he said, Go forth, and stand upon the mount before the* L<small>ORD</small>*. And, behold, the* L<small>ORD</small> *passed by, and a great and strong wind rent the mountains, and brake in pieces the rocks before the* L<small>ORD</small>*; but the* L<small>ORD</small> *was not in the wind: and after the wind an earthquake; but the* L<small>ORD</small> *was not in the earthquake: And after the earthquake a fire; but the* L<small>ORD</small> *was not in the fire: and after the fire a* **still small voice**. *And it was so, when Elijah heard it, that he wrapped his face in his mantle, and went out, and stood in the entering in of the cave. And, behold, there came a voice unto him, and said, What doest thou here, Elijah?* (1 Kings 19:11–13).

Example of Use: *The Final Days* commemorates a rare episode in Nazi Germany when the **still, small voice** of conscience rang out loud and clear. It's an authentic, harrowing tale of heroism. ("'Sophie Scholl' Pits Conscience against Nazi Power," Michael Sragow, Apr. 21, 2006, *Baltimore Sun*)

S

Still waters

Means: A situation or a person manifested by peace and contentment, without disturbance

Biblical Text: *He maketh me to lie down in green pastures: he leadeth me beside the **still waters*** (Psalm 23:2).

Example of Use: I went again, from the country of flux, To the country of **still waters**. . . . ("The Country of **Still Waters**," Harry Clifton, Mar. 22, 2003, *The Southern Review* Vol 39, Issue 2, p. 242)

Stolen waters are sweet

Means: Concealed, unlawful acts thrill some people

Biblical Text: *Stolen waters are sweet, and bread eaten in secret is pleasant* (Proverbs 9:17).

Example of Use: *Stolen Waters are Sweet* Written and Directed by Anthony Harper. It's the summer of 1964 and a young woman discovers the consequences of adultery. As she attempts to cope with her discovery, she embroils her husband and the congregation of her church into a web of deceit, scandal, violence, family and ultimately redemption. Come and witness this gripping journey as one woman's deception leads her husband on a journey to one of the darkest paths of human nature. Will her deception ultimately destroy her and her family as she learns a painful lesson of love, honesty, faith and forgiveness? (Dec. 2009, 3foodllc.com)

Stone someone, To

Means: To punish someone, implying a desire to stone the person

Biblical Text: *When they heard these things, they were cut to the heart, and they gnashed on him [Stephen] with their teeth. But he, being full of the Holy Ghost, looked up stedfastly into heaven, and saw the glory of God, and Jesus standing on the right hand of God, And said, Behold, I see the heavens opened, and the Son of man standing on the right hand of God. Then* *they cried out with a loud voice, and stopped their ears, and ran upon him with one accord, And cast him out of the city, and **stoned him**: and the witnesses laid down their clothes at a young man's feet, whose name was Saul. And **they stoned** Stephen, calling upon God, and saying, Lord Jesus, receive my spirit* (Acts 7:54–59).

Example of Use: "He just kind of takes games away from you with saves like that," said the Flyers Geoff Sanderson, who looked stunned after Brodeur **stoned him** with a remarkable save midway through the second period. ("Flyers Fall to Devils," Ray Parrillo, Dec. 8, 2006, *Philadelphia Inquirer*)

Stones into bread, Turn

Means: Do what is or seems to be impossible

Biblical Text: *And Jesus being full of the Holy Ghost returned from Jordan, and was led by the Spirit into the wilderness, Being forty days tempted of the devil. And in those days he did eat nothing: and when they were ended, he afterward hungered. And the devil said unto him, If thou be the Son of God, **command this stone that it be made bread**. And Jesus answered him, saying, It is written, That man shall not live by bread alone, but by every word of God* (Luke 4:1–4).

Example of Use: Moderate smoking and drinking are not, in themselves, sinful; gambling is. Gambling is the activity that most resembles government itself; it, too, promises to **turn stones into bread**. ("Sinfully Lucrative; Smokers, Drinkers and Gamblers All Have 'Addictions,' and Are Milked for Billions," Kevin Michael Grace, Aug. 12, 2002, *The Report Newsmagazine*)

Stones would cry out, The

Means: Trying to suppress some truths is useless because the truth will be revealed eventually

Biblical Text: *And he answered and said unto them, I tell you that, if these should hold their peace,* **the stones would** *immediately* **cry out** (Luke 19:40).

Example of Use: With an unforgettable performance that was enough to make the **stones cry out**, Denman gave us all an imperishable second Hennessy yesterday, and the beauty of this great bruiser of a chaser is that he is as big-hearted as he is brilliant. ("Horse with Iron in His Soul Stands Alongside Immortals; Alastair Down Sees Denman Deliver a Victory That Had the Crowd Roaring and Left His Trainer Mute," Nov. 29, 2009, *The Racing Post*, London)

Stony ground, To fall on

Means: To be ignored or received with a response that is unfriendly, negative, unsympathetic, or unemotional

Biblical Text: *And some [seed]* **fell on stony ground***, where it had not much earth; and immediately it sprang up, because it had no depth of earth: But when the sun was up, it was scorched; and because it had no root, it withered away* (Mark 4:5–6).

Example of Use: Pleas to the French Federation for a qualifying wildcard **fell on stony ground**. ("Dad's Unforced Error Denies Liam Open Run," May 26, 2011, *Daily Mail*, London)

Straight and narrow, The

Means: Morally correct behavior

Biblical Text: *Enter ye in at the strait gate: for wide is the gate, and broad is the way, that leadeth to destruction, and many*

there be which go in thereat: Because **strait is the gate, and narrow is the way,** *which leadeth unto life, and few there be that find it* (Matthew 7:13–14).

Example of Use: Eric Zahnd had a pretty clear message for sixth-grade students at Plaza Middle School—**follow the straight and narrow**. The Platte County prosecutor shared a modern morality tale with students last week in describing the fate of three teenagers who played a prank at a Weston high school. The prank snowballed into other crimes, including trespassing, burglary and vandalism. "Little mistakes can lead to serious mistakes," Zahnd said. ("Prosecutor Gives Kids His Case for **Straight and Narrow**," Linda Man, Nov. 29, 2006, *Kansas City Star*)

Strain at a gnat and swallow a camel

Means: To become exercised over minor matters while overlooking major ones

Biblical Text: *Ye blind guides, which* **strain at a gnat, and swallow a camel** (Matthew 23:24).

Example of Use: Regrettably we still live in an era when some among us choose to "**strain at a gnat and swallow a camel**" when it comes to racial issues. They choose to allow slight physiological variations to be an impediment to acceptance of others as part of a common human family. ("Racism and Bigotry Right Here in Idaho," Mar. 27, 2011, *Idaho State Journal*)

Stranger in a strange land, A

Means: One who feels isolated and uncomfortable in unaccustomed surroundings

Biblical Text: *And she bare him a son, and he called his name Gershom: for he said, I have been **a stranger in a strange land*** (Exodus 2:22).

Example of Use: Dennis Lawrence is **a stranger in a strange land**. The 50-year-old Livermore man offered a unique perspective on the goings-on inside the Calaveras County Jail—and he is appalled. Lawrence never had been in trouble before he found himself one of the jail's longest-serving inmates. He's serving a year for manslaughter. ("It Just Doesn't Matter to Them," Aug. 5, 2007, *The Record*)

Stranger within thy gates

Means: A person who does not belong to a particular group, especially if ostracized or treated unfairly by members of the group

Biblical Text: *But the seventh day is the sabbath of the LORD thy God: In it thou shalt not do any work, thou, nor thy son, nor thy daughter, thy manservant, nor thy maidservant, nor thy cattle, nor thy **stranger that is within thy gates*** (Exodus 20:10).

Example of Use: Gambino and colleagues published the results of their research in History of Psychiatry ("These **Strangers within Our Gates**: Race, Psychiatry and Mental Illness among Black Americans at St. Elizabeths Hospital in Washington, D.C., 1900–40." *History of Psychiatry*, 2008;19(4):387–408). ("New Psychiatry Findings from University of Illinois Published," Jan. 7, 2009, *Biotech Week*)

Streets of gold

Means: Signs of affluence

Biblical Text: *And the twelve gates were twelve pearls; every several gate was of one pearl: and **the street of the city was pure gold**, as it were transparent glass* (Revelation 21:21).

Example of Use: An Italian émigré who sailed into the United States in 1903 with just $2.50 in his pocket, Ponzi himself seemed to embody the **streets-of-gold** potential of his adopted homeland. By summer of 1920, dapper in daily tuxedos, sporting an ivory cigarette holder and a gold-tipped cane, the 40-ish swindler was tooling around Beantown in a blue limo and talking of a run for mayor. ("He Came, He Saw, He Conned. (Charles Ponzi, Creator of the Ponzi Pyramid Scheme)," Joellen Perry, Aug. 26, 2002, *U.S. News & World Report*)

Strength to strength, From

Means: To become stronger; to experience ever-increasing success

Biblical Text: *Blessed is the man whose strength is in thee; in whose heart are the ways of them. Who passing through the valley of Baca make it a well; the rain also filleth the pools. They go **from strength to strength**, every one of them in Zion appeareth before God* (Psalm 84:5–7).

Example of Use: The Indian pharmaceutical industry is going **from strength to strength** in establishing itself across the world. That's the verdict of Chiltern International, a leading independent clinical research organisation which is carrying out a range of projects with international clients. "The Indian pharmaceutical industry has made no secret of its desire to globalise and eventually compete with its counterparts in Europe, Japan and the USA," explained Chiltern`s Dr. Faiz Kermani. "But there is still a long way to go before it can truly regard itself as a major international force." ("India Goes **from Strength to Strength**," Dec. 1, 2004, *M2 Presswire,* Bath, England)

S

Stricken in years (or in age)

Means: To be old or advanced in years

Biblical Text: *Now king David was old and **stricken in years**; and they covered him with clothes, but he gat no heat* (1 Kings 1:1).

Example of Use: It sounds like a 1960s dream band line-up. Gerry Marsden, Mike d'Abo, Dave Berry, Brian Poole and Mike Pender, all five of them—just count 'em—on the same bill. No groups, just a handful of the great rock and roll lead singers from the legendary decade backed by the Big Beat Band. And, if all that wasn't enough, there was a brace of Nolan Sisters thrown in for good measure. . . . The inescapable *Ferry 'Cross the Mersey* and *You'll Never Walk Alone* eventually brought things to a close. They may be well **stricken in years**, but these pop veterans have proved once again that rock 'n' roll is here to stay. ("Blasts from the Past, but Rock 'n' Roll Still Lives Music Reelin' and a Rockin' Southport Theatre," Stan Woolley, Apr. 1, 2002, *Daily Post*)

Strong meat

Means: A challenging idea to comprehend or accept

Biblical Text: *For when for the time ye ought to be teachers, ye have need that one teach you again which be the first principles of the oracles of God; and are become such as have need of milk, and not of **strong meat*** (Hebrews 5:12).

Example of Use: The black American feminist writer-critic and social commentator bell hooks is **strong meat**. Take the way she spells her name, militantly lower case. ("Books: *O Brother, Where Art Thou? We Real Cool* by Bell Hooks," Bonnie Greer, Mar. 12, 2004, *The Independent,* London)

Stumbling block

Means: A hindrance, impediment, or obstacle

Biblical Text: *As it is written, Behold, I lay in Sion a **stumbling-stone** and rock of offence: and whosoever believeth on him shall not be ashamed* (Romans 9:33).

Example of Use: Despite a move toward democracy, bureaucracy remains a **stumbling block** for those who want to set up businesses in Mexico, according to a study by the World Bank. ("Study Shows Mexico's Bureaucracy Remains **Stumbling Block** for Businesses," Jenalia Moreno, Oct. 4, 2002, *Houston Chronicle*)

Sudden fear

Means: Panic or fright

Biblical Text: *Be not afraid of **sudden fear**, neither of the desolation of the wicked, when it cometh* (Proverbs 3:25).

Example of Use: While it's not yet keeping me up at night, the anxiety surrounding that first job out of college has begun to spark more than a few existential questions. I was warned about this feeling—the **sudden fear** of life's shapelessness, the terror of having no structure. ("Diploma, Done. Now What?" Benjamin Toff, July 31, 2005, *The Boston Globe*)

Suffer fools gladly

Means: To tolerate or agree with stupid or unwise people; to fail to use discernment in evaluating other people's ideas or advice

Biblical Text: *Seeing that many glory after the flesh, I will glory also. For ye **suffer fools gladly**, seeing ye yourselves are wise* (2 Corinthians 11:18–19).

Example of Use: "Rumsfeld Stars During War Coverage; Secretary Enjoys Reporters but Doesn't **Suffer Fools Gladly**," Apr. 30, 2003, *The Washington Times*

Suffer little children

Means: An admonition to allow little children to do a particular thing

Biblical Text: *And they brought young children to him, that he should touch them: and his disciples rebuked those that brought them. But when Jesus saw it, he was much displeased, and said unto them, **Suffer the little children** to come unto me, and forbid them not: for of such is the kingdom of God* (Mark 10:13–14).

Example of Use: Perhaps most chillingly, scholars at the University of Michigan Survey Research Center have documented a stunning decline in unstructured, unorganized "free time," with kids losing a dozen hours a week of unfettered hang time since the late '70s. As any pint-sized Pete Rose could tell you, time in organized sports has doubled during the same period and, as a *Pittsburgh Post-Gazette* account grimly notes, "the amount of homework increased dramatically between 1981 and 1997. . . . The amount given to 6- to 8-year-olds tripled during that time." **Suffer the little children** (and, in this case at least, their parents)! ("**Suffer the Little Children**: The Grim 'Fun' of Highly Partisan Kid Lit," Nick Gillespie, May 1, 2006, *Reason*)

Sufficient unto the day is the evil thereof

Means: Enough wrongs have been committed without adding more

Biblical Text: *Take therefore no thought for the morrow: for the morrow shall take thought for the things of itself. **Sufficient unto the day is the evil thereof*** (Matthew 6:34).

Example of Use: Apologies for the past hide the evils of today. Now is the time for our legislature, the president and faculty of Duke University, the members of the Greensboro Truth and Reconciliation Commission, the Ku Klux Klan, the NAACP and all other racially oriented groups to shake off their blinding focus on skin color and clothe themselves with some love, forgiveness, respect and color-blindness. It is certainly not a time to rekindle the sins of the past. "**Sufficient unto the day is the evil thereof.**" ("Nothing Is Gained by Classifying a Whole Group of People as 'Victims.' We All Deserve Better. Letters to the Editor," Apr. 29, 2007, *The News & Record,* Piedmont Triad, NC)

Sun go down on your wrath, Don't let the

Means: In your anger, do not sin or bear a grudge against someone

Biblical Text: *Be ye angry, and sin not: let not the sun go down upon your wrath* (Ephesians 4:26).

Example of Use: Remedies. Establishing a perfect love in the beginning constitutes a preventive. Fear that they are not truly loved usually paves the way for "spats." Let all who make any pretension guard against all beginnings of this reversal, and strangle these "hate-spats" the moment they arise. "**Let not the sun go down upon thy wrath,**" not even an hour, but let the next sentence after they begin quench them forever. And let those who cannot court without "spats," stop; for those who spat before marriage must quarrel after. ("Health Secret News," Aug. 2007, healthsecret.performancefitness.info)

Sun rises on the evil and on the good, The

Means: Good things happen to good people as well as bad.

Biblical Text: *He maketh his sun to rise on the evil and on the good, and sendeth rain on the just and on the unjust* (Matthew 5:45).

Example of Use: After Sept. 11, it can no longer be believed that science, technology, and industry are only good or that they serve only one "side." That never has been more than a progressivist and commercial superstition. Any power that belongs to one side belongs, for worse as well as better, to all sides, as indifferent as **the sun that rises "on the evil and on the good."** ("Two Minds," Wendell Berry, Nov. 1, 2002, *The Progressive*)

Sun stood still, The

Means: Time seems to stop

Biblical Text: *Then spake Joshua to the LORD in the day when the LORD delivered up the Amorites before the children of Israel, and he said in the sight of Israel, Sun, stand thou still upon Gibeon; and thou, Moon, in the valley of Ajalon. And **the sun stood still**, and the moon stayed, until the people had avenged themselves upon their enemies. Is not this written in the book of Jasher? So **the sun stood still** in the midst of heaven, and hasted not to go down about a whole day. And there was no day like that before it or after it, that the LORD hearkened unto the voice of a man: for the LORD fought for Israel* (Joshua 10:12–14).

Example of Use: The sun stood still, birds stopped singing and motorists and passersby watched. Even policemen just stood and watched. Some people joined us in song. After the letter had been delivered to the Provincial Magistrate we marched up past Tredgold turning left into H Chitepo Street. We started singing Seliwile Babylon (Babylon has fallen). As we reached 9th Avenue, we started singing Kunini Sahlupheka Kuletilizwe (We have suffered long in our country). ("Bulawayo,

S

24 July 2003: 'Women Were So Brave That Day,'" Patricia Tshabalala, Nov. 1, 2003, *Sister Namibia,* Zimbabwe)

Sun, Under the

Means: In the world; on earth; anywhere

Biblical Text: *The thing that hath been, it is that which shall be; and that which is done is that which shall be done: and there is no new thing **under the sun*** (Ecclesiastes 1:9).

Example of Use: Where to eat and where to stay requires some tough decision-making because the range is wide; from delis and grills to five-star dining, quaint B & B's to elegant beach-front resorts. Families are finding just about everything **under the sun** under one roof at Disney's Vero Beach Resort, with its charming turn-of-the-century style. ("Florida's Indian River County: From Water Sports to Grapefruit Groves, the Vero Beach Area Offers Everything **under the Sun**," Alice Ross, May 1, 2002, *Travel America*)

Sweat blood

Means: To wait anxiously or to worry; to be under great stress

Biblical Text: *And being in an agony he prayed more earnestly: and **his sweat was as it were great drops of blood** falling down to the ground* (Luke 22:44).

Example of Use: Coventry City boss Iain Dowie takes charge of the team for the first time tonight having told his players to go out and "**sweat blood** for the Sky Blue shirt." ("Football: **Sweat Blood** for This Shirt; Dowie's Call to City Players Ahead of His First Game," Andy Turner, Feb. 20, 2007, *Coventry Evening Telegraph,* England)

S

Sweeter than honey

Means: Someone or something that is superlative; sometimes an exaggerated expression of praise

Biblical Text: *More to be desired are they than gold, yea, than much fine gold:* ***sweeter also than honey*** *and the honeycomb* (Psalm 19:10). See also Judg. 14:18; Ps. 119:103.

Example of Use: With voices **sweeter than honey**, the cast of *Beehive* is ready to entertain audiences with "everything 60's" nostalgia. Music, hair-do's, dress and spirit from that bygone era! ("Beehive," June 24, 2002, *San Diego Business Journal*)

Swift to hear and slow to speak, Be

Means: An admonition to listen more than one talks

Biblical Text: *Wherefore, my beloved brethren, let every man* ***be swift to hear, slow to speak,*** *slow to wrath* (James 1:19).

Example of Use: His longtime law clerk, Leslie Marant, said Judge Green "was a scholar and a distinguished jurist, but certainly not self-important." "He was a very patient, measured man—**slow to speak but quick to listen**," she said. "Everything that the rest of us try to be? That's what he was." ("Pioneering Jurist Clifford Scott Green Dies," John Shiffman, June 1, 2007, *Philadelphia Inquirer*)

S

Sword, Two-edged (or Double-edged)

Means: Something that has or can have both favorable and unfavorable results or consequences

Biblical Text: *For the word of God is quick, and powerful, and sharper than any* ***two-edged sword***, *piercing even to the dividing asunder of soul and spirit, and of the joints and marrow, and is a discerner of the thoughts and intents of the heart* (Hebrews 4:12).

Example of Use: However, technology is said to be a **two-edged sword**. While technological initiatives generally can reduce the likelihood of fraud, it can at the same time open the door to another type of criminal activity hacking into electronic systems. ("Technology, a **Double-Edged Sword**," Apr. 16, 2001, *Investor Digest,* Malaysia)

S

RAISING CAIN

T

"HOLD ONE'S TONGUE"

Tabernacle

Means: Any place or house of worship, whether actual or metaphorical; a temporary dwelling or shelter

Biblical Text: *And the LORD spake unto Aaron, saying, Do not drink wine nor strong drink, thou, nor thy sons with thee, when ye go into the **tabernacle** of the congregation, lest ye die* (Leviticus 10:8–9).

Example of Use: Oscar Night. . . . The Kodak Theater was transformed into a **tabernacle** of talent. . . . Absolutely breathtaking, Beyoncé stole the show. ("Obnoxious: Beyoncé Rocks at the Oscars, Chris Rock Doesn't," William McCray III, Mar. 29, 2005, *Oakland Post*)

Take root

Means: To become established, settled, or fixed

Biblical Text: *And the remnant that is escaped of the house of Judah shall again **take root** downward, and bear fruit upward* (Isaiah 37:31).

Example of Use: Ken Milliken, head of forensic for KPMG in Scotland, said: "Given the repeated and extended nature of most frauds, companies need to work extremely hard to detect frauds earlier, through tighter internal controls, data analytical tools, and more widely publicised fraud reporting mechanisms. Engendering the right culture is also important, to create an environment where it is less likely that fraud can **take root**." ("Tighter Internal Controls Crucial in Helping Stop Business Fraud Take Root," Apr. 23, 2007, *The Aberdeen Press and Journal*, UK)

T

Take up thy bed and walk

Means: A command to get up

Biblical Text: *Whether is it easier to say to the sick of the palsy, Thy sins be forgiven thee; or to say, Arise, and **take up thy bed, and walk?*** (Mark 2:9).

Example of Use: "When I give them an opportunity to draw, they say, 'I can't do this, I'm blind,'" explains Kennedy. "I feel a bit like I'm saying, **'Take up thy bed, and walk.'** But I'm saying, **'Take up thy pen and draw.'** And they say, 'Okay, I'll try.' And then they start, and within seconds they say, 'I didn't know that I could do this.'" ("Unseen Forces: What Blind People Draw; Professor's Findings Hint at How Art Enters the Mind," Blake Gopnik, Apr. 29, 2001, *The Washington Post*)

Tale that is told, A

Means: A story, myth, or legend, especially one that has been told many times and circulated widely, over a long period of time; a proverbial or archetypical story

Biblical Text: *Lord, thou hast been our dwelling place in all generations. Before the mountains were brought forth, or ever thou hadst formed the earth and the world, even from everlasting to everlasting, thou art God. Thou turnest man to destruction; and sayest, Return, ye children of men. . . . For all our days are passed away in thy wrath: we spend our years as **a tale that is told*** (Psalm 90:1–3, 9).

Example of Use: Very gradually, yet very quickly, Dickie learned about this new boy who was, and wasn't, himself. [His nurse] would sit by his side by the hour and tell him of things that had happened in the short life of the boy whose place he filled. . . . And as soon as she had told him a thing he found he remembered it—not as one remembers **a tale that is told**, but as one remembers a real thing that has happened. ("Partners in Crime: E. Nesbit and the Art of Thieving," Marah Gubar, Sept. 22, 2001, *Style*)

Talents

Means: Special natural abilities or aptitudes given to a person for use and improvement; an ancient unit of weight or money

Biblical Text: *For the kingdom of heaven is as a man travelling into a far country, who called his own servants, and delivered unto them his goods. And unto one he gave five **talents**, to another two, and to another one; to every man according to his several ability; and straightway took his journey. Then he that had received the five **talents** went and traded with the same, and made them other five **talents**. And likewise he that had received two, he also gained other two. But he that had received one went and digged in the earth, and hid his lord's money. After a long time the lord of those servants cometh, and reckoneth with them. And so he that had received five **talents** came and brought other five talents, saying, Lord, thou deliveredst unto me five **talents**: behold, I have gained beside them five **talents** more. His lord said unto him, Well done, thou good and faithful servant: thou hast been faithful over a few things, I will make thee ruler over many things: enter thou into the joy of thy lord. He also that had received two **talents** came and said, Lord, thou deliveredst unto me two talents: behold, I have gained two other **talents** beside them. His lord said unto him, Well done, good and faithful servant; thou hast been faithful over a few things, I will make thee ruler over many things: enter thou into the joy of thy lord. Then he which had received the one **talent** came and said, Lord, I knew thee that thou art an hard man, reaping where thou hast not sown, and gathering where thou hast not strawed: And I was afraid, and went and hid thy **talent** in the earth: lo, there thou hast that is thine. His lord answered and said unto him, Thou*

T

*wicked and slothful servant, thou knewest that I reap where I sowed not, and gather where I have not strawed: Thou oughtest therefore to have put my money to the exchangers, and then at my coming I should have received mine own with usury. Take therefore the talent from him, and give it unto him which hath ten **talents**. For unto every one that hath shall be given, and he shall have abundance: but from him that hath not shall be taken away even that which he hath. And cast ye the unprofitable servant into outer darkness: there shall be weeping and gnashing of teeth* (Matthew 25:14–30). See also 2 Sam. 12:30; 2 Kings 5:23; 18:14; 2 Chron. 9:13.

Example of use: Dive in. If you're sick of an office or boss, use your **talents**—like jewelry making—to begin your own business. "First, test your chops in a relevant class," says Margit Feury Ragland, author of *Get a Freelance Life*. ("Ditch Your 9-to-5 Job. [Start Your Own Job]," Sara Bodnar, Oct. 1, 2006, *Cosmopolitan*)

Taste death

Means: To die or be near death

Biblical Text: *But we see Jesus, who was made a little lower than the angels for the suffering of death, crowned with glory and honour; that he by the grace of God should* ***taste death*** *for every man* (Hebrews 2:9).

Example of Use: I think I'd come to understand that Terry had **tasted death** when he had cancer. He didn't know if he was going to live or die so he had come to an acceptance of the fact that he might die out there. ("Canada at a Glance: AM," Apr. 11, 2005, *Resource News International*, Winnipeg, Manitoba)

T

Tell it not in Gath

Means: A command not to relay bad news to an enemy

Biblical Text: *Tell it not in Gath, publish it not in the streets of Askelon; lest the daughters of the Philistines rejoice, lest the daughters of the uncircumcised triumph* (2 Samuel 1:20).

Example of Use: But it is fungi and not bacteria that engage Mother Noella and unfortunately she had no time in Paris to admire the splendid St. Nectaire rinds just a few blocks away, at Barthelemy, the famous cheese store that is about the size of a wheel of Gruyere and offers an astonishing variety. But these days—**tell it not in Gath**—the store also stocks Philadelphia Cream Cheese. Does this packaged supermarket-style product sell? "I wouldn't have it if it didn't," snaps the patronne. Heavens above. ("A Master Pursues the Secrets of Cheese," Mary Blume, Jan. 23, 2004, *International Herald Tribune*)

Tender mercies

Means: Kindness of a particularly generous nature, often used ironically to refer to attention or treatment not in the best interests of its recipients

Biblical Text: *Bless the LORD, O my soul, and forget not all his benefits: Who forgiveth all thine iniquities; who healeth all thy diseases; Who redeemeth thy life from destruction; who crowneth thee with lovingkindness and tender mercies* (Psalm 103:2–4).

Example of Use: All proceeds will go to **Tender Mercies**, which provides permanent housing and support services to homeless persons with histories of mental illness. ("Designer Trees Aid **Tender Mercies**," Dec. 2, 2003, *The Cincinnati Post*)

Tentmaker

Means: Someone who makes a living through one job in order to support another role or job, more enjoyable or personally satisfying, in which he makes less income or none at all, often as a minister

Biblical Text: *After these things Paul departed from Athens, and came to Corinth; And found a certain Jew named Aquila, born in Pontus, lately come from Italy, with his wife Priscilla; (because that Claudius had commanded all Jews to depart from Rome) and came unto them. And because he was of the same craft, he abode with them, and wrought: for by their occupation they were **tentmakers** (Acts 18:1–3).*

Example of Use: Dr. James Fennelly, who earned his living teaching about the history of religion at a Long Island university but was best known locally as the "**tentmaker** minister" of the First Presbyterian Church in Maywood, died Saturday. He was 70. Known as a "**tentmaker** minister" because he was not paid in his post, Dr. Fennelly took over the pulpit in Maywood in 1984. ("Dr. James Fennelly, 70; Led Flock as '**Tentmaker** Minister,'" Seamus McGraw, Jan. 11, 2000, *The Record*, Bergen County, NJ)

They who follow vain persons will have poverty enough

Means: One who imitates unwise people will fail and fall into poverty

Biblical Text: *He that tilleth his land shall have plenty of bread: but **he that followeth after vain persons shall have poverty enough*** (Proverbs 28:19).

Example of Use: I've been hearing this a lot lately from some part-time entrepreneurs. The idea is to get a loan to start a business or buy real estate. A lot of midnight infomercials promote this strategy. Here's the problem: Proverbs 28:19–20[:] He who tills his land will have plenty of bread, But **he who follows frivolity will have poverty enough**! ("'Other People's Money': No Such Thing," Mar. 30, 2007, geredml.blogspot.com)

Thief in the night, Like a

Means: To appear or arrive swiftly, stealthily, and unexpectedly

Biblical Text: *But the day of the Lord will come as a **thief in the night**; in the which the heavens shall pass away with a great noise, and the elements shall melt with fervent heat, the earth also and the works that are therein shall be burned up* (2 Peter 3:10).

Example of Use: Daley moved in **like a thief in the night**. As a Chicago resident, I am appalled at the unprofessional way Mayor Richard M. Daley shut down Meigs Field. Meigs has not only been a part of our economic system but a historic asset to Chicago. **Like a thief in the night**, after midnight, he came in the form of his city workers and took away one of our city's most vital assets. How dare he use the seriousness of this war and the possibility of terrorist attack as his platform for making yet another bad decision in the mayoral reign of the Daley family? (Fence Post, Letter to the editor. *Daily Herald*, Arlington Heights, IL, Apr. 24, 2003)

Thirty pieces of silver

T

Means: Compensation, not necessarily money, received for taking the life of another person; anything paid or given for a treacherous act

Biblical Text: *Then one of the twelve, called Judas Iscariot, went unto the chief priests, And said unto them, What will ye give me,* *and I will deliver him unto you? And they covenanted with him for **thirty pieces of silver*** (Matthew 26:14–15).

Example of Use: Princess Diana was betrayed by many men in her life. It is a tragedy that it should continue after her death. The latest parasite to emerge is Patrick Jephson. When he was her private secretary he pledged personally to her that all that passed between them would remain secret. For eight years she trusted him.

Now she is in her grave, Diana's confidant has turned betrayer. He is another in a line of Judases to know Diana, and has sold his soul for a sordid book contract worth a lot more than **thirty pieces of silver**. ("Record View; A Traitor to Diana's Trust," Sept. 16, 2000, *Daily Record* Glasgow, Scotland)

Thorn in the flesh

Means: A persistent difficulty or annoyance

Biblical Text: *And lest I should be exalted above measure through the abundance of the revelations, there was given to me **a thorn in the flesh**, the messenger of Satan to buffet me, lest I should be exalted above measure* (2 Corinthians 12:7).

Example of Use: The adequate supply of wet blue leather has been singled out as a **thorn in the flesh** for the newly launched Tannery Industries Botswana (TIB), the country's only tannery. ("Leather Industry Needs Protection—Tanners," May 8, 2007, *All Africa Global Media*)

Thou shalt not . . . (See also "Commandments")

Means: A command not to take a particular action

Biblical Text: *Thou shalt have no other gods before me. **Thou shalt not** make unto thee any graven image, or any likeness of any thing that is in heaven above, or that is in the earth beneath,*

T

*or that is in the water under the earth. **Thou shalt not** bow down thyself to them, nor serve them: for I the L*ORD* thy God am a jealous God, visiting the iniquity of the fathers upon the children unto the third and fourth generation of them that hate me; And shewing mercy unto thousands of them that love me, and keep my commandments. **Thou shalt not** take the name of the L*ORD* thy God in vain; for the L*ORD* will not hold him guiltless that taketh his name in vain. Remember the sabbath day, to keep it holy. Six days shalt thou labour, and do all thy work: But the seventh day is the sabbath of the L*ORD* thy God: in it thou shalt not do any work, thou, nor thy son, nor thy daughter, thy manservant, nor thy maidservant, nor thy cattle, nor thy stranger that is within thy gates: For in six days the L*ORD* made heaven and earth, the sea, and all that in them is, and rested the seventh day: wherefore the L*ORD* blessed the sabbath day, and hallowed it. Honour thy father and thy mother: that thy days may be long upon the land which the L*ORD* thy God giveth thee. **Thou shalt not** kill. **Thou shalt not** commit adultery. **Thou shalt not** steal. **Thou shalt not** bear false witness against thy neighbour. **Thou shalt not** covet thy neighbour's house, **thou shalt not** covet thy neighbour's wife, nor his manservant, nor his maidservant, nor his ox, nor his ass, nor any thing that is thy neighbour's* (Exodus 20:3–17).

Example of Use: Thou shalt not desecrate thine windows with suction-cup Garfields or Baby on Board signs, nearly three decades after they were considered de rigueur. Repent. ("**Thou Shalt Not** Ignore Pope's Rules of the Road," Paige Wiser, June 24, 2007, *Chicago Sun-Times*)

Though he slay me, yet will I trust in him

Means: A declaration stating that, despite the apparent betrayal of someone, one will continue to have confidence and trust in him

Biblical Text: *Though he slay me, yet will I trust in him: but I will maintain mine own ways before him* (Job 13:15).

Example of Use: New Yorkers want serenity, and they will have it, despite all distractions. Each can pull a cone of quiet over himself; in the middle of Penn Station during rush hour, or the Sheep Meadow on a Sunday afternoon, or Times Square at intermission, they can walk, sit, or stand and think, "**Though he slay me, yet will I trust in him**," or "The jewel is in the eye of the lotus." They need the gift of serenity, for they have much to fend off. ("Internal Émigrés: Efforts of New Yorkers to Find Peace and Quiet," Richard Brookhiser, June 11, 2001, *National Review*)

Threefold cord is not quickly broken, A

Means: The unity of a group is strong and resistant to opposition

Biblical Text: *Two are better than one; because they have a good reward for their labour. For if they fall, the one will lift up his fellow: but woe to him that is alone when he falleth; for he hath not another to help him up. Again, if two lie together, then they have heat: but how can one be warm alone? And if one prevail against him, two shall withstand him; and **a threefold cord is not quickly broken*** (Ecclesiastes 4:9–12).

Example of Use: "We picked Fredericksburg as the area where we wanted to live," said Mike Jones. "It was obvious that Fredericksburg was destined to experience a tremendous amount of growth. We wanted to get in the path of growth and let it run over us." They incorporated under the name Tricord, which was inspired by Ecclesiastes 4:12: "And if one prevail against him, two shall withstand him; and **a threefold cord is not quickly broken**." "That communicates a value that we bring to our business—our teamwork," said Mike Jones. "You work together, you get more done. We maximize each others' strengths." ("Virginia-Based Development Firm's Owners Try to Be Good Stewards," Cathy Jett, Sept. 30, 2004, *Free Lance-Star*, Fredericksburg, VA)

Threescore years and ten

Means: The span of one's allotted life span, or seventy years

Biblical Text: *The days of our years are **threescore years and ten**; and if by reason of strength they be fourscore years, yet is their strength labour and sorrow; for it is soon cut off, and we fly away* (Psalm 90:10).

Example of Use: As the eighth best-selling male artist of all time, with more than 100 million record sales to his name, Kenny Rogers is the undisputed King of Country, so it was quite an honour to witness him performing for the first time at Plymouth Pavilions last night. Judging from his appearance on stage at Plymouth Pavilions last night he's in pretty fine fettle for his **three-score and ten**. ("Canny Kenny Bets on a Sure Thing," Apr. 3, 2009, *The Plymouth Evening Herald*, England)

Through fire and water

Means: Endurance of life's trials

Biblical Text: *Thou hast caused men to ride over our heads; we went **through fire and through water**: but thou broughtest us out into a wealthy place* (Psalm 66:12).

Example of Use: Bugsy does everything he's told by his trainer and owner Rick Schubert. Bugsy, a protection dog, is trained to bite on command, and he's the best in the business. Schubert knows because he and Bugsy won the K-9 Pro Sports championship for professional protection dogs in Fort Worth, Texas, in October. "He'd go **through fire and water** to protect you,"

Schubert said. ("Bugsy's Best; Manlius Trainer's Pit Bull Wins National Championship," Jim Read, Nov. 25, 2004, *The Post-Standard*, Syracuse, NY)

Thy will be done (See also " Lord's Prayer")

Means: A statement signifying acceptance of another person's authority

Biblical Text: *Thy kingdom come, **Thy will be done** in earth, as it is in heaven* (Matthew 6:10). See also Matt. 26:42.

Example of Use: "The referendum happened," Birmingham says. "We had a full and fair debate. The side that supported 5 percent prevailed and by a sizable majority. . . . It is about keeping faith with the voters. In a democracy it has to be about '**thy will be done**.'" ("Thy Will Be Done," Steve Bailey, Oct. 26, 2005, *The Boston Globe*)

Time and a place for everything, There's a

Means: Different things are appropriate on different occasions

Biblical Text: *To every thing there is a season, and a time to every purpose under the heaven: A time to be born, and a time to die; a time to plant, and a time to pluck up that which is planted; A time to kill, and a time to heal; a time to break down, and a time to build up; A time to weep, and a time to laugh; a time to mourn, and a time to dance; A time to cast away stones, and a time to gather stones together; a time to embrace, and a time to refrain from embracing; A time to get, and a time to lose; a time to keep, and a time to cast away; A time to rend, and a time to sew; a time to keep silence, and a time to speak; A time to love, and a time to hate; a time of war, and a time of peace* (Ecclesiastes 3:1–8).

Example of Use: Everyone praises your elevator speech, the 30-second message that tells prospects the benefits of doing business with you. Your wording is good, and so is your delivery. But are you getting business from all that networking? If not, you may be breaking an unwritten rule—namely, **there's a time and a place for everything**, including your commercial. ("There Is a Time and a Place for Your 30 Second Elevator Speech," Adina Genn, Feb. 25, 2005, *Long Island Business News*)

Time to be born, a time to die, A

Means: An appropriate occasion exists for all things, including death

Biblical Text: *To every thing there is a season, and a time to every purpose under the heaven: A time to be born, and a time to die; a time to plant, and a time to pluck up that which is planted* (Ecclesiastes 3:1–2).

Example of Use: In February of 2005, she moved from Massachusetts to Madison to live out her remaining months in the home of her brother and sister-in-law, Duane and Pat Smith. She filled out an end-of-life directive: no ventilators, no feeding tubes, no efforts to resuscitate. "I'm so scared some idiot will start sticking tubes in me. **There's a time to live and a time to die**. My time will be my time." ("Time to Reflect: A Death Well Planned," Doug Erickson, May 20, 2007, *Wisconsin State Journal*, Madison, WI)

Time, Spend

T

Means: To use time in a particular way

Biblical Text: *For all the Athenians and strangers which were there **spent their time** in nothing else, but either to tell, or to hear some new thing* (Acts 17:21). See also Acts 18:23; 20:16; 27:9.

Example of Use: In a statement, the lobbying firm called Ridge and Girard-diCarlo "close personal friends for more than a decade." The firm said, "Their wives are close friends, and they often **spend time** together as families. They talk and get together on a regular basis, as good friends do." ("Ridge Spent Time with Lobbyist," Pete Yost, Jan. 12, 2005, AP Online)

Tithe

Means: A tenth of one's income contributed voluntarily or as a tax, especially for the support of a religious institution

Biblical Text: *And Melchizedek king of Salem brought forth bread and wine: and he was the priest of the most high God. And he blessed him, and said, Blessed be Abram of the most high God, possessor of heaven and earth: And blessed be the most high God, which hath delivered thine enemies into thy hand. And he gave him **tithes** of all* (Genesis 14:18–20).

Example of Use: Dues-paying members of medical societies who join this new federation automatically would become members of the AMA, but the Chicago-based doctors' group would have few if any direct dues-paying members of its own. Instead, an as-yet undetermined portion of the dues paid by doctors to their specialty society or local medical association would be funneled to the AMA, an automatic "**tithe**" that has upset some groups in the past. It's not clear whether the AMA's dues would rise or fall under this plan. ("Revolutionary Change May Be Next for a Tired AMA; with Dues Declining, Doc Group Could Collect '**Tithe**' as Umbrella Organization for Specialty, Medical Societies," Michael Romano, Mar. 11, 2002, *Modern Healthcare*)

To and fro

Means: Any action or movement back and forth; restless or turbulent movement

Biblical Text: *And the* LORD *said unto Satan, Whence comest thou? Then Satan answered the* LORD, *and said, From going **to and fro** in the earth, and from walking up and down in it* (Job 1:7).

Example of Use: A small craft motors **to and fro** in the Potomac, methodically puttering toward the shoreline and back out again to river's midsection, over and over in the raw chill. ("Tide's Turned for a Way of Life in Prince William," Marc Fisher, Dec. 7, 2004, *The Washington Post*)

To everything there is a season

Means: An appropriate moment exists for all things

Biblical Text: *To every thing there is a season, and a time to every purpose under the heaven* (Ecclesiastes 3:1).

Example of Use: To everything, there is a season. Stomp, squish, swat. No sooner had we finished sweeping the cicada carcasses off the driveway than the next summer scourge appeared, this one unannounced. Itch mites. ("Editorial: Mitey Irritated," Aug. 18, 2007, *Chicago Tribune,* Chicago, IL)

To him who hath will more be given

Means: Successful people will have more than will those who are unsuccessful

Biblical Text: *His lord answered and said unto him, Thou wicked and slothful servant, thou knewest that I reap where I sowed not, and gather where I have not strawed: Thou oughtest therefore to have put my money to the exchangers, and then at my coming I should have received mine own with usury. Take therefore the talent from him, and give it unto him which hath ten talents. **For unto every one that hath shall be given**, and he shall have abundance: but from him that hath not shall be taken*

T

away even that which he hath. And cast ye the unprofitable servant into outer darkness: there shall be weeping and gnashing of teeth (Matthew 25:26–30).

Example of Use: Perhaps Frayling has done too much ever to have done anything well. He is, above all, a committee man, unable to resist another and another membership or chairmanship—and to the committees on all sorts of arts, on planning, publications, projects and photography, we must add trusteeships and working parties by the dozen. With so much to do, can he have given the Royal College the leadership it needs? Perhaps he prefers the diversions. He has clearly long been on the little lists that civil servants keep of minor public figures worthy of unimportant appointments—and **to him that hath shall more be given**. ("The Worst Man to Run the Arts? Sir Christopher Frayling Is the New Chairman of the Arts Council—a Foolish Appointment to a Useless Institution," Brian Sewell, Dec. 9, 2003, *Evening Standard*, London)

To whom much is given, much is expected

Means: Those who are gifted are expected to be more productive than others

Biblical Text: *And the Lord said, Who then is that faithful and wise steward, whom his lord shall make ruler over his household, to give them their portion of meat in due season? Blessed is that servant, whom his lord when he cometh shall find so doing. Of a truth I say unto you, that he will make him ruler over all that he hath. But and if that servant say in his heart, My lord delayeth his coming; and shall begin to beat the menservants and maidens, and to eat and drink, and to be drunken; The lord of that servant will come in a day when he looketh not for him, and at an hour when he is not aware, and will cut him in sunder, and will appoint him his portion with the unbelievers. And that servant, which* *knew his lord's will, and prepared not himself, neither did according to his will, shall be beaten with many stripes. But he that knew not, and did commit things worthy of stripes, shall be beaten with few stripes.* **For unto whomsoever much is given, of him shall be much required**: *and to whom men have committed much, of him they will ask the more* (Luke 12:42—48).

Example of Use: To whom much is given, much is expected. The Lions are counting on Johnson to make an immediate impact, not just with the balls he catches, but with how his presence opens up the offense for others. ("Now That Top Pick Johnson Is Signed, Much Is Expected," Aug. 4, 2007, *Detroit Free Press*)

Toil not, neither do they spin, They

Means: Someone who does no labor

Biblical Text: *And why take ye thought for raiment? Consider the lilies of the field, how they grow;* **they toil not, neither do they spin** (Matthew 6:28).

Example of Use: One effect of the Cuban campaign has been the rehabilitation of the dude in the popular respect. When the war broke out, the young rich, **who toil not, neither do they spin**, enlisted in considerable numbers and in the lowest rank often. ("The Dude Goes to War," May 1, 2003, *Canadian Speeches*)

Tomorrow will take care of itself

Means: Preparation for the present will tend to make preparation for the future unnecessary; an attitude of ambivalence, causing one not to prepare for the future

Biblical Text: *Take therefore no thought for the morrow: for **the morrow shall take thought for the things of itself**. Sufficient unto the day is the evil thereof* (Matthew 6:34).

Example of Use: Lynn also says that small business owners often get caught up in the daily operations of their business and don't take the time to look at a broader scope. . . . "They will often feel that they need to live for today and **tomorrow will take care of itself**," she says. ("In Case of Emergency. (Contingency Planning)," Doug Donaldson, Sept. 1, 2007, *Hardware Retailing*)

Tongue, Bridle one's

Means: To control what one says, especially in subduing one's emotions that might cause one to make inappropriate comments

Biblical Text: *If any man among you seem to be religious, and **bridleth not his tongue**, but deceiveth his own heart, this man's religion is vain* (James 1:26). See also Ps. 39:1.

Example of Use: Bridle Your Tongue. Words really do hurt and children take your unkind words to heart. Teasing, insulting or berating them over their looks, intelligence, athletic ability and other traits can lead to poor school performance, bad behavior, health problems and low self-esteem. Rather than criticizing your child for their faults, offer constructive advice. ("Five Ways to Boost Your Child's Confidence," Feb. 2, 2004, *Jet*)

Tongue, Hold one's

Means: Keep quiet, remain silent

Biblical Text: *And a man's uncle shall take him up, and he that burneth him, to bring out the bones out of the house, and shall say unto him that is by the sides of the house, Is there yet any with*

*thee? and he shall say, No. Then shall he say, **Hold thy tongue**: for we may not make mention of the name of the LORD* (Amos 6:10).

Example of Use: And when that idiot pulls in front of you in the parking lot, remember to **hold your tongue**. ("Try to Hold Your Tongue This Holiday Season," Tom Schaefer, Dec. 6, 2000, Knight Ridder/Tribune News Service)

Tongues, To speak in

Means: To speak in a language unknown to the speaker; to speak in ecstatic utterances, not a known language; to speak gibberish

Biblical Text: *When they heard this, they were baptized in the name of the Lord Jesus. And when Paul had laid his hands upon them, the Holy Ghost came on them; and **they spake with tongues**, and prophesied* (Acts 19:5–6).

Example of Use: The Blood Brothers force listeners to **speak in tongues** of superlatives, metaphors and exaggerations. Words like "manic," "schizophrenic" and "varied" fall as phenomenal understatements. These judgments would be true of their first two albums as well, but here they move further away from the idea of a clear concept album. ("CD Review: Listeners Should Get Stranded on 'Piano Island,'" Steve Marshall, Mar. 18, 2003, *University Wire*)

Touch (1)

Means: To harm someone

Biblical Text: *And when he saw that he prevailed not against him, he **touched** the hollow of his thigh; and the hollow of Jacob's thigh was out of joint, as he wrestled with him* (Genesis 32:25).

Example of Use: Jarrod Washburn pitched a masterful one-hitter over six shutout innings against the Minnesota Twins on

T

Tuesday night. Unfortunately for him and the Mariners, however, Washburn pitched seven innings. And the odd inning out, in which the Twins **touched** him for six hits and four runs in the second, proved the Mariners' undoing in a 5–1 loss at the Metrodome. ("Twins' Santana Outduels Mariners' Washburn," Larry Stone, May 2, 2006, *Seattle Times*)

Touch (2)

Means: To mention; to refer to or consider briefly, especially in a light or passing way

Biblical Text: *As **touching** our brother Apollos, I greatly desired him to come unto you with the brethren: but his will was not at all to come at this time; but he will come when he shall have convenient time* (1 Corinthians 16:12).

Example of Use: What is the effect of DB or PLB on dynamic hyperinflation? Studies cited in the article barely **touched** this subject. ("Diaphragmatic Breathing Training: Further Investigation Needed," Christine R. Wilson, Apr. 1, 2005, *Physical Therapy*)

Touch me not

Means: A command not to touch someone

Biblical Text: *Jesus saith unto her, **Touch me not**; for I am not yet ascended to my Father: but go to my brethren, and say unto them, I ascend unto my Father, and your Father; and to my God, and your God* (John 20:17).

Example of Use: But I'm not going to be impressed because, besides icing me out with her frosty "**Touch me not**" supermodel vibes, she's bound to start preaching her youthful idealism at me, like some catwalk version of Bono. She does, after all, have a bit of a reputation that way, does caring, ecofriendly, flame-haired, miss smarty pants Lily Cole. ("Queen of the

CABs (Clever, Ambitious and Beautiful) . . .," James Delingpole, Mar. 12, 2007, *Evening Standard,* London)

Train up a child in the way he should go, . . .

Means: A child who receives proper and consistent discipline will continue to be a responsible person, even as he grows old

Biblical Text: *Train up a child in the way he should go: and when he is old, he will not depart from it* (Psalm 22:6).

Example of Use: I may have contributed to the next generation of fashionistas who shall learn to shop like the pros. **Train up a child,** as they say. ("Gift Cards; Easy Out or Thoughtful Present?" Lori Price and Joy Oglesby, Dec. 17, 2006, *The Milwaukee Journal Sentinel*)

Treasure in heaven

Means: Eternal benefits or consequences as a result of certain temporal activity

Biblical Text: *Now when Jesus heard these things, he said unto him, Yet lackest thou one thing: sell all that thou hast, and distribute unto the poor, and thou shalt have **treasure in heaven**: and come, follow me* (Luke 18:22).

Example of Use: One man's junk is another man's treasure, the saying goes. And Tim Hansen has been laying up **treasure in heaven**. Salvage Heaven, that is. Through his West Allis business, Salvage Heaven, Hansen, in short, "recycles houses," among other buildings. ("Spare Parts: Salvage Heaven a Handyman's Paradise," Steve Watrous, Sept. 19, 1999, *The Milwaukee Journal Sentinel*)

T

Treasure is there your heart will be also, Where your

Means: One tends to keep a close emotional attachment to that in which he invests his tangible assets

Biblical Text: *Where your treasure is, there will your heart be also* (Matthew 6:21).

Example of Use: infoUSA believes that the best guardians of shareholder value have personal and financial interests that are aligned with shareholders. Mr. Gupta, the founder of infoUSA is the Company's largest shareholder. He and his family have a huge portion of their net worth invested in infoUSA. Dr. Haddix and Dr. Raval have each made personally significant financial investments in the Company as well. Each of our nominees brings an owner-orientation to the Board which is invaluable. "**Where your treasure is, there will your heart be also.**" ("infoUSA Calls ISS Recommendation 'Absurd'; Company Urges Shareholders to Vote FOR Its Director Nominees and AGAINST Shareholder Proposal 2," May 16, 2006, *Business Wire*)

Tree is known by its fruit, A

Means: One's commitment or motives will be known by one's actions

Biblical Text: Either make the tree good, and his fruit good; or else make the tree corrupt, and his fruit corrupt: for *the tree is known by his fruit* (Matthew 12:33).

Example of Use: The Kurikulum Bersepadu Sekolah Rendah (KBSR) generation had been exposed to formal music education for at least six years. As a consequence, we should see informed music appreciation and an active music culture in Malaysian society. Sadly, this is not happening. **A tree is known**

by its fruit and Malaysian parents clearly do not see the fruit of music education. ("Don't Cut Down the Music Tree," Joe Chelliah, July 24, 2009, *New Straits Times*, Malaysia)

Tree of knowledge

Means: A source of information, providing knowledge

Biblical Text: *But of **the tree of the knowledge of good and evil**, thou shalt not eat of it: for in the day that thou eatest thereof thou shalt surely die* (Genesis 2:17).

Example of Use: I don't buy the idea that Gingrich was struggling with donors because his wife wanted him to take it easy in the past two weeks. . . . This story was fresh when Eve was at the **tree of knowledge**, but it's getting kind of stale. ("Same Old Storyline," June 10, 2011, States News Service)

Tree of life

Means: Reference to the tree of life in the Bible's Creation story; a list of one's ancestors and their relationships; a particular kind of tree

Biblical Text: *And the LORD God said, Behold, the man is become as one of us, to know good and evil: and now, lest he put forth his hand, and take also of the **tree of life**, and eat, and live for ever: Therefore the LORD God sent him forth from the garden of Eden, to till the ground from whence he was taken* (Genesis 3:22–23).

T

Example of Use: This argument against the reality of evolution is found in his chapter "Darwin's **Tree of Life**," where Wells contends not only that the Cambrian explosion turns the **tree of life** upside down, but that it also was too fast to have occurred by evolution. ("Intelligent Design: Jonathan Wells and the **Tree of Life**," Thomas Gregg, July 1, 2007, *Journal of College Science Teaching*)

Trumpet gives an uncertain sound, who will be ready for battle?, If the

Means: A rhetorical question implying that a group will fail to perform as intended without proper leadership and communication

Biblical Text: *For if the trumpet give an uncertain sound, who shall prepare himself to the battle?* (1 Corinthians 14:7–9).

Example of Use: No army could operate if individual soldiers started distancing themselves from orders with which they disagreed. The same principle applies even more strongly to the top brass. **If the trumpet give an uncertain sound, who shall prepare himself to the battle?** ("An **Uncertain Trumpet**," Apr. 29, 2003, *Daily Telegraph,* London)

Truth shall make you free, The

Means: Knowing truth frees one from bondage

Biblical Text: *As he spake these words, many believed on him. Then said Jesus to those Jews which believed on him, If ye continue in my word, then are ye my disciples indeed; And ye shall know the truth, and **the truth shall make you free.*** (John 8:30–32).

Example of Use: My mission here is to teach you to think and amass wealth for yourselves, once you have it and know how to use it no one or thing shall make you slaves and hold you in financial bondage again. For you have discovered truth and **truth shall make you free**. ("Your Money; Money and Your Thoughts," Robert Henderson, July 12, 2005, *Miami Times*)

Truth?, What is

Means: A rhetorical question about the meaning of truth, sometimes implying that its meaning cannot be known

Biblical Text: *Pilate saith unto him,* **What is truth?** *And when he had said this, he went out again unto the Jews, and saith unto them, I find in him no fault at all* (John 18:38).

Example of Use: Liberal blogger Arianna Huffington charges that "too many in the Washington press corps want to pretend they are leaving the question of **'what is truth'** to their readers—refusing to admit that there is even such a thing as truth. ("The Lukewarm Truth: Unable to Lock In on Elusive Facts, News Outlets Hear It from All Sides," Howard Kurtz, Sept. 17, 2007, *The Washington Post*)

Turn the other cheek

Means: To accept injuries and not to seek revenge

Biblical Text: *But I say unto you which hear, Love your enemies, do good to them which hate you, Bless them that curse you, and pray for them which despitefully use you. And* **unto him that smiteth thee on the one cheek offer also the other***; and him that taketh away thy cloak forbid not to take thy coat also. Give to every man that asketh of thee; and of him that taketh away thy goods ask them not again. And as ye would that men should do to you, do ye also to them likewise* (Luke 6:27–31).

Example of Use: Jesus' way of dealing with aggression is *revolutionary!* It's so wise, so beautiful, so strong, and so different from what is normally done. If someone hits you on the cheek and you strike him back then they know what to do next: hit you harder! But if, in strength and love, you **turn your other cheek** then he doesn't know what to do! He's never seen that response. It confuses him. It may frighten him. It may convict him. You've turned the tables on your offender. ("Jesus Jujitsu: The Power to **Turn the Other Cheek**," Bill Gaultiere © 2005, 2010, http://www.soulshepherding.org/2012/08/jesus-jujitsu-the-power-to-turn-the-other-cheek)

T

Turn the world upside down

Means: To cause drastic change

Biblical Text: *And when they found them not, they drew Jason and certain brethren unto the rulers of the city, crying, These that have **turned the world upside down** are come hither also* (Acts 17:6).

Example of Use: The Internet is **turning the TV world upside down**. Just when CBS was about to pull the plug on "Jericho" and NBC was about to shut off "Friday Night Lights" due to low ratings, fans persuaded network executives to renew the shows through concerted online campaigns. ("Viewers' Efforts Rescued Other Shows from Chopping Block," Tenley Woodman, Nov. 18, 2007, *The Boston Herald*)

Twinkling of an eye, In the

Means: In an instant, an extremely short period of time

Biblical Text: *Behold, I show you a mystery; We shall not all sleep, but we shall all be changed, In a moment, **in the twinkling of an eye**, at the last trump: for the trumpet shall sound, and the dead shall be raised incorruptible, and we shall be changed* (1 Corinthians 15:51–52).

Example of Use: Step inside the booth, strip down to your underwear, and **within the twinkling of an eye**, a laser beam scans your body and records your measurements—some 100 of them. It's safe, fast, clean, objective and noninvasive. Body scanning is the new technology that's going to be a major change in the fashion industry and retail marketplace. ("The Body Scanner Is the Future of Fit," Judith Rasband, May 17, 2007, *Deseret News*, Salt Lake City)

T

Unknown God

Means: Designation for any divine being unfamiliar to one

Biblical Text: *Then Paul stood in the midst of Mars' hill, and said, Ye men of Athens, I perceive that in all things ye are too superstitious. For as I passed by, and beheld your devotions, I found an altar with this inscription, TO THE **UNKNOWN GOD**. Whom therefore ye ignorantly worship, him declare I unto you* (Acts 17:22–23).

Example of Use: Laws of Newton supported the possibility of such a model of [the] universe, viewed as a designed clock with purposeful and accurate motions, actions and functions, being controlled by an **unknown God**. This theory is also compatible with theories of motion by Bruno, Copernicus, and Galileo. ("Universe As the Interaction of Its Parts with Limitations," Rostam Khorsandian, Aug. 1, 2003, *Journal of Evolutionary Psychology*)

Unpardonable sin

Means: A serious transgression against a recognized authority, so heinous that no forgiveness can be expected

Biblical Text: *And whosoever shall speak a word against the Son of man, it shall be forgiven him: but **unto him that blasphemeth against the Holy Ghost it shall not be forgiven*** (Luke 12:10).

Example of Use: That is, until Sunday night, when the people who run the Big 12 committed what should be an **unpardonable sin**. Faced with the decision of how to break the tie between Texas, Oklahoma and Texas Tech to represent the South Division in the Big 12 championship game, the league simply decided to send whichever team the BCS ranked higher. ("BCS Beats Texas in Red River Sellout," Michael Wilbon, Dec. 2, 2008, *The Washington Post*)

U

Unspotted

Means: Morally upright; free from moral blemish

Biblical Text: *Pure religion and undefiled before God and the Father is this, To visit the fatherless and widows in their affliction, and to keep himself **unspotted** from the world* (James 1:27).

Example of Use: Carlyon's depiction of the chief Australian players is objective. He is generous to find merit wherever he can, but promotes no shining and **unspotted** heroes. ("The Burdens of War," Peter Ryan, Jan. 1, 2007, *Quadrant*)

Upon this rock will I build. . .

Means: A statement signifying that one will establish something on the characteristics or principle of someone or something

Biblical Text: *And I say also unto thee, That thou art Peter, and **upon this rock I will build** my church; and the gates of hell shall not prevail against it* (Matthew 16:18).

Example of Use: So it's true then. Rugby really IS a religion in Wales. Along comes a Messiah, a Great Redeemer. And yea, verily, this Fisher of Men gathers about him a band of true believers. And first among them is Brother Alfie, he who is called Slaphead because of his celebrations. And to him the Great Redeemer doth say: "Thou art Alfie, and **upon this rock I will build my team**." ("Let's All Remember Rugby's Just a Game," Dan O'Neill, Feb. 20, 2006, *South Wales Echo*, Cardiff, Wales)

U

RAISING CAIN

V

"VOICE OF THE TURTLE"

Valley of the shadow of death

Means: The perils of life, especially relating to death

Biblical Text: *Yea, though I walk through the **valley of the shadow of death**, I will fear no evil: for thou art with me; thy rod and thy staff they comfort me* (Psalm 23:4).

Example of Use: When the gallant 600 rode into **the valley of the shadow of death**, they didn't ask reason why. Not at all. They kept the British upper lip stiff and galloped into a thunderous cannonade. You might say the charge didn't do the Light Brigade a lot of good. ("It's Official—Big Boys Shouldn't Cry," Karreny Brady, June 10, 2008, *Birmingham Mail*, England)

Vanity of vanities, all is vanity

Means: Human activity to find meaning or satisfaction in life is pointless

Biblical Text: *Vanity of vanities, saith the Preacher, **vanity of vanities**; all is vanity* (Ecclesiastes 1:2). See also Eccl. 12:28.

Example of Use: The expression **"vanity of vanities"** is not ordinary English, but we end up understanding what the Bible seems to be saying. In Hebrew, *havel havelim* (literally *"breath of breaths"*) is a superlative form that might be translated literally as *"ultimate vaporousness."* In other words, in the context of all that might be thought of as vaporous, Qoheleth evokes a supreme instance, like the terminal value in calculus of a function, expressed as the sum of a series of increasingly-infinitesimal elements, when the number of summations approaches infinity. ("Antipodes: Reflections from an Australian Expatriate in France, William Skyvington, http://skyvington.blogspot.com/2012/05/is-bible-good-english-literature.html)

V

Veil of the temple rent

Means: Reference to the curtain of the temple in Jerusalem that was torn when Jesus died; some cataclysmic event that ushers in a new era

Biblical Text: *And, behold, **the veil of the temple was rent in twain** from the top to the bottom; and the earth did quake, and the rocks rent* (Matthew 27:51).

Example of Use: We have been warned that the vault of the heavens would crack, and the **veil of the temple would be rent** in twain, if "the religious right" came to power. Note the lack of cracking and renting. ("Bush's Conservatism," George F. Will, Apr. 29, 2001, *The Washington Post*)

Vengeance is mine

Means: A statement affirming that one particular person, and no one else, will exact a penalty

Biblical Text: *Dearly beloved, avenge not yourselves, but rather give place unto wrath: for it is written,* **Vengeance is mine;** *I will repay, saith the Lord* (Romans 12:19).

Example of Use: *Death Sentence* is as hard and violent as you'd expect from James Wan, the director of *Saw*. But, in the same year as the horrendous *Outlaw* and *Straightheads*, this "**vengeance is mine**" trend is becoming a real worry. ("Movie Reviews: Saving Your Bacon in a World of Violence; the Razz Movie Reviews Death Sentence," Alan Morrison, Aug. 31, 2007, *Daily Record,* Glasgow, Scotland)

V

Vials of wrath

Means: Severe punishment

Biblical Text: *And I heard a great voice out of the temple saying to the seven angels, Go your ways, and pour out **the vials of the wrath of God** upon the earth.* (Revelation 16:1).

Example of Use: Those national members of Congress from the former solid Democratic South, turned solid Republican South, cling as ardently to state sovereignty as ever. We are witnessing on the floor of Congress the **pouring out of their vials of wrath** upon those whom they desire to re-enslave: poor whites and blacks. ("Budget Debacle a Smoke Screen," James Cameron, Jan. 17, 1996, *The Milwaukee Journal Sentinel*)

Voice from the whirlwind

Means: An answer derived from chaotic forces or conditions

Biblical Text: *Then the LORD answered Job out of the whirlwind, and said, Who is this that darkeneth counsel by words without knowledge? Gird up now thy loins like a man; for I will demand of thee, and answer thou me* (Job 38:1–3).

Example of Use: The turbidity of the opening of *The Voice out of the Whirlwind* at first obscures recognition that the piece is an arrangement of Galliard of the Sons of the Morning from Job. ("Vaughan Williams: Mass in G. The Voice out of the Whirlwind. Valiant-for-truth. Three Choral Hymns. Nothing Is Here for Tears. A Vision of Aeroplanes. The Souls of the Righteous. A Choral Flourish," Ronald E. Grames and James A. Altena, July 1, 2010, *Fanfare*)

Voice of the turtle, The

Means: The pleasant cooing of turtle doves; a phrase used to indicate the arrival of spring

Biblical Text: *The flowers appear on the earth; the time of the singing of birds is come, and **the voice of the turtle** is heard in our land* (Song of Solomon 2:12).

Example of Use: Remember the glorious '40s and '50s? Great years for college football. We had a lot of good friends among the coaches and enjoyed every one of their flights of fancy. None more than **the voice of the turtle** in Columbus, Ohio. Woody Hayes loved to hear himself speak and he was never afraid of leading with his chin. It was Woody who acquainted us with one of the most awful metaphors of the 20th century— that football is the closest thing we have to war. ("Football & War . . . (Here Below)," Herman L. Masin, Oct. 1, 2004, *Coach and Athletic Director*)

V

RAISING CAIN

W

"WOLF IN SHEEP'S CLOTHING"

Wages of sin

Means: The results or consequences of doing wrong

Biblical Text: *For the **wages of sin** is death; but the gift of God is eternal life through Jesus Christ our Lord* (Romans 6:23).

Example of Use: Shamed peer Jeffrey Archer sparked outrage yesterday by profiting from crime after selling his jail diaries for pounds 600,000. . . . MP [Member of Parliament] Paul Flynn said: "The **wages of sin** are handsome." ("**Wages of Sin**; Liar, Cheat and Jailbird Archer to Make Pounds 600,000 from His Prison Diaries," Lynn McPherson, Oct. 6, 2002, *Sunday Mail*, Glasgow, Scotland)

Wages of sin is death, The

Means: Those who sin will receive death, deserved by their actions

Biblical Text: *For the **wages of sin is death**; but the gift of God is eternal life through Jesus Christ our Lord* (Romans 6:23).

Example of Use: It is around 3:54 a.m. when I hear the empty rattler making its way from Temple Meads to Westonsuper-Mare. Funny sort of place, Weston. A while back they had a sign at the station saying: And Remember, **the Wages of Sin is Death**. To be honest I have no strong opinion on that either way, though I can see it would be a bit of a downer if you were arriving for an illicit weekend. The grammar looks a bit suspect as well. ("Let me Loose at Brighton and Forget Forever," Ian Carnaby, Apr. 10, 2011, *The Racing Post,* London)

W

Walk, To

Means: To conduct oneself or behave in a particular manner; to live

Biblical Text: *If we **walk** in the light, as he is in the light, **we** have fellowship one with another, and the blood of Jesus Christ his Son cleanseth us from all sin* (1 John 1:7).

Example of Use: And we bear witness as an African people that as our beginning was great and good so shall our development throughout eternity be if we dare struggle, speak truth, do justice and **walk** in the way of rightness. ("The Millions More March and Movement; Mission, Meaning and Struggle," Maulana Karenga, Oct. 26, 2005, *Los Angeles Sentinel*)

Walk by faith, not by sight

Means: To live on the basis of trust instead of observation

Biblical Text: *Therefore we are always confident, knowing that, whilst we are at home in the body, we are absent from the Lord: (For **we walk by faith, not by sight*** (2 Corinthians 5:6–7).

Example of Use: He [Evander Holyfield] follows the scripture on his boxing shorts which says "**For we walk by faith, not by sight.**" ("Holyfield Is Finer with Age," Sept. 2, 2007, *South Florida Sun-Sentinel*, Ft. Lauderdale, FL)

Walk on water

Means: To do what seems impossible

Biblical Text: *And when he had sent the multitudes away, he went up into a mountain apart to pray: and when the evening was come, he was there alone. But the ship was now in the midst of the sea, tossed with waves: for the wind was contrary. And in the fourth watch of the night Jesus went unto them, walking on the sea. And when **the disciples saw him walking on the sea**, they were troubled, saying, It is a spirit; and they cried out for fear* (Matthew 14:23–26).

Example of Use: Parramatta coach Brian Smith thought the Eels were "dead in the water" tonight when they trailed New Zealand Warriors by 14 points with 11 minutes remaining. But the Eels somehow managed to **walk on water**, scoring three tries in the final 10 minutes to pull off an incredible 28–26 victory in the National Rugby League clash at Parramatta Stadium. ("RL: Eels **Walk on Water** to Pull off Incredible Win over Warriors," June 15, 2003, *AAP Sports News,* Australia)

Walls of Jericho

Means: An apparently impregnable obstacle that can be breached

Biblical Text: *Now* **Jericho** *was straitly shut up because of the children of Israel: none went out, and none came in. And the* LORD *said unto Joshua, See, I have given into thine hand* **Jericho***, and the king thereof, and the mighty men of valour. And ye shall compass the city, all ye men of war, and go round about the city once. Thus shalt thou do six days. And seven priests shall bear before the ark seven trumpets of rams' horns: and the seventh day ye shall compass the city seven times, and the priests shall blow with the trumpets. . . . So the people shouted when the priests blew with the trumpets: and it came to pass, when the people heard the sound of the trumpet, and the people shouted with a great shout, that the* **wall** *[of* **Jericho***] fell down flat, so that the people went up into the city, every man straight before him, and they took the city* (Joshua 6:1–4, 20).

Example of Use: Without this testing, without its capacity to at the very least throw a caution into the worst of the cheats, Sydney would have been as vulnerable as the **walls of Jericho**. The Olympics would have stood before the spectre of blood-doping about as imposingly as Florence Nightingale confronting the Black Death with a bowl of water and a clean towel.

W

("Olympics: IOC Wages a War on Damage Limitation 'Without Testing, Without Throwing a Caution to Cheats, Sydney Would Be As Vulnerable As the **Walls of Jericho**,'" James Lawton, Aug. 30, 2000, *The Independent,* London)

Wander in the wilderness

Means: To continue without direction or focus

Biblical Text: *And the* LORD's *anger was kindled against Israel, and he made them* **wander in the wilderness** *forty years, until all the generation, that had done evil in the sight of the* LORD, *was consumed* (Numbers 32:13).

Example of Use: National Democrats continue to **wander in the wilderness**, searching for the path to the Promised Land. Along the way, the debate is heated and emotional because it's not only a squabble about tactics, but a battle for the soul of the party. ("Three Wise Men 'Get It'? Remaking the Party's Image," Gary J. Andres, Dec. 30, 2004, *The Washington Times*)

War in heaven

Means: Reference to the biblical conflict between God and opposing angels

Biblical Text: *And there was* **war in heaven**: *Michael and his angels fought against the dragon; and the dragon fought and his angels, And prevailed not; neither was their place found any more in heaven. And the great dragon was cast out, that old serpent, called the Devil, and Satan, which deceiveth the whole world: he was cast out into the earth, and his angels were cast out with him. And I heard a loud voice saying in heaven, Now is come salvation, and strength, and the kingdom of our God, and the power of his Christ: for the accuser of our brethren is cast down, which accused them before our God day and night. And*

W

they overcame him by the blood of the Lamb, and by the word of their testimony; and they loved not their lives unto the death (Revelation 12:7–11).

Example of Use: "**War in Heaven**; The Arms Race in Outer Space," May 1, 2007, *Reference & Research Book News*

Wars and rumors of wars

Means: Actual fighting or rumors of such fighting between nations and groups; presence of warlike conditions

Biblical Text: *And ye shall hear of **wars and rumours of wars**: see that ye be not troubled: for all these things must come to pass, but the end is not yet* (Matthew 24:6).

Example of Use: Amid **wars and rumors of wars**, my 84-year-old mother, Mary, and I beat a hasty retreat to Loudoun County for a day of reading (historic markers), riding (in a car) and relaxation. ("Echoes of Wars Past; In Nearby Leesburg, Ball's Bluff Brings Cost of Battle Close to Home," Linton Weeks, Mar. 12, 2003, *The Washington Post*)

Was blind, but now I see, I

Means: One's perception has changed dramatically, now enabling one to understand

Biblical Text: *He answered and said, Whether he be a sinner or no, I know not: one thing I know, that, whereas **I was blind, now I see*** (John 9:25).

Example of Use: Greeks invented the Olympics, but I've been shut out of the real Chicago Olympic sport: Cashing In. To cement this pact, I will pray at the shrine of St. Richie the Benign for advice on how the heck I'm going to endorse Patrick Daley for mayor someday. Yes, **I was blind but now I see**. I understand my errors in judgment. Sorry, mayor, for all

W

that stuff I said. I love you, man. ("Seeing the Light, Praying for a Contract," John Kass, Mar. 1, 2007, *Chicago Tribune*)

Washed in the blood

Means: (1) Totally committed to something; (2) initiated into a group or a cause; (3) related to someone or a group

Biblical Text: *And I said unto him, Sir, thou knowest. And he said to me, These are they which came out of great tribulation, and have **washed their robes, and made them white in the blood of the Lamb*** (Revelation 7:14).

Example of Use: Eprile, a South African writer now living in the United States, doesn't deal in bright futures. In *The Persistence of Memory* he dedicates himself to scrutinizing the South African past through the consciousness of a single individual, one Paul Sweetbread, a Jewish man whose inner life is **washed in the blood** of South African history. ("Out of Africa: Tony Eprile's Latest Novel Joins the Jewish Literature of Memory; The Persistence of Memory," Mark Shechner, May 21, 2004, *Forward*)

Waste howling wilderness

Means: A dangerous and uninhabitable place or condition

Biblical Text: *He found him in a desert land, and in the **waste howling wilderness**; he led him about, he instructed him, he kept him as the apple of his eye* (Deuteronomy 32:10).

Example of Use: China's "go west" enterprise is an epic project to industrialize, repopulate, and transform the **waste-howling wilderness** that makes up one-sixth of mainland China. ("Go West: China Looks to Transform Its Frontier; Beijing Is on a 50-Year Plan to Build Colleges, Hospitals, and Roads in the Resource-Rich Region," Robert Marquand, Sept. 26, 2003, *The Christian Science Monitor*)

Watch and pray

Means: Be alert and diligent and seek divine intervention.

Biblical Text: *Take ye heed, **watch and pray**: for ye know not when the time is* (Mark 13:33). See also Matt. 26:41.

Example of Use: Of the two jobs—coach and parent—Rivers didn't hesitate in regard to a question about which is more difficult. "Oh, a parent," he said. "Easy. As a coach, you can have an impact." . . . "But (as a coach), you can call a timeout. You can do something. As a parent, you can just sit there. You basically just **watch and pray** a lot." ("Doc Has Son in His Eyes: Enjoys Run of Hoyas," Steve Bulpett, Mar. 27, 2007, *The Boston Herald*)

Water into wine, Change

Means: Reference to Jesus' miracle of turning water to wine

Biblical Text: *And the third day there was a marriage in Cana of Galilee; and the mother of Jesus was there: And both Jesus was called, and his disciples, to the marriage. And when they wanted wine, the mother of Jesus saith unto him, They have no wine. Jesus saith unto her, Woman, what have I to do with thee? mine hour is not yet come. His mother saith unto the servants, Whatsoever he saith unto you, do it. And there were set there six waterpots of stone, after the manner of the purifying of the Jews, containing two or three firkins apiece. **Jesus saith unto them, Fill the waterpots with water**. And they filled them up to the brim. And he saith unto them, Draw out now, and bear unto the governor of the feast. And they bare it. When the ruler of the feast had tasted **the water that was made wine**, and knew not whence it was: (but the servants which drew the water knew;) the governor of the feast called the bridegroom, And saith unto him, Every man at the beginning doth set forth good wine; and*

W

when men have well drunk, then that which is worse: but thou hast kept the good wine until now. This beginning of miracles did Jesus in Cana of Galilee, and manifested forth his glory; and his disciples believed on him (John 2:1–11).

Example of Use: Turning water into wine may be among the most venerable of miracles, but for Greg Allgood, the real miracle has been turning dirty water into drinkable water. ("A Clear Solution for Dirty Water," Tim Lougheed, July 1, 2006, *Environmental Health Perspectives*)

Water, Like

Means: (1) Something that is abundant or ubiquitous; (2) lavishly, freely, as if something has no value; (3) of, containing, or similar to the qualities of water

Biblical Text: *Their blood have they shed **like water** round about Jerusalem; and there was none to bury them* (Psalm 79:3).

Example of Use: He [Gordon Brown] borrowed like an 18th century rake suddenly coming into a fortune. He spent his tax revenue **like water**. ("Spending Our Money **Like Water**," Andrew Alexander, Aug. 1, 2008, *Daily Mail*, London)

Way of a man with a maid, The

Means: The nature of romance

Biblical Text: *There be three things which are too wonderful for me, yea, four which I know not: The way of an eagle in the air; the way of a serpent upon a rock; the way of a ship in the midst of the sea; and **the way of a man with a maid*** (Proverbs 30:18–19).

Example of Use: One journalist inquired if [Everett] Dirksen would vote for Knowles when his nomination reached the Senate floor. "Four things I know not of," he said, paraphrasing Pr. 30:18–19: "They are the way of a ship with the sea, **the way**

of a man with a maid, the way of an eagle on the rock, and the way of a minority leader under certain circumstances." ("The Knowles Affair: Nixon's Self-Inflicted Wound," Dean J. Kotlowski, Sept. 1, 2000, *Presidential Studies Quarterly*)

Way of transgressors is hard, The

Means: Those who commit misdeeds have a difficult life because of their misconduct.

Biblical Text: *Good understanding giveth favour: but the **way of transgressors is hard*** (Proverbs 13:15).

Example of Use: The greatest deterrent to wrongdoing is early detection and the certainty of suitable punishment: **the way of transgressors must be seen to be hard.** ("Hospital Is Diligent in Infection Control," Archie Smith, Sept. 11, 2007, *The Western Morning News*, Plymouth, UK)

Weaker sex, The

Means: Women

Biblical Text: *Likewise, ye husbands, dwell with them according to knowledge, giving honour unto the wife, as unto **the weaker vessel**, and as being heirs together of the grace of life; that your prayers be not hindered* (1 Peter 3:7).

Example of Use: The **weaker sex** are the stronger sex because of the weakness of the stronger sex for the **weaker sex**. ("I Wish That Sofa Had Swallowed Me Up!" June 16, 2011, *Daily Mail*, London)

W

Weary in well-doing, Do not be

Means: Continue doing good deeds, even when it is difficult

Biblical Text: *Be not deceived; God is not mocked: for whatsoever a man soweth, that shall he also reap. For he that soweth to his flesh shall of the flesh reap corruption; but he that soweth to the Spirit shall of the Spirit reap life everlasting. And **let us not be weary in well doing**: for in due season we shall reap, if we faint not* (Galatians 6:7–9).

Example of Use: Living wills attempt what undertakers like to call "pre-need planning," and on inspection they are as otiose as the mortuary version. Critically, empiricists cannot show that advance directives affect care. This is damning, but were it our only evidence, perhaps **we might not be weary in well doing**: for in due season we might reap, if we faint not. However, our survey of the evidence suggests that living wills fail not for want of effort, or education, or intelligence, or good will, but because of stubborn traits of human psychology and persistent features of social organization. ("Enough: The Failure of the Living Will," Angela Fagerlin and Carl E. Schneider, Mar. 1, 2004, *The Hastings Center Report*)

Weaver's shuttle, Swifter than a

Means: Fast

Biblical Text: *My flesh is clothed with worms and clods of dust; my skin is broken, and become loathsome. My days are **swifter than a weaver's shuttle**, and are spent without hope* (Job 7:5–6).

Example of Use: Like Greg, I too am nearing the retirement that always loomed in the distant future. It's true. The years do go by "**quicker than a weaver's shuttle**." ("DAU Visual Arts and Press Director Retires: Greg Caruth—A Career by Design," Collie J. Johnson, May 1, 2003, *Program Manager*)

W

Weeping (or wailing) and gnashing of teeth

Means: Extreme suffering due to despair and remorse

Biblical Text: *But the children of the kingdom shall be cast out into outer darkness: there shall be* **weeping and gnashing of teeth** (Matthew 8:12).

Example of Use: That great **weeping and gnashing of teeth** you hear is hypocritical Southern Californian politicians decrying Ventura County's decision to authorize the first stage of the Ahmanson Ranch development. ("Ahmanson Anguish a Scapegoat for Decades of Government Failure," Dec. 23, 2002, *Daily News,* Los Angeles, CA)

Well done, good and faithful servant (See also "Parable of the talents")

Means: A climactic assessment of praise for one's faithfulness and service

Biblical Text: *His lord said unto him,* **Well done, thou good and faithful servant**: *thou hast been faithful over a few things, I will make thee ruler over many things: enter thou into the joy of thy lord. He also that had received two talents came and said, Lord, thou deliveredst unto me two talents: behold, I have gained two other talents beside them. His lord said unto him,* **Well done, good and faithful servant**; *thou hast been faithful over a few things, I will make thee ruler over many things: enter thou into the joy of thy lord* (Matthew 25:21–23).

Example of Use: In the parable of the talents (Matthew 25:14–20) Jesus praised the faithful servant that increased his talents. [Editor's Note: A talent was a Roman measure of gold of approximately 33 kg worth roughly 1 Million US$, a substantial amount of money on the same scale as many folk's retirement savings] Jesus condemned the unfaithful servant that

W

buried his talents in the ground. I invest because I want to be a faithful servant to my Lord. I want to use my talents to produce more talents for the glory of God. We must be careful when investing that our success does not lead to a lust for money. What we make investing is for our basic needs and for the kingdom of God. We must keep our eyes focused on Jesus and not the temptations of this world. (**"Well Done Good and Faithful Servant,"** Roger Davis, http://www.worldofwallstreet. us/2008/04/well-done-good.html)

What God has joined together, let no man put asunder

Means: A command that no one dissolve any union, especially a marriage, that God has made

Biblical Text: *What therefore God hath joined together, let not man put asunder* (Mark 10:9).

Example of Use: Although "Asunder'" takes its title from Matthew 19:6 and the Book of Common Prayer (**"Those whom God hath joined together let no man put asunder"**), don't expect the sweetness of his "Once upon a Time" film. This one is about greed and obsession. ("Tim Reid's Thrill Ride 'Asunder' Is First Film to Be Completed at Petersburg Studio," Mal Vincent, Apr. 7, 2000, *The Virginian Pilot,* Hampton Roads)

What hath God wrought?

Means: A rhetorical question, implying that God has done some great deed directly or indirectly

Biblical Text: *Surely there is no enchantment against Jacob, neither is there any divination against Israel: according to this time*

it shall be said of Jacob and of Israel, ***What hath God wrought!*** (Numbers 23:23).

Example of Use: On the twenty-fourth of that month (May, 1844) Samuel Morse sat before his instrument in the room of the Supreme Court at Washington. His friend Miss Ellsworth handed him the message which she had chosen: **"What hath God wrought!"** Morse flashed it to Vail forty miles away in Baltimore, and Vail instantly flashed back the same momentous words, **"What hath God wrought!"** ("The Communication Revolution: Samuel Morse & The Telegraph" Mary Bellis, About. com Guide)

What is man?

Means: A rhetorical question implying mankind's relative insignificance to God and all Creation

Biblical Text: *What is man, that thou art mindful of him? and the son of man, that thou visitest him?* (Psalm 8:4).

Example of Use: The fact that the great Harvard philosophers inhabited Emerson Hall struck me as extraordinarily ironic, but not only because this building had co-starred in *Love Story*. Rather, the irony of ironies had to do with what was engraved in stone on the outside of Emerson Hall. There, in giant letters, was a portion of Psalm 8: **"WHAT IS MAN THAT THOU ART MINDFUL OF HIM."** ("Harvard Ironies" © 2010, Rev. Mark D. Roberts, http://www.patheos.com/blogs/markdroberts/series/harvard-ironies)

Whatever you do, do quickly

Means: An admonition to be decisive and act with speed

Biblical Text: *And after the sop Satan entered into him. Then said God unto him,* ***That thou doest, do quickly*** (John 13:27).

Example of Use: The Securities and Exchange Commission is under more pressure to do something—opinions vary as to what—about two proxy access proposals it has been considering since this summer, and to **do whatever it's going to do quickly**. ("Proxy Season upon Us, but Rules Remain Uncertain," Christopher Faille, Nov. 21, 2007, *Daily News*, NY)

Whatsoever thy hand findeth to do, do it with thy might

Means: An admonition to do well what one does

Biblical Text: *Whatsoever thy hand findeth to do, do it with thy might; for there is no work, nor device, nor knowledge, nor wisdom, in the grave, whither thou goest* (Ecclesiastes 9:10).

Example of Use: Indeed his chosen motto, framed and hung on his study wall, read "**Whatsoever thy hand findeth to do, do it with thy might**." It was this drive to pursue active sports that some years later may have tragically contributed to his untimely death. ("Whitby Produces England Footballer," July 26, 2010, *Whitby Gazette*, Whitby, England)

Wheat and tares

Means: The approved and the disapproved

Biblical Text: *Another parable put he forth unto them, saying, The kingdom of heaven is likened unto a man which sowed good seed in his field: But while men slept, his enemy came and sowed* **tares** *among the* **wheat**, *and went his way. But when the blade was sprung up, and brought forth fruit, then appeared the tares also. So the servants of the householder came and said unto him, Sir, didst not thou sow good seed in thy field? From whence then hath it tares? He said unto them, An enemy hath done this. The servants said unto him, Wilt thou then that we go and gather*

*them up? But he said, Nay; lest while ye gather up the tares, ye root up also the wheat with them. Let both grow together until the harvest: and in the time of harvest I will say to the reapers, Gather ye together first the **tares**, and bind them in bundles to burn them: but gather the **wheat** into my barn* (Matthew 13:24–30).

Example of Use: The anniversary of Sept. 11 leads to comparisons, a search through history for clues about how to deal with landmark events of our own experience. *The New Criterion*, a magazine that consistently **separates the tares from the wheat** of what's new, measuring current writers, artists and ideas against the standards of the past, dares to draw on the unfashionable to measure the fashions of our day. ("An Oasis to Celebrate; New Criterion Turns 25," Suzanne Fields, Sept. 14, 2006, *The Washington Times*)

Wheel within a wheel

Means: A conundrum

Biblical Text: *And there appeared in the cherubims the form of a man's hand under their wings. And when I looked, behold the four wheels by the cherubims, one wheel by one cherub, and another wheel by another cherub: and the appearance of the wheels was as the colour of a beryl stone. And as for their appearances, they four had one likeness, as if **a wheel had been in the midst of a wheel*** (Ezekiel 10:8–10).

Example of Use: The problem arises in that we get bad government because the decisions that occur cannot be challenged as they are being made. The decision by the Cabinet to proceed with the Dome is a perfect example of this. What **wheels within wheels** exist behind Legacy getting the Dome will never be known with certainty. ("**Wheels within Wheels** of Political Donation," John Hemming, Jan. 8, 2001, *Birmingham Post*)

W

When I was a child . . .

Means: A statement introducing a childhood recollection

Biblical Text: *When I was a child, I spake as a child, I understood as a child, I thought as a child: but when I became a man, I put away childish things* (1 Corinthians 13:11).

Example of Use: When I was a child, I spoke as a child, I felt as a child, I thought as a child. Indeed, I drank hot chocolate as a child—from a packet of dry powder stirred into scalded milk, with the occasional small white dehydrated cube reputed to be a marshmallow. And I was happy. But now that I am grown, I have put away (some) childish things, and chief among them is inferior hot chocolate. ("Classy Chocolate Is Hot: We've Moved on from Watery Kids' Stuff to a Brew So Rich That It's Like Drinking Molten Candy," Dianna Marder, Nov. 30, 2006, *Philadelphia Inquirer*)

Where is thy sting?

Means: A rhetorical question implying the missing effect of some expected force or power; sometimes used as a taunt

Biblical Text: *O death, where is thy sting? O grave, where is thy victory? The sting of death is sin; and the strength of sin is the law. But thanks be to God, which giveth us the victory through our Lord* (1 Corinthians 15:55–57).

Example of Use: Despite it all, Lincoln still gets cut way more slack than the average perp. He wasn't even arrested Friday. According to the indictment, the feds aren't going after his Brockton pension of $77,090.45 a year. Indictment, **where is thy sting?** ("Dem Hacks Ready to Pig out on Deval Meal Ticket," Howie Carr, Oct. 29, 2006, *The Boston Herald*)

W

Where is thy victory?

Means: An exclamation asking about the missing effect of some expected force or power; sometimes used as a taunt

Biblical Text: *O death, where is thy sting? O grave, **where is thy victory?*** (1 Corinthians 15:55).

Example of Use: Since then, Sunday morning has become a major shopping day, but now, at last, come signs that the worms are turning and answering the call of the wild. They are starting to abandon the shopping trolleys and seek instead healthy, outdoor Sunday mornings on the course. Tesco, where is thy sting? M & S, **where is thy victory?** ("Sports Active: Tesco, Where Is Thy Sting?" Peter Corrigan, Jan. 16, 2005, *The Independent on Sunday,* London)

Where there is no vision, the people perish

Means: Without ambition and a plan for the future, a group will fail.

Biblical Text: *Where there is no vision, the people perish: but he that keepeth the law, happy is he* (Proverbs 29:18).

Example of Use: In Proverbs 29:18, we are advised that **"where there is no vision, the people perish."** With your assistance, we have developed and approved a new Chemical Corps Vision. . . . A successful Vision must be believable, positive, and appealing to all members of the community. Our new Vision meets these goals and is a great beacon to guide future efforts. ("The U.S. Army Chemical Corps: Serving a Nation at War, Today and Tomorrow," Thomas Spoehr, Jan. 1, 2007, *CML Army Chemical Review*)

W

Where two or three are gathered together . . .

Means: An allusion to Jesus' statement indicating his presence among even a small assembly of people who are devoted to him

Biblical Text: *Verily I say unto you, Whatsoever ye shall bind on earth shall be bound in heaven: and whatsoever ye shall loose on earth shall be loosed in heaven. Again I say unto you, That if two of you shall agree on earth as touching any thing that they shall ask, it shall be done for them of my Father which is in heaven. For **where two or three are gathered together** in my name, there am I in the midst of them* (Matthew 18:18-20).

Example of Use: As a visitor to the U.S., you won't much enjoy being fingerprinted, photographed and asked to supply a "biometric" passport; nor will you relish being shooed away from the toilet on the plane because **where two or three are gathered together** they might constitute a terrorist cell. ("The Secret State of America: George Bush Is Using the 'War against Terrorism' to Justify Frightening Change, Says Jonathan Raban," Jonathan Raban, Jan. 11, 2004, *The Independent on Sunday,* London)

Which of you, if his son asks for bread, will give him a stone?

Means: A rhetorical question implying that one would not give bad or useless things to someone he loves

Biblical Text: *Or what man is there of you, whom if his son ask bread, will he give him a stone?* (Matthew 7:9).

Example of Use: "What man is there of you, whom if his son ask bread, will he give him a stone?" It's a biblical question, but parents of every clime would answer it the same way: No caring parent would ever hand a child a poisonous snake. Yet according to findings by two national groups—The Sight and

Hearing Association and U.S. Public Interest Research Group—parents do give children toys that can be just as dangerous. ("Harmful Toys for Girls and Boys," Dec. 16, 2006, *Deseret News*, Salt Lake City)

White as snow

Means: (1) Purely white; (2) perfect or uncorrupted

Biblical Text: *Come now, and let us reason together, saith the* LORD: *though your sins be as scarlet, they shall be as **white as snow**; though they be red like crimson, they shall be as wool* (Isaiah 1:18).

Example of Use: "I'm not dumb enough that I'm going to go out there and declare this guy innocent and **white as snow**," Sacks told the *Herald* yesterday. "But I think there are a lot of very tangible problems with the prosecution's case that point to possible innocence." ("Yakker Eyes Hopkins Case," Jessica Heslam, Jan. 16, 2009, *The Boston Herald*)

Whited sepulcher

Means: A person who is inwardly evil but outwardly professes to be virtuous; a hypocrite

Biblical Text: *Woe unto you, scribes and Pharisees, hypocrites! for ye are like unto **whited sepulchres**, which indeed appear beautiful outward, but are within full of dead men's bones, and of all uncleanness* (Matthew 23:27).

Example of Use: "White Lies and **Whited Sepulchres** in Conrad's *Heart of Darkness*, Philip V. Allingham, Contributing Editor, Victorian Web; Faculty of Education, Lakehead University, Thunder Bay, Ontario. http://www.victorianweb.org/authors/conrad/pva52.html

W

Whither thou goest, I will go

Means: I will go with you wherever you go

Biblical Text: *And Ruth said, Intreat me not to leave thee, or to return from following after thee: for **whither thou goest, I will go**; and where thou lodgest, I will lodge: thy people shall be my people, and thy God my God: Where thou diest, will I die, and there will I be buried: the* LORD *do so to me, and more also, if aught but death part thee and me* (Ruth 1:16–17).

Example of Use: So the incensed motorist did what she could about the uninsured motorist. She leaped into the back of the truck as it sped away. "I don't know why," she confessed. "I just wanted to be wherever he was." For those who know the Bible, it was kind of a Ruth moment: **Whither thou goest, I will go,** sucker. And thus began a real circus. Warnecia pitched around in the back of the truck. Sideboards and a tarp over the top prevented her from seeing where she was going. She suddenly remembered she had her roommate's cellphone with her. ("Steve Blow Column: Freeway Full of the Uninsured and Unhinged," Steve Blow, Oct. 1, 2006, *Dallas Morning News*)

Whole duty of man, The

Means: Mankind's supreme reason for existing

Biblical Text: *Let us hear the conclusion of the whole matter: Fear God, and keep his commandments: for this is **the whole duty of man*** (Ecclesiastes 12:13).

Example of Use: As I was mowing my lawn today, making intersecting zigzag patterns, I was thinking about my poor husband. He is the reason I was mowing in such an interesting configuration. Perhaps I should explain. You see, I consider it part of my cosmic commission to demonstrate that **the whole duty of man** is NOT to disprove the second law of thermodynamics (everything tends to disorder). He does not share this point of view. (May 11, 2006, itreallyisadogslife. blogspot.com)

Whore after, To

Means: To pursue something that is immoral or depraved

Biblical Text: *And the* LORD *said unto Moses, Behold, thou shalt sleep with thy fathers; and this people will rise up, and go a* **whoring after** *the gods of the strangers of the land, whither they go to be among them, and will forsake me, and break my covenant which I have made with them* (Deuteronomy 31:16).

Example of Use: We have allowed a system to develop in Wisconsin whereby **whoring after** campaign cash is not only allowed, it has become necessary to be "competitive." The corrosive effect of that fact cannot be overstated. ("Troha Case Stresses Necessity of Reform," Rick Berg, Mar. 10, 2007, *The Capital Times*, Madison, WI)

Whore, Play the

Means: Commit fornication or prostitution; to devote oneself to immoral or unworthy purposes

Biblical Text: *And the daughter of any priest, if she profane herself by* **playing the whore,** *she profaneth her father: she shall be burnt with fire* (Leviticus 21:9). See also Deut. 22:21; Judg. 19:2.

Example of Use: It is because your crucial concept, whether you know it or not, is that sterility is better than fecundity, that children are bad and contraception is good, that marriage is oppression but whoredom is freedom, that authority is oppression, the femininity is weakness, that masculinity is tyranny, that sex itself is unfair because the two sexes are not one (and

W

you reject marriage, the one why where the two sexes can in truth become one), and that everything is opposed to your independence and self-expression and self-esteem, and you want to whore around and **play the whore**, because you wish you lived in a world where you could get away with every sin without every paying any price. ("Antifatherhood, or A Belated Father's Day Thought", John C. Wright, *Live Journal,* http://johncwright.livejournal.com/520692.html)

Why hast thou forsaken me?

Means: Why have you abandoned me?

Biblical Text: *My God, my God, **why hast thou forsaken me?** why art thou so far from helping me, and from the words of my roaring?* (Psalm 22:1). See also Matt. 27:46; Mark 15:34.

Example of Use: Those haunting words that were uttered on a hill on Calvary: My God, my God, **why hast thou forsaken me?** Despair is a natural emotion at a time like this. They're all natural. They're all appropriate. But let me ask one thing of you, this community: As you wrestle with your sadness, as you wrestle with your own feelings of anger and confusion, as you wrestle with the despair, even you family members who have lost people close to you, do not, do not let hold of that spirit of community that makes Virginia Tech such a special place, do not lose hold of that. ("Gov. Tim Kaine Delivers Remarks at Convocation at Virginia Tech," Apr. 17, 2007, Washington Transcript Service)

Widow's mite

W

Means: A generous contribution made by one who has little

Biblical Text: *And Jesus sat over against the treasury, and beheld how the people cast money into the treasury: and many*

*that were rich cast in much. And there came **a certain poor widow, and she threw in two mites**, which make a farthing. And he called unto him his disciples, and saith unto them, Verily I say unto you, That this poor widow hath cast more in, than all they which have cast into the treasury: For all they did cast in of their abundance; but she of her want did cast in all that she had, even all her living* (Mark 12:41–44).

Example of Use: A Plympton schoolboy was so upset to see his beloved Argyle in financial difficulties he offered all his money to help. Jack Wilkinson had just 53p in his wallet but declared to his grandparents after his usual Saturday trip to Home Park, that he wanted to help save his club. His grandparents, Ken and Irene Miners, said they hoped this **"Widows Mite"** gesture might hit home to the Argyle Directors more than anything else, since he represented the club's future. ("Jack Offers Up His 53p in a Bid to Help Argyle," Feb. 17, 2011, *The Plymouth Evening Herald,* England)

Wind blows where it will, The

Means: Some people or things move without any apparent control by another force or by reason.

Biblical Text: *The wind bloweth where it listeth, and thou hearest the sound thereof, but canst not tell whence it cometh, and whither it goeth: so is every one that is born of the Spirit* (John 3:8).

Example of Use: There's an old adage that says, **"The wind blows where it will."** The winds of change blew through Wisconsin with gale force strength in the past two years and those winds swept one governor out, a new one in and other politicians into court. ("Doyle Gets It Right: What's Best for People of Wisconsin?" Jan. 13, 2003, *The Capital Times,* Washington, DC)

W

Wind of something, Every

Means: Uncertainty and relativism

Biblical Text: *That we henceforth be no more children, tossed to and fro, and carried about with **every wind of doctrine**, by the sleight of men, and cunning craftiness, whereby they lie in wait to deceive* (Ephesians 4:14).

Example of Use: It's the roadmaps or guidance tools that help drive performance and ensure the organization is not thrown off by **every wind of change**. ("Financial Solutions for Nonprofit Organizations; Mirror, Mirror on the Wall," Andrea Morrow, Nov. 22, 2005, *Michigan Chronicle*)

Wine for your stomach's sake, Take a little

Means: Drink wine to help one's digestion.

Biblical Text: *Drink no longer water, but **use a little wine for thy stomach's sake** and thine often infirmities* (1 Timothy 5:23).

Example of Use: In its earliest days, the primary motive for the illegal distilling of liquor was for family or social use. Residents often quoted Paul's Biblical advice to Timothy to "**take a little wine for thy stomach's sake.**" Later, unlicensed distilling became a matter of economics. ("Running the Blockade, Franklin County Style," Ken Lauterstein, Oct. 3, 2008, *Roanoke Times & World News*, VA)

Wing, To be under one's

Means: Under one's care as patron, guardian, mentor, tutor, or in a similar role

W

Biblical Text: *O Jerusalem, Jerusalem, which killest the prophets, and stonest them that are sent unto thee; how often would I*

*have gathered thy children together, as a hen doth gather her brood **under her wings**, and ye would not!* (Luke 13:34).

Example of Use: "I trusted Dr. Holderman because he had been my mentor for many years, " Diaz said at his sentencing. "**He took me under his wings** and tried to serve as a second father to me. . . . I made the mistake of letting the situation drive my conduct." ("Ex-Official Sentenced in Money Laundering," Catherine Wilson, Sept. 5, 2003, AP Online)

Wings of a dove

Means: The means by which one rises above one's circumstances

Biblical Text: *And I said, Oh that I had **wings like a dove!** for then would I fly away, and be at rest* (Psalm 55:6).

Example of Use: Tired of nearly four decades of guerrilla war, Colombians turned in 1998 to the presidential candidate who promised peace, and Andres Pastrana was carried to victory on the **wings of a dove**. ("Hardliner Winning in Colombia: Front-Runner Uribe Set to Win Sunday's Presidential Election," Howard LaFranchi, May 24, 2002, *The Christian Science Monitor*)

Wings of the morning

Means: Means of flight or escape

Biblical Text: *If I take the **wings of the morning**, and dwell in the uttermost parts of the sea; Even there shall thy hand lead me, and thy right hand shall hold me* (Psalm 139:9–10).

Example of Use: In front of him spread the blue expanse of the world's most heavenly harbor. Sailboats and cruise ships elegantly framed the **wings of the morning**'s stage. ("Olympic

W

Journal," Gil Lebreton, Sept. 17, 2000, Knight Ridder/Tribune News Service)

Wink at

Means: To deliberately overlook or pretend not to see, especially in order to connive with someone

Biblical Text: *And the times of this ignorance God **winked at**; but now commandeth all men every where to repent* (Acts 17:30). See also Job 15:11–13; Ps. 35:19; Prov. 10:10.

Example of Use: The principal allegation against the University of Colorado football program is that it used sex and alcohol as tools of recruitment, or **winked at** their use by athletes who hosted high school prospects. ("Gary Barnett and a Skeptical Panel Commission Needs More Testimony before Its Verdict," Apr. 15, 2004, *Rocky Mountain News,* Denver)

Wisdom of words

Means: An effective ability to communicate

Biblical Text: *For Christ sent me not to baptize, but to preach the gospel: not with **wisdom of words**, lest the cross of Christ should be made of none effect* (1 Corinthians 1:17).

Example of Use: Writing, [Julie] Andrews said, is an extension of her singing voice. "There is no greater gift that we can give ourselves than a sense of wonder at the miracles that are under our noses every single day," Andrews said. "And one of the best ways that I know to access that wonder is through **wisdom of words**." ("Awe and Advice Julie Andrews Enchants Naperville Crowd, Offers Tips," Melissa Jenco, Apr. 25, 2006, *Daily Herald,* Arlington Heights, IL)

W

Wise and foolish virgins

Means: People who are prudent and prepared and those who fail to prepare for unexpected situations

Biblical Text: *Then shall the kingdom of heaven be likened unto ten* **virgins**, *which took their lamps, and went forth to meet the bridegroom. And* **five of them were wise, and five were foolish.** *They that were foolish took their lamps, and took no oil with them: But the wise took oil in their vessels with their lamps. While the bridegroom tarried, they all slumbered and slept. And at midnight there was a cry made, Behold, the bridegroom cometh; go ye out to meet him. Then all those virgins arose, and trimmed their lamps. And the foolish said unto the wise, Give us of your oil; for our lamps are gone out. But the wise answered, saying, Not so; lest there be not enough for us and you: but go ye rather to them that sell, and buy for yourselves. And while they went to buy, the bridegroom came; and they that were ready went in with him to the marriage: and the door was shut. Afterward came also the other virgins, saying, Lord, Lord, open to us. But he answered and said, Verily I say unto you, I know you not. Watch therefore, for ye know neither the day nor the hour wherein the Son of man cometh* (Matthew 25:1–13).

Example of Use: There are other consolations to be found, although we cannot possibly condone the sudden flurry of cancelled visits to aunts and dentists. And then, away from the protests, there are the strangely empty roads. Have you been bowling along, discovering the carefree joys your parents have told you about? Or are you with the prudent, carefully conserving that nearly full tank, shaking your head as others go tootling by? There has not been such a clear-cut division since the **wise and foolish virgins** faced their oil crisis. Something to think on, in the queue. ("Leading Article: Making Tracks," Sept. 14, 2000, *The Independent,* London)

Wise as serpents and harmless as doves, Be as

Means: Be shrewd and intelligent yet innocent in dealings with others.

Biblical Text: *Behold, I send you forth as sheep in the midst of wolves: be ye therefore wise as serpents, and harmless as doves* (Matthew 10:16).

Example of Use: Sometimes people don't want to relinquish power or are too fearful to consider anything other than their own self-interest. Other people may wish to take the high road, but they don't know how to do it without worrying that people will take advantage of them. The biblical admonition to "be wise as serpents and innocent as doves" certainly applies. There are tools to level the playing field and make it safe for participants to come out of their shells. ("Business Success Column," Don Maruska, Jan. 30, 2002, *The Tribune*, San Luis Obispo, CA)

Wise in thine own eyes, Be not

Means: Do not think oneself wiser than one actually is.

Biblical Text: *Be not wise in thine own eyes: fear the LORD, and depart from evil* (Proverbs 3:7).

Example of Use: Anderson serves as producer on Baumbach's autobiographical tale of a **wise-in-his-own-eyes** teen (Jesse Eisenberg) struggling through the absurdities and the hurt of watching his intellectual parents (Jeff Daniels and Laura Linney) split messily. ("Intellectual Family, Absurdly Messy Divorce," Tom Russo, Mar. 19, 2006, *The Boston Globe*)

W

Wise men

Means: Persons of wisdom, not necessarily male; sometimes used ironically

Biblical Text: *Now when Jesus was born in Bethlehem of Judaea in the days of Herod the king, behold, there came **wise men** from the east to Jerusalem, Saying, Where is he that is born King of the Jews? for we have seen his star in the east, and are come to worship him* (Matthew 2:1–2). See also Matt. 2:3–12.

Example of Use: The European Committee of **Wise Men** warns that the EU cannot afford to delay integration of financial markets. ("**Wise Men's** Warning," Brendan Bracken, Dec. 1, 2000, *The Banker*)

Wit's end, To be at one's

Means: Completely puzzled and perplexed, not knowing what to do

Biblical Text: *They reel to and fro, and stagger like a drunken man, and are at their **wits' end*** (Psalm 107:27).

Example of Use: Wit's end is so much closer these days. With unpredictable Hurricane Ivan churning through the Caribbean, threatening to further ravage what Frances already stomped, many South Florida residents have reached their **wit's end** and taken that step beyond. ("Hurricane Triggers Mostly Flight Response," Rachel Sauer, Sept. 11, 2004, *The Palm Beach Post*, FL)

Witch of Endor

Means: Reference to the medium King Saul consulted in the OT

Biblical Text: *Then said Saul unto his servants, Seek me a woman that hath a familiar spirit, that I may go to her, and*

*inquire of her. And his servants said to him, Behold, there is **a woman that hath a familiar spirit at En-dor**. And Saul disguised himself, and put on other raiment, and he went, and two men with him, and they came to the woman by night: and he said, I pray thee, divine unto me by the familiar spirit, and bring me him up, whom I shall name unto thee* (1 Samuel 28:7–8).

Example of Use: As this issue of *Liberty* goes to press, there is absolute certainty about two things: the nation's finances will remain in shambles, and the next president of the United States will be someone who never saw the crisis coming. Now, with all appropriate modesty, I have to mention the fact that *Liberty's* writers and readers did see it coming. Even I saw it coming. No magic was involved. We didn't study Nostradamus. We didn't use a Ouija board. We didn't visit the **witch of Endor**. We didn't haruspicate or scry. But somehow we—and millions of other people—managed to know all those important things that the wizards of government and commerce now proclaim they did not know, and could never have even guessed. ("From the Editor," Stephen Cox, Dec. 1, 2008, *Liberty*)

Without blemish

Means: Faultless

Biblical Text: *Your lamb shall be **without blemish**, a male of the first year: ye shall take it out from the sheep, or from the goats* (Exodus 12:5). See also Eph. 5:25–27; 1 Pet. 1:18–21.

Example of Use: Netanyahu insisted the police recommendations are "insignificant because all the accusations are totally unfounded. . . . We are **without blemish**." ("Netanyahu: We're **without Blemish**," Mar. 29, 2000, United Press International)

W

Woe is me

Means: A declaration expressing regret about one's despair

Biblical Text: *Then said I, **Woe is me!** for I am undone; because I am a man of unclean lips, and I dwell in the midst of a people of unclean lips: for mine eyes have seen the King, the* LORD *of hosts* (Isaiah 6:5).

Example of Use: With the eyes of the world upon us, Minnesotans resisted the urge to wail in front of cameras, scream about mistakes, demand more help and so much as mutter a **"woe is me."** Instead, we went to work, doing what had to be done to assist with rescues, to take care of victims, to help each other recovery. Emergency officials were well-prepared and acted promptly and efficiently without seeking glory. ("Editorial: Amid Tragedy, Minnesotans Show Their Mettle," Aug. 15, 2007, *Post-Bulletin*, Rochester, MN)

Wolf and the lamb, The

Means: Enemies, especially if one is dominant; predator and prey

Biblical Text: *The wolf also shall dwell with the lamb, and the leopard shall lie down with the kid; and the calf and the young lion and the fatling together; and a little child shall lead them* (Isaiah 11:6). See also Isa. 65:25.

Example of Use: Politics makes strange bedfellows, but so, too, do national tragedies. In the wake of the events of Sept. 11, we have seen new alignments in the ideological constellations. Congressional Democrats and Republicans literally have sung together and political-action groups whose differences once were deemed intractable now are laboring side by side. If the **wolf and the lamb** were to lie down together, it scarcely could be more surreal. ("Symposium. [Homeland Security Interview]," Lamar Smith, Oct. 22, 2001, *Insight on the News*)

W

Wolf in sheep's clothing

Means: Someone or something that conceals its evil intentions or character beneath an innocent exterior

Biblical Text: *Beware of false prophets, which come to you* **in sheep's clothing**, *but inwardly they are ravening* **wolves** (Matthew 7:15).

Example of Use: Charley Ellis, founder of Greenwich Associates, has warned pension schemes against allocating money to alternative investments, describing them as "**wolves in sheep's clothing**." ("Ellis Brands Alternatives '**Wolves in Sheep's Clothing**,'" Ben Wright, Oct. 14, 2003, *Financial News*)

Wolves

Means: Fierce or destructive people

Biblical Text: *Beware of false prophets, which come to you in sheep's clothing, but inwardly they are ravening* **wolves** (Matthew 7:15).

Example of Use: An old shepherd was talking to his sons and he had this to say: It is not the **wolves** you can see that you must protect your flock from, but the ones that you can't see. The analogy seems to fit in today's competitive business environment. ("Real Threat Is from the **Wolves** You Can't See," Karen Fukumura, Aug. 21, 2000, *Business Times*, Malaysia)

Word and deed, In

Means: Speech and action, as distinct from each other

Biblical Text: *My little children, let us not love* **in word**, *neither in tongue; but* **in deed** *and in truth* (1 John 3:18).

Example of Use: Finally, trust is the foundation for all effective partnerships. We can only forge meaningful partnerships when those of us with the responsibility for public safety demonstrate, **in word and deed**, that we understand the issues that matter to our Muslim-, Arab- and Sikh-American communities. ("Protecting Civil Liberties a Vital Goal," May 29, 2011, *Los Angeles Daily News*)

Word in season, A

Means: An appropriate comment at an appropriate time, especially advice or comforting words

Biblical Text: *The Lord GOD hath given me the tongue of the learned, that I should know how to speak **a word in season** to him that is weary: he wakeneth morning by morning, he wakeneth mine ear to hear as the learned* (Isaiah 50:4).

Example of Use: Twenty feet from the window I realized I had missed a wonderful opportunity. Here was a Bruised Reed Person who needed **a word in season**, and the best I could do was say nothing. Here was a wounded individual who needed binding up, and I didn't even try. ("Spirit of Scornful Censorship Is Not Religion," Dec. 8, 2002, *The News & Record*, Piedmont Triad, NC)

Word made flesh, The

Means: An abstract idea made practical or incarnate

Biblical Text: *And **the Word was made flesh**, and dwelt among us, (and we beheld his glory, the glory as of the only begotten of the Father,) full of grace and truth* (John 1:14).

Example of Use: There is an only-in-America quality about Elvis that accounts for much of his enduring appeal. Leave aside his artistic merits (and camp value) and, for a moment, consider seriously what Elvis represents: As much as anything else, the King of Rock and Roll is the embodiment of America's embrace of free-market capitalism. He is **the word** of free-market

W

philosopher Friedrich Hayek **made flesh**. ("Why the Free Market Is King," Jonathan V. Last, Oct. 17, 2006, *Philadelphia Inquirer*)

Word, In the beginning was the

Means: Reference to Jesus, the Word, in John's gospel

Biblical Text: *In the beginning was the Word, and the Word was with God, and the Word was God* (John 1:1).

Example of Use: Last week *Cooks Source* magazine, based in Western Massachusetts, was accused of publishing an entire article without getting the writer's permission or paying her. When the writer, Monica Gaudio, complained, the magazine's editor, Judith Griggs, told Gaudio in an e-mail that all content on the Internet is "public domain" (which of course is not true). The story quickly exploded on the Web, and an apology was posted Friday on the magazine's Facebook page. We decided to help *Cooks Source* out by writing the Editor's Note for its next issue:

A note to readers from the editor of Cooks Source: It was a dark and stormy night, four score and seven years ago, when I said to myself: **In the beginning was the word, and the word was with God, and the word was God**. Yet, in the course of human events, it becomes necessary for one people to dissolve the political bands which have connected them. Darn it if we don't hold these truths to be self-evident. ("Unoriginal Thoughts; An Apology? We Took the Words Right Out of Their Mouths," Steve Greenlee, Nov. 8, 2010, *The Boston Globe*)

Words of the wise

Means: Good advice

Biblical Text: *The **words of wise men** are heard in quiet more than the cry of him that ruleth among fools* (Ecclesiastes 9:17).

Example of Use: "The Presidency of the United States was an office neither to be sought nor declined. To pay money for securing it directly or indirectly was in my opinion incorrect in principle," wrote John Quincy Adams in 1828. These are wise words from one of the nation's first leaders. Unfortunately, the **words of the wise** are not always followed. Money and politics go hand in hand, and the presidency is no exception. ("Taxpayer Money Should Not Fund Presidential Election Campaigns," Adam Scharn, Mar. 10, 2005, *University Wire*)

Work, one doesn't eat, If one doesn't

Means: One will receive no benefit without commensurate labor

Biblical Text: *For even when we were with you, this we commanded you, that **if any would not work, neither should he eat*** (2 Thessalonians 3:10).

Example of Use: As a taxpayer, still a worker-bee at age 64 and proud of it, I want to say that I don't mind my taxes and Social Security money going to those who need it: the truly elderly and those who just cannot work because of physical and mental disabilities. If you check history in this country, go back to Jamestown, people who were healthy and able-bodied but **did not work did not eat**. ("Employee Benefits," Apr. 16, 2011, *Maryland Gazette*)

Wrath to come

W

Means: Future difficulties or cataclysms

Biblical Text: *Then said he to the multitude that came forth to be baptized of him, O generation of vipers, who hath warned you to flee from **the wrath to come**?* (Luke 3:7).

Example of Use: Repent Now! The end is at hand! A panel of eminent scientists testified yesterday at a congressional hearing on global warming, showing up just short of wearing sandwich boards splashed with warnings of **the wrath to come**. ("Inconvenient Truth," Wesley Pruden, June 23, 2006, *The Washington Times*)

Writing (or Handwriting) on the wall

Means: A sign of future judgment

Biblical Text: *Then they brought the golden vessels that were taken out of the temple of the house of God which was at Jerusalem; and the king, and his princes, his wives, and his concubines, drank in them. They drank wine, and praised the gods of gold, and of silver, of brass, of iron, of wood, and of stone. In the same hour came forth* ***fingers of a man's hand, and wrote over against the candlestick upon the plaister of the wall*** *of the king's palace: and the king saw the part of the hand that wrote. Then the king's countenance was changed, and his thoughts troubled him, so that the joints of his loins were loosed, and his knees smote one against another* (Daniel 5:3–6). See also Dan. 5:1–30.

Example of Use: No one expects the coordinating board to close programs arbitrarily or capriciously, and everyone expects such programs will be given a reasonable time to improve. Nevertheless, the **writing on the wall** puts Texas's public universities on notice that regular academic review of doctoral programs will be the norm. (**"The Writing on the Wall**: Doctoral Education in Texas and Elsewhere," Philip Cohen, Nov. 1, 2006, *Change*)

Written in the book

Means: Included in an important and desirable list

Biblical Text: *And at that time shall Michael stand up, the great prince which standeth for the children of thy people: and there shall be a time of trouble, such as never was since there was a nation even to that same time: and at that time thy people shall be delivered, every one that shall be found **written in the book*** (Daniel 12:1).

Example of Use: "I'm a big man," 6–9 sophomore center Eric Williams said. "It's been **written in the book** of basketball that big men have to follow point guards no matter how old they are. So that's the way I've been coming at it." ("Odds and Ends," J. P. Pelzman, Mar. 25, 2004, *The Record*, Bergen County, NJ)

W

RAISING CAIN

Y

"UNEQUALLY YOKED"

Yoke is easy, My

Means: One's demands are not difficult

Biblical Text: *Come unto me, all ye that labour and are heavy laden, and I will give you rest. Take my yoke upon you, and learn of me; for I am meek and lowly in heart: and ye shall find rest unto your souls. For* **my yoke is easy**, *and my burden is light* (Matthew 11:28–30).

Example of Use: For now, at least, Chastain sounds like he's ready for the new challenges ahead. If the money isn't there to build the plan as he envisioned, he's willing to go back to the voters. But, he quickly adds, the money should be there. "I'm interested in cooperating and Kansas City being rewarded for their generosity and their courage," he says. He likes how people see him, although he says that what's most important is how he views himself. "**My yoke is easy**, and my burden is light," he says. "Now it is." ("Victory Recasts Chastain As Hero: The Approval of the Activist's Light-Rail Plan Changes Many People's Perceptions of Him," Steve Kraske, Dec. 16, 2006, *Kansas City Star*, MO)

Yoke, Break the

Means: To bring undesirable conditions to an end

Biblical Text: *And by thy sword shalt thou live, and shalt serve thy brother; and it shall come to pass when thou shalt have the dominion, that thou shalt* **break his yoke** *from off thy neck* (Genesis 27:40).

Example of Use: King and his generation did not fully eradicate poverty and racial disparities in the United States. Nevertheless, they **broke the yoke** of America's version of racial apartheid, which makes the United States a better

Y

country today than when he died nearly 40 years ago. ("King's True Legacy," Jan. 14, 2007, *The Washington Times*)

Yoke, Take (or Bear) one's

Means: To take responsibility for or make a commitment to someone or something; a mark of servitude

Biblical Text: *Take my yoke upon you, and learn of me; for I am meek and lowly in heart: and ye shall find rest unto your souls* (Matthew 11:29).

Example of Use: Physicians need permission to admit errors. They need permission to share them with their patients. The practice of medicine is difficult enough without having to **bear the yoke** of perfection. ("Why Clinics Now Admit Mistakes," Jan. 24, 2005, *Grand Forks Herald*, ND)

Yoked, Unequally

Means: Poorly balanced or matched in a relationship

Biblical Text: *Be ye not **unequally yoked** together with unbelievers: for what fellowship hath righteousness with unrighteousness? and what communion hath light with darkness?* (2 Corinthians 6:14).

Example of Use: In the Americas, meanwhile, the North American Free Trade Agreement (NAFTA) has **unequally yoked** the United States to both Canada and Mexico, and the planned Free Trade Area of the Americas would extend a NAFTA-type arrangement to the entire Western Hemisphere (except Cuba) and possess more powers than NAFTA. ("New World Order Strategist: Thirty Years Ago Richard N. Gardner Proposed a 'Piecemeal' Approach to World Government. The Internationalist Insiders Have Followed His Blueprint Ever Since," Steve Bonta, May 3, 2004, *The New American*)

Y

You can't take it with you

Means: One cannot keep one's possessions after death.

Biblical Text: *As he came forth of his mother's womb, **naked shall he return to go as he came, and shall take nothing of his labour**, which he may carry away in his hand* (Ecclesiastes 5:15).

Example of Use: "Beware the Person Who Reminds You That **You Can't Take It with You**. He'll Try to Take It with Him" ("A 'Friend's Help,'" Thomas LaMance, July 1, 2007, *Saturday Evening Post*)

Young lions

Means: People who claim more personal importance than is warranted, especially when younger than their competitors

Biblical Text: *Their roaring shall be like a lion, they shall roar like **young lions**: yea, they shall roar, and lay hold of the prey, and shall carry it away safe, and none shall deliver it* (Isaiah 5:29).

Example of Use: Why do I need to go back to square one and fight these **young lions** only to win back the same belts that I have already won? ("The Defining Moment of Thomas Hearns' Career," May 9, 2004, www.eastsideboxing.com)

Y